AT EMERSON'S TOMB
The Politics of Classic
American Literature

John Carlos Rowe

COLUMBIA UNIVERSITY PRESS

New York

Columbia University Press
Publishers Since 1893
New York   Chichester, West Sussex
Copyright © 1997 Columbia University Press
All rights reserved

Library of Congress Cataloging-in-Publication Data
Rowe, John Carlos
    At Emerson's tomb : the politics of classic American literature /
John Carlos Rowe.
        p.   cm.
    Includes bibliographical references (p.) and index.
    ISBN 0-231-05894-2 (cl).—ISBN 0-231-05895-0 (pa)
        1. American literature—19th century—History and criticism.
    2. Politics and literature—United States—History—19th century.
    3. Emerson, Ralph Waldo. 1803–1882—Political and social views.
    4. American literature—20th century—History and criticism.
    5. Literature and society—United States. 6. Antislavery movements—
    United States. 7. Women's rights in literature. 8. Liberalism in
    literature. 9. Sex role in literature. 10. Race in literature.
    I. Title.
    PS217.P64R69   1997

                                                                    96-24554
    814'.3—dc20
                                                                    CIP

∞

Casebound editions of Columbia University Press books are printed on
permanent and durable acid-free paper.

Printed in the United States of America
c 10 9 8 7 6 5 4 3 2 1
p 10 9 8 7 6 5 4 3 2 1

In memory of Joseph N. Riddel

*"his mind leaping
        like dolphins"*

Contents

Preface

⟟⟍ In this book, I reassess the liberal tradition of American literature in terms of its relevance to the two great rights movements of modern American history: the abolition of slavery and the women's rights movement. In more general terms, this book examines the ways in which classic American writers from Emerson to Faulkner responded to changing attitudes toward race and gender from the 1840s to 1940s. My methodological assumption is that the claims for social reform made so often by liberal culture should be evaluated in terms of the political and social achievements of specific historical movements.

Of course, demonstrable political changes are not the only ways in which social reforms occur, and I try in the following chapters to suggest some of the ways that literary works change psychological attitudes and thus humans' behaviors in ways that go beyond political and legal reform. Even as I recognize the uniqueness of the changes literature and the arts can bring in individuals' attitudes, I also argue that psychological transformations of readers and viewers are most effective when they are linked with larger social and political reforms. Too often and for too long, the Emersonian tradition of "aesthetic dissent" has defined itself as distinct from those political movements through which historical progress has been achieved in America.

The term "classic" is used in this study in a deliberately ambiguous manner. On the one hand, it refers to the writings by authors associated primarily with the Emersonian tradition that has shaped what several generations of readers have understood to be the distinctive qualities both of American literature and the American experience. In this century, Emerson, Poe, Melville, Whitman, Twain, Henry James, and Faulkner have been crucial figures of this literary experience for readers both in this country and around the world. This "American Exceptionalism" has been rightly challenged by many recent cultural critics, and it is one of my primary purposes in this book to contribute to that critique. Yet, the aim of my criticism is not to abandon the writings of some of our most powerful social critics for the sake of other literary traditions that have been unjustly ignored and excluded from that tradition. Instead, I hope to construct a new literary tradition that will have closer intellectual and practical alliances with the political and social reform movements that have improved democratic opportunities and broadened our understanding of what it means to be an American. "Classic American literature" in this latter sense, then, must include works that have contributed to this ongoing process of democratization, whether or not those works have been previously recognized as literary masterpieces. Thus the works I discuss by Frederick Douglass, Harriet Jacobs, and Kate Chopin are interpreted as "classics," because their enduring values derive less from their transcendence of time than from their profound involvement in our history. Most readers will agree that the classic achieves its status because it still has something to tell us, and I would add that such continuing relevance indicates human problems that still command our attention.

I have tried to connect the ten chapters that focus on specific literary works by means of certain complementary and supplementary gestures from which the writers themselves did not always benefit in their own times and mutual relations. Emerson, Melville, and Whitman would have learned much from their contemporaries, Frederick Douglass and Harriet Jacobs, and we must conclude that racial divisions and gender hierarchies discouraged such education. In my argument, the respective intellectual impasses reached by Emerson, Melville, and Whitman—the inapplicability of transcendentalism to the politics of abolition and the complicity of literary authority with the ideological authorities of modern America—are overcome in Douglass' and Jacobs' uses of literature for explicit political ends. My purpose in emphasizing such complementarities is to stress the intellectual and educational advantages of bringing together different literary traditions, especially when their differences can be made the basis of debate. The point of contact between such different historical and cultural traditions is often the site of historical change, and scholarly books may sometimes help effect such change by establishing such contact.

In the same regard, Twain, James, Chopin, and Faulkner would have benefited from the influences of more politically pragmatic and equally profound literary writers like Douglass, Jacobs, Hurston, and Morrison. What Chopin's Edna Pontellier misses in her bid for freedom is precisely the sisterhood with women of color whose labor and identity are so profoundly marginalized by Creole society in New Orleans. In their advocacy of communal agency and their critique of self-reliance, Douglass and Jacobs offer alternatives to what Henry James and Faulkner anxiously experience as their reproduction of the aristocratic pretensions of European and Southern feudalism. Taken together, women and African-American writers in this study represent some of the different modes of political, social, and literary agency by means of which these writers not only criticized but also helped transvalue the dominant American ideology of their times. In this respect, they offer positive responses to Twain's pessimism about the chances for genuine freedom available to African Americans and immigrants in the post-Civil War period.

There is yet another, less explicitly acknowledged, critical narrative that links the ten major American writers discussed in this book. Each struggles in turn with the elements of what today we recognize as postmodern social life: the unanchored, multiple self; the discursive basis for all experience and thus the socially constructed character of such experience; the attenuation of the body and the material world; the consequent crises of authority and value. These and many other characteristics of our postmodern condition are already central to the concerns of these nineteenth- and early twentieth-century writers. In some cases, we can conclude that they were indeed prescient, anticipating our contemporary concerns because of their understanding of the social structures of a modernity from which our postmodernity surely derives. In other cases, their prescience was also informed by their experiences as women and/or oppressed minorities, often the first of us to experience the full consequences of social hypocrisy and ideological contradiction. As several of the writers in this study continue to warn us, the means of oppression first used to control those in the weakest social position are the same as those used to achieve more comprehensive social control in subsequent periods.

The postmodern dimension of my argument is not intended to be a deliberate anachronism for the purpose of reviving interest in texts now fifty to one hundred and fifty years old. Our current postmodern society has deep roots in the American modernity that begins with industrialization, westward expansion, and the contemporary efforts to reconceptualize the agrarian economy that had relied in significant part on slavery. The questions we ask today about authority, agency, the production of value, and the modes of economic and social production are by no means utterly new or original questions. Each of the writers interpreted in this book has something explicit to say about how our postmodern condition developed out of this modernity, whether it be Poe's aggressive effort to situate his poetic authority at the center of the postmodern economy, Jacobs' use of the increasingly malleable definitions of family and feminine identity to construct alternative meanings, or Twain's and Warner's satire of a speculative economy and thus their nostalgia for an older, more stable system of social values. Recognizing the many different approaches currently available for the study of our postmodern condition, I begin this study by claiming unequivocally that such postmodernity is the consequence of complex historical processes that are nevertheless open to our collective understanding as intellectuals.

Cultural critics are happily less embarrassed by their exclusions and omissions than scholars of other schools and movements, in part because cultural studies takes the vast and untotalizable field of "culture" for its object of study. There is, of course, properly no such "object," but myriad subjects and disciplines that can be comprehended only with the help of other specialists. I have selected works that stretch from the 1840s to the 1940s without any presumption that I have thereby "represented" the complexity of American cultural and political realities in this hundred-year period. Nevertheless, there are certain areas of emphasis that might properly have figured in this book, given its argument and focus on political rights movements of the modern period. My discussion of race in this book is almost exclusively informed by literary and ideological conceptions of white and African-American peoples and cultures. Yet, the ideological construction of racial hierarchies in the United States relies profoundly on its caricature of Native American cultures according to a wide variety of myths intended to justify our genocidal policies toward native peoples. From Roy Harvey Pearce and Richard Slotkin to Gerald Vizenor, Arnold Krupat, and Louis Owens, specialists in Native American studies have not only analyzed the "Myth of the Vanishing American" and its ideology, but added to the work of Native American writers, like Leslie Silko and Louise Erdrich, that "writes back" to reaffirm the different cultures of Pueblo, Ojibway, Lakota, and other native peoples in the face of their continuing exclusion by the dominant American ideology.

I also do not address the developing nineteenth-century ideologies of sexuality that established the terms that would be used by the end of the century to marginalize lesbian and gay sexual preferences. Critics like Eve Sedgwick, Richard Dellamorra, Michael Moon, and Scott Derrick have taught us much about how ideologies of race, gender, and sexuality are mutually constructed and thus must be disentangled in related ways. My interpretation of Whitman's bid to renew his poetic power in the face of the political crisis and the human damage of the Civil War draws on their theories of nineteenth-century homosociality (and its inherent homophobia), but my approach in no way develops what such critics distinguish as the very different homosexual identity articulated by gays and lesbians in response to their marginalization and demonization. Quite clearly, Whitman's career is a major example of just such an alternative sexuality and how it challenged the strict binaries of acceptable gender roles and sexual identities in the nineteenth century.

These are only two of the most important exclusions in a study that attempts to establish the terms for enriching the description and interpretation of "classic" American literature by including not just the works but also the intellectual challenges and literary experiments of some of the different cultures that compose America. The study of Asian-American challenges to "American" literature, especially in the period of the Chinese Exclusion Laws, and the rich heritage of the several different cultures associated with Chicano and Latino communities are areas of complementarity with the present study that must be sought in the writings of many other contemporary scholars who have published work in what are by now well-established intellectual disciplines. Just as our students cannot know America without studying the many different cultures that compose this society, so we must read a wide variety of different books to be capable of teaching that America to those students.

I have incurred too many debts in the writing of this book to repay them properly in a brief list of acknowledgments. Many of these chapters were first presented as papers at colleges, universities, and scholarly conferences. I am grateful to my hosts and audiences for their invitations and valuable discussion of these ideas at Princeton University, Pennsylvania State University (and the Poe Studies Association), the Tudor and Stuart Club of Johns Hopkins University, the Institute for North American Studies of Johann-Wolfgang Goethe University (Frankfurt), the American Literature Association, the University of California at Santa Cruz, the Philosophy and Literature Association, Northwestern Louisiana State University, and the Modern Language Association. I benefited greatly from the editors of journals and volumes in which portions of several of these chapters were first published: Richard Kopley, Bainard Cowan, Joseph Kronick, Günter Lenz, Kathryne Lindberg, Forrest Robinson, Susan Gillman, Martha Banta, Lynda Boren, Sara de Saussure Davis, and J. Gerald Kennedy.

I wish to thank the following presses for permission to publish substantially revised versions of work that first appeared as chapters in books they published: Duke University Press for the portions of chapter 3 that first appeared in *Poe's 'Pym': Critical Explorations*, ed. Richard Kopley, and for the portions of chapter 8 that first appeared in *Mark Twain's "Pudd'nhead Wilson:" Race, Conflict, and Culture*, eds. Forrest Robinson and Susan Gillman; Louisiana State University Press for the portions of chapter 4 that first appeared in *Theorizing American*

Literature: Hegel, the Sign, and History, eds. Bainard Cowan and Joseph Kronick, for the portions of chapter 7 that first appeared in *America's Modernisms: Re-Valuing the Canon: Essays in Honor of Joseph N. Riddel*, eds. Joseph Kronick and Kathryne Lindberg, and for the portions of chapter 10 that first appeared in *Kate Chopin Reconsidered: Beyond the Bayou*, eds. Lynda S. Boren and Sara deSaussure Davis; St. Martin's Press for the portions of chapter 5 that first appeared in *Reconstructing American Literary and Historical Studies*, ed. Günter Lenz; Cambridge University Press for the portions of chapter 9 that first appeared in *New Essays on James's "The American,"* ed. Martha Banta, and for the portions of chapter 11 that first appeared in *Modern American Short Story Sequences*, ed. J. Gerald Kennedy.

My wife, Kristin, who is also a teacher, and my sons, Sean, Kevin, and Mark, have been part of all my book projects; to them, I am forever grateful: *I migliori fabbri.*

AT EMERSON'S TOMB

*The Politics of Classic
American Literature*

1   At Emerson's Tomb

Death is seen as a natural event, and is met with firmness. A wise man in our time caused to be written on his tomb, "Think on living." That inscription describes a progress in opinion. Cease from this antedating your experience.

—Emerson, "Immortality"

In the following chapters, I interpret the limitations and possibilities of political critique in the Emersonian tradition of *aesthetic dissent*. By "aesthetic dissent," I mean the romantic idealist assumption that rigorous reflection on the processes of thought and representation constitutes in itself a critique of social reality and effects a transformation of the naive realism that confuses truth with social convention. This utopian dimension of Euroamerican romanticism is the basis of the literary modernism that would find its primary critical function in the aesthetic irony practiced by the high moderns and theorized by Anglo-American New Criticism. This is the "aesthetic modernism" that has often been transformed from an historically specific artistic movement to a transhistorical "modernity," an avant-gardism often considered essential to literature. In the study of American literature, it has also served to bolster a certain "American Exceptionalism," to which my 1982 book, *Through the Custom-House*, certainly contributed, despite my explicit effort in that book to challenge traditional conceptions of American literary nationalism by introducing Continental theoretical and philosophical models to read American literature.[1]

"Emersonianism" is easily written but very difficult to trace in any comprehensive way, not simply because the definitions of Emerson's chief influence vary but also because that influence is so vast. The enormous impact of

Emerson's ideas, however those ideas have been "misinterpreted," as both Emerson's defenders and critics claim, is not attributable solely to Emerson's singular genius; it is also a consequence of the adaptability of those ideas to key features of the American ideology. A comprehensive survey of the "critical reception" of Emerson's ideas, then, cannot be attempted in a brief introduction to a study that proposes to examine other traditions existing alongside Emersonianism and yet frequently marginalized or silenced. Instead, I shall use only one excellent example of a careful and dedicated defense of Emersonianism by an influential critic, whose arguments are sufficiently recent to draw together many of the strongest parts of this tradition.

In *The Renewal of Literature: Emersonian Reflections* (1987), Richard Poirier treats Emerson as a writer and thinker who understands the essential features of literary language as polysemantic, process-oriented, ceaselessly subversive of convention, and thus performative. For Poirier, literature creates a textual space that is an alternative to the world of ordinary experience, physical materiality, and denotative meaning.[2] This is the aesthetic "world elsewhere" that was the title of an earlier book by Poirier, in which Poirier had argued that an Emersonian "style" established firmly the distinctive qualities of American literature from the transcendentalists to the moderns. Poirier opened *A World Elsewhere* (1966) by claiming: "The most interesting American books are an image of the creation of America itself, of the effort, in the words of Emerson's Orphic poet, to 'Build therefore your own world.' "[3] By the time Poirier published *The Renewal of Literature*, his previous book had been understood by critics to be one of the important contributions to the general proposition that American literature is a version of literary modernism.

America's literary "modernity" is, according to this argument, deeply ingrained in a certain "American" way of thinking and being. As Poirier puts this idea in the opening pages of *The Renewal of Literature*:

> Literature generates its substance, its excitements, its rhetoric, and its plots often with the implicit intention, paradoxically, to get free of them and to restore itself to some preferred state of naturalness, authenticity, and simplicity. . . . Another way to put it, which will help explain why my emphasis on the Emersonians is not merely an American emphasis, is to say that literature implicitly idealizes that condition of bareness, that thinness of social and cultural circumstances, which, according to Henry James and other observers, was supposed to be the special plight of American writers.[4]

As literary modernism became an "international" movement, it merely revealed this essential characteristic of literary idealization that had long been a part of

American literature. Thus the tradition that Poirier traces in *The Renewal of Literature* from Emerson through William James to Wallace Stevens and T. S. Eliot is an *American* tradition that may happily be adapted to *international* literary schools and movements.

William James figures interestingly in Poirier's account of Emersonianism, because Poirier insists that Emerson's idealism is the actual origin of America's only native philosophy, pragmatism. Of course, Poirier develops this argument in his effort to defend Emerson and the tradition he represents against the charge that it has advocated ideas and values that tend to trivialize political praxis, but it is an argument that sounds convincing when Emerson and William James are brought together:

> The effort of reading, like the effort of writing, is entirely its own reward. To ask for more, to seek security in meaning, is a cheat upon literature and upon life. It is like a surrender to Fate. "The truth of an idea is not a stagnant property inherent in it," [William] James instructs us in *Pragmatism*, "truth *happens* to an idea. It *becomes* true, is *made* true by events"—including the acts and operations of writing and reading. "Its verity," he continues, "*is* in fact an event, a process: the process namely of verifying itself, its *verification*. Its validity is the process of its valid-*ation*." (Renewal, 44)[5]

What we might term "rhetorical" or "textual" pragmatism in Emerson and William James must be distinguished by Poirier from concrete political action even as such pragmatism must be judged in its own right as a kind of politics of moral reform. Emerson has far more in common with William James, because both are "essentially" philosophers of "language and literature." As Poirier acknowledges, "this will please no one who wants writers to be more politically engaged than Emerson managed to be, and I leave the possible reprimands to them."

Let me say immediately, then, that my argument in this book is part of that "reprimand" of Emerson and the "Emersonianism" Poirier claims can be traced in the tradition of American pragmatism. I take issue with the sort of logical trap into which such Emersonianism forces us, especially where the "politics of literature" is concerned:

> One reason for his emphasis on language as the instrumentality of culture has already been suggested: that there was not much else, institutionally, to be concerned about, not so far as he could see. Slavery, "the woman question," American imperialism in Mexico, all these excited a degree of spirited outrage. But he never imagined that any of them resulted from essential defects in the American system, and in fact could not recognize the presence of a "system." (Renewal, 33–34)

Poirier refers here to Emerson's confidence that America is built upon the antibureaucratic, antisystematic, and ultimately antigovernmental Self that discovers its strength in its capacity to represent itself as "other" from all the conventional determinations (institutions) that threaten it.

For Emerson, such radical selfhood is ultimately "genius": "Through his concept of 'genius' he manages to hold onto an idea of the self, even though it is a self far more shadowy than his rhetoric of individualism has led people to suppose. The self in Emerson is not an entity, not even a function; it is an intimation of a presence, and it comes upon us out of the very act by which the self tries to elude definition" (Renewal, 86–87). Linked with other passages in which Poirier discusses the anti-activist "politics" of such a rhetorical self, it becomes clear that he is *defining* such selfhood and genius by virtue of its capacity to escape political engagement. Poirier explains: "Literature is not in itself an effective political form of action, except under the rather limited conditions described later in this book" (48). Those "conditions" turn out to be the very familiar ones by which the high moderns criticized the social circumstances of a profoundly alienated and alienating industrial age from which all sensitivity to the subtleties of rhetoric and the pragmatics of language had vanished. Modernism at its best reaffirms the Emersonian conviction that "language is . . . the place wherein we can most effectively register our dissent from our fate by means of troping, punning, parodistic echoings, and by letting vernacular idioms play against revered terminologies. Through such resistances, more than through directly political ones, sporadic evidences might emerge of some truer self or 'genius.' Language is the only way to get around the obstructions of language, and in his management of this paradox Emerson shows why he is now and always essential" (72).

Poirier states clearly and succinctly the basic qualities of an Emersonianism that has been used variously to justify an American Exceptionalism and to describe the contours of the international modernism that challenged such national boundaries. It is the naïveté of this theory of literary modernity regarding the workings of ideology that is perhaps the most striking and finally enables this position so easily to be manipulated for purposes contrary to its own lofty goals. Failing to take into account the subtle arts and rhetorical ruses of ideology, the theory of literary modernity assumes that any rhetoric that imitates its style and follows its philosophical predicates will qualify as ethically proper. Yet as so many of the authors studied in the following chapters demonstrate, the powers of patriarchy, slavery, and urban capitalism were profoundly rhetorical and textual in the *real* effects they had on their victims. Indeed, the problems of textual and rhetorical domination are very often the first ones to be addressed by writers, like Douglass and Jacobs and Chopin, who are explicitly committed to the political functionality of literary representation. What these writers reveal is the degree to which the Emersonianism analyzed so accurately by Poirier is subject to transformation into an aesthetic ideology in the service of the very social and political forces for which Emerson, William James, T. S. Eliot, and Wallace Stevens expressed the greatest contempt.

There is little need at this date to interpret the subtleties of this *aesthetic ideology* and how its overt claims to political critique disguised exclusions and rationalizations that have been quite capably revealed by the new American cultural studies of the last ten years. The great emancipatory movements of the American nineteenth century—women's rights and the abolition of slavery—were unquestionably subordinated by this aesthetic ideology to the "higher laws" of an American Romanticism established firmly by Emerson, Thoreau, and Whitman and institutionalized by several generations of professional interpreters. In my opening chapter on Emerson's responses to the specific political issues of his times in such essays as "Emancipation in the British West Indies," his addresses on the Fugitive Slave Law, "American Civilization," and "Woman," I try to show how the subordination of such urgent political and social issues to an aesthetic dissent is endemic to Emerson's transcendentalism, not simply a failure of attention or a "blind spot." Indeed, it is when Emerson talks the *most* about questions of race and gender, as well as about the specifics of political reform, that the complicity of his aesthetics with nineteenth-century U.S. ideology becomes the most apparent. What the admirable work of *rehistoricizing* Emerson has shown us (in the work of scholars as different as Carolyn Porter, Maurice Gonnaud, Barbara Packer, Len Gougeon, and Howard Horwitz) is that Emersonian transcendentalism had an important ideological function to serve in nineteenth-century America: the legitimation of those practices of intellectual abstraction required to rationalize the contradictions of the new industrial economy.[5] As Porter has argued so persuasively, Emersonianism is a mode of reification, despite Emerson's vigorous objections to what he understood as the alienation and commodification inherent in the industrial economy.[6]

It is not surprising, then, that those most committed both to reclaiming their rights to their own labor, both in the economic sphere and the equally important realm of self-representation, should have viewed Emersonianism with such suspicion. In our own times, the most effective critique of Emersonianism has been the rejection of its literary and cultural canons. The successful deconstruction of Emerson is not the work of some Derrida or Harold Bloom, but that of Women's Studies and Afro-American Studies programs (and research initiatives) in the 1960s and 1970s that reconstructed their own traditions, in part by proposing alternatives to Emersonian individualism, the self-sufficient and powerfully gendered genre of the novel (or that special blend of romance and novel that came persuasively to be known as the "American Novel"), the assumed "privacy" of literary experience (and thus its class-specificity), and the *aesthetic politics* that assumed ideology to be a sort of naive realism or, at best, a crude form of domination.

Of course, this work was not accomplished by way of professional interpretations of Emerson or the traditions with which he was associated: American transcendentalism and European romanticism. The very political efforts of nineteenth-century abolition and the women's rights movement turned crucially on issues of educational opportunity and rights to literacy as basic components of the legal rights to one's identity, self-expression, and control of the labor of one's body. Alienation from one's body as socially, legally, and economically constructed was the shared experience of women and African Americans in the nineteenth-century, however divided post-Civil War political groups representing African Americans and women may have become over such issues as suffrage and economic rights.[7] The rediscovery of just how women and African Americans variously constructed new subject-positions, their own communities, and in this work employed new forms of expression was bound to involve a searching critique of the hegemonic modes of domination that had marginalized these important American cultural legacies. Such cultural criticism was necessary in order for these other voices to be heard in their own terms, rather than as mere "echoes," the ventriloquized "characters" women and African-Americans heard too frequently in both the theater of the everyday and the narratives of high culture speaking *for* them.

Eric Sundquist's *To Wake the Nations: Race in the Making of American Literature* is a splendid example of this work of cultural reconstruction, and it influences profoundly my argument in the chapters that follow. Sundquist's work is the culmination of the work of many scholars committed to representing more adequately the unique cultural and political contributions of African-American activists, intellectuals, and artists from Abolition to Civil Rights, from the so-called "fugitive slave narrative" to the diverse arts and politics of the Harlem Renaissance. Sundquist foregrounds the ways African Americans have introduced new modes of expression into American culture by drawing on their African legacies in myth, folklore, music, and dance, as well as the strategies both of survival and affirmation African-Americans developed in folklife, music, song, dance, religion, and storytelling in response to their oppression and exclusion throughout American history. For Sundquist, these different means of cultural representation require "a redefinition of the premises and inherent significance of the central literary documents of American culture."[8] Despite his emphasis on African-American writings, music, song, and political acts, Sundquist is anxious to explain that his intention is:

. . . not to depose canonical figures but to see their less often celebrated works—Herman Melville's *Benito Cereno*, Frederick Douglass' *My Bondage and My Freedom*, and Mark Twain's *Pudd'nhead Wilson*—from the new point of view provided by the introduction of comparatively ancillary but nonetheless important works such as Nat Turner's "Confessions" and Martin Delany's *Blake; or the Huts of America*, and the more extended serious treatment of major authors such as Chesnutt and Du Bois, who are the equals of most any writer in the history of American Literature. (7)

I would describe this sort of literary criticism as *comparative*, even if it deals primarily with U.S. works and cultures.[9]

Sundquist's emphasis is on African-American writers, but his book is "not a study of them alone, nor is it a study . . . of contrasting 'black' and 'white' approaches to the problem of race. Rather, I would like to keep alive the necessary contradiction that the two traditions can be seen as both one and separate. I entertain the assertion of 'separate but (and) equal' European American and African American literary critical traditions."[10] Sundquist's ultimate aim is to make possible the sort of dialectical interchange between the independent traditions of Euroamerican and African-American literatures that ought to have been one important focus of American literary scholarship and too often failed to operate reciprocally even in the production of these two American literatures. For if there is a great tradition of mutual literary influences, frequently ignored by the dominant scholarly and critical schools, there have also been conscious refusals of influence that have not only exemplified racial division in U.S. history but also missed opportunities for crucial political and cultural alliances.

Although they shared the podium on significant occasions in their mutual fight for Abolition, Emerson and Douglass barely refer to each other in their major writings and even correspondence. Of the three references to Emerson in Douglass' three autobiographies, none suggests a substantial influence of transcendentalism on Douglass' thought.[11] By the same token, Emerson's writings, especially those most vigorously critical of slavery, betray no trace of the rhetorical strategies African-American orators, activists, and writers, like Douglass and Harriet Jacobs, had developed in the interests of persuading their auditors and moving the thoughts and emotions of their readers. Melville is familiar with and contemptuous of the proslavery ideology of the southern romances by writers like William Gilmore Simms, John Pendleton Kennedy, and even arguably Edgar Allan Poe, but he relies obliquely and erratically on African-American traditions and then in only selected works, such as *Benito Cereno* and *The Confidence-Man*. Of course, Toni Morrison is profoundly influenced by William Faulkner, just as her writing is fully involved in African-American cultural traditions;

Faulkner is attentive to the vernacular culture of southern African Americans, even if he fails adequately to represent their views and modes of cultural self-representation. There are complex reasons for this history of the uneven interchange between African-American and Euroamerican traditions, but it is safe to say that those reasons are too often traceable to racial divisions that the two cultures still need to overcome both in literary production and scholarly understanding. My interpretation of what Sundquist has achieved in *To Wake the Nations* is a major step toward putting these separate literary and cultural traditions into conversation with each other regarding the issues that have been primarily responsible for dividing them. Because he has insisted on treating African-American cultural traditions in terms of their own integrity—formal inventiveness, social functionality, and political effect, Sundquist has avoided the tendency of so many other studies to subordinate African-American culture to the "models" of the dominant Euroamerican culture.

I very much want my own study to follow Sundquist's example, adding what I can to this new dialectical understanding of these two important nineteenth-century and early modern cultural traditions—helping, in short, to constitute a dialectic that has too often been missing at the productive and interpretive levels of our social understanding. Even as I am attentive to the limitations and exclusions of my own argument—such as the notable absence of the contributions of Native Americans to early modern U.S. culture, I recognize that this dialectic should not be elaborated in our critical and scholarly debates without the incorporation of women's voices in both the political struggles for Abolition and women's rights and in the formation of a national culture composed of several different cultures (a "national multiculture" would be more appropriate as a term). Thus I am critical of Sundquist's explanation about why "neither gender nor sexuality is often foregrounded" in *To Wake the Nations*: "The fact that I do not treat women authors in detail (Harriet Jacobs, Harriet Beecher Stowe, Pauline Hopkins, and Zora Neale Hurston in particular provide significant points of reference throughout) would be a decided shortcoming if my intention had been to write a comprehensive study."[12] The chapters that follow are by no means as comprehensive in their scope as Eric Sundquist's work, whose historical and generic scope is enormous. Even in my more modest argument, however, I must consider the challenge posed to the American literary canon both by American women writers and the literary and cultural politics that follow from their commitments to the women's rights movement and to Abolition.

The efforts to construct independent cultural traditions for women and African-Americans have been extremely successful, in large part because of richness of the materials and because of their self-evident importance for understanding the roles played by culture in political and social change. In my view, some of what has been learned about cultural politics from the women's movement and African-American rights' movements in the nineteenth century now needs to be used to reinterpret and evaluate works and authors associated somewhat unreflectively with the Emersonianism I have described above. The traditional American literary canon need no longer be "expanded," because other traditions have been established independently. But many works and authors in that canon ought to be reassessed in terms of the political efficacy achieved by women's and African-American cultures, to mention here only the two that most powerfully shape the nineteenth and twentieth-century issues in this book.

I view this project as part of what Sacvan Bercovitch calls for in *The Rites of Assent* as a large-scale revaluation of what America's " 'subversive literary tradition' " now should mean, even as we should continue to articulate the different kinds of "subversive" and "critical" literary and cultural strategies that have been employed in our self-consciously "revolutionary" postures as "Americans."[13] Bercovitch does this work in *The Rites of Assent* by drawing out the challenges to ideology in Emerson, Hawthorne, and Melville while detailing their complicity in a mid-nineteenth-century ideology slow to abolish slavery and perversely resistant to changes in gender hierarchies (while simultaneously eradicating American Indian cultures in pursuit of liberal policies). Rehistoricizing classic American literature means for Bercovitch articulating its conflicted qualities, and I agree that any act of cultural transformation must be understood within the constraints of its specific historical moment, including the limitations inevitable in every political practice. What Bercovitch fails to do, even as he recognizes its importance, is provide an effective hermeneutic for distinguishing literary "subversions" that contribute to progressive change from nominally "liberal" or "progressive" sentiments that merely help ideology adapt to new circumstances. In contrast, Sundquist provides us with the terms for judging when Douglass has been coopted by the bourgeois ideology of the nuclear and patriarchal family, for example, and distinguishing this from Nat Turner's use of millennial rhetoric to refuse the cooptation of his words or his deeds by the dominant culture.[14] Failing to make this distinction, Bercovitch can only show how any "major work" of American literature (the phrase is his) potentially challenges ideology, potentially transforms ideology, and just as potentially is recaptured by ideology. Just such a capacity to negotiate between an easy consensus and a more difficult and perhaps actual dissensus is what constitutes the "major" or "classic" literary work for Bercovitch.

Thus when Bercovitch turns to works that may rightly claim to have contributed demonstrably to social change, he finds in them many of the same ideological conflicts as he had found in his earlier (and much more detailed) interpretations of classic American literature. Nowhere is this more evident than in Bercovitch's reading of Frederick Douglass' 1845 *Narrative* and the apparent appeal at the end of the *Narrative* to "the *liberating* appeal for Douglass of free-enterprise ideology."Acknowledging in passing Douglass' manipulation of that ideology for his own rhetorical purposes, Bercovitch nonetheless emphasizes how "Freedom for Douglass means self-possessive individualism."This does not "necessarily . . . de-radicalize" the 1845 *Narrative*, Bercovitch claims, in part because what Bercovitch wants to do is use the self-evident political efficacy of Douglass' work of abolition to *reradicalize* the Emersonianism that Bercovitch draws finally from Douglass. It is an "Emersonianism" that Bercovitch must put in a long footnote as an explicit equation, but the point is clear—Emerson and Douglass are similarly caught in the radicalism *and* ideological constraints of an American ideal of "freedom" that is the paradox of liberal democracy.[15]

Bercovitch creates his own problem by insisting on reading Douglass (or Stowe, as Bercovitch does in pages just preceding these involving the 1845 *Narrative*) in terms of an American ideology sustained as it was problematized by the very literary tradition he knows we must now transform. My own approach is to read that literary tradition of Emersonianism *through* Douglass. Far from being an enthusiastic endorsement of "free-enterprise ideology" and thus of the ontology of "self-possessive individualism," the conclusion of Douglass' 1845 *Narrative* connects economic self-determination with rhetorical self-determination and the necessary complement of a shared discursive community. Douglass' ability to earn his own wages cannot be distinguished from the political symbolism of "self-purchase," which is a symbolic act made so by virtue of the collective work of abolitionists (in this case, the English abolitionists who raised the funds and the Northern abolitionists who arranged the legal transfer). And the coordinated work of abolitionists serves as a sign, like the collective "I" of this political "autobiography," to the "brothers and sisters" in the South who will join this communal action as abolition succeeds. Having experienced in Durgin and Bailey's shipyard in Baltimore some of the limitations of "free-enterprise," Douglass is hardly a naive propagandist for laissez-faire capitalism.

By the same token, Douglass is fully aware of the importance of signs, whether they be words or money, in self-determination, and he encourages the reader to respect the authority over earnings and self-representation that the rights to one's own being should bring. The point of ideological contradiction is not so much Douglass' apparent naïveté before the new slavery of wage-exploitation, although it is fair to say that the 1845 *Narrative* does not provide a comprehensive interpretation of Northern social and economic practices. Rather than collapse Douglass into Emerson, effectively minimizing the differences between abolitionist rhetorical practices and the "aesthetic dissent" of

Emerson, I develop that aspect of Douglass' political practice that seems logically necessary and yet strangely underdetermined in his narrative: the revolution in gender that ought to accompany the revolution against slavery.

What prevents Douglass' *Narrative* from being translated into the "self-possessive individualism" that underwrites the tradition of American autobiography from the Puritans to Moderns is a deliberate identification with the victimization of African-American women under slavery. I will not repeat here what I develop at some length in my reading of Douglass' fictional recovery of his childhood witnessing of the whipping of Aunt Hester—that scene both of voyeuristic eroticism and sympathetic terror—except to say that it exemplifies for me the political efficacy of a certain literary identification, in which it is possible for the subject—in this case white Northern readers and the African-American male author—to experience imaginatively (and thereby sympathetically) the process of the other's victimization.

Such literary experiences are for me profoundly political, and I privilege them in my interpretations of the texts that constitute this narrative of classic American literature. Such moments are often divided between appeals to the reader either for conventionalization—the erotic satisfaction of the white male reader anxious to witness the African-American woman's vulnerability—or for transformation—the sympathy of the recollected child in his awareness that this could "happen to him," that such victimization should awaken revolutionary solidarity. There is for each such literary experience a fundamental horizon or boundary beyond which the text does not go, and it is often at this impasse that the text's complicity with ideology may be read the most easily. The limitation in Douglass' representation of gender in the 1845 *Narrative* is the extent to which African-American women are made essential to the work of abolition and yet given voice and presence (both body and being) only through Douglass' narrative "I."

Douglass' inability to represent African-American women in the 1845 *Narrative* may not be fully confessed by the narrator, but the victimization of African-American women is represented as one of the chief injustices of slavery. Thus the limitation in Douglass' *Narrative* virtually invites, rather than forecloses, supplementary accounts, such as Harriet Jacobs' *Incidents in the Life of a Slave Girl*, which not only details the social and human costs of such victimization but also begins to resist it in the very act of narration. The sheer power of telling the secrets of the domestic household of a slave-holding community like Edenton, North Carolina, empowers Linda Brent and, of course, Harriet Jacobs in her abolitionist purposes. Mrs. Flint's jealousy and shame prompt not only her cruelty toward Linda but also her willingness to keep secret her husband's sexual harassment of Linda. What makes Jacobs' *Incidents* such an important supplement to the African-American narrative of emancipation is its special insight into how the ideology of slavery and racism divides women and confounds the apparently natural affections in families. Yet if Jacobs' narrative develops this critical analysis of the gender-specific consequences of slavery, it encourages a sympathy between white, middle-class women readers and the African-American narrator that is thoroughly utopian, which is to say, "literary." In that famous moment of moral ambiguity when Jacobs' Linda Brent "gives herself" to Sands rather than be raped by Dr. Flint, she knows how the moral dilemma posed by this choice provokes an imaginative sympathy in her readers by way of her appeal to the rhetoric of religious morality (as supported not only by the Church but also by sentimental romances): "But, O, ye happy women, whose purity has been sheltered from childhood, who have been free to choose the objects of your affection, whose homes are protected by law, do not judge the poor desolate slave girl too severely! If slavery had been abolished, I, also could have married the man of my choice; I could have had a home shielded by the laws; and I should have been spared the painful task of confessing what I am now about to relate."[16]

Brent's "painful task of confessing" is, of course, less the moral dilemma confronting her (or Jacobs in her own experience) than it is the "painful task" of exposing the contradictions of American democracy with its racism and sexism at mid-century. The goal of *Incidents* is hardly the self-reliant "individual" we associate with Emersonianism (and its ideals of authorship), but the coalition of women across class and racial lines that occasionally "happens" in Linda Brent's experiences (hints of utopia) but more often is the aim of Jacobs' work with other feminists and abolitionists, like Lydia Maria Child: political work in which literary narrative (or fictional autobiography) plays only one part. If I have stressed these fictional experiences of sympathetic identification in Douglass and Jacobs, I should add that much as I prize them for their unique political value they nevertheless cannot exclusively do the work of social reform. One conclusion to be drawn from the progressive political functions claimed by many of the classic American texts in this study is that social reform never is achieved exclusively by cultural means. Insofar as cultural work can be critical, then it must be linked with specific political practices, as Douglass' 1845 *Narrative*, Jacobs' *Incidents*, and Stowe's *Uncle Tom's Cabin* were variously intended to serve the political agenda of abolition. The literary works treated in this text that offer only lucid analyses of social problems generally conclude in political impasses or contradictions, unable to imagine how literary experience could be transformed into political functionality.

I identify such impasses in Emerson's political writings, Melville's critique of such idealism in *Pierre*, Whitman's struggle to represent the damage of war in

Drum-Taps, James' treatment of the consequences of historical ignorance in *The American*, and Chopin's interpretation of the commodification of women in *The Awakening*. Each of these authors takes recourse in his or her own vocation as writer and intellectual either by affirming its special authority and social vantage, as Emerson, Whitman, James, and Chopin do, or by mocking a literary perspective that reveals only the futility of one's knowledge, as Melville does in *Pierre*. What used to be the essential metaliterary turn in any literary text becomes in this context an expression of the impotence of pure social critique without at least imagined solutions to such problems. By the same token, I do not judge such works to be without social value or as exclusive expressions of an "aesthetic ideology." Each calls for some supplementary act either by way of another literary text that offers practical alternatives, as I think Douglass and Jacobs do in their works, or specific political and social organizations that will accomplish what literature alone is powerless to achieve, as I think Abolition and the nineteenth-century women's rights movements did.

The political coalitions imagined in literature and organized in civil rights' movements are based on the assumption that discursive communities have real power. Women's rights activists, African Americans, and abolitionists discovered this as a consequence of the powerful rhetorics of nineteenth-century ideologies of race, class, and gender.[17] At least part of this book deals, then, with *aesthetic dissent* that draws on just this power of ideological rhetoric, claiming for literature new powers of ideological control and authority. This is the case with my reading of the thematics of racism and sexism in Poe as functions of a new hierarchy of "textual competency," in which the subtleties of poetic language, along with its techniques, become tokens of privilege and power. Thus the fetishized, even dismembered feminine body in Poe, like the "natives" (of Tsalal in *Pym*, for example) and the "masses," are excluded from poetic speech, except as its negation, and all power of representation belongs to the uncanny poet-detective, who can read what is profoundly hidden from these Others. Twain offers an interesting variation on just such a theme, albeit with very different political consequences. Poe's effort to reinvent poetic power is explicitly racist and sexist: it depends crucially upon the poetic construction of the Other as savage, woman, victim. Twain reads critically just this inclination of those who understand the powers of language in the new speculative economy of the late nineteenth century, and he tries to retheorize the function of the author as social critic when the primary object of criticism is itself a social text. For Twain, the proliferation of new popular discourses, ranging from mass media to elaborate marketing schemes and political scams, offers the serious writer and intellectual a new opportunity to establish standards of judgment or discrimination by which the reader can be taught how to distinguish "true fiction" from "true lies."

Reread in terms of the successful work of literary rhetoric in the causes of women's and African-American rights movements, the politics of American literature must thus be revaluated in terms of both its critique of ideology—the traditional function of *aesthetic dissent*—and the discursive communities such literature helps constitute. In my brief account to this point, it may appear that I merely privilege texts like Douglass' and Jacobs' that are self-evidently political in purpose and subordinate texts traditionally or canonically literary, like those by Emerson, Poe, Whitman, and James. Even avowedly emancipatory texts, like Kate Chopin's *The Awakening*, can now be read as "limited," not just in terms of the political standards represented by Douglass and Jacobs but also by way of more traditionally literary texts that take on new significance when read in terms of these larger political purposes.

Chopin's Edna Pontellier is thus an utter failure when measured in terms of Douglass' and Jacobs' successful efforts to connect their voices to the discursive communities of abolition and women's rights. Like Pierre or some other romantic ironist, Edna experiences only her alienation from her body, and like Pierre she can find no filiation with other alienated or oppressed people or groups in her South. There are, of course, many opportunities for her to connect with victimized women of color—both African- and Spanish-American—as well as children and servants. Unlike Poe or his surrogates, Edna does not *desire* such alienation, but she has no means of overcoming it and the once-prevalent scenario for the woman heroine of madness or death is thus romanticized and *aesthetic dissent* relegitimated just in proportion as political connections have been missed.

On the other hand, a more recognizably modernist literary work like Faulkner's *Go Down, Moses* reveals some surprising coalitions and social filiations when read in terms of these criteria for political efficacy. Although unable to speak *for* Southern African Americans, Faulkner at least identifies the discursive and rhetorical trap in which they have been placed, unable to "speak" except through the grammar and conventions of a white Southern culture that depends upon their virtual silence. The ideological contradictions embodied in Lucas Carothers McCaslin or Molly Beauchamp generally reflect the contradictions of a Southern culture that has forced the descendants of slavery to live out their "freedom" according to the logic of a slaveholding society. Quite brilliantly and courageously, Faulkner lets his text overtake his own literary authority and predict its demise along with the other tattered and unreliable authorities of the Old South.

The "politics" of classic American literature, then, are by no means evenly distributed according to the customary division between canonical and marginalized writers and texts. The literary history I have reconstructed by way of representative literary texts is uneven and sometimes unpredictable according to the sides that have been taken in debates over the American literary canon in the past decade. None of the literary texts selected to represent "classic" American literature is ideologically innocent; none escapes fully the ideological factors influencing American culture when that text was produced. Each work benefits by being read in a critical narrative that causes established literary works to be read together with works whose canonical status has often been in question, as is the case with Douglass' 1845 *Narrative*, Jacobs' *Incidents*, and Chopin's *Awakening*. Critical studies that attempt to read representative texts across a very wide historical span—this book deals with texts from the 1840s to the 1940s— are still uncommon for very good reason. There is no final way to justify the selection of texts as "representative," and those works omitted tend to invalidate most of the general claims made in such studies. It is also difficult in such stud- ies to avoid the impression that the author's "selection" is intended to serve in itself or synecdochally for some "great tradition" based on the values enunciated by the scholarly author.

This book is subject to all these criticisms, but I think it is well worth these costs to try to read anew our classic literature for the sake of some new defini- tion of what constitutes "classic American literature." I have retained this trou- blesome term, "classic," precisely because I think writers like Douglass, Jacobs, and Chopin ought to be included in that definition even as they force us to rede- fine what the American "classic" means. I have also given prominence to the term in my title and throughout this book, because I want to reconsider the degree to which the "classic" American literary text has become the site of dehistoricized, depoliticized "aesthetic" representation that has been so frequently criticized. In some respects, such criticism has been well-deserved not only by the critical and scholarly traditions that so defined our "classic" works but also by the literary authors themselves, who did their own parts to inaugurate these same critical and scholarly methods. Yet when many of our "classic" texts are read in the rehis- toricized, repoliticized contexts made possible by comparing them with more self-consciously designed political writing, then the "classic" American literary text takes on in many circumstances a new significance, a wider political rele- vance, and a revived value for this generation of readers.

The important task before scholars and critics of American literature today is how we shall coordinate the several traditions of literary and cultural expression now available to us. We might appeal broadly and enthusiastically to the "dissensus" they make possible, as Bercovitch has done in *The Rites of Assent*. We might follow Eric Sundquist's suggestion that there is some value in keeping "alive the necessary contradiction that the two traditions" of "European American and African American literary-critical" interpretation are "separate

but (and) equal," adding to this equation the equally important and often separate traditions of American women's writing. Yet a third possibility would be for
us to read comparatively these three established traditions, looking along the
way for the points of incompatibility as well as for their possible intersections
and supplementarities. It is this possibility, which becomes possible after reading Bercovitch and Sundquist, as well as the new American scholarship and criticism on which they have drawn, that I try to realize in my arguments in the following chapters.

The stakes of such negotiation among these three traditions to shape the
cultural realities of modern America from Emerson to Faulkner are not exclusively historical. To be sure, a better understanding of the three traditions and
their negotiations is an obvious way to organize many of the important historical changes of the nineteenth century and modernity, even if certain exclusions
are obvious, such as the treatment of native peoples. But there is simply a more
pressing pedagogical need that is also at stake, and any book that claims to
address "classic" American literature or "our" literary tradition (or traditions)
must be understood as a contribution to such pedagogy insofar as synthetic critical books are implicitly courses of study or curricular designs. As literary scholars and interpreters, we are historians, not only of the past but also of the present. We help make history as teachers by enabling our students to work through
the political, social, and cultural crises and conflicts that may still be with us.
Scholarly books do this sort of teaching as well, and I have tried to show in my
book how certain negotiations among the several traditions can now be articulated in ways that will allow students of whatever gender, race, or class background to imagine the other, to occupy sympathetically another's political and
social psychological space. And finally, at the furthest theoretical reach, to know
the difference between such imaginative participation with and ideological
domination of the other. Knowing the difference will enable our students to turn
the adversarial politics of the past decade into the coalition politics needed for
this decade.

2 "Hamlet's Task":
Emerson's Political Writings

Freedom all winged expands,
Nor perches in a narrow place;
Her broad van seeks unplanted lands;
She loves a poor and virtuous race.

. . . .

She will not refuse to dwell
With the offspring of the Sun;
Foundling of the desert far,
Where palms plume, siroccos blaze,
He roves unhurt the burning ways
In climates of the summer star.
He has avenues to God
Hid from men of Northern brain,
Far beholding, without cloud,
What these with slowest steps attain
—Emerson, "Voluntaries" (1863)

Very sad was the negro tradition, that the Great Spirit, in the beginning, offered the
blackman, whom he loved better than the buckra, or white, his choice of two boxes,
a big and a little one. The black man was greedy, and chose the largest. "The buckra
box was full up with pen, paper, and whip, and the negro box with hoe and bill; and
hoe and bill for negro to this day."
—Emerson, "Emancipation of the Negroes in the British West Indies" (1844)[1]

Emerson wrote "Voluntaries" to memorialize Colonel Robert Gould
Shaw and his Massachusetts regiment, "among the first to enlist blacks, many of
them ex-slaves."[2] Shortly after Shaw and most of his regiment were killed on July
18, 1863, during their assault on Fort Wagner in South Carolina, Emerson wrote
"Voluntaries" in the spirit of Northern consensus that Gay Wilson Allen has
termed "the *righteousness* of the cause for which, after Emancipation, there was
no longer any doubt."[3] By 1863, Emerson could count nearly two decades of
writing and speaking against slavery, often on occasions charged powerfully with
the political passions of the times. Allen describes how Emerson's "Boston
Hymn" was received when it was first read publicly at the Jubilee Concert in the
Boston Music Hall to celebrate "January 1, 1863, the day the Emancipation
Proclamation went into effect." "One might think that the twenty-two stanzas,
rehearsing the spirit of American freedom from the Puritans to the Emancipation, would have been tedious," Allen writes, "But if so, two stanzas near the end
brought the crowd—many of its members former slaves—to their feet, shouting and singing wildly."[4]

No one can dispute Emerson's profound commitment to and his activism
regarding the abolition of slavery in the United States in the years following

Daniel Webster's "great betrayal" in giving his support to the Compromise of 1850, which included passage of the Fugitive Slave Bill. Yet the criticism that Emerson did not join any of the many antislavery societies that had urged him do so continues to haunt his reputation as the intellectual model of the American reformer. Emerson certainly struggled with the issues of slavery and abolition well before 1850; his writings in the 1840s frequently address the curse of slavery and the intellectual challenge of solving this great social problem. As he wrote Whittier in 1844: "Since you are disposed to give so friendly a hearing to opinions of mine, I am almost ready to promise you as soon as I am free of this present coil of writing, my thought on the best way of befriending the slave and ending slavery."[5]

Yet long after his declaration of war on Webster and on slavery in general in the decisive year 1850, Emerson still felt the anxiety and defensiveness of the intellectual whose commitments to political causes are often likely to appear publicly less substantial than judges' laws or soldiers' acts. As late as 1855, Emerson could write his brother William: "I am trying hard in these days to see some light in the dark Slavery question to which I am to speak next week in Boston. But to me as to many tis like Hamlet's task imposed on so unfit an agent as Hamlet. And the mountains of cotton & sugar seem unpersuadeable [sic] by any words as Sebastopol to a herald's oration. Howbeit, if we only drum, we must drum well."[6] His "Boston Hymn" opens with an invocation of the power of God's word:

> The word of the Lord by night
> To the watching Pilgrims came,
> As they sat by the seaside,
> And filled their hearts with flame.[7]

God's word may be uttered with apocalyptic tongues of flame, especially at such critical historical moments as when Emerson calls for divine sanction of Emancipation, but Emerson had doubted the sufficiency of his own transcendental moral authority to respond to slavery as an evil at least since he had delivered "An Address on the Emancipation of the Negroes in the British West Indies" in August of 1844.[8]

In the opening lines of "Voluntaries," conventional though they may be for an elegy of this sort, Emerson reproaches himself for a philosophical treatment of slavery that ignores the real suffering of the slave:

> Low and mournful be the strain,
> Haughty thought be far from me;
> Tones of penitence and pain,

Moanings of the tropic sea;
Low and tender in the cell
Where a captive sits in chains,
Crooning ditties treasured well
From his Afric's torrid plains.[9]

"Haughty thought" may refer conventionally enough to the inappropriateness of the poet using the tragic circumstances of an elegy as occasion for displaying his own learning, but the phrase also puns on Emerson's understanding of the transcendentalist's obligation to "higher laws."[10] The "tones of penitence and pain," even though sounded by the "moanings of the tropic sea," belong properly to those who have permitted slavery to continue, not to the African "captive" who "sits in chains." As Emerson makes clear in the second verse paragraph, the African has no reason to feel guilty and thus be in any way repentant: "What his fault, or what his crime?" (539). In both "Boston Hymn" and "Voluntaries," geography plays an important part in these poems' rhetorical motifs, not surprisingly since Emerson addresses in both the conflicts between North and South.[11] As the lines from "Voluntaries" quoted in the epigraph to this chapter indicate, Emerson causes a personified Freedom to wing from her traditional region in the North to the "dwell / With the offspring of the Sun," by which he refers at once to the American South and Africa. Freedom's "flight" to southern regions is not simply the customary paternalism offered by New England abolitionists to Southern slaves. Emerson insists that the African:

. . . has avenues to God
Hid from men of Northern brain,
Far beholding, without cloud,
What these slowest steps attain.[12]

Emerson clearly appeals here for New England transcendentalism to be changed significantly by its exposure to the African-American's experiences under slavery. As the opening figure of the captive African "crooning ditties treasured well" suggests, the "sole estate" of enslaved African-Americans are the spirituals—"the wailing song he breathed"—that challenge an exclusively abstract, dispassionate consideration of the issues in the debate over slavery.

In his earlier writings, such sentiments are unimaginable; Emerson establishes transcendentalism on values and ideals that are measured by their *distance* from a secular ignorance repeatedly metaphorized as "effeminate," "savage," or "childish." In *Nature* (1836), the transcendental spirit is approached by the "man thinking" who uses language in a decidedly patriarchal fashion: "That which intellectually considered we call Reason, considered in relation to nature, we call

Spirit. Spirit is the Creator. Spirit hath life in itself. And man in all ages and countries embodies it in his language as the FATHER."[13] What Emerson so confidently
claims true "in all ages and countries" is measured against the primitive use of language: "Children and savages use only nouns or names of things, which they con-
vert into verbs, and apply to analogous mental states."[14] The truly "spiritual" must
meet the demands of "the high and divine beauty which can be loved *without
effeminacy*," reminding us that Emerson's allegorization of nature as feminine in
Nature serves more than a conventional purpose: nature without the supplement
of man's art remains incomplete, "effeminate," childish, and primitive.[15]

Thus Emerson's self-reliant man may happily aspire beyond the limitations
of woman, child, slave, even as he claims to point the way for them to follow.
Transcendence is a matter of disciplined reflection, gnostic surrender to a higher
power, and careful use of language to embody such visionary experience. In the
course of representing such transcendental experience, Emerson incorporates
childish innocence, feminine submission, even the slave's bondage into the figure of the transcendental *Cogito*. In the famous image of the "I" as "transparent
eye-ball," Emerson borrows from each of these others in turn to construct his
transcendent figure. "In the woods, too, a man casts off his years . . . and . . . is
always a child. In the woods is perpetual youth." These symbolic woods are
explicitly "plantations of God," which for all its evocation of the rhetoric of the
King James translation of the Bible nonetheless still resonates with the meaning
of "plantation" in the slaveholding South. For it is, after all, as an absolute servant
to God that Emerson figures his transcendental man, whose spiritualization is
achieved by a divine circulation that is nearly erotic: "Standing on the bare
ground,—my head bathed by the blithe air, and uplifted into infinite space,—all
mean egotism vanishes. I become a transparent eye-ball; I am nothing; I see all;
the currents of the Universal Being circulate through me; I am part or parcel of
God." In such an ecstatic moment, Emerson argues, human relations lose their
meaning, precisely because the "I" has been so thoroughly *possessed* by divine
spirit, both within and without: "The name of the nearest friend sounds then foreign and accidental: to be brothers, to be acquaintances,—master or servant, is
then a trifle and a disturbance."[16]

In such a transcendental ethos, all men are "servants" (and "women" and
"children") and all men equally capable of liberation from these bonds. The ease
with which Emerson can command us to "build therefore your own world," so
that "a correspondent revolution in things will attend the influx of the spirit,"
also accounts for his curious association of the abolition of the slave-trade with
a variety of "miracles" he cites just a few paragraphs earlier in the closing section
("Prospects") of *Nature*. In "the thick darkness" of human history, Emerson
writes:

There are not wanting gleams of a better light,—occasional examples of the action of man upon nature with his entire force,—with reason as well as understanding. Such examples are, the traditions of miracles in the earliest antiquity of all nations; the history of Jesus Christ; the achievements of a principle, as in religious and political revolutions, and in the abolition of the slave-trade; the miracles of enthusiasm, as those reported of Swendenborg, Hohenlohe, and the Shakers; many obscure and yet contested facts, now arranged under the name of Animal Magnetism; prayer; eloquence; self-healing; and the wisdom of children. These are examples of Reason's momentary grasp of the sceptre; the exertions of a power which exists not in time or space, but an instantaneous in-streaming causing power.[17]

Eight years later in "Emancipation in the British West Indies," Emerson would argue that the emancipation of Jamaican slaves was the consequence of long, careful legal struggles against slavery that could be traced back to the eighteenth century. In *Nature*, the abolition of the slave-trade in 1808 is accounted a "miracle," explicable only by "the action of man upon nature with his entire force," and comparable with hypnotism ("Animal Magnetism"), prayer, and self-healing.

When Emerson in the mid-1840s did turn seriously to the political issues of his day—women's rights and the abolition of slavery, he was faced with the problem of adapting his transcendentalism to the pragmatics of political activism. Len Gougeon argues that in his 1844 "Address on Emancipation in the British West Indies," Emerson "shows his willingness to consider, now, the possibility of a collective rather than an exclusively individualistic development of society."[18] Yet herein lies the fundamental problem with Emerson's political writings from 1844 to 1863—the period of his most active commitment to the cause of abolition as well as the period of his 1855 lecture, "Woman": Emerson either must abandon the fundamentals of transcendentalism or the principles of political activism. Transcendentalism reveals itself to be at fundamental odds with the social reforms regarding slavery and women's rights. This conflict is at the heart of what can be viewed in no other way than as the intellectual schizophrenia of Emerson in these writings in this period. When he endorses a liberal political position, he must abandon transcendentalist principles; when he embraces transcendentalism, his politics are as patronizing and impractical as the formula for "reform" in *Nature* and his other early writings. In short, Emersonian transcendentalism and political activism in mid-nineteenth-century America were inherently incompatible.

Yet in the century that followed Emerson's passionate commitment to abolition and his public discussion of women's rights, what has survived has primarily been Emersonian transcendentalism. Only recently, in work by Carolyn Porter, Maurice Gonnaud, Len Gougeon, and Barbara Packer, has the political writing of Emerson been read with any care. In the Riverside edition of his collected works, Emerson's essays from this period are exiled to chapter 11, "Miscellanies." Not until 1995, with the publication of Gougeon's and Joel Myerson's fine edition of *Emerson's Antislavery Writings* have we had available to us a scholarly edition of many of Emerson's important political writings.

At issue, then, is not Emerson's political commitment to anti-slavery in the 1850s; Emerson had demonstrated publicly his advocacy of abolition well before the Compromise of 1850 and the "great betrayal" by Massachusetts' own, Daniel Webster. Emerson's passions against slavery are not in question, but the adequacy of his transcendentalism to serve the cause of abolition certainly is. In the 1850s, Emerson clearly changed his mind regarding his earlier commitment to self-reliant man resisting the fashions and even the laws of his day for the sake of transcendental genius. As Barbara Packer writes of Emerson's "American Slavery" lecture of 1855: "Society . . . is more than the joint-stock company he had contemptuously termed it in 'Self-Reliance.' Now he argues that the state is a reality, and 'God is certain the societies of men, a race, a people, have a public function, a part to play in the history of humanity."[19] Yet the transcendentalist values persist in these writings, effectively preventing them from contributing to the practical politics necessary for the abolition of slavery and the furtherance of women's rights at mid-century. Gougeon may argue that Emerson's 1844 "Address on Emancipation in the British West Indies" "brought him into firm contact with a group whom he had mostly avoided, and he forged thereby a de facto alliance with them," but this does not change the fact that Emerson's political writings from 1844 to 1863 remain so profoundly divided internally between transcendentalist values and practical politics as to be practically useless, except as far as the value of their political rhetoric might be measured.[20]

It has often been argued that Emersonianism, despite Emerson's vigorous criticism of industrialism and materialism in his own time, nevertheless provides a splendid intellectual rationale for Jacksonian democracy and thus emergent industrial capitalism.[21] If Emerson's radical individualism cannot be aligned with his political activism in the 1850s—that is, with the explicit instances of his work toward social reform—then the argument that Emersonianism supports, rather than refutes, the values of Jacksonian America seems strongly supported. Given the fact that Emersonianism has so profoundly shaped our traditional understanding of classic American literature, then that same American literature would appear to be profoundly implicated in the ideology of American commercialism that stretches from Jacksonian America to the present. In short, the classic American literature founded on Emersonian values would be an explicit instance of an "aesthetic ideology" working to support the very social forces it overtly criticizes.

In *The Rites of Assent*, Sacvan Bercovitch has tried explicitly to refute this criticism of Emerson and Emersonian transcendentalism. Relying on two journal entries from 1842, Bercovitch wants to carry back as far as he can in Emerson's career the notion that "individuality" or "self-reliance" is fundamental to a new conception of "community." To do so, Bercovitch must distinguish between "individuality" and "individualism," as the latter term was used by nineteenth-century utopian socialists as a code word for everything the socialists rejected in industrial capitalism. For Bercovitch, Emerson's task was compounded by his own need to reject clearly and explicitly the rhetoric of Jacksonianism in the early 1840s, which had enshrined "individualism" as the highest goal of civilization.[22] Steering a narrow course between an unqualified endorsement of the European socialism of the 1840s, which was hardly popular with Americans, and overt criticism of Jacksonian democracy, Bercovitch's Emerson intellectually "hesitates" as he searches "for the proper paradox that would connect" European socialism's and Jacksonian capitalism's very different ideas about "individuality" and "individualism" (Rites, 318). What Emerson manages to achieve paradoxically in his early essays, then, is a curious synthesis of these two powerful cultural oppositions:

> "America" was for him alternately the facts of liberal individualism and the ideals of individuality—a symbolic polarity which appeared sometimes as sheer antagonism, sometimes as probation or trial, and whose divergent meanings he somehow combined, in the early essays (1836–1841), in his consummate figure of dissent, the representative/adversarial American Self. (319)

For Bercovitch, this paradox becomes the energetic center of Emersonianism as demonstrated both by the rest of Emerson's career and the legacy of a "liberal dissent" that has had such a powerful influence in the modern definition of American culture. Relying on essays from the 1840s, Bercovitch argues that Emerson "subsumes the goals of socialism under the actualities of the developing Northern United States" and thereby claims social "revolution" is to be found properly in the normal course of "liberal individualism." By the time of the actual revolutions in Europe, 1848, Emerson can advocate in "Natural Aristocracy" a "more or less outright identification of individuality with industrial-capitalist 'Wealth' (1851) and 'Power' (1860), with 'American Civilization' (1862), and summarily with 'The Fortune of the Republic' (1864)" (Rites, 336, 340). Acknowledging that Emerson capitulates to American ideology, especially progressive capitalism, Bercovitch refuses to argue that Emerson has been coopted by the dominant culture and that the legacy of "Emersonianism" is one designed to support rather than challenge that culture:

> I am not arguing that Emersonian individualism is a form of liberal co-optation. It is a form of utopian consciousness developed within the premises of liberal culture. It carries with it the profoundly unsettling energies released by that culture in its formative phase—well designated 'the era of boundlessness'—and it sustains that profoundly energizing, destabilizing, centrifugal thrust by an appeal to subjectivity as the sine qua non of union. (345)

Recognizing the problems in Emerson's thought, especially as Emerson attempted to come to terms with the new economics and thus new social relations of modern America, Bercovitch nonetheless redeems Emersonianism, especially as it is founded on Emerson's writings before 1850, which have generally been used by scholars to connect the supposed Puritan Origins of American culture with modern American culture by way of what Bercovitch terms "the combined sacred and secular authority of Protestant non-conformity and the theory of natural rights" (Rites, 345). Bercovitch's careful argument allows him to do more than simply redeem Emerson from ideological critique; it enables Bercovitch to find within liberal progressivism a critical dimension that fits admirably the social criticism of many classic American writers. Indeed, *The Rites of Assent* effectively uses this theory of "liberal dissent" to find the critical substrate in Hawthorne and Melville, as well as Emerson.

Bercovitch's argument skips over, however, Emerson's essays on the political issues of slavery and women's rights, with the exception of "American Civilization" (1862), an essay that does deal with slavery together with industrial capitalism. My contention is that the "liberal dissent" Bercovitch reads in Emerson's canon is not the energetic "paradox" of these political writings, but rather the fundamental contradiction beyond which Emerson cannot take his transcendentalism. Acknowledging as early as 1844 the political and civil rights of African Americans as crucial to the future spiritual and physical survival of the nation, Emerson tries valiantly to avoid the sort of idealist rhetoric that characterizes his early and most often cited works, such as *Nature*, "Self-Reliance," and "The American Scholar." But transcendental and practical politics continue to collide in his essays from 1844 to 1862, demonstrating the inappropriateness of Emersonianism for any practical social reforms. What Bercovitch concludes is an enabling, fundamentally *poetic* "paradox" at the heart of Emerson's thought is in my view an essential contradiction fundamental to nineteenth-century liberal progressivism and its legacy in the twentieth century.

Because the political writings of this period so fundamentally challenge Emersonianism, they have remained largely unread in that tradition. They have been interpreted ably in their historical contexts by scholars like Len Gougeon in *Virtue's Hero: Emerson, Antislavery, and Reform*. Gougeon's task is to redeem Emerson's reputation as a social reformer in two important ways. First, he demonstrates that Emerson "was a committed social reformer all of his life. . . deeply concerned with and involved in the major social reform movement of his time, antislavery."[23] Second, Gougeon wants to correct the late nineteenth-century misinterpretation of Emerson as a supporter of laissez-faire capitalism and Social Darwinism.[24] Just as Bercovitch only treats Emerson's philosophical transcendentalism, so Gougeon treats only Emerson's political affiliations and commitments. When treated together, Emersonian transcendentalism and Emerson's political commitments from 1844 to 1863 are fundamentally at odds with each other. What this suggests ultimately is that Emersonianism is ill-suited to social and political reform and that the scholarly reliance on such Emersonianism to interpret (even *organize*) the modern American literary tradition has effectively depoliticized that tradition. To read the political dimensions of American literature we may, of course, simply reject Emersonianism and the tradition it has constructed. Yet another way to approach the problem would be to identify just those blindnesses and limitations in Emerson's treatment of concrete political issues. Assessing other classic American literary authors in terms of the degrees to which they overcome or reproduce such limitations will enable the critic to construct a different "classic" American literature without inevitably subscribing to the values of Emersonianism.

Emerson delivered "An Address on the Emancipation of the Negroes in the British West Indies" on August 1, 1844, in Concord at the invitation of the Women's Anti-Slavery Society, which annually celebrated the anniversary of the British abolition of slavery in the West Indies (meaning primarily Jamaica). Emerson was the keynote speaker, but "Samuel Joseph May and Frederick Douglass, among others, delivered lectures."[25] Although Emerson's address marked the tenth anniversary of legal emancipation on August 1, 1834, the British had adopted a policy of "gradual" emancipation that indentured former slaves to landowners during a six-year "apprenticeship" plan. As Emerson points out in his lecture, "300,000 [Jamaican] negroes, early in 1838, resolved to throw up the two remaining years of apprenticeship, and to emancipate completely on the 1st August, 1838."[26] Emancipation also occurred two years early in part because Parliament paid that year the £20,000,000 awarded landowners for the "loss" of their "property." Although Emerson discusses this system of compensation, he chooses to stress Jamaicans liberating themselves as a more effective example of the human desire for freedom.

Emerson's main arguments in this lecture, however, follow the relatively conservative abolitionist position in the 1840s that Southern slaveholders should be led to recognize the evils of slavery and the degree to which the slaveholding economy is not in their own self-interest. Gougeon traces such ideas to Emerson's mentor, William Ellery Channing, who claimed that "slavery would soon disappear 'were the obligation to remove it thoroughly understood and deeply felt.' "[27] These are the same attitudes that inform Emerson's earliest writings, which urge individuals to discover their own moral grounds for social action. What usually accompanies this argument when applied to slavery is some practical appeal to the slaveowner that plantations run by wage-earning laborers will be more economically successful: "If the Virginian piques himself on the picturesque luxury of his vassalage, . . . I shall not refuse to show him, that when their freepapers are made out, it will still be their interest to remain on his estate, and that the oldest planters of Jamaica are convinced, that it is cheaper to pay wages, than to own the slave" (BWI, 8).

Emerson's reference to the luxury of the Virginian's vassalage prompts an extended reflection on the history of slavery as the commodification of Africans and the theft of their labor: "From the earliest time, the negro has been an article of luxury to the commercial nations. So it has been, down to the day that has just dawned on the world" (BWI, 9). Relying on a transcendentalist convention regarding excess (*luxus*) and dependency as unnatural, Emerson verges here on a brilliant understanding of what Marx and Engels would subsequently theorize as the "surplus theory of value" fundamental to capitalism. Later in his lecture, he will return to this theme of unnatural luxury in slaveowning to make clear he means more than just that the slaveowner "only wants the immunities and the luxuries which the slaves yield him." Emerson disagrees with this view, commonly used to support arguments that slavery might simply be abolished by economically compensating slaveowners: "I think experience does not warrant this favorable distinction, but shows the existence, beside the covetousness, of a bitterer element, the love of power, the voluptuousness of holding a human being in his absolute control" (BWI, 17). The obvious unnaturalness of such a love of power nonetheless contradicts earlier transcendentalist claims, such as the famous passage in "Self-Reliance": "Power is, in nature, the essential measure of right. Nature suffers nothing to remain in her kingdoms which cannot help itself."[28]

Such voluptuousness of unnatural power also seems to argue against gradual solutions and strengthens the appeal to violent revolution, but when Emerson comes to praise "such men as Toussaint [L'Ouverture] and the Haytian heroes," recalling the Haitian revolution of 1791 against the French, he does so in a manner that explicitly links such revolution with the "progressive" history of antislavery that he has traced in British law (BWI, 31). What Emerson advocates practically, amid transcendentalist enthusiasms for intellectual "miracles" and "spiritual progress," is the long history of British emancipation that he carefully traces in British law from 1772 to 1834.[29] This history brings about an eventual "moral revolution," but Emerson insists on its humble and quotidian sources: "Here was no prodigy, no fabulous hero, no Trojan horse, no bloody war, but all was achieved by plain means of plain men, working not under a leader, but under a sentiment." The collective work Emerson here celebrates is not the consequence of the moral persuasion and conversion he would associate with his transcendentalism, but the hard and time-consuming work of legal decisions joined with the moral conversion of slaveowners: "Other revolutions have been the insurrection of the oppressed; this was the repentance of the tyrant. It was the masters revolting from their mastery. The slave-holder said, I will not hold slaves" (BWI, 26).

Of course, Emerson has shifted the referent for slaveholder from those Jamaican planters who love irrationally their power over other human beings to the British parliamentarians and justices—"All the great geniuses of the British senate, Fox, Pitt, Burke, Grenville, Sheridan, Grey, Canning, ranged themselves on its side" (BWI, 27)—who contributed to the ultimate legal abolition of slavery in the British West Indies. Emerson thereby connects the history of the abolition of slavery with a general progressive spirit in modern civilization, and he does so in ways that are contrary to his transcendentalist critique of modern commercialism. The Jamaican planter may be "the spoiled child of his unnatural habits," which include "the need of excitement by irritating and tormenting his slave," but Emerson nonetheless endorses the compensation of planters for "so much of the slaves' time as the act took from them" on practical rather than moral grounds. To be sure, the idea of applying the British model of compensation to Southern slavery was often debated in the antebellum years, usually as a moderate solution to slavery. Yet Emerson goes on to argue that this "practical" solution grows out of the planters' recognition that slavery has produced an economically and morally depressed society in the West Indies. "It was shown to the planters that they, as well as the negroes, were slaves; that though they paid no wages, they got very poor work; that their estates were ruining them, under the finest climate; and that they needed the severest monopoly laws at home to keep them from bankruptcy. The oppression of the slave recoiled upon them. They were full of vices; their children were lumps of pride, sloth, sensuality, and rottenness" (BWI, 21).

There is no historical evidence that the economic impracticality of slavery caused West Indies' planters to accept the terms of the British courts and Parliament. Nevertheless, Emerson is intent upon making his moral argument in terms acceptable to commercial interests, and his strategy is not without merit. Six years later, 800 Boston merchants would sign a letter in support of Daniel Webster's participation in Clay's Compromise of 1850, to the disgust of Emerson and other committed abolitionists.[30] In 1844, however, Emerson acknowledges that the British and Americans share a commercial character that must be considered by abolitionists: "The English lord is a retired shopkeeper. . . . And we are shopkeepers, and have acquired the vices and virtues that belong to trade. . . . The national aim and employment streams into our ways of thinking, our laws, our habits, and our manners" (BWI, 20). For such societies, Emerson argues, slavery has a special appeal: "We had found a race who were less warlike, and less energetic shopkeepers than we; who had very little skill in trade. We found it very convenient to keep them at work, since, by the aid of a little whipping, we could get their work for nothing but their board and the cost of whips. What if it cost a few unpleasant scenes on the coast of Africa?" (BWI, 20).

Such contempt for commercialism and its inherent exploitation of those weaker follows the rhetorical logic of Emerson's transcendentalism, but in this lecture it becomes the economic basis of social values that must be turned to the work of abolition. Actual moral persuasion is slight in the remainder of Emerson's argument; instead, he offers the practical advantages likely to accrue to such commercial interests from the abolition of slavery:

> Slavery is no scholar, no improver; it does not love the whistle of the railroad; it does not love the newspaper, the mailbag, the college, a book. . . . For these reasons, the islands proved bad customers to England. It was very easy for manufacturers less shrewd than those of Birmingham and Manchester to see, that if the state of things in the islands was altered, if the slaves had wages, the slaves would be clothed, would build houses, would fill them with tools.   (BWI, 21)

It is just a step from this argument in favor of liberal progressivism in its commercial guise to a benign imperialism that would "enlighten" the African slave, not only in America and Britain's colonies but in Africa itself: "In every naked negro of those thousands, they saw a future customer. Meantime, they saw further, that the slave-trade, by keeping in barbarism the whole coast of eastern Africa, deprives them of countries and nations of customers, if once freedom and civility, and European manners could get a foothold there"   (BWI, 22).

Although Emerson continues by insisting that economic and legal considerations were by no means the only factors in British emancipation, he does not successfully separate the altruistic motives of British abolitionists from their economic interests. To the end of his lecture, Emerson connects the moral aims of abolition with the commercial interests of the Western nations, whose aims in increasing trade ought ultimately to be the spread of Western civilization. Following the convention of many New England abolitionists, Emerson describes the African-American or West Indies' slave as "child-like" and "barbaric," in effect requiring the enlightenment of civilization. Toward the end of his lecture, he comments on Thomas Clarkson's "collection of African productions and manufactures, as specimens of the arts and culture of the negro. . . . These he showed to Mr. Pitt, who saw and handled them with extreme interest. 'On sight of these,' says Clarkson, 'many sublime thoughts seemed to rush at once into his mind.' . . and hence appeared to arise a project which was always dear to him, of the civilization of Africa" (BWI, 29). Clarkson, who together with William Wilberforce won the passage of the 1807 law abolishing the British slave trade, is thus represented by Emerson as one of the late eighteenth-century originators of the British movement to abolish slavery by way of a scene in which he introduces to Prime Minister William Pitt (prime minister 1783–1801) the commercial and imperial advantages of such a righteous cause.

Far from meeting the lofty demands of Emerson's transcendentalist ethics, his argument in "Emancipation of the British West Indies" embraces thoroughly practical solutions that are in the best interests of the expanding commercial, capitalist, and Northern interests he had hitherto claimed to criticize so profoundly. Yet, Emerson has not simply abandoned his earlier positions; in his efforts to maintain the high ground of morally "persuading" slaveowners of the "advantages" to be gained from emancipation, he subordinates his own transcendentalism to the Jacksonian values he had traditionally abhorred. The late nineteenth-century "misreading" of Emerson's ideas that Gougeon cites as justifications for corporate interests and Social Darwinism are not entirely the work of cynical capitalists searching for some innocent philosopher's authorizing ideas. As he struggled to find the terms to appease Northern commercial interests and yet still satisfy his own moral convictions, Emerson turned from radical individualism toward a new collectivity.[31] It was not, however, a socialist community that sustained this new vision of reform; it was a decidedly capitalist ruling class that would do the work of abolition and subsequent "civilization." It is but a step from Emerson's vision in this essay to the late nineteenth-century doctrine of the "White Man's Burden."

In his first lecture on the Fugitive Slave Law, "Address to the Citizens of Concord" on May 3, 1851, Emerson passionately denounces Daniel Webster, appeals in support of this new law for preservation of the Union and patriotism, and the failure of the political process to serve a higher moral law. "Not since 1844 had he been moved to such emotional heights by a social cause," Gougeon writes. It is a powerful speech, fueled by Emerson's "pyrotechnical ferocity" against "politicians, crass materialism, and especially the cultivated barbarism of the polite classes who defend a moral outrage on the basis of its constitutionality."[32] In his rage, Emerson understandably reverts to the radical individualism of his early transcendentalism, effectively rejecting the careful legal processes he had encouraged his auditors to adapt from the British model in his 1844 address. Clay's and Webster's Compromise had, of course, so corrupted the American political process as to mock confidence in a legal process of emancipation in America comparable to the sixty-two year history of legal reforms Emerson had traced in his 1844 address.

Condemning leaders like Webster for their lack of character and the legal and political processes for their "metaphysical debility," Emerson appeals for the renewal of virtue in civil disobedience: "An immoral law makes it a man's duty to break it, at every hazard. For virtue is the very self of every man."[33] Emerson will build upon this appeal to our inherently moral individuality to promote finally what Gougeon terms "a collective rather than an individualist response to the evil at hand."[34] Not only are the grounds for such collective action profoundly transcendental, the political "action" is by no means compatible with the other economic and political solutions Emerson will offer in the essay. In short, the Concord address is stirringly righteous and passionate in its commitment to moral law as "natural" to men, but it is also fundamentally contradictory, nowhere more so than in its effort to revive transcendentalist values to fight Webster's and Clay's "treason."

"All men that are born are, in proportion to their power of thought and their moral sensibility, the natural enemies of this law. The resistance of all moral beings is secured to it" (Concord, 58). Emerson knew well and was in fact inspired to his towering rage by the fact that many Bostonians and other New Englanders applauded the Compromise of 1850.[35] Thought, morality, and nature must therefore be taken in the preceding quotation as predicates of Emersonian transcendentalism, which is to say: a certain kind of thinking results in a morality that is natural and proper to man. Certainly Emerson is striving here to link his philosophy with the traditional abolitionist arguments based on every human being's natural rights to life, liberty, and control of one's own labor-power. But he has made it appear that the best resistance to the new law is to be found in a transcendentalist temper, which supports disobedience of the law.

In direct response to Daniel Webster's mockery of Seward's appeal to "higher laws" in opposition to the Compromise of 1850, Emerson invokes just such "higher laws" now in the guise of his transcendentalism:

I thought that all men of all conditions had been made sharers of a certain experience, that in certain rare and retired moments they had been made to see how man is man, or what makes the essence of rational beings, namely, that, . . . men have to do with rectitude, with benefit, with truth, with something which *is*, independent of appearances: and that this tie makes the substantiality of life, this, and not their ploughing or sailing, their trade or the breeding of families. I thought that every time a man goes back to his own thoughts, these angels receive him, talk with him, and, that, in the best hours, he is uplifted in virtue of this essence, into a peace and into a power which the material world cannot give.   (Concord, 58)

Here Emerson transcendentalizes the "natural law" arguments of abolitionists, and he does so explicitly to express his contempt for the commercial and property interests that would "make the world a greasy hotel" if not transformed by some higher purpose (Concord 59). Emerson then proceeds to demonstrate how "the great jurists, Cicero, Grotius, Coke, Blackstone, Burlamaqui, Montesquieu, Vattel, Burke, Mackintosh, Jefferson" all "affirm" that "it was a principle in law that immoral laws are void" (Concord 59).

Yet the civil disobedience that Emerson counsels does not lead relentlessly either to a call to arms or comparable revolutionary practice. Despite his condemnation of commercial interests in the debate over slavery, insisting as he does that "property" in no way satisfies our spiritual natures, and his fiery condemnation of political and legal processes in America, Emerson reverts to the same solutions to slavery he had proposed in 1844: economic and legal. Whereas he had associated slavery in "Emancipation in the British West Indies" with economic decadence and impracticality, he associates Southern slavery in this lecture with a perverse industry, progress, even Manifest Destiny: "Slavery . . . is very industrious, gives herself no holidays. No proclamations will put her down. She got Texas, and now will have Cuba, and means to keep her majority" (Concord, 69). Alluding to the political successes of proslavery interests in Congress, Emerson treats these, perhaps correctly, as primarily economic advantages that can be combated only by the superiority of Northern technological and commercial energies. Indeed, it is just such technology that makes the agrarian labor of the Southern slave less necessary and thus easier for the Southern landowner to give up: "By new arts the earth is subdued, roaded, tunneled, telegraphed, gas-lighted; vast amounts of old labor disused; the sinews of man being relieved by sinews of steam. We are on the brink of more wonders" (Concord, 69).

Emerson does not explicitly link this technological progress with the spiritual progress of transcendental man, but it seems clear enough that the former will make possible greater spiritual self-realization. The subtle difference between technology and commerce, scientific advances and the curse of "property" is sufficient for Emerson to align the technology of urban capitalism on the side of abolition, making the stubborn maintenance of agrarian slavery appear to be an anachronism. In such a "progressive" context, Emerson may reintroduce his idea from his 1844 address of compensating Southern owners for their "loss" of slaves' time, as the British had paid Jamaican planters. Emerson's paean to technological achievement is also a rhetorical way of addressing the huge amount estimated such compensation would cost Americans—"a thousand millions" in Emerson's biblical rhetoric (Concord 70). In fact, the vision of accelerating technological and thus commercial development that Emerson outlines is on such a grand scale as to trivialize the "thousand millions" that would be paid Southern slaveowners.

Emerson can now return to the idea of legal and political processes for emancipation working on the model of British constitutional law, but only after he has aligned the spiritual progress of the transcendental self with that of urban industrialism and its technology. As in "Emancipation in the British West Indies," this leads him to a conclusion that endorses the imperialist project of "advancing" Western civilization to the furthest reaches of the globe as a direct consequence of the abolition of slavery. In his "Address to the Citizens of Concord," however, such imperialism is explicitly linked with the idea of representative man. Personifying Massachusetts as the goddess of liberty, comparable to ancient Greece and Judaea in her potential influence on subsequent civilizations, Emerson then peoples this Massachusetts with representative men:

> We must make a small State great, by making every man in it true. . . .
> Every Roman reckoned himself at least a match for a province. Every
> Dorian did. Every Englishman in Australia, in South Africa, in India, or in
> whatever barbarous country their forts and factories have been set up,—
> represents London, represents the art, power, and law of Europe. Every
> man educated at the northern schools carries the like advantages into the
> south.   (Concord, 71)

Taken together with his remarks on the advantages opened to British imperialism in Africa after the slave trade was abolished, Emerson's extended metaphor here is much more than merely figurative in the connection he makes between British imperialism in "barbarous" lands and the "enlightenment" Northern intellectuals could bring to the South. To be sure, the moral values of abolitionists committed to disobeying immoral proslavery laws would be a most welcome "invasion" of the antebellum, slaveholding South, but it is not quite this moral crusade that Emerson has endorsed in the final pages of his address. The moral purpose of the representative man has been confused with the commercial and technological enlightenment of the new industrial capitalism, which had so often been at the root of Emerson's criticism of Jacksonian America. Powerless in himself, the transcendentalist has had to make his own difficult compromise to respond concretely to this historical crisis.

Emerson's effort to connect abolition with the "progress" of industrial capitalism is made particularly clear in his 1861 lecture, "American Civilization," which he delivered at the Smithsonian on January 31, 1862, "in the presence of President Lincoln and some of his cabinet," in a specific effort to speed Lincoln's formal declaration of emancipation.[36] Developing at some length a democratic theory of labor that has its roots in his analysis of slavery's "surplus theory of value" in "Emancipation in the British West Indies," Emerson gives up even the divine right to "mastery" he had affirmed in *Nature*: "Use, labor of each for all, is the health and virtue of all beings. *Ich dien*, I serve, is a truly royal motto. . . . Nay, God is God because he is the servant of all" ("Civilization," 277). Slavery epitomizes, of course, the corruption of this ideal and thus the ignoble essence of those slaveowners who aspire to feudal aristocracy. Indeed, the Civil War itself is recast by Emerson as a second revolution against feudalism:

> We have attempted to hold together two states of civilization: a higher state, where labor and the tenure of land and the right of suffrage are democratical; and a lower state, in which the old military tenure of prisoners or slaves, and of power and land in a few hands, makes an oligarchy. . . . But the rude and early state of society does not work well with the later, nay, works badly, and has poisoned politics, public morals and social intercourse in the Republic, now for many years.   (Civilization, 279)

Creating a strict binary between the decadent South and progressive North, Emerson is forced by his own rhetoric to celebrate with patriotic zeal the "march" of Northern civilization: "We live in a new and exceptional age. America is another word for Opportunity. Our whole history appears like a last effort of the Divine Providence in behalf of the human race" (Civilization, 279–80). Later, such enthusiasm will expand to include Emerson's zeal for Manifest Destiny, which will be the work of united and free African-American and white laborers in the aftermath of Emancipation and the Civil War: "There does exist, perhaps, a popular will that the Union shall not be broken,—that our trade, and therefore our laws, must have the whole breadth of the continent, and from Canada to the Gulf" (Civilization, 285).

In fairness to Emerson, the prospect of free labor that he describes is utopian, predicated on the solidarity of several different labor interests, notably those of "the poor white of the South" with both the African American and "the

Northern laborer." In this respect, he attempts to adapt his philosophical thinking to the practicalities of the contemporary economy in ways as forthright as
Frederick Douglass in his reflections on a man's right to his labor in the 1845
Narrative.[37] Nevertheless, the prevailing view in "American Civilization," like
that in "To the Citizens of Concord" is that progressive, laissez-faire urban capitalism offers the most likely means both toward enduring emancipation of
African Americans and toward the "civilization" of "barbarous lands," whether
the latter be in Africa or India or the American South.

In "The Fugitive Slave Law," delivered at the New York Tabernacle on
March 7, 1854, Emerson addresses formally the hated law for the second time,
now two years after Webster's death. Relying on many of the same ideas and
occasionally on the same paragraphs, Emerson stresses in this lecture the failure
in Webster of the promise of the representative man. Throughout the essay,
Emerson argues that Webster's rhetorical powers were insufficient to compensate for a lack of moral principle most evident in what Emerson terms Webster's
ultimate lack of "genius":

> It is the office of the moral nature to give sanity and right direction to the
> mind, to give centrality and unity. Now it is a law of our nature that great
> thoughts come from the heart. It was for this reason I may here say as I
> have said elsewhere that the moral is the occult fountain of genius,—the
> sterility of thought, the want of generalization in his speeches, and the
> curious fact, that, with a general ability that impresses all the world, there
> is not a single general remark, not an observation on life and manners, not
> a single valuable aphorism that can pass into literature from his writings.[38]

Thus despite the appearance in Webster, especially before 1850, of all the
qualities Emerson would count in his representative man, Webster's rhetorical
power reveals ultimate sophistry rather than moral action. In the size of his person and his oratory, Webster gave audiences the impression of his "Adamitic
capacity," such that his famous oration at Bunker Hill on June 17, 1843 could
seem equivalent to the symbolism of the monument itself: "I remember his
appearance at Bunker Hill. There was the monument, and here was Webster"
(Fugitive, 76).

In "The Fugitive Slave Law," Emerson abandons his vision of collective
reform as indispensable for so great a task as the abolition of slavery and reverts
to the individualism of his early transcendentalism. Daniel Webster's greatest
betrayal is his failure to sustain his role as the representative man, the exemplary
figure of statesmanship that was once served as the citizen's ideal. In the wake of
the Compromise of 1850, Emerson could write in his journals that Webster rep-

resented "the American people just as they are, with their vast material interests, materialized intellect, and low morals."[39] Emerson's disappointment with Webster reflects Emerson's own anxieties about the potential of transcendentalist rhetoric to effect social reform. In no place does he equate his own rhetoric with Webster's sophistry and rationalization of immoral laws, but it is clear that Emerson sets his own considerable rhetorical talents in competition with the failure of Webster's rhetoric—his want of "genius" and "inspiration."

In the face of duplicitous laws, traceable in part to the Constitution's silence regarding slavery, only character can serve the true leader, either political or spiritual, in a time of crisis: "There are always texts and thoughts and arguments; but it is the genius and the temper of the man which decides whether he will stand for Right or for Might" (Fugitive 78). In his 1851 address, Emerson condemns the corrupt legal and political processes that have resulted in such an immoral law, but in 1854 he stresses that "Covenants are of no use without honest men to keep them. Laws are of no use, but with loyal citizens to obey them. To interpret Christ, it needs Christ in the heart" (Fugitive, 83). In effect, Emerson reverts in 1854 to the arguments of his earlier transcendentalist essays from 1836 to 1841 that social reform must begin with the individual's discovery of his spiritual nature.

There is a defensiveness in this posture, as well as in Emerson's rhetorical demonstration in the lecture of *his* inspiration and genius as transcending Webster's merely apparent rhetorical powers. The appeal to self-interest that so structures the argument of both "Emancipation in the British West Indies" and "To the Citizens of Concord" is here condemned as mere selfishness: "The national spirit of this country is so drowsy, so preoccupied with interest, deaf to principle. The Anglo-Saxon race is proud and strong but selfish. They believe only in Anglo-Saxons" (Fugitive, 86). Recounting the diverse emergent nations that had been rejected by America for assistance in their revolutions—Greece, Poland, Italy, Hungary, France—Emerson concludes that "the like torpor exists here throughout the active classes on the subject of domestic slavery and its appalling aggressions" (Fugitive, 86). In his conclusion, Emerson will no longer call for practical economic and legislative solutions to slavery, but rather for a "Crusade" for "Liberty" that ought to be an inspiration "to every poetic; to every heroic; to every religious heart." In effect, the "revolution" against slavery's aggression is couched by Emerson in terms of "our learning, our education, our poetry, our worship"—in sum, the disciplines and powers encompassed by Emerson's "Man Thinking." In his 1863 poem, "Voluntaries," Emerson would ask:

In an age of fops and toys,
Wanting wisdom, void of right,
Who shall nerve heroic boys

To hazard all in Freedom's fight,——
Break sharply off their jolly games,
Forsake their comrades gay
And quit proud homes and youthful dames
For famine, toil and fray?

(Voluntaries, 180)

At the end of the stanza, Emerson will answer with Duty's call, which derives from God, in a much-quoted patriotic refrain: "When Duty whispers low, *Thou must*, / The youth replies, *I can*." For all his rhetorical passion, Emerson in "The Fugitive Slave Law" appears to be subordinating his rhetoric to just such an emotional call to political or military arms and encouraging his listeners to "follow" leaders who can sustain the charismatic appeal of this "Crusade."

Emerson's changes of emphasis in these lectures on slavery from practical reforms that rely on Northern commercial support and interests to the rediscovery of transcendentalist values in the "representative man" as the only leader capable of revolutionizing the corrupt legal and economic system of modern America are perfectly understandable for an intellectual who chose to assume a central position in the heated political debates surrounding slavery in these years. Emerson's personal courage cannot be denied, just as we must admire his intellectual struggles to negotiate his own settled values with the dramatic changes in public events. Nevertheless, the contradictions in Emerson's arguments regarding concrete social reforms drive him into two equally unacceptable positions for the future of a democracy based on the philosophical principles of "self-reliance" and the "representative man." On the one hand, spiritual progress will have to rely crucially on the material progress of industrialism and its technology if the former is to have any practical impact on such demonstrable evils as Southern slavery. On the other hand, the "collective" promise of industrial capitalism will have to be *directed* at the political, economic, and cultural levels of social experience by the "representative man," whose capacity to incarnate the ideals of the republic will serve a crucial symbolic purpose for Americans otherwise inclined to pure self-interest. In "American Civilization," Emerson carries this second option to an extreme that verges on fascism: "I wish I saw in the people that inspiration which, if Government would not obey the same, would leave the Government behind and create on the moment the means and executors it wanted" (Civilization, 282). The "democracy" promised by industrial capitalism's progress and the "liberty" offered by the strong political leader have both turned out to be horrible delusions of our modernity, pasteboard masks behind which exploitation, new forms of wage-slavery, and assorted fascisms have first paraded.

An important test of Emerson's endorsement of the Northern industrial economy as an answer to Southern feudalism and immorality must be the degree to which Emerson addresses the existing problems within Northern society. In his antislavery writings, he returns frequently to the theme that Northern citizens remains "slaves" to their government, their economy, and immoral laws as long as they permit slavery to continue. Although less righteous in his condemnation of American commercialism than in his early writings, Emerson still finds occasion to criticize the narrow materialism and selfishness of commercial interests untouched by higher laws. Yet throughout these explicitly reformist writings, in which Emerson has frequently alluded to the "higher civilization" of the North, "where labor and the tenure of land and the right of suffrage are democratical," he has said hardly anything about those members of Northern society largely excluded from these rights of the higher civilization: women (Civilization, 279).

Excusing himself on the grounds he was too busy editing Margaret Fuller's *Memoirs*, Emerson had declined Lucy Stone's invitation that he address the women's rights convention held in Worcester in 1851.[40] As Allen points out, five years later, he did accept an invitation to "address a Woman's Rights Convention in Boston, and on September 20 he delivered an address called simply 'Woman.' His attitude toward women had not basically changed since 1851, but he had come around to accepting 'the benefits of [public] action having for its object a benefit to the position of Woman."[41] Emerson's argument in "Woman" relies on key transcendentalist concepts to urge woman's subordination to man and thus maintenance of the existing patriarchal ideology, even as Emerson endorses women's claims to such basic rights as education, property, voting, and judicial process. In effect, Emerson employs his rhetoric to mystify women in a way that comes dangerously close to what Emerson had accused Webster of doing to abolitionists.

In his opening paragraphs, Emerson endorses most of the popular stereotypes of nineteenth-century American bourgeois men and women. Men are strong, and women are delicate. "Man is the will, and Woman the Sentiment." Man is the "rudder," and woman is the "sail" in the "ship of humanity." Women are decorative and "embellish trifles," which explains for Emerson why "no mastery in either of the fine arts . . . has yet been obtained by them, equal to the mastery of men in the same."[42] Given Margaret Fuller's careful account of the achievements of women in politics and the arts throughout history in *Woman in the Nineteenth Century*, it seems especially ignorant of Emerson to make such a claim about women so shortly after editing Margaret Fuller's *Memoirs*. Yet for all his fitful admiration of Fuller's intellect, he nonetheless identifies her in his Journals and letters with the sort of dilettantism that lacks "mastery" in literature. Even her noted skills as a conversationalist, not only in general social converse but also in her structured "Conversations" with women in Boston, are treated by Emerson as examples of women's special talent for conversation and thus the medium of their "social influence": "But there is an art which is better than painting, poetry, music, or architecture—better than botany, geology, or any science; namely, Conversation. . . . Conversation is our account of ourselves" (Woman, 340).[43]

Through their conversation "and their social influence," Emerson argues, "Women are. . . the civilizers of mankind. What is civilization? I answer, the power of good women" (Women, 340). To be sure, these are common patriarchal clichés in this period, and Emerson works hard to connect them with his transcendental values: "Society, conversation, decorum, flowers, dances, colors, forms, are their homes and attendants. . . . More vulnerable, more infirm, more mortal than men, they could not be such excellent artists in this element of fancy if they did not lend and give themselves to it. They are poets who believe their own poetry" (Woman, 343). In short, women are more *transcendental* for Emerson than men, at least as far as visionary experience is concerned: "There is much in their nature, much in their social position which gives them a certain power of divination. . . . Women know, at first sight, the characters of those with whom they converse. . . . And in every remarkable religious development in the world, women have taken a leading part" (Woman, 345). Thus clichés about "women's intuition," the "angel in the house," and the "feminine muse" are repeated here in a context that unsubtly transcendentalizes them, granting a sort of specious philosophical respectability to stereotypes without intellectual credibility.

Emerson repeats such stereotypes, even as he recognizes the important roles women have played in the struggle for the abolition of slavery. Indeed, "the antagonism to Slavery" is cited by Emerson as the third stage in a short history of women's rights that he traces from "the deification of Woman in the Catholic Church" of the Middle Ages through emergence of the intellectual woman of the salon in Louis XIV's France to the activist contemporary woman whom "it was impossible not to enlist" in the fight against slavery (Woman, 346–47). As if recalling his own intellectual and political struggles with Abolition between 1844 and 1855, Emerson claims that this Cause was a great educator:

> But that Cause turned out to be a great scholar. He was a terrible metaphysician. He was a jurist, a poet, a divine. . . . It took a man from the plough and made him acute, eloquent, and wise, to the silencing of doctors. There was nothing it did not pry into, no right it did not explore, no wrong it did not expose. And it has, among its other effects, given Woman a feeling of public duty and an added self-respect.   (Woman, 347)

Emerson had often referred to Abolition or its opposite, proslavery and the Fugitive Slave Law, for example, as an "education" of an entire people, as he had in his 1851 "To the Citizens of Concord."[44] It would follow, then, from Emerson's own political zeal on behalf of Abolition and in defiance of the Fugitive Slave Law that the "education" achieved by women regarding their own rights "by argument and by association" with the issues of antislavery would be endorsed thoroughly by Emerson as well.

After all, woman's "progressive" achievement of her own self-consciousness fits well the transcendental path Emerson typically charts for "civilization," and Emerson carefully establishes the terms by which such enlightenment can be achieved by women who follow the basic tenets of transcendental self-realization. Eleven paragraphs from the end of his lecture, at what must have been the rhetorical climax of his oratorical performance, Emerson affirms in quick succession women's rights to all that had been proposed at women's rights conventions from Seneca Falls in 1848 to the 1855 meeting in Worcester: "They have an unquestionable right to their own property. And if a woman demand votes, offices and political equality with men, . . . it must not be refused. . . . Educate and refine society to the highest point" (Woman, 350). Yet Emerson appears only to be playing rhetorically with his audience, because in the remaining ten paragraphs of the lecture he will rely on a mystified version of transcendentalist choice or self-reliance to argue: "I do not think it yet appears that women wish this equal share in public affairs. But it is they and not we that are to determine it" (Women 354). Of course, Emerson was not entirely mistaken in this regard, because many women active in the antebellum women's rights conventions shared this more conservative view that women should not yet have the vote or otherwise participate directly in politics.

The end of Emerson's lecture rationalizes precisely this conservative position with regard to nineteenth-century women, and it does so by way of very familiar romantic conventions. Men and women are inextricably bound together in their social self-interest, so Emerson may claim that if you "improve and refine the men, . . . you do the same by the women, whether you will or no" (Woman 355). Women in their relations to men are the latter's ideal complement, so that spiritually understood "wife, daughter, sister, mother" serve the same purpose of mediating between man and nature through the family. In his internal critique of romantic idealism in *Pierre*, Melville will focus on just this idealization of Woman as basic to romanticism's political impasse. For Emerson, however, this very abstraction of the "feminine," achieved in "Woman" by way of his own transcendental values and rhetoric, is used to offer his listeners a meliorist position that sounds daring and emancipatory while it returns women to their customary bondage:

Slavery it is that makes slavery; freedom, freedom. The slavery of women happened when the men were slaves of kings. The melioration of manners brought their melioration of course. It could not be otherwise, and hence the new desire of better laws. For there are always a certain number of passionately loving fathers, brothers, husbands and sons who put their might into the endeavor to make a daughter, a wife, or a mother happy in the way that suits best. Woman should find in man her guardian. Silently she looks for that, and when she finds that he is not, . . . she betakes her to her own defences. . . . But when he is her guardian, fulfilled with all nobleness, knows and accepts his duties as her brother, all goes well for both.

(Woman, 356)

As I shall point out in my discussion of Melville's treatment of relations between brothers and sisters in *Pierre*, this well-established romantic convention regarding idealized relations between genders was clearly intended to maintain gender hierarchies. As Mary Wollstonecraft and other preromantic women intellectuals had challenged the patriarchal order, romantic idealists like Hegel and Emerson would develop subtler but still no less constraining rhetorical bonds than their enlightenment predecessors to keep women subordinate.

In his political writings from 1844 to 1855, Emerson struggles to adapt the predicates of transcendentalism to the concrete social issues of abolition and women's rights. More often than not, transcendentalism works to rationalize present wrongs rather than bring about actual social change. Pressed by his own personal commitment to the cause of antislavery, Emerson leaps from philosophical abstractions to specific legal, economic, and political remedies that contradict the "spiritual progress" he had advocated so passionately in his earlier writings. When he does attempt to synthesize his transcendentalism with the practical demands of the new age, then he subordinates his philosophy to the progressive forces of the new urban capitalism in ways that contradict his own earlier contempt for material wealth and commercialism.

The examples I have chosen from Emerson's writings are by no means his greatest essays, when measured by the standard of the American romanticism he helped establish under the name of transcendentalism. By the same token, these writings are by no means exceptions in Emerson's canon; they represent an internal contradictoriness between the anticommunal, ahistorical aspects of his philosophy and the demand he placed upon that philosophy to effect social reform. Sacvan Bercovitch is, of course, right that this internal division in Emerson's writings reflects microcosmically the conflict within the American symbology, especially as that conflict has been understood to pit the individual against society: "The appeal of Emersonian dissent lies in an extraordinary conjunction of forces: its capacity to absorb the radical communitarian visions it renounces, and its capacity to be nourished by the liberal structures it resists. It demonstrates the capacities of culture to shape the subversive in its own image, and thereby, *within limits*, to be shaped in turn by the radicalism it seeks to contain."[45]

Insofar as Bercovitch claims that the "paradoxes" of such an internally divided cultural symbology "remain a central tension in American literary, cultural, and political dissent," then I think he has failed to distinguish between what might sometimes be enabling paradoxes and at other times disabling contradictions in the Emersonianism that has been for too long fundamental to our cultural self-definition as Americans. In sum, what Bercovitch finds as the primary cultural *value* of liberal dissent in Emerson is for me our long-standing problem. The "critical imperative" that Bercovitch reminds us is also our inheritance from "the Emersonian legacy" has too often served false gods or made Americans appear tolerant of differences when in fact they are intent on maintaining the same old powers.[46] It is this friendly disagreement over the Emersonian legacy that I intend to let play through the rest of this study as I assess the degrees to which classic American writers have solved this problem of the political efficacy of literary representation.

3 Antebellum Slavery and Modern Criticism: Edgar Allan Poe's *Pym* and "The Purloined Letter"

Mr. Poe is decidedly the best of all our young writers—I don't know but that I may say, of all our old ones.

—James Kirke Paulding

My argument is on the face of it simple: Poe was a proslavery Southerner and should be reassessed as such in whatever approach we take to his life and writings. This is by no means an original claim. From Ernest Marchand in the 1930s to Bernard Rosenthal in the 1970s, the pro-slavery case against Poe has been argued again and again, usually on the very specific grounds of the infamous review of pro-slavery books by James Kirke Paulding and William Drayton published in 1836 in *The Southern Literary Messenger* while Poe was an assistant editor under Thomas Wylkes White, the general editor.[1] For these earlier critics, Poe's sympathies with the Southern aristocracy, plantation life, and the institution of slavery have been treated as personal prejudices, which are not consistently displayed in his literary writings. Marchand, F. O. Matthiessen, and Rosenthal, among others, have found elements of Poe's racism at the heart of certain key works, notably *The Narrative of Arthur Gordon Pym*, but in most cases have treated the literary work as an allegory of Poe's antebellum prejudices. My own argument is that Poe's proslavery sentiments are fundamental to his literary production and thus demand a searching reconsideration of his aesthetic canon. Of equal interest, I think, is the history of Poe's twentieth-century canonization as modernist and the ways it has compounded the problem. Thus the reinterpretation of Poe's writings in terms of his pro-slavery sentiments involves an equally comprehensive reconsideration of twentieth-century critical approaches to Poe, as well as their theoretical assumptions.

My thesis is complicated by several factors that cannot always be kept clear and distinct, so I shall simply make a preliminary effort to identify them and then let these factors play throughout the rest of this chapter. First, the critical neglect of the historical circumstances surrounding Poe's literary production has been the work both of traditional literary historians and critical theorists. Ironically, the only literary historians who seem to have been *right* about Poe's complicity with antebellum Southern legitimists are those who have been demonstrated to have been factually *wrong* on several scores. In a similarly ironic manner, the vigorous efforts of poststructuralist theorists to modernize Poe and thus remove him (and his writings) from any historical context other than our own has had the effect of complementing what I contend was precisely Poe's racist strategy of literary production in the antebellum period. Second, Poe's racism is inextricably entangled with his attitudes toward women and his conception of the literary author as the new aristocrat. Racism, sexism, and aristocratic pretensions, of course, often go hand-in-hand, but in the case of Poe these prejudices are finely woven into the fabric of his art.

I will entangle Poe's name and thus meaning in contemporary debates about the psychoanalytical dimensions of literature (or the inevitable literariness of psychoanalysis) with a much-needed review of the historical study of Poe's proslavery sentiments, even as I warn against a narrow reliance on strictly empirical evidence. Such documentary evidence as the review of Paulding and Drayton in the 1836 *Messenger* and the possible sale of a slave by Poe in Baltimore should not be ignored, but they should not be treated in purely archival and historical terms.[2] Treated in a strictly positivist manner, they can be easily enough refuted or ignored, as has been the case with these two significant "details" from Poe's life. The ruses by which willful critics separate and discriminate "life" from "letters" are sufficiently familiar to all of us, and the text-bound myopia of literary criticism is by no means restricted to that brief historical moment we have so obsessively monumentalized in the ominous name "Anglo-American New Criticism." Textualists have often done the same work, trivializing biographical and historical facts, even when they know well enough that such facts ought to be incorporated into rhetorical history, rather than conveniently forgotten.

The stakes of my argument are by no means exclusively concerned with Poe's reading by modern scholars and critics. In his own time, Poe enjoyed a reputation as a poetic extremist who challenged the transcendentalists' confidence in the correspondence between natural and supernatural realms. Writing as an avowedly anti-Emersonian idealist, Poe advocated a seemingly more radical, posttheological idealism that often uses scientific rhetoric and pseudoscientific evidence to legitimate its concepts. In these respects, Poe was often judged in his own times as a radical and even "revolutionist," insofar as what has been termed his "romantic irony" criticized the established values of "the New England transcendentalist clique he would dub the 'Frogpondians.'"[3] Joan Dayan interprets Poe as a nineteenth-century alternative to Emerson and thus to "the Emersonian strain of American literary history, best represented by Charles Feidelson's *Symbolism and American Literature* and Sacvan Bercovitch's *The Puritan Origins of the American Self*" (Dayan, 5).

Yet even as the nineteenth-century Poe seems to offer an idealist alternative to American transcendentalism and Continental romanticism, he ends up representing simply a more systematic or logical idealism: "Poe is not interested in any simple opposition between 'scientific reason' and 'poetic intuition' or 'material fact' and 'visionary knowledge.' He works his language so that such oppositions become convertible. Instead of arguing against materialism and rationalism, Poe shows how the arch-rationalist can engender the most amazing fanaticism, how the facts of matter can be turned into suppositions of mind" (Dayan, 9). In my view, this qualifies the nineteenth-century Poe as the obverse of the Emersonian coin, the unconscious of a transcendentalist idealism that would overtly endorse liberal progressive ideals and still be liable to a philosophical "imperialism" isomorphic with nineteenth-century social and economic hierarchies. In the case of Emerson and the New England transcendentalists, I have argued that their views often reproduced the social system they criticized: the entreprenuerial expansion of Jacksonian-era capitalism and its general tendency toward Manifest Destiny. In the case of Poe, philosophical and aesthetic idealism props up reactionary politics that reject any sign of liberal progressivism for the sake of a "radical" retreat to feudal hiearchies, albeit redefined to survive in Poe's nineteenth century (Dayan, 9).

The marginal, eccentric, supercilious nineteenth-century Poe has thus done specific cultural work in legitimating the American Self, even if Dayan is right to argue that he has more often seemed to represent the opposite or negative of the Emersonian "self-reliant man." The attenuated, gnostic, even obliterated self is often enough Poe's literary theme, and it is the necessary other of Emerson's "man thinking" (Dayan, 5–6). The construction of such a "Poe," pushed to the margins of American culture and yet nonetheless a figure who continues to exert an obsessive fascination for interpreters of nineteenth-century America, must be considered part of the cultural work that made Emersonianism such an enduring and defining legacy of American identity. Enduring as an "exile" of this tradition, thereby serving to frame it, Poe has also escaped reconsideration in terms of the central political issues of his age: abolition and women's rights. Protected by his aesthetic supernaturalism, hiding behind his pose as poetic rebel, Poe has realized his own grandest ambition: to escape history.

Literary historians have also played a part in this work of historically reconstructing, if not outright protecting Edgar Allan Poe from his own Southern identity. In this regard, let me turn to the fate of the review of Paulding and Drayton in the twentieth century. The misattribution of that infamous review to Poe seemed to be settled decisively by William Doyle Hull's 1941 doctoral dissertation at the University of Virginia, "A Canon of the Critical Reviews of Edgar Allan Poe."[4] Arraying an impressive variety of circumstantial evidence, Hull argued that the review was most likely written by Judge Beverly Tucker, the proslavery advocate. Hull's scholarship is in no way concerned with Poe's literary writings, except in their connection with the literary taste demonstrated in his reviews. Hull equally ignores the wider cultural context in which proslavery works appeared in the antebellum period. "Authorship" for Hull is not a theoretical matter; it is simply a question of assessing the surviving empirical evidence to determine the authorship of an unsigned work.

Yet as the scandal about Paul de Man's wartime writings for *Het Vlaamsche Land* and *Le Soir* has once again taught us, the moral responsibilities of writing are hardly covered by conventional notions of historical "authorship." Those defending de Man's writings on the grounds that they display only occasional and then debatable anti-Semitic and pro-Nazi sentiments can do so only by ignoring or trivializing the virulent anti-Semitic and vigorously pro-Nazi views published along with de Man's "cultural" reviews in *Le Soir* during the German occupation of Belgium. Wary as we should be of the dangers of charging "guilt by association," we must acknowledge that the association of publication in the same newspaper or journal can be the basis for a substantial case.[5]

In the case of Poe, such an association with the likes of Judge Beverly Tucker, should he in fact be the author of the disputed review, is made even more invidious when we consider Poe's "heavy correspondence" with Tucker in the spring of 1836 while Poe was working as an assistant editor for Thomas Wylkes White of *The Southern Literary Messenger*. Although there is no evidence that Poe commissioned the review by Tucker, Poe was serving effectively as the "review editor" when the review of Paulding and Drayton's books was published.[6] In 1974, responding in part to criticism that his *Race and the American Romantics* (1971) had mistakenly included the Paulding-Drayton review as the work of *Poe*, thus ignoring the evidence of Hull's doctoral dissertation, Bernard Rosenthal carefully argued both the "guilt by association" thesis and challenged the circumstantial evidence of Hull's thesis in "Poe, Slavery, and the *Southern Literary Messenger*: A Re-examination."[7] In that essay, Rosenthal argues the case in historically concrete terms, but he includes as part of that history Poe's deferential correspondence with Judge Tucker, his great admiration for and gratitude to Paulding himself, and Poe's undisputed admiration for Thomas R. Dew in his October 1836 review of Dew's address to the students at William and Mary—the Thomas R. Dew, who Rosenthal calls "the architect of the South's intellectual position in defense of slavery" and who subsequently became president of William and Mary (Rosenthal, 30).

Yet, since Rosenthal reopened the debate concerning the authorship of the infamous Paulding-Drayton review, there has been very little scholarly discussion of Poe and slavery, with the exception of interpretations of *Pym* as a "fantasy of white slaveholding paranoia" that have followed the leads of Walter Bezanson and Rosenthal himself.[8] The "modern" or "postmodern" Poe hardly lends himself to this debate, which turns so crucially on historical details and the very regional identification that Poe himself seemed to do everything possible to disavow in his major literary productions. Rosenthal made an understandable, albeit strategic, error in framing his 1974 argument primarily in historical terms. Although he broadened the historical context of Hull's argument, he kept the argument primarily in an archival context at the very moment Poe was about to reemerge as a major figure in what has come to be termed "Deconstruction in America."

Rosenthal's arguments were virtually ignored, even by Poe scholars. One notable exception was the distinguished Poe scholar G. R. Thompson, who reviewed Rosenthal's argument in *American Literary Scholarship* for 1974 and concluded: "Although his argument depends on a number of ambiguities and a few improbabilities, he does a good job of showing greater improbability that the review is Tucker's."[9] Such grudging acknowledgement of Rosenthal's challenge to Hull, appearing as it did in the annual *ALS* review of Poe scholarship, was not likely to have much impact on poststructuralists working on Poe, especially since their interest derived hardly from the study of Poe as an American author but from the study of Poe primarily in the context of comparative literature and Continental theory.

Thompson himself seems to have forgotten what he wrote in 1975 about Rosenthal, because in his contribution to the new *Columbia Literary History of the United States*, Thompson argues in "Poe and the Writers of the Old South" that "Poe's conception of letters is virtually devoid of regionalist sentiment" and that: "(The notorious review of two books defending slavery in the *Messenger* in 1836, upon which some critical interpretations of Poe's *Narrative of Arthur Gordon Pym* have been based, was written not by Poe but in all likelihood by Beverly Tucker)."[10] Acknowledging that "Poe's Southernness" remains a question "of recurrent critical debate," Thompson judges Poe's "high formalism of prose style, . . . idealization of women, . . . scorn for democracy and the idea of progress, and an uneasiness about the age of the machine" as "not . . . specifically Southern" (269). Further, in his volume for the Library of America, *Poe's Criticism and Reviews*, Thompson pays little attention in his "Notes" to Poe's Southern sentiments, despite his inclusion of Poe's long, admiring review of Beverly Tucker's chivalric romance, *Balcombe*. Throughout the reviews and criticism that Thompson selects for this volume, there is frequent evidence of Poe's preferences for Southern literature and the chivalric romance, including Poe's praise for William Gilmore Simms' melodramatic novel about Southern honor and romance, *Beauchamp*. In his introduction to the notes for this volume, Thompson cites Hull's dissertation as one of his sources for establishing the canon of Poe's reviews and criticism, which seems to explain why Thompson makes no reference to the Paulding-Drayton review.[11]

In *The Word in Black and White*, Dana Nelson has woven together a number of the same strands in this critical reception of Rosenthal's 1974 essay to conclude that Thompson's version of Poe in the *Columbia Literary History of the United States* "most directly voices the recent trend to sweep Poe's politics under the rug."[12] Nelson is careful not to decide hastily the question of Poe's racism, appealing instead for a reconsideration of how "a depoliticized and dehistoricized reading of the Poe oeuvre concomitantly 'saves' Poe for a canon increasingly skeptical of texts that support human oppression."[13] What Nelson's approach enables us to do is judge not merely Poe's Southern sentiments and racist values, but also reexamine political consequences of the several critical traditions from the New Critics and phenomenological critics to post-structuralists that have canonized Poe by depoliticizing his writings.

My argument, like Nelson's, then, is not directed simply at the critical blindness of a single critic, such as G. R. Thompson, or at the fate of a single essay, such as Bernard Rosenthal's work of 1974, but at the politics of the hermeneutic and historical principles that have helped limit such critics' understanding. Since my own earlier writings on Poe are taken as objects of critique in both Nelson's study and this chapter, I recognize fully the ease with which our own theoretical commitments can overwhelm our interpretive judgment and historical knowledge.[14]

Thompson's assessment of Poe in the *Columbia Literary History* as a protomodern cosmopolitan writer without "specifically Southern" identity in his writings is the place to begin reinterpreting Poe's significance for our own time as well as in the antebellum South. Rosenthal's mistake, like Marchand's and Matthiessen's before him, was to treat the historical Poe and the modernist Poe as different figures, involving drastically different intellectual issues. The consequence has been that the rise of the "modernist Poe" has left the historical Poe in the archives, virtually ignored in our generation and, unfortunately, for the next generation reading the *Columbia Literary History of the United States.*

Let me now try to weave together some of these specific historical questions, including Poe's critical reception in the twentieth century, together with the theoretical Poe, whose circulation in the past twenty years has given him a new currency, but one that has strategically ignored his nineteenth-century political affiliations. Since the recovery of Poe by the French Symbolistes, "Poe" has been treated as an invention or an occasion for a wide variety of different language games—Symbolist poetry, psychobiography, psychoanalysis, deconstruction—that would seem to have little to do with the historical Poe. Edgar Allan Poe, of course, would have loved this transcendence; he himself never much cared to live in his own age. The translation of his literary works into the language game of psychoanalysis has accomplished precisely what Edgar Allan Poe had hoped: the substitution of an immaterial world for the threatening world of material history. The immaterial poetic world of the language game that Poe worked so hard to distinguish from ordinary reality is in no way an "unreal" or purely "fictional" world. The very appropriateness of post-Freudian psychoanalytical and textualist approaches to Poe's writings argue just the opposite, and I have no intention of attacking their claims according to some specious criteria for "truth" and "falsehood." My contention is that there is a rhetorical and psychoanalytical relation between the immaterial, poetic world of Poe's writing and the material history from which it flees. It is just this differential relation between the material and the immaterial that modern psychoanalytical theories using Poe's writings have missed—not only in Poe, but also in themselves.

Lacan, Derrida, Barbara Johnson, Jean Ricardou, I myself—none of these interpreters of Poe, I suspect, would be disturbed by the accusation: "You have not been historical enough." That, it would appear, is beside the point. Even John Irwin's *American Hieroglyphics*, which so brilliantly translates many of the chief issues in the Lacan-Derrida debate into the rhetoric and ideas of nineteenth-century romanticism, demonstrates this discrepancy between intellectual and material history. The rich history that Irwin offers us is the grand narrative in which Poe is a single chapter: the narrative of romanticism's defensive substitution of its own text (the Text of texts) for the increasingly unmanageable text of nineteenth-century social life.[15]

Let us be historical. And let us begin in the most improbable place for such work, "The Purloined Letter." Suffice it to say that Lacan and Derrida have so charged the title of this story that I can hardly utter it without invoking the fantastic narrative of twentieth-century psychoanalysis.[16] The analysis is truly interminable. It is a story that encourages just such fantastic narration, because it is itself so tenuously connected with any history. A monarchy. Paris. Minister D. An unread message. In the first paragraph, as if to confirm this ahistorical mise-en-scène, there is a mocking date: "18——."[17] It is as if Poe works here, as in so many other fictive spaces, to make the intrusions of material history as insignificant as possible, serving the barest of technical functions to permit us to imagine what is otherwise unimaginable, unpresentable. Like the furnishings in Minister D's apartments, which the Prefect so diligently and futilely destroys, these historical details seem given only to be discarded.

"18——."The date can be uttered only clumsily and with explanations; it is a nearly pure *grapheme* that emphasizes the space of writing we are entering. Yet, even Poe's textual formalism is still penetrated by history, for this date *follows* the French Revolution, in a text that plays with the threat posed to the monarchy by a message stolen by a Minister of State. Dupin's clever narrative saves the monarchy from this threat by recourse to two simulated "revolutions." The distraction that allows Dupin to substitute his forgery for the actual message is a "disturbance in the street" occasioned by "the frantic behavior of a man with a musket. He had fired it among a crowd of women and children. It proved, however, to be without ball, and the fellow was suffered to go his way as a lunatic or a drunkard" (Poe, 992). We shall have more to say of women and children, as well as of revolutions. The other revolution is the real challenge Poe offers to the French Revolution: the poetic "counterrevolution" (the term is quite precise here) by which he appears to save the monarchy, but in fact institutes his own power. It is, quite obviously, the power of rhetoric, of poetry: Poe's power claimed by way of the "new" nobility of the Author.

In the disputed review of J. K. Paulding's *Slavery in the United States* and [William Drayton's] *The South Vindicated from the Treason and Fanaticism of the Northern Abolitionists*, which appeared in the April 1836 issue of *The Southern Literary Messenger*, we find the following remarks on the French Revolution: "It should be remembered now, that in that war against property [the French Revolution], the first object of attack was property in slaves; that in that war on behalf of the alleged right of man to be discharged from all control of law, the first triumph achieved was in the emancipation of slaves. The recent events in the West Indies, and the parallel movement here, give an awful importance to these thoughts in our minds. They superinduce a something like despair of success in any attempt that may be made to resist the attack on all our rights, of which that on Domestic Slavery (the basis of all our institutions) is but the precursor" (267). The "disturbance in the street" is a mock-enactment of a "lunatic" or anarchic act of revolution; it motivates the reasoned act of "counterrevolution": the apparent restoration of the monarchy with the subtler effect of the instantiation of Dupin's power as master of rhetoric.

We must keep in mind the familiar psychobiographical interpretation of

Poe, especially as developed by Marie Bonaparte. Poe's own Southern aristocratic pretensions, fuelled just as they were frustrated by his foster father, John
Allan, find here their curious realization in the will-to-power of the artist, whose
"property" is the ultimate defense against "the attack on all our rights" that is the
Abolitionist movement.[18] Derrida's critical reading of Lacan may be recalled in
general terms here. For Derrida, what marks Lacan's contradiction, his blindness, is precisely his insistence upon the route by which the psychic narrative of
"The Purloined Letter" restores the monarchy, reaffirms the Law-That-Is-the-
Name-of-the Father, in this case, the King. For Derrida, this transforms the
Signifier of the Unconscious into a Signified, restoring the phallic authority of
the King/Father, just as Dupin's "forgery" inseminates that obvious vaginal
scene: the clitoral card rack dangling above the yawning, burning opening of the
fireplace in the Minister's apartments.[19] For Lacan, Dupin's forgery is a
metonymic displacement (his coded message for the Minister's theft, itself a
substitution for the original performative of the message to the Queen) that
reroutes the letter, only for the letter of the Unconscious to return to its proper
service: affirmation of the centered authority of the Father/King in the circuits
of psychic signification.[20] For such clever insemination, Derrida substitutes *dis-
semination*, whereby the rhetoric of Dupin initiates a "wandering" that makes
possible the scene of writing itself: the possibility that a letter does not always
reach its proper destination. For Derrida, it is the subversive, the deconstructive
moment, which would align Dupin with a revolution against monarchy, the
Minister, the Prefect—all the putative authorities of this world "recentered" in
the wake of the decentering of the French Revolution. For Derrida, Dupin
would have to be understood as a revolutionary, shadowy precursor to the
deconstructor himself, and here, of course, is the dilemma for those interested
in claiming Poe as proto-deconstructive writer.

Returning to history, to the proslavery cant in the 1836 *Messenger*, we must
pursue a different reading, albeit one that grants the validity of Derrida's deconstruction of Lacan. Poe/Dupin has "seized" a certain "property," and it is, of
course, the property of language. As we know from Poe, such property must be
distinguished strictly from the material property that is finally an illusion for his
characters, even kept apart from the specious "empiricism" of science and journalism: that is, the properties of a referential language. In the decidedly immaterial domain of poetic rhetoric, "possession" is no longer mere theft, the sheer cru-
dity of what Marx would consider the "primitive accumulation of capital."
"Possession" is now achieved by ruses that declare the intelligence, even the
genius, of the poet. Thus the allusive texture of "The Purloined Letter" culminates
in the ultimate "forgery," Dupin's strategic "quotation" from Crébillon, the line
itself an allusion to Aeschylus' *Oresteia*, Sophocles' *Electra*, Euripides' *Electra* and

Orestes, and these classical tragedies themselves allusions to their mythic prototypes: " 'Un dessein si funeste, / S'il n'est digne d'Atrée, est digne de Thyeste.' " Dupin's "theft" is legitimated by means of literary and mythic history, in ways far more subtle and finally subversive than the Minister's crude attempt at blackmail.

Even so, a certain strategic will-to-power has been enacted, whereby these "literary properties" have been made to conclude in the name of Dupin/Poe. For whom? The reader, of course, whose interest in the story turns precisely on the rhetorical moves by which Dupin solves the puzzle by constituting a new narrative. The very appearance of the "ahistorical" setting for this tale leads us inevitably to an interest in literary history: a history far more compelling in this tale than anything that speaks of that despicable aftermath of the French Revolution, that threat to aristocracy and monarchy, that anarchic rebellion against what "the few possess." Again, from that troublesome 1836 proslavery review in the *Southern Literary Messenger*: man's "prevailing interest" is "happiness. . . . Foremost among these, and the equivalent which is to purchase all the rest, is property. . . . Under such excitement, the many who want, band themselves together against the few that possess; and the lawless appetite of the multitude for the property of others calls itself the spirit of liberty" (267). I confess that this sounds too crude for Poe, too naively utilitarian, and nevertheless I "quote" it here, in a reading of "Poe."

There is yet another historical detail in "The Purloined Letter," albeit one that requires considerable speculation. It is in *Vienna* that the Minister once did Dupin "an evil turn, which I told him, quite good-humoredly that I should remember" (225). For those worried about aristocratic privilege in the years leading up to the Paris Commune and to the American Civil War, "Vienna" has one large significance among others. It was at the Congress of Vienna in 1814–1815 that the last desperate effort was made by the European and Russian monarchies to consolidate their powers and territories in the wake of Napoleon's abdication. Even so, the Congress was a reminder that the old order was changing, that monarchy was in jeopardy and royal territories increasingly arbitrary. Admittedly, I can only speculate here, but in ways that make the most of these bare historical traces in a designedly literary displacement of history into the psychopoetic history that is so often the wish-fulfillment of the embattled aristocrat, the would-be plantation owner: the apotheosis of "property" into the ultimate property of language. The Congress of Vienna, the great political event of the early nineteenth century, now becomes the occasion for Dupin's revenge against a Minister of State. "The Purloined Letter" is Dupin/Poe's own "Congress of Vienna," in which the territory of Europe is not simply reapportioned, but remapped onto the coordinates of poetry. Crébillon, we ought to remember, was one of the official censors of the French Academy in the first half of the eighteenth century. Dupin has effected his own repetition of such censorship by creating a discursive field in which the materiality of the letter forbids the intrusions of the more threatening materiality of history.

Jacques Derrida is thus the winner of the battle, but perhaps he has lost the war. Which war? Well, the Civil War, among others, which brings us to *Pym*, written twenty-four years before the American Civil War and yet addressing all the fears that the Southerner would revolve in the turbulent years leading to the necessity of battle. I make no claim for originality here; the interpretation of *Pym* as a thinly disguised allegory of Poe's manifesto, "Keep the South white," belongs to others.[21] I add only a few touches, delicate strokes, as it were, not the least of which involves the entanglement of scholarly debates over historical, psychoanalytical, and theoretical issues.

The date of *Pym*'s first appearance in *The Southern Literary Messenger* is 1837, but the date of the voyage on the *Grampus* is "June 1827."[22] Poe probably got the idea for *Pym* from James Kirke Paulding's suggestion in a letter of March 1836 that Poe "undertake a Tale in a couple of volumes, for that is the magical number." Paulding was trying to soften the blow Poe certainly felt when Paulding had notified him two weeks earlier that Harpers had turned down Poe's manuscript, *Tales of the Folio Club*.[23] This is the same period of Poe's work as assistant editor at the *Southern Literary Messenger*, his correspondence with Beverly Tucker, and weeks before the proslavery review was published in the *Messenger*. The significant event on board the *Grampus* is a mutiny, which seems distinguished for its extraordinary brutality and its utter irrationality. Emancipation in the British West Indies was formally declared on August 1, 1834. Three years earlier, Nat Turner's Rebellion—the Southampton Insurrection—occurred in August 1831, in Southampton County in southeastern Virginia.

Following the much-publicized trial and execution of Nat Turner in November 1831, much stricter laws regulating Southern slaves (especially laws regarding travel passes) were passed in most Southern states. Just as the earlier slave revolts by Gabriel Prosser and Denmark Vesey had fueled Southern white paranoia, so Turner's revolt had the effect of what Eric Sundquist judges an instance of nineteenth-century terrorism: "The white paranoia that followed the revolt bred distortions that in turn heightened apprehension—accounts suggesting that the rebels wore outfits ceremoniously dyed red in their victims' blood or, more strikingly, that they drank the blood of the slaveholders."[24] Poe writes this long narrative in the historical context of decades of Southern white anxieties regarding the possibility of widespread slave revolts, recently made real in Turner's revolt. As Nelson points out in *The Word in Black and White*, this Southern cultural anxiety is complemented by wider nineteenth-century Anglo-European defenses of "Anglo racial superiority," arguments that helped support various imperialist projects as well as the more specific ideology of Southern slavery.[25]

The Narrative of Arthur Gordon Pym of Nantucket is thus not a mere allegory of proslavery values; in this regard, the historical interpretations have been too crude, rather than simply "inaccurate" or falsely "historical," as defenders of Poe against proslavery charges have argued. Poe's own repressed fears regarding slave rebellions in the South and the deeper fear that Southern aristocratic life itself might be passing are the psychic *contents* that provoke the poetic narrative. The defense of the poetic narrative against just these fears is its argument that language, the essence of reason, is the basis of all reality and thus the only proper "property." As the "enlightened ruler" of language, its rational governor, the poet works to recontain savagery—the mob, the black, the lunatic—within poetic form.

In *Beneath the American Renaissance*, David Reynolds shows how Poe "had learned from America's pioneering penny newspaper a lesson in conscious manipulation of sensational themes through a double-sided fiction that possessed both novelty and tact, excitement and control." For Reynolds, *Pym* combines the irrational sensationalist and the pseudoscientific in a narrative that, if "not altogether successful," nonetheless constitutes a defensive parody of such popular styles.[26] Nat Turner's Southampton Insurrection provoked sensationalist journalism of the most hysterical kind, often focusing on Turner's gory use of a broad-axe to murder his master and the master's wife.

Poe's defensive fantasy about savage, rebellious blacks is not exclusively enacted on the island of Tsalal. The first outbreak of such savagery is on board the *Grampus* during the mutiny. As I argued in "Writing and Truth in *The Narrative of Arthur Gordon Pym*," it is during the mutiny that *writing* assumes the virtual bodily character of the blood Augustus desperately uses to send his warning to Pym in the hold.[27] From this point on, writing will become the primary referent for reality, and it will be represented commonly in metaphors of the body and/or physical reality. Chief among the savages of the crew is the Black Cook, who is a virtual "demon" and executes bound seamen who have not joined the mutiny by "striking each victim on the head as he was forced over the side of the vessel" (86). The Black Cook tells Augustus "that he should never put his foot on deck again 'until the brig was no longer a brig' " (89). As Reynolds points out, piracy was a common topic for sensational literature of the time. In Poe's narrative, this conventional subject is poetically, perversely metaphorized to cross "piracy" as a literary topic with the historical threat of the "theft" of property posed by slave insurrection and Abolition in general. Like Nat Turner, the Black Cook strikes his victims on the head, testifying to the symbolic danger to reason posed by the emergence of irrational savagery so many Southern whites imagined would accompany slave rebellion or even legal emancipation.[28]

The mutiny unleashes a terrible savagery that belongs for Poe to the uncivilized state. The providential "storm" that saves Augustus and Pym from butchery seems to argue against Poe's thesis that the "savagery" of the pirate or the black belongs to a "state of Nature" that civilization must control. In the Paulding-Drayton review, the reviewer endorses the extended "family" of the Southern slaveowner as the basis for "the moral influences flowing from the relation of master and slave, and the moral feeling engendered and cultivated by it" (270). In a perfectly conventional manner, the reviewer argues for the happy "patriarchal character" and the essential "clanship" in the extended "family" of the black's childlike relation to his/her benign master. These are typical proslavery views, certainly more compatible with Tucker, Paulding, and Dew on that subject than the subtler, more ambivalent Poe.

Even so, in *Pym* nature is nothing but the site of savagery and precisely what the unnatural family of master and slave, and thus of the institution of slavery itself, are designed to control. The providential storm arrives, however, at precisely the moment that the *Narrative of Arthur Gordon Pym* has been transformed from the pseudo-realism of either sensational or scientific voyages and travels into the *poetic* voyage constituted by Augustus' and Pym's writing and reading. It is the very moment, in fact, when Pym learns to *impersonate* the dead mutineer, Hartman Rogers. This impersonation will be followed by the *ingestion* of the other surviving mutineer, Richard Parker.

The scene of cannibalism enacted by the survivors on the drifting hulk of the *Grampus* only appears to identify them with the savagery they have miraculously escaped. The "horrible purpose," "the most horrible alternative which could enter the mind of man," is proposed initially by Parker, who becomes the victim of his own plan. Although Pym's efforts to convince Parker to "abandon his design" or "at least . . . defer it for another day" seem motivated by Pym's reason and humanity, Pym's arguments have the consequence of turning Parker's savage instinct for survival into a rational, even democratic "lottery" (132). In short, Pym tricks Parker into agreeing to a rational choice of victim. Once he is chosen in this manner, Parker is utterly unmanned, mastered by Pym's trick, no less than the mutineers were mastered by the ghostly apparition of Hartman Rogers: "He made no resistance whatever, and was stabbed in the back by Peters, when he fell instantly dead" (135).

Translated into the rhetoric of the poetic voyage, such cannibalism figures doubly. On the one hand, as empirical event, it represents the savagery exploited by sensationalist literature. Read as poetic enactment, it is the *internalization* of white power, the transformation of the "blood" of Augustus' message into the perverse Transubstantiation of Poe's Poetic Mystery. As Poe's version of the Southern white reaction to the Turner revolt, such figurative "cannibalism" appropriates the "savagery" attributed to Turner and his rebels, such as the myth that they drank the blood of their victims. The cannibalism in *Pym*, however, is not simply a defensive enactment of the savage custom of eating an enemy to defeat his spirit, although it certainly partakes of that ritual. Internalizing his power, consuming his own body, the poet transforms the threatened body of the White Master into the rhetoric of the White Poet. Without offering a full analysis, I shall merely note here the curious rhetoric of *inversion*, of a *topsy-turvy* world, that characterizes the experiences of the survivors on the capsized *Grampus*.

There is yet one more touch that, speculative as it must remain, I cannot help adding to this account. Of the six judges signing the November 5, 1831, order for Nat Turner's execution, one was "James W. Parker." Conventional as the name is, the association of these "Parkers" is at least suggestive. Judge Parker, of course, can hardly be identified with a "mutineer" in league with that savage executioner with his hatchet, the Black Cook, but the wayward tracks of condensation and displacement hardly meet the requirements of logic. Even so, if the "Parker" eaten by Pym is not just his threatening enemy but also the authority of the Court in Jerusalem, Viriginia, that condemned Nat Turner, then Pym is invested with the power of the Law, now transposed into the fictional frame.[29]

In *Pym*, the narrative begins in Nantucket as Augustus enchants Pym with stories of romantic adventure at sea, not unlike, we might guess, the sensational stories of pirates that appeared contemporaneously in the popular press. Reborn first in the accident of the *Ariel*, then again from the mutiny and shipwreck of the *Grampus*, Pym and Augustus leave behind the nuclear family of Pym's own family of lawyers and Augustus' family of sea-captains. In the place of those conventional forms of bourgeois control and civilization, Augustus and Pym substitute their own friendship, which is based on their adolescent rebellion against family authority (especially various father figures for Pym and Augustus). This friendship is repeatedly linked with story-telling and writing, as if to suggest that this, rather than the bourgeois family, is the real source of social authority. Augustus' wounded arm, which rots disgustingly as they drift on the *Grampus*, has its obvious sexual suggestiveness, which few critics have missed. The threat of castration that Augustus makes sensuously present to Pym provokes Pym's own narrative of compensation. Insofar as the "savagery" of the mutineers and, above all, the Black Cook threaten the powers of reason represented by Augustus and Pym, the pencil that Pym wields as he keeps that soggy diary of events following the mutiny becomes his best defense. But so does his subsequent companion, Dirk Peters.

As a "half-breed," Peters offers an alternative to the "savagery" of the Black Cook. Like the black slaves who would serve their masters faithfully and often to the death during the Civil War, Dirk Peters is Poe's fantasy of the faithful and grateful servant. It is Peters, of course, who embodies the "fierceness of the tiger" that grips Pym when the decision is made to sacrifice Parker to save the others from starvation. Peters' savagery is of a fundamentally different character than the Black Cook's, because it enacts what has already been conceptualized by Pym, who is from this moment on Peters' white master. Peters both resembles and is distinguished from the natives of Tsalal, who "were among the most barbarous, subtle, and bloodthirsty wretches that ever contaminated the face of the globe" (180). In his July 1835 review of Theodore Irving's *The Conquest of Florida, by Hernando De Soto*, Poe observes that "the Floridian savage was a more formidable foe than his Mexican brother—more hardy of frame, and more implacable in his revenge."[30] In his favorable review of James Hall's *Sketches of History, Life, and Manners in the West* in the December 1835 *Messenger*, Poe praises Hall's "undoubted abilities as a writer" and claims that he is "excellently qualified to write precisely such a book as he has written," which includes "the policy of our government in regard to the Aborigines."[31]

Peters is from a Missouri tribe, his father a fur-trapper, but he resembles these Floridians and the "Aborigines" William Henry Harrison, old "Tippecanoe," helped subdue by defeating Tecumseh in 1811. Let us not forget that Poe would campaign vigorously for Harrison in the 1840 Election, along with his friend Frederick W. Thomas.[32] Peters reenacts the fate of the faithful crewmen on the *Grampus* met at the hands of the Black Cook: "We had proceeded some hundred yards, threading our route cautiously between the huge rocks and tumuli, when, upon turning a corner, five savages sprung upon us from a small cavern, felling Peters to the ground with a blow from a club." With pistols in hand, Pym kills two "savages" and frees Peters, who promptly "seizing a club from one of the savages who had fallen . . . dashed out the brains of the three who remained, killing each instantaneously with a single blow of the weapon, and leaving us *completely masters of the field*" (199, my italics). Like Native Americans who scouted for and fought with the American Cavalry against tribal foes in the course of Manifest Destiny, like the East Indian Sepoys who fought faithfully for the British in India, Dirk Peters exemplifies one common "colonial solution" to the problem of a native population: subjugation by way of ideological conversion. As "half-breeds," either biologically or ideologically, such colonized people are indentured to the colonizer's values. It is an "art" never raised to a higher level than that of the British in their vast Empire, practiced more crudely in the American West and in our ventures in Southeast Asia.

The black prisoner, Nu-Nu, whom Peters and Pym take along on their escape from the savagery of Tsalal, wastes away as they advance toward the whiteness of the Pole. As Orlando Patterson and Toni Morrison have interpreted respectively the sociology of slavery and the cultural rhetoric of "blackness," the social death of the slave and the destruction of the racially marked other are crucial strategies in the invention of "white" authority.[33] The incomplete "family" of Augustus and Pym is here fully constituted, albeit in appropriately *masculine* form. With the help of the servile half-breed, the white master affirms his mastery and takes possession of the savagery that so threatens him. He does so not by means of legal and economic domination, but in and through the poetic domination that is figured in the *writing* in the interior of the island of Tsalal. Like Nantucket, the poeticized Tsalal now becomes a place of civilization, thanks to the powers of reading and, above all, the power of *writing* that has helped insinuate this fiction—*The Narrative of Arthur Gordon Pym of Nantucket*—into reality. It should not surprise us that the author of the "Note" tells us that "Peters, from whom some information might be expected, is still alive, and a resident of Illinois, but cannot be met with at present. He may hereafter be found, and will, no doubt, afford material for the conclusion of Mr. Pym's account" (207). I shall not belabor this passage, although I am tempted to do so. Suffice it to say that Illinois is a free-state, and the convenience of Peters' status as "half-breed" (Native American and white) allows Poe's Pym to liberate a "savage" without succumbing to the Southern heresy of liberating a perfectly good piece of property, that is, a slave. Having served his murderous purposes—the murder of Parker, the vengeful murder of the natives on Tsalal, the indirect cause of Nu-Nu's death, Peters has earned his just desserts: the "free-state" that only the white slave master, now turned poet and parodist, can award for service against the savagery that threatens him and his kind. That Peters remains a potential authority able to verify the authenticity of Pym's posthumous narration only underscores this point.

Much could still be said of the translation of black and white oppositions into the manageable black letters and white field of Poe/Pym's written text. Even Poe's apparent anticipation of Freud's thesis about the "antithetical sense of primal words" (in his review of Karl Abel's philological work of the same title) seems to confirm Pym's will-to-power in this instance. If the psychic script has the power to transform opposites into uncanny relations, if black is nothing but the repression of *white* (and, of course, vice versa), then the psychic narrative is little more than a confirmation of Poe's own thesis: that the transformation of material history into poetic history will save the reign of Reason from the savage intrusions of the real. Freud would not stop at such a conclusion, but reveal, as we have crudely attempted to do, how the "black savagery" so frightening to both Pym and Poe is little other than the repressed contents of their own white psyches. Such an interpretation would matter little to Poe, however, for it would depend crucially upon a reading in which the Ego would read the authority of its own unconscious. In fact, Poe has constituted a narrative in which the reader is by no means the Ego of Poe/Pym, but yet another Dirk Peters, the faithful "half-breed" who discovers only the authority of the white master.

I return at the end to those twentieth-century narratives of psychoanalysis provoked by Poe's *Narrative*. In his reading of the uncanny relation between black and white in *Pym*, John Irwin concludes: "For though Pym says that they 'noticed no light-colored substance of any kind on the island' and though the anonymous author of the note adds that 'nothing *white* was to be found at Tsalal, and nothing otherwise in the subsequent voyage to the region beyond,' Pym himself points out the white arrowhead flints in the chasm. And just as whiteness lies at the core of the dark realm of Tsalal, so darkness must be present in the white realm of Tekeli-li, otherwise there would be no color boundary, no figure/ground differentiation, no signification. The shadow image haunts the lone regions of Tekeli-li—whether Pym recognizes it or not. . . . What the ending of *Pym* acts out, then, is 'a certain *tendency* of the human intellect' (inscribed within it by the very structure of its birth) to try to survive death by projecting an image of itself (the self as image) into the infinite void of the abyss" (204–5). In the subtle optical reading he offers of the appearance of the white figure at the Pole, Irwin contends that it is the shadow cast by Pym that establishes the figure/ground relation. Irwin has already made clear that such an optical scene is always already a psychic scene of representation, that the "shadow" of Pym is nothing other than his fear of death, the ghostly double of Freud's Uncanny. Without for a moment disagreeing with this reading, I would supplement that shadow—the shadow of the White Man as Poet—with the corpse of Nu-Nu: the black body that as slave chattel or as "soulless" corpse is the necessary shadow for the poetic representation of *Pym*. The "whiteness" found at the heart of the chasms is, after all, that of "arrowhead flints," which are instruments of the kill. As images of the savage threat posed by the black natives and by black slaves, they are metonymies for their targets: not animals of the hunt, but the whites tabooed in the cry, "Tekeli-li!" Poetically repossessed both by the white poet and the "half-breed" with whom arrowhead flints are so conventionally identified, the "white arrowhead flints" become the "invisible bullets" of Poe's poetic mastery, his poetic colonialism.

Such a reading is thus not the radical "other" of the psychoanalytical debate occasioned by Poe's writings between Jacques Lacan and Jacques Derrida, unless that other is the uncanny double of just what psychoanalysis threatens to consolidate as the "law" of psychic signification. In her account of that debate, Barbara Johnson summarizes the consequences for the reader of the Poe text and the psychic Signifier of the Unconscious:

> The reader is comprehended by the letter: there is no place from which he can stand back and observe *it*. Not that the latter's meaning is subjective rather than objective, but that the letter is precisely that which subverts the polarity subjective/objective, that which makes subjectivity into

something whose position in a structure is situated by the passage through it of an object. The letter's destination is thus *wherever it is read*, the place it assigns to its reader as his own partiality.[34]

The "letter" thus quite by design "takes dominion everywhere," so constituting the reader's relation to his psychic text that he can find nothing but the letter's dominion, its specular *shadowing-forth* of his own identity. In this way, Lacan, Derrida, Barbara Johnson, and I myself (among other textualist readers of Poe) would institutionalize the domain of language, both as psychic and literary landscape, as the ineluctable field of our historical acts. The appropriateness of these gestures to Poe's own intentions is thus perfect; the textualist has read, even as he/she has disregarded Poe's own historical situation, in a manner that perfectly realizes Poe's very contemporary poetic purpose. Johnson continues:

> The opposition between the "phallus" [Lacan] and "dissemination" [Derrida] is not between two theoretical objects but between two interested positions. And if sender and receiver are merely the two poles of a reversible message, then Lacan's *substitution* of "destin" for "dessein" in the Crébillon quotation—a misquotation that Derrida finds revealing enough to end his analysis upon—*is* in fact the quotation's message. The sender (*dessein*) and the receiver (*destin*) of the violence that passes between Atreus and Thyestes are *equally* subject to the violence the letter *is*.[35]

Once again, we can find no fault with this reading, insofar as we stay within the frame of psycholinguistic reference. The revenge-cycle of the ancient struggle between Atreus and Thyestes, which turns upon the subtle arts by which each attempts to destroy the lineage of the other's house, is precisely the incestuous violence initiated by this postmodern poetic: that of Poe's art and of psychoanalysis itself. Internalizing the violence of material history, the immaterial history of poetry and psychoanalysis transforms such violence into the very principle of its perverse power.

My conclusion, then, is that the modern Poe and the antebellum, proslavery Poe are far more intricately connected than we want to believe. Spiller and Thorp's *Literary History of the United States* (1947) and Arthur Hobson Quinn's *Edgar Allan Poe—A Critical Biography* (1941) consider Poe as a Southern writer, whose ambivalence toward his own Southern identity is treated both literarily and psychobiographically.[36] They are history and biography respectively that are perfectly readable in the context of Ernest Marchand's 1934 essay, "Poe as Social Critic," which uses a wide variety of materials other than the disputed Paulding-Drayton review to make the proslavery case against Poe. I have for sheer histrionic effect not mentioned the author of "Edgar Allan Poe" in Spiller and Thorp's

1947 *Literary History of the United States*. I myself could not remember as I quickly looked back through my copy. The author writes: "To be sure, he sometimes betrayed a provincialism of his own. He was so eager to prove himself a Virginian that he followed Allan's tradition, which was that of Marshall and not that of Jefferson. Poe went so far as to deplore the French Revolution, to defend slavery as 'the basis of all our institutions,' and to assume the scorn held by the propertied classes for the democratic 'mob.' "[37] The references are obviously to the infamous Paulding-Drayton review, but they are also to Poe's general politics and his psychobiography. The author was F. O. Matthiessen, often the target of critics intent on establishing Poe's centrality to American literature. Is it any wonder, then, that Matthiessen should have so neglected Poe in *American Renaissance*?

The answer to that rhetorical question is not as self-evident as I have implied. At the end of his article in the *History*, Matthiessen concludes: "In opposition to the romantic stress on the expression of personality, he insisted on the importance, not of the artist, but of the created work of art."[38] And then, as if fearing we had missed his reference to Eliot's "Tradition and the Individual Talent," Matthiessen writes: "He stands as one of the very few great innovators in American Literature. Like Henry James and T. S. Eliot, he took his place, almost from the start, in international culture as an original creative force."[39] There it is: Poe the precursor to the international modernism of James and Eliot that is the ultimate goal of the nineteenth-century literature Matthiessen studied in *American Renaissance*. Six years later is Matthiessen changing his mind, or is this merely an explicit address to the "Poe" otherwise pushed to the margins of a book, *American Renaissance*, whose theoretical boundaries welcomed him and accounted for him perfectly? No. Matthiessen simply didn't know what to *do* with Poe in that context. Poe's Southernness, his proslavery arguments and regional sentiments, corrupted Matthiessen's modernism. Matthiessen, then, was wrong as well, and he let himself in for just what G. R. Thompson and subsequent Poe critics have done: repress the subtle complicity of literary modernism with racist ideology, which now Poe may be said to represent both in his antebellum historical context and his modern revival.

But just what *is* the complicity of literary modernism with the proslavery sentiments we have tried to impute again to E. A. Poe, now in his proto-modern as well as antebellum identities? Poe's prose and poetry is full of abused, murdered, dismembered women, of native peoples represented as the emodiment of primitive evil, of visionary aristocrats, of royalty saved by poetic manipulation, of the hateful masses. Such literary thematics, although we should not neglect their evidence, will only take us so far in the direction of a revaluation of Poe's aristocratic pretensions and slaveholding mentality. Behind these obsessive themes in Poe's writings is the gnostic idealism, together with its hatred of the material and the temporal, of the body and its decay, that found such powerful resonance in the Symbolists, Decadents, and High Moderns. It is a virtual Nietzschean *ressentiment*—that hatred of time, change, and becoming—that Nietzsche attributes to the "priestly abnegation of life" he finds so central to Romantic Idealism.

Its characteristics are, Nietzsche knew well enough himself, the very predicates of a modernism from which Nietzsche would work futilely to distinguish himself: contempt for history, disdain of labor, disgust with the body, avoidance of the crowd, abhorrence of nature. Out of such negativity, aesthetic modernism constructed its own anti-terra, a Laputa that seemed once populated only by harmless Swiftian cranks. Its geography is perfectly mental or verbal, and it can be travelled only by those clever enough to follow its precharted paths. Access to this territory can be gained only by a certain literacy, defined by competency in those ideas and texts that in our own age have challenged the status of the landed estate and other signs of privilege marking the ruling class.

This critique of the "ideology of modernism" is familiar enough by this late date, but it has generally led merely to an indictment of aesthetic modernism—and of idealism in general—as powerless, reactive, or narcissistic. We need to recognize the will-to-power that is involved in such modernist negativity in the larger context of the new class configurations that have emerged in our own postindustrial age. Poe's contempt for the material world enables his glorification of the imagination, visionary experience, and the ultimate transcendence of the alienated body. Even in *Eureka*, Poe's sublime is language, but only when it is employed in very specific ways. Only in its poetic, self-referential, metamorphic dimensions does language escape the instrumentality of everyday life. And such poetic language demands a special literacy, a competency of poetic reading and writing that would develop into the sorts of *institutions* of sophisticated interpretation that have their origins in aesthetic modernism. For all their avant-gardism, the modernists yearned for a new aristocratic order, a secret society, whose signs and symbols could be read only by those initiated properly and strictly.

However powerless, irrelevant, or insignificant the institutions of academic criticism might seem in the larger context of our postindustrial age of information, they have helped legitimate hierarchies of language use that are today the structural foundations for what I would term a "hermeneutics of class."[40] The calls for "cultural literacy" are only the most recent echoes of this modern appeal for the reorganization of human activity along the lines of signifying authority. Abolitionists like Frederick Douglass knew well enough that the postbellum fight for genuine economic and social freedom would have to be conducted at all levels in terms of verbal authority—in politics, in the courts, in the press, as well as in literature. Those with *access* to language, both in terms of their educations (the capabilities to speak in technically proper ways) and the availability to them of actual media (who controls the presses of the papers, journals, and publishing industry), control the political economy. The rest constitute the "mob," which Poe fears as profoundly as any of his literate contemporaries. Like Poe's "Man of the Crowd," the mob represents all that which "does not permit itself to be read," a fearful collective unconscious.

Yet, it is just this unconscious that the *flâneur* of Poe's story, "amusing" himself with a cigar, a newspaper, and the comings and goings of the London crowd, does read, translating the apparently indiscriminate mob first into a carefully articulated hierarchy of classes and then into a single figure, the "Man of the Crowd" himself, whose passage from downtown London to the Gin Palace at the outskirts of the City and back again seems to describe the senseless repetition of the mob's apparent "industry." It should not surprise us that Poe's *flâneur* reads the unconscious of London in a manner that recalls the Editor's interpretation of the writings of and in the chasms on the Island of Tsalal in *The Narrative of Arthur Gordon Pym*, published serially three years before "The Man of the Crowd." What remains unreadable to Pym and simply a part of the natural environment of the Tsalalian natives is for "Mr. Poe" a complex "text," whose origins are the same as those of our own western, literate, rational tradition and whose end is, as Jean Ricardou has argued so eloquently, the signature of the Author.

Poe's insistence upon a new *authority* capable of reading what remains profoundly unconscious either to the malevolent Tsalalian native or to the London mob becomes his warrant for a new class system predicated on linguistic competency. The new property of words may have seemed to have little practical value for the Poe harassed by money worries and dependent on his Southern patrons, whose capital was counted in human beings and acreage. But today we may conclude, as we so often have, that Poe was profoundly clairvoyant, even if we must insist that his was a perverse vision. Today one's class identification and one's virtual earning power are tied intimately to the "Power of Words." If we hope to revive the important historical question of Poe's antebellum politics, then we will have to reconsider its continuity with the postbellum politics of aesthetic language and its powerful hierarchies of verbal competency and cultural literacy, which is to say we must rethink the entanglement of the antebellum Southern writer with his shadowy other: the modern, cosmopolitan trickster, Edgar Allan Poe.

4 A Critique of Ideology: Herman Melville's *Pierre*

> The founders of Rome . . .—Romulus and Remus—are, according to the tradition, themselves freebooters—represented as from their earliest days thrust out from the Family, and as having grown up in a state of isolation from family affection. . . .
>
> The immoral active severity of the Romans in this private side of character necessarily finds its counterpart in the passive severity of their political union. For the severity which the Roman experienced from the State he was compensated by a severity, identical in nature, which he was allowed to indulge towards his family—a servant on the one side, a despot on the other.
>
> —Hegel, *The Philosophy of History*

In his introduction to the 1949 Hendricks House edition of *Pierre*, Henry A. Murray criticizes Melville for not providing a clearer cultural motivation for Pierre's alienation: "Melville does not present us with a pertinent spectacle or analysis of American society, nor does he state explicitly what forces of the culture are so inimical to his spirit that he and his hero are driven to condemn it in toto. . . . This hiatus in emotional logic is one of the outstanding structural defects of the novel."[1] Murray very clearly identifies a central problem that has caused both contemporary reviewers and twentieth-century scholars to judge *Pierre* as Melville's most incoherent work. What little explicit commentary Melville gives the reader about social issues appears in those chapters in New York, after Pierre has crossed his Rubicon and rebelled against his family. Indeed, what Murray terms "this hiatus in emotional logic" applies equally well to the customary division critics make between the pastoralism of the domestic romance at Saddle Meadows and the surrealism of the episodes in the city. Instead of offering us the naturalist's microscopic examination of urban corruption, Melville focuses on Pierre's efforts to write his "infernal book." Instead of the pastoral romance of Saddle Meadows giving way to the gritty realism of New York, we find pastoralism transformed into a metafictional romance, in which virtually every urban experience relates to Pierre's problem of artistic creation. The social issues in *Pierre* thus appear to be forgotten as Melville shifts his attention from the domestic conflicts at Saddle-Meadows to Pierre's artistic problems in the city.

Yet, this problem may well be a consequence of our critical methods rather than an inherent defect in the work's composition and structure. This is not to say that *Pierre* is an unacknowledged masterpiece. Quite the contrary, the novel is full of difficulties I shall not try to resolve, but instead use to clarify Melville's contempt for "the man of letters" and thus for himself. Melville's thorough critique of authorship is not, however, simply a symptom of madness or uncontrolled ranting. His indictment of idealist philosophy and literary practice, especially focused on the transcendentalists, is coherent and profound, because it recognizes how powerfully such abstractions would serve the political purposes of the new American ruling classes. At the same time, he could find no acceptable alternative to this complicity of the author with those more powerful authorities whom Melville judged to have ruined the republican dream from the beginning. Intricately worked out in the very novelistic form Melville had come to detest, his critique of ideology in *Pierre* remains a testament to the limits of literature as a force for political reform. In *Pierre*, Melville bids farewell to the literary forms of romance and the novel neither because he had lost control of them nor because he had lost control of his own life, unless we understand that life to be inseparable from his conception of his vocation as an author. What he recognizes instead is how powerfully these forms contribute to the very social forces of domination they so often claim to contest. The argument of *Pierre* is thus *too* coherent and *too* convincing to result in any other conclusion than that literature, at least as Melville understood it, is more often the agent of domination than emancipation.

Above all, it is literature's inclination to make credible its fantasy that troubles Melville, because he recognizes this tendency toward "fictional realization" as comparable to the work of ideology in naturalizing otherwise arbitrary social fictions. Among many literary forms, the romance and novel are particularly prone to accomplish this work of naturalization by way of characters and dramatic situations that substitute interpersonal psychologies for more complex social and economic forces. In *Pierre*, Melville focuses on family relations both at Saddle Meadows and in New York, because he recognizes that the family is that institution through which the dramatic social changes of Jacksonian America would be rendered acceptable and normal. And it is the family as the focus of the fiction of manners—whether it be the sentimental romance or the novel of social manners—that had such a powerful influence on Melville's readers. As a primarily bourgeois form, the nineteenth-century novel of social manners quite obviously helped legitimate its middle-class readers and their values, often by criticizing ruthlessly aristocratic pretensions. Insofar as bourgeois values are identified with democratic sentiments, the novel became the primary literary form of urban and industrial America. It is, of course, quite conventional to notice how the novel of social manners from Jane Austen to Henry James concentrates on the specific social functions of a fictional family. More often than not, the family's class identification governs other mimetic criteria, even in writers like Trollope and James for whom bourgeois values are considered necessary to the well-ordered state. Even so, it is surprising how often literary critics treat such family relations in phenomenological and psychological terms. By personalizing characters and dramatizing interpersonal conflicts, novelists tempt readers to identify with characters in ways that encourage the use of psychological and phenomenological terms to understand the narrative functions of character. One consequence of this critical inclination is the relative neglect of the social and political significance of family relations in fiction. In short, the form of the novel and the reader-competence it constructs often work contrary to the larger class significance that "character" and "the family" are supposed to convey.

Social historians traditionally have had as much difficulty studying the social functions of the family as literary scholars. Whereas literary critics tend to treat fictional families in psychological terms, social historians have relied on demographic statistics and other empirical data that do not adequately reflect the family as a form of social behavior. As Mark Poster has written: "While quantitative, demographic studies are needed, they cannot provide historians with a concept of the family that can pose the important questions and render the family intelligible in premodern and modern Europe."[2] Only recently have works like Philippe Ariès' *Centuries of Childhood: A Social History of Family Life* and Jacques Donzelot's *The Policing of Families* begun to combine psychological and traditional sociological approaches to the family in order to understand the very particular mediatory function played by families in the relation of individual behavior to communal practices.[3]

The rediscovery of the family by the social historian has interesting consequences for the literary critic. Literary critics interested in the political functions of artistic forms should find theoretical suggestions in the work of those social historians who have begun to write the social psychology of the family as an historical institution. The analogy between the family and art is not merely coincidental; both employ discursive practices that explicitly combine public and private terms and values. Both the family and the artistic work are representational forms that must address the bases for their actual and nominal authorities (parent and author), the origins and ends of such authority (biology and genius; history and tradition), and the status of those subject to such authorities (children and readers).

I have suggested that Melville's concentration on family relations and artistic creation in the two major movements of *Pierre* has encouraged critics like Murray to consider Melville's often strident social criticism to be unjustified or inexplicable. I want to argue that Melville's social criticism in *Pierre* is focused primarily on the social psychologies of the nineteenth-century family and romantic theories of art. I shall demonstrate not merely how the family and art serve different social purposes, which are often disguised by the naturalness and privacy of the family and the idealism of art, but how the family and art participate with each other in maintaining a nineteenth-century American politics of self-reliance within the larger context of what I have been terming in this book "Emersonianism." *Pierre* is a comic send-up of popular literature of mid-nineteenth-century America, but Melville's criticism of "high" literature has a more serious purpose. Challenging the "great tradition" of his age, which culminates in American transcendentalism, Melville challenges the very terms on which "American culture" was being established. As Sacvan Bercovitch has written: "*Pierre* is valuable as a critique of the inner dynamics of the best-seller . . . at the very moment that the literary marketplace was emerging in antebellum America. But the critique itself extends to include the classic forms implicit in the popular. . . . As the plot unfolds the satire turns increasingly against the would-be antithesis to that popular mode, the spiritual pattern of self-reliant dissent provided by Emerson and Thoreau."[4] As Bercovitch succinctly puts the matter, *Pierre* "is the reductio ad absurdum" of "Emerson's 'Self-Reliance,' " by which I take Bercovitch to mean both Emerson's famous essay and the American myth with which it has been associated.[5]

Emory Elliott has argued that the "classic American writers" of this period "created literary works that internalized, quarreled with, but invariably preserved the values, myths, and beliefs that constituted an American ideological consensus."[6] In *Pierre*, however, Melville strikes at the very heart of that nineteenth-century consensus: "family values." By allegorizing Pierre's frustrated oedipal rebellion as a national project trapped by the sins of the fathers, rebelling only to repeat their mistakes, Melville calls in admittedly oblique ways for a comprehensive overturning of our cultural and intellectual traditions. Elliott focuses on how "the complex details of Pierre's experience convey the significance of New England Calvinism and the American Revolution as cultural facts that have helped to shape his individual identity, foster his ideological inflexibility, and thereby profoundly affect his ability to become a successful artist."[7] While building on Elliott's argument, I want to focus on Melville's critique of the adaptation of romantic philosophy to the national ideology in the first half of the nineteenth century, a dimension of Pierre's ideologically petrified soul that Elliott recognizes quite clearly: "Pierre remains trapped between Jonathan Edwards' doctrine of divine sovereignty and Emerson's declaration of self-reliance, unable to believe in a higher authority and incapable of trusting himself."[8]

The social history of the nineteenth-century American family is one of the principal concerns of Michael Paul Rogin's *Subversive Genealogy: The Politics and Art of Herman Melville*. In its attention to the socioeconomic impact of Jacksonian America on the family, Rogin's study gives historical specificity to Eric Sundquist's psychoanalytical approach to the question of nineteenth-century literary authority, so often figured in metaphors of paternity, in his 1979 study, *Home as Found: Authority and Genealogy in Nineteenth-Century American Literature*. Both critics pay special attention to *Pierre* as Melville's defensive autobiography. *Pierre* is both Melville's willful rebellion against the aristocratic pretensions of his mother's family, the Gansevoorts, and the fictional confession of his failure to live up to his aristocratic ancestry. Characterizing himself in Pierre as a dilettante and literary dabbler, Melville also associates himself with Pierre's unsuccessful efforts to champion those characters exploited by the Glendinnings: the illegitimate Isabel, the vanishing Indian, the African-American slaves kept by Pierre's ancestors. Rogin calls *Pierre* a "bourgeois family nightmare" that employs Pierre's initiation into urban life to explore the crisis of the family occasioned by the rapid industrialization of Jacksonian America: "The adolescent male, coming of sexual age, symbolized the disruptive forces at work in Jacksonian America. Poised to break free from his family of origin, sexually and in his working life, he was the locus for Jacksonian anxieties about the disruption of the preindustrial family. The chaste woman . . . was society's agent to discipline him."[9]

The nineteenth-century bourgeois family is one of the primary social forces that constructed subjectivity, especially as Americans confronted the social transformations brought about by industrialization and urbanization. The family is a discursive formation that contributes to the ideological work of *interpellating* subjects in new social contexts. Because the family appears at once to be based on a natural relation among its members and yet depends crucially upon the production of its members, both in its domestic space and in the larger economy, the family serves a crucial function in naturalizing individuals' relations to ideology.[10] Because the family's means of production seems so self-evidently *natural* and *biological*, the family is an especially attractive medium for disguising ideological messages and thus contributing to the naturalization of new social relations. Engels' *The Origins of the Family, Private Property, and the State* is the classic Marxian work on the relation between private psychological relations and ideology, but both Marx and Engels treat the family as secondary to the mode of production. As Mark Poster observes, for Marx and Engels, "the family is epiphenomenal compared to the mode of production. In general their writings relegated the family to the backwaters of superstructure."[11]

Engels' note to the third German edition of *Capital* makes clear that the origin of the family was a troublesome issue for Marx: "Subsequent and very thorough investigations into the primitive condition of man led the author to the conclusion that it was not the family that originally developed into the tribe, but that, on the contrary, the tribe was the primitive and spontaneously developed form of human association, based on consanguinity, and that out of the first incipient loosening of the tribal bonds, the many and various forms of the family were afterwards developed."[12] As sketchy and sometimes contradictory as Marx's critical remarks on the family are, they focus with some consistency on the *bourgeois* family. Yet even the vulgar Marxian distinction between economic base and ideological superstructure permits Marx and Engels to comprehend the mystification of economic motives as *natural* attachments and the legitimation of a deceptive "individualism" achieved in the bourgeois family. For in its reflection of capitalist alienation, the bourgeois family is where the "private individual" is at home, rather than in the more public groups Marx associates with the historical origins of social organization. As Raymond Williams observes, "the dominance of the sense [of the family as a] small kin-group was probably not established before the early nineteenth century."[13] In effect, the *biological* legitimacy of the "family" belongs to nineteenth-century capitalism, and such modern kin relations are integrally related to historically contemporary conceptions of the individual. As I shall argue later in chapters 5 and 6, the imbrication of the family with the ideology of nineteenth-century capitalism makes it extremely difficult for writers like Frederick Douglass and Harriet Jacobs to appeal to "family values" without being misunderstood as referring to *bourgeois* family values.

Hegel has a great deal to say about the family, in part because his own philosophical project so explicitly attempts to legitimate bourgeois individualism. Hegel understands the family as the active and historical mediation between individual and social forms of self-consciousness. The very centrality of the family in Hegel's philosophy reflects his emphasis on individual self-consciousness, which would serve nineteenth-century American capitalism as a convenient philosophical justification for entrepreneurial practices. Nevertheless, the main thrust of Hegel's idealism was toward a concept of "self-consciousness" that would find its dialectical realization in a larger social self-consciousness, rather than in the mere exchange of the father's authority for that of the capitalist or ruler. In Hegel, the family is the virtual unconscious of man's social impulse, and the historical process by which such an unconscious achieves conscious form involves the transformation of the family's privacy into public forms of social existence. For Hegel, the state does not merely imitate the structure of familial authority, it dialectically transforms that authority with the aim of achieving the ultimate self-governance citizens would achieve in Hegel's ideal community. In the course of such transformation, the limited authority of the family is replaced by that of the state, in keeping with Hegel's liberal progressive scheme.[14]

In *Pierre*, Melville seems to criticize urban America for having forgotten or neglected the significant social role played by the family. In the pastoral world of Saddle-Meadows, social life is organized around such ruling families as the Glendinnings. In New York, Pierre encounters unruly mobs, decadent aristo-crats, eccentric artists and philosophers. The carnivalesque world of the city is distinguished by the alienation of different groups and individuals, as well as the absence of those family ties that offered Pierre some stability in the country. Even in his rebellion against his family, Pierre attempts to create a surrogate fam-ily, composed of Lucy, Isabel, and Delly, as if to compensate for the isolation they all experience in the city. In this view, Melville's social criticism appears to be quite conventional; Pierre's "fall," like that of industrial America, is his loss of those stable family associations that ought to have been the bases for his initia-tion into social life. Such allegories of the decline of family values in the face of urban alienation and temptation are central to many nineteenth-century senti-mental romances.[15]

Pierre's rebellion against his family and his rejection of the stability of Saddle-Meadows, however, cannot be so easily allegorized as urban America's repudiation of the stable, preindustrial family. Like Hegel, Melville understands family and social relations to function dialectically. Melville devotes a great deal of attention to the Glendinnings' ordered and closed world, in order to prepare the reader for Pierre's discovery of Isabel's illegitimacy and his subsequent rejec-tion of his heritage. The father's sin is not just his adultery with Isabel's mother, but his even more pernicious refusal to accept publicly his responsibility for Isabel: that is, establish visible signs of kinship with her. The customs and prac-tices that encourage such secrecy are those of the preindustrial family and the class relations governed by a landed gentry. Thus it is understandable that Murray finds Melville's social criticism in *Pierre* unmotivated. Rather than exploring the significance of the Glendinnings' fatal flaw in the particular social world they govern, Melville seems to change the subject from rural to urban social issues, from aristocratic to bourgeois discursive registers. By the same token, the landed aristocracy represented by the Glendinnings seems hardly a worthwhile object for Melville's criticism. Given the rapid change from rural to urban economies in Jacksonian America, Melville's attack on an outmoded form of aristocratic rule seems unnecessary. In fact, the Glendinning family and its "secret" refer more tangibly to the plot of some European romance than to con-crete social problems in nineteenth-century America.

Viewed from the perspective of Hegel's conception of the family as the "unconscious" of the state, however, Melville's concentration on the preindustrial, aristocratic family may be an indirect approach to his criticism of American capitalism. Melville stresses the European character of the Glendinning family, as if reminding democratic Americans that they might be working to produce a society that will merely repeat the hierarchical class systems of Europe. Nineteenth-century Americans were very familiar with the ways Southern planters imitated the pretensions of the European aristocracy. Northern industrialists frequently justified urbanization as a way of encouraging democratization and overcoming the inherent hierarchies of landed estates. By the same token, the common nineteenth-century American assumption that agrarianism and industrialism constituted two distinct spheres is by no means historically accurate. As Carolyn Porter has argued: "Farming was no more impervious to the forces of specialization, rationalization, and commodification than was household manufacture or urban life, once we recognize that America was not merely a predominantly agrarian society, but a *capitalist* agrarian society."[16] American capitalism had a vested interest in promoting the different mythologies of the country and the city, preindustrial feudalism and the "free-exchange" of labor under capitalism, Old World aristocracy and American democracy. By developing the narrative contiguity of country and city, aristocratic family and democratic mob, Melville may be suggesting in *Pierre* that the origins of urban corruption are to be found in the well-ordered estates of the landed gentry.

Hegel's idealist treatment of the family's relation to the state may help us formulate this problem in terms pertinent to the romantic ethos of *Pierre*. In Hegel, the ultimate function of the family is to serve the state, virtually by acknowledging the insufficiency or limitation of the family structure as an enduring historical principle. Hegel's version of oedipal triangulation is supposed to effect the rite of passage from family to state, from biological repetition to historical time and change. Within the narrow family, Hegel's unrealized self is metaphorized as "brother and sister," both of whom remain in bondage to an external, abstract notion of authority that is at once the father and the divine. In the family, the dialectic of self and other is worked out in terms of "brother and sister," precisely because "the brother . . . is in the eyes of the sister a being whose nature is unperturbed by desire and is ethically like her own; her recognition in him is pure and unmixed with any sexual relation."[17]

In one sense, Hegel here repeats the nineteenth century's ideology of the ideal, chaste, unsexed "family," which served the purpose of repressing and controlling those sexual energies threatening a rational social order. In this regard, Hegel's metaphors of "sister and brother" for the familial dialectic of self and other merely reinforces the ideology's spiritualization of family relations in the manner Rogin has analyzed so well: "Family ideologists sought not only to intensify the bonds between mother and son, but also to spiritualize the relations of husband to wife. Pierre's game of brother and sister is supposed to establish the closeness of this son to his mother. But it also calls attention to those family reformers who, purifying the marriage bond of power and appetite, modeled the relations of husband and wife on those of brother and sister."[18] Pierre's habit of calling his mother "sister" certainly follows this ideology of the family. The spiritualization of family relations helps maintain a sharp distinction between the "proper family" and the impropriety or illegitimacy associated with sexuality. Melville's use of the conventions of the fair lady and dark woman to represent respectively Lucy and Isabel suggests how feminine propriety depended upon the repression of the sexual. In keeping with Melville's general critique of American transcendentalism, *Pierre* identifies idealization and spiritualization with psychic and cultural repression of basic drives and appetites. This idealization of family relations is the object of Melville's critique of ideology in *Pierre*, because it is one of the principal means of disguising the ruling class's legitimation of its right to rule. By doubling Pierre's treatment of his mother as "sister" and his incestuous relation with Isabel, Melville renders extremely ambiguous the customary distinctions between the proper family and illegitimate sexual relations.[19]

Hegel's interpretation of the unsexual relation of "brother and sister" as a model for familial self-consciousness thus appears to work in accord with those nineteenth-century family ideologists criticized by Melville. In terms of his larger social argument, however, Hegel stresses this relation of brother and sister in order to identify the limitation of the family and its necessary transcendence in the social order. Dividing unrealized self-consciousness into "brother and sister," Hegel establishes an unsexual relation of self and other that is the abstract model for proper citizenship in the state. Within the narrow circle of the family, the metaphors "brother and sister" are reminders of the self's dependence on external authorities—God, father, Nature. Hegel wants to demonstrate that the apparently self-moving history of the family produces no genuine historical growth and change but merely reproduces the same structure. Given the ways the European aristocracy based its power on complex family genealogies, Hegel's argument has immediate relevance for the changing class structures of early nineteenth-century Europe. The *desire* of the family remains purely sexual or reproductive—natural and thus not yet spiritual (or self-conscious) in the proper sense of historical *Weltgeist*. Within the family, the individual remains in bondage to natural authority, which rules that the "individual" has no particularity beyond his/her identification with the species reproduced. The *unsexual* relation of brother and sister signifies for Hegel that neither brother nor sister possesses an independent and reproductive power equivalent to the natural sexuality that continues to govern the family.

By the same token, the apparent authority of the father and mother is equally dependent upon the law of biological reproduction that they merely follow. No matter what venerable origins or trappings of power the family employs to claim its independent identity, it continues to perform the same subservient function: the reproduction of the species. Within the family form, the child's rebellion is thus always doomed merely to repeat what it attempts to escape: the hierarchical relation of the individual to an external law. *Working* at that relation, *laboring* to overcome such externality—father, God, Nature—the son or daughter merely reproduces it in the subsequent role of husband or wife. Insofar as the son's oedipal aggression fails to negate the family and transform it into the larger forms of social law and *citizenship*, the son must experience his transformation into a father as incestuous. Metaphorically, *spiritually*, such philosophical incest does weaken successive generations, since it reminds the individual that his "freedom" is already fated, that his "rebellion" is merely natural, that his "self-consciousness" is simply a biological mirage rather than a genuine product of human reason. The consequence of recognizing such a limitation to individuation in the reproduction of an unchanging and external natural law can result only in what Hegel terms "unhappy consciousness," which is his own version of philosophical madness, of absolute "ambiguity."

The "illegitimacy" of the family depends upon its failure to bring its own natural legitimacy to self-consciousness: the transformation of natural law into social practice. The son realizes this potential in the family by rebelling against the father and discovering his destiny as a citizen: "The individual who seeks the 'pleasure' of enjoying his particular individuality finds it in the family life, and the 'necessity' in which that pleasure passes away is his own self-consciousness as a citizen of his nation." In short, rebellion against the family works ideally to transform the natural and biological family into the more populous social "family," insofar as Hegelian dialectics may be read in organic, evolutionary terms. Within the natural family, there are only sons and daughters, fathers and mothers; the son doubles the father, the daughter the mother. Within its own reproductive cycle, then, the natural family always grows more abstract and general, working against the destiny of the human spirit to individuate itself, to realize and complete natural law as human history. What remains purely external to the "son" within the confines of the family ought to become the internal and self-regulating principle of ethical authority within the well-ordered state: "It is knowing the 'law of his own heart' as the law of all hearts, knowing the consciousness of self to be the recognized and universal ordinance of society: it is 'virtue', which enjoys the fruits of its own sacrifice, which brings about what it sets out to do, viz. to bring the essential nature into the light of the actual present,—and its enjoyment is this universal life."[20]

For Melville as well, the nineteenth-century family is an inadequate substitute for a truly democratic society. Melville understands, however, both how the family deceives the individual with the illusion of its own self-sufficient "community" and is also the primal site of transformation—from self to other, nature to culture. In the former case, the "family" remains a formalist work; in the latter case, the "family" is an active social and historical force. These different functions of the "family" may be understood primarily in the ways they organize the *labor* of those identified with the elementary "society" of the family. Indeed, it is the labor *of* the family—in the double sense of what the family produces and what is the social consequence of a certain family structure—that Melville understands as an indirect means of understanding the power and function of nineteenth-century ideology.

Isabel is, of course, a key to Melville's social theory of the American family, not only because her supposed illegitimacy allows Melville to question class boundaries but also because Isabel represents a wide variety of exploited people. As Bercovitch puts it, "Isabel's shadow falls across all aspects of Saddle Meadows: across Indian mounds and traces of slave-quarters; across Mary Glendinning's abuse of Delly Ulver; across Falsgrave's abuse of religious principle; across the relation between master and servant, lady and tenant farmer; across the class hierarchy thriving 'in the heart of the republic.' "[21] By her own account, Isabel achieves her initial awareness of herself as a consequence of her labor:

> I must have been nine, or ten, or eleven years old, when the pleasant-looking woman carried me away from the large house. She was a farmer's wife; and now that was my residence, the farm-house. They taught me to sew, and work with wool, and spin the wool; I was nearly always busy now. This being busy, too, this it must have been, which partly brought to me the power of being sensible of myself as something human. Now I began to feel strange differences. When I saw a snake trailing through the grass, I said to myself, That thing is not human, but I am human.   (Pierre, 122)

Indeed, Isabel's sense of the "old bewilderings" that haunted her adolescence are certainly associated with her sense of alienation from a stable human community. When she has grown and become a burden on the farmer's family, she asks the farmer's wife to "hire me out to some one, let me work for some one" (Pierre, 124–25). Knowing little of the ways of the world, Isabel still senses that her departure from even this adoptive family requires some change in the conditions of her labor. Whereas her labor for her adoptive family had seemed to her equivalent to the physical and psychological maintenance the family gave her, her adult labor involves her in an exchange economy, in which wages mark the difference between the labor that produces the self (labor *for* the self) and the

work that produces *society*. Melville uses "The Story of Isabel" to present a critical reading of the conventional paradigm for romantic self-consciousness. In her
spiritual and physical growth, Isabel—unlike Wordsworth in *The Prelude*—learns
how integral concrete labor is to the development of a psychological personality. And she experiences as well the first consequences of the alienation of the
worker from her proper labor, her only true product: that sensuous human
activity realizable only within a social community.

Isabel's mystical guitar is a metaphor for the sort of social product that
ought to issue from such human labor. Isabel tells Pierre that she bought the guitar from a peddler, who "had got it slyly in part exchange from the servants of a
grand house." It is especially important, I think, that Isabel specifies that "with
part of my earnings, I bought the guitar. Straightway I took it to my little chamber in the gable, and softly laid it on my bed" (125). A few sentences earlier,
Isabel also indicates just what sort of labor had earned her the means of buying
the guitar: "My work was milking cows, and making butter, and spinning wool,
and weaving carpets of strips of cloth." These bucolic labors are conventional
enough, except that in series they offer a little genealogy of human labor from
agrarian activities to cottage industry. Measured against Isabel, Pierre is especially inexperienced in the ways of ordinary labor, particularly those involving
even the most elementary manufacturing. His labor in the course of the novel
includes his work as a writer, occasional hunting, and the "work" of honor, which
is to say the labor of melodrama.

Nevertheless, Isabel's labor does not signify some growth in the direction
of social integration, even though the development of the series clearly suggests
such socialization. Milk produces butter, just as wool produces cloth for carpets.
Like Hester Prynne, Isabel is often shown sewing, and her labor as a seamstress
seems nearly to objectify in the work of her hands the weaving and vining of her
black hair. All such labor, however, fails to produce her own image, as labor in
Hegel's ideal society promises. Exchanging money for the guitar, Isabel is
prompted by some intuition or identification with the instrument, even though
she confesses she "had never seen a guitar before." "There was a strange humming
in my heart," she says, and it is this claim (and many others like it) that convince
us that she is some version of Hawthorne's mystical women. As it turns out, the
guitar is a crucial figure in the melodramatic plot, because it contains the mysterious, gilt signature, *Isabel*, which Isabel takes as her *own* name. And in
Melville's romance of coincidences, it is revealed to have been acquired by the
peddler from the mansion at Saddle-Meadows, fuelling Isabel's intuition that it
was her *mother's* guitar. All this would account for the guitar being in the possession of the servants, to whom it must have been given by Mary Glendinning in
some equally intuitive understanding of its illegitimate associations. The peddler

acquires it from the servants "slyly," suggesting some cheat in the exchange, as if the guitar must perpetuate its illegitimacy in its repeated circulation: the economy of illegitimacy. The peddler, of course, lives upon an exchange economy, insofar as he makes nothing in his own right. His "slyness" is precisely his "craft," because perfectly honest, market-value exchanges would leave him penniless. To the value of the goods he offers, he must add the "cost" of his labor, which more than anything else amounts to his "slyness."

Ironically, Isabel's wages are part of an exchange economy in which the *need* to purchase some means of self-expression (the guitar) reflects the fact that Isabel's actual labor is alien, not an integral part of her spiritual and psychological development. Indeed, Isabel's sense of her alienation from *any* society may well be her intuition of the conditions governing the laborer in such an exchange economy. And it is this sense of alienation that provokes her not just to "uncover" her family origins, but also to imagine that family to be the means of *protecting* her from a hostile, alienating world. It should not surprise us, then, that guitar and family origins are so intimately related in the plot: art as a "leisure-time" expression of the inner self and the family as a "private" validation of the self are related defenses against alienating labor. Isabel's regression from socialization to the narrow circle of her lost family heritage may also be understood as her rebellion against the romantic ideal of *Bildung* that her own story tries to sketch out. And this regression, like Pierre's own failure to grow beyond the love or conflict of the Glendinning family, expresses the failure of the larger social order to overcome (or at least *use productively*) the alienation of its workers.

What the guitar does for Isabel is effectively swerve her labors from her own socialization (from cows to carpets, Nature to Culture) in the direction of a self-expression that is at once sexual and illegitimate. In the context of the explicit sexual themes of *Pierre*, Isabel's first act of placing the guitar on her bed reminds us of the feminine form of the instrument. Insofar as it hides Isabel's own *assumed* name beneath a removable panel (I assume this is a decorative cover of the opening in the sound-box: a sort of hymen), the guitar serves as a sexually suggestive metonymy for Isabel herself. In this regard, we might conclude that her labor has provided her the concrete means (wages) of achieving self-expression that may communicate with the world.

Unlike the Memnon Stone, which is a mere ancient "gimmick" that simulates the voice of the divine, and unlike Westervelt's "trick" of the "Veiled Lady" in *The Blithedale Romance*, Isabel's guitar represents a genuine artistic desire to give objective and thus communicable form to her self-consciousness. By transforming work into wages, then into the music of the guitar, Isabel's labor initiates the transformation of individual activity into a social function, of mere existence into socially significant being. This constant metamorphosis is Emersonian, and it would place metaphor at the *heart* of the human project of bringing the world to self-consciousness. As a genuine product of Isabel's own labor, the guitar assumes a "real body," much in the manner of Whitman's poetic body, insofar as it embodies those universals by which human beings recognize each other as fundamentally *social*. Yet, we must remember that the guitar is initially *not* the product of Isabel's own labor. The guitar *becomes* her own only as she *labors* upon it, learning how to make the music by which her story is alternately told to others.

The guitar plays, however, as if independent of Isabel herself, the dreamy story of her life, and Isabel understands the music to have only one purpose: to establish contact with her brother, Pierre. In this sense, then, the music of the guitar merely plays the *family tune*, thus guaranteeing that Isabel will legitimate the name within the guitar as her origin, her mother. As such, the guitar does not serve the higher function of art in Hegel of mediating between citizen and divine, between social history and universal order, but merely mystifies and enchants both Isabel and Pierre in the magic circle of the family. In effect, the guitar *negates* Isabel's more earthly labors, and it does so precisely by serving as a fetish for her *absent* family. This lost family is Isabel's imaginary compensation for her lack of social integration. The nineteenth-century sentimental romance used plots like Isabel's story to suggest the uniqueness of the illegitimate child's social exclusion; Melville's more encompassing plot eventually transforms Isabel's eccentric fate into the repressed story of respectable sons and daughters. By the end of the narrative, virtually every important character will have been revealed as inherently *illegitimate*. A substitute for her social labor, the guitar offers two compensations in place of a true democracy. In the plot, the guitar offers the secret of Isabel's family lineage and origins. As a musical instrument, the guitar offers the spiritual and ideal pleasures of art in compensation for labor that within this social context fails to produce any psychic or social growth.

Without claiming much knowledge of nineteenth-century guitar production in America, I want to suggest that the name in the guitar may well be simply a *trade* or *model* name. Even in cottage industry, the name inside a guitar would normally be taken as that of its *producer* rather than its *owner*, except in the case of some expensive custom guitar designed for a titled aristocrat. The cottage industry serving a feudal aristocracy like that at Saddle-Meadows could *only* sign the *same name* for producer and owner, since the lord or lady of the tenant lands "owns" both the means of production and the identity of the producers. The landed gentry gives title to all the products of its lands, legitimating those products only with its signature. One of the functions of art in such feudal societies is to provide the tokens of that name, ranging from the architecture of the manor house to the trophies and objets d'arts in the great hall.

Yet the secret signature in the guitar is an *illegitimate* name, even if we assume that it is *not* the real name of Pierre Glendinning, Sr.'s Frenchwoman. The unconscious of the aristocratic Glendinning line is its very illegitimacy, which is not to say simply that the veneer of respectability is maintained to hide the unauthorized affair of the father. Critics as various as Murray, Milton Stern, Sundquist, and Rogin have called attention to the genealogy of the Glendinnings out of Pierre's paternal great-grandfather, who "mortally wounded, had sat unhorsed on his saddle in the grass, with his dying voice, still cheering his men" in battle against the Indians in the French and Indian Wars (5–6). This event, of course, gives its *name* to "Saddle-Meadows," which continues to be haunted by the usurpation that initiated this American aristocratic line. As Carolyn Karcher observes: "Melville in fact comments on the double irony that America may have sold her democratic birthright for an aristocratic mess of pottage, and that the ingredients constituting that pottage—lineage, title, landed property—are all tainted."[22]

The history of aristocratic pretensions is described by Melville in terms of those "incessant restorations and creations" designed to mask their artificial origins, which on close examination generally betray the theft, piracy, and military conquest that Marx considered the means of the precapitalist accumulation of capital. Critics have often connected the Glendinnings' aristocratic pretensions with Pierre's fantastic conception of himself and the melodrama that such a self-image seems to require. More interesting is Melville's contention that the rise of the bourgeoisie, which he generally traces to the execution of Charles I and the exile of Charles II, does not lead to an authentic democracy, but merely to the manufacture of new and explicitly arbitrary titles in the place of those social institutions that would transcend the family and thereby *realize* a larger human community. The history of the English peerage is a chronicle of such artificial titles: "For not Thames is so sinuous in his natural course, not the Bridgewater Canal more artificially conducted, than blood in the veins of that winding or manufactured nobility" (Pierre, 10).

Anticipating subsequent critics who would complain that his aristocratic romance has little to do with American democracy, Melville calls attention to the Dutch Patroons, like the Gansevoorts, whose lineages dwarf the more limited spans of their English equivalents, "those grafted families" who "successively live and die on the eternal soil of a name" (10). The difference between these American aristocrats and the English is that the former stake their claims to nobility on the property that they possess, whereas the English gentry make vain appeals to the past, often to fictionalized lineages:

> But our lords, the Patroons, appeal not to the past, but they point to the present. One will show you that the public census of a county, is but part of the roll of his tenants. Ranges of mountains, high as Ben Nevis or

Snowdon, are their walls; and regular armies, with staffs of officers, crossing rivers with artillery, and marching through primeval woods, and
threading vast rocky defiles, have been sent out to distrain upon three
thousand farmer-tenants of one landlord, at a blow.   (Pierre, 11)

Murray points out that Melville is recalling in this passage the militiamen
who set out from Albany on December 9, 1839 to subdue "a strong force of anti-
rent farmers assembled on the Helderbergs" (435). The Anti-Rent protests in
New York between 1839 and 1846 give historical credibility to Melville's argument that America does indeed have a powerful, feudal aristocracy. The conventional reading of this passage as Melville's effort to defend America against
English jibes at its "newness" and its "lack of history" does not address Melville's
curious insistence on the appeal of American aristocrats to the present, rather
than the past. Melville foresees in this passage the peculiarly American aristocrat that by the end of the Civil War would be known in caricature as the Tycoon.
This aristocrat makes no appeal to the past, but relies instead on the accumulated wealth that quite literally *expands* his present, giving him authority over the
historical moment. Indeed, this aristocrat's power is essentially anti-historical,
bent as it is upon turning the "resources" of the past into the enduring image of
this master. In this regard, the urban capitalist and the landed Patroon have
much in common.

Melville stresses the size of these feudal Dutch estates in New York by
observing that they often exceed county boundaries and may include greater
populations on their "rent-rolls." The very mountains of the region serve as the
"walls" of these estates, suggesting that the Patroons' rule is not simply very
extensive but presumed to be *natural*. In Melville's landscape, the New York State
Militia enters the picture on the provocation of the Anti-Rent agitators. It would
not have been lost of the mid-nineteenth-century reader that such rebellion parallels quite explicitly the motives for the American Revolution.

Melville specifically associates this American aristocracy with Eastern and
pre-Christian cultures: "These far-descended Dutch meadows lie steeped in a
Hindooish haze; an eastern patriarchalness sways its mild crook over pastures,
whose tenant flocks shall there feed, long as their own grass grows, long as their
own water shall run. Such estates seem to defy Time's tooth, and by conditions
which take hold of the indestructible earth seem to cotemporize their fee-sim-
ples with eternity. Unimaginable audacity of a worm that but crawls through the
soil he so imperially claims!" (Pierre, 11). On the one hand, Melville merely
seems to make these associations to stress the unexpectedly venerable character
of these American princes. On the other hand, he understands how these Dutch
Patroons imitate the chaotic and irrational despotism that nineteenth-century

westerners popularly associated with the "mysterious" Orient. Hegel is a familiar figure of this orientalizing by which nineteenth-century Europeans rationalized their ethnocentrism and imperialism, and he repeatedly uses India to represent the moral anarchy of the East: "If China may be regarded as nothing else
but a State, Hindoo political existence presents us with a people but *no State*.
Secondly, while we found a moral despotism in *China*, whatever may be called a
relic of political life in *India*, is a despotism *without a principle*, without any rule
of morality and religion: for morality and religion (as far as the latter has a reference to human action) have as their indispensable condition and basis the freedom of the Will. In India, therefore, the most arbitrary, wicked, degrading
despotism has its full swing."[23] Melville stresses the *military* claims to rule both
of the Glendinnings and the Dutch Patroons he considers typical of an American
landed aristocracy. Like Hegel's Indian monarchs, Melville's American princes
are products of a social situation lacking any rational political principle that
might coordinate the various and conflicting claims to power and authority. This
seems confirmed by the New York State Militia, on order of Governor Seward,
acting as if it were the private army of these threatened landowners.

Hegel considers the "history" of India to be no history at all, merely the
record of the acts and possessions of different princes and their numerous wars.
In particular, Hegel stresses how family genealogies take the place of the public
events we normally associate with history: "It is the struggle of an energetic will
on the part of this or that prince against a feebler one; the history of ruling
dynasties, but not of peoples; a series of perpetually varying intrigues and
revolts—not indeed of subjects against their rulers, but of a prince's son, for
instance, against his father; of brothers, uncles and nephews in contest with each
other; and of functionaries against their master."[24] For Hegel, the Hindu prince
merely serves as a fetish for the still struggling spirit of social self-governance—
a spirit that Melville understands as America's democratic dream. Hegel's Hindu
genealogies of princely families find their equivalence in Melville's conception
in *Pierre* of the *image* or *portrait* of the father as the ultimate product or fetish of
a patriarchal aristocracy. The Patroon or Patriarch is possible only as a consequence of a fragmented, essentially *unpolitical* society, like the anarchic New
York that Pierre discovers on his first evening in the city with Delly and Isabel.
Just this *chaos* of the urban realm gives special credibility to the apparently *pastoral order* represented by the Patroon's country estate.

In *Capital*, Marx develops Hegel's arbitrary Hindu despot as a historical
and rhetorical figure for the development of capitalism. Sketching the history of
cooperative labor, Marx notes: "The colossal effects of simple co-operation are
to be seen in the gigantic structures erected by the ancient Asiatics, Egyptians,
Etruscans, etc." For Marx, co-operation in the labor process of precapitalist soci-

eties generally depends upon "the common ownership of the conditions of production." In Marx's own myth of social origins, cooperative labor reminds us of
the essentially collective motives for socialization. On the other hand, Marx recognizes that the "sporadic application of cooperation on a large scale in ancient
times, in the Middle Ages, and in modern colonies, rests on direct relations of
domination and servitude, in most cases on slavery." Marx is careful to distinguish
this cooperation of slave-labor from capitalist cooperation, which seems to begin
with the "free wage-labourer" selling "his labour-power to capital." This mystified
"free-exchange" enables the capitalist to make "co-ordinated labor" appear to be
a consequence of his ownership and management of the labor-power that he has
purchased. Less explicit because more subtly contrived as a "free exchange" in
the rhetoric of capitalism, the capitalist's exploitation of labor nonetheless finds
a precedent in the forced labor of slaves in ancient times rather than in the tribal
cooperation of primitive hunting tribes or agrarian societies.[25]

In particular, Marx calls attention to the "colossal works" of this coordinated slave labor in terms designed clearly to gloss his theory of surplus value.
The monumental projects undertaken by such coordinated labor forces are generally made possible by large state surpluses often generated by military con-
quests. These monuments are thus testaments to the surplus value on which the
ancient despot based his political power—the capital of domination. Indeed, the
very labor-force is itself often composed of just such a surplus, insofar as the
slaves committed to such great works were often the spoils of war. In addition,
the monuments built by such despots often serve no other purpose than to represent that arbitrary power in the form of such purely ceremonial structures as
tombs, pyramids, and obelisks. Failing to recognize that it is their coordinated
labor alone that produces such objects of wonder, these workers take such productions as symbols for the despot's power and authority. As such, these ancient
monuments—so often appropriately dedicated to death and/or a religious or
military ideal—are testaments to social waste as well as dramatic illustrations of
the kind of reification that will be the ultimate product of capitalism. Having
quoted a long section of Richard Jones' *Textbook of Lectures* on the economics of
such colossal projects among the ancients, Marx concludes by making explicit
the implications of such despotism for the rise of capitalism: "This power of
Asiatic and Egyptian kings, of Etruscan theocrats, etc. has in modern society
been transferred to the capitalist, whether he appears as an isolated individual
or, as in the case of joint-stock companies, in combination with others."[26]

The colossal works of Hegel's and Marx's ancient despots have a curious
association with Terror Rock, or the Memnon stone, in *Pierre* and with the *name*
of the Glendinning Estate, "Saddle-Meadows," which memorializes Pierre's
great-grandfather's subjugation of the Indian. In subtler ways than the Oriental

despot, however, Melville's American aristocrat legitimates his usurpation of Nature, "savage," and tenant-farmer by means of those signs and symbols (representational forms) that constitute his estate or property. It is thus little wonder that Pierre burns the "mementoes and monuments of the past" that he had so fondly collected over the years on the eve of his break with his family. With special deliberation, he burns the chair-portrait of his father, whose image now seems to speak to him only of the father's adultery and illegitimate child, Isabel: "It speaks merely of decay and death, and nothing more; decay and death of innumerable generations, it makes of earth one mold. How can lifelessness be fit memorial for life?" (Pierre, 197). What the coordinated labor of soldiers, tenant-farmers, artisans, and painters produces is merely the *personality* of the ruler. And that personality is already a fetish for the labor of others that has actually produced such an image: the portrait of a father or the military saddle of a great-grandfather.

This transformation of the living labor of the community into "heirlooms" is precisely a labor that "speaks merely of decay and death," a subtler version of Marx's "commodity fetishism" and an anticipation of Luckács' more developed conception of reification in *History and Class Consciousness*. It is a lineage without a proper history, insofar as it merely repeats the illegitimate authority of the ruler. Viewed in this manner, Pierre's grandfather's patriotism in defending "a rude but all-important stockaded fort, against the repeated combined assaults of Indians, Tories, and Regulars" during the Revolutionary War can no longer be understood as unqualified valor in the name of democratic ideals (Pierre, 6). Re-read according to the aristocratic lineage that such patriotism has produced, the grandfather's sacrifice serves only to maintain his family's power rather than the ideals of a social democracy. The grandfather merely repeats the conquering will—and its anti-historical bias—that the great-grandfather initiated in his combat with the Indian during the French and Indian Wars. In the course of making these close associations between the acts of founding the American Glendinnings by the great-grandfather and the founding of America in the Revolutionary War, Melville renders ambiguous the presumed origin of America's break with its European heritage. And by suggesting an ironic repetition of such origins in the New York State Militia's suppression of the Anti-Rent protesters in 1839, Melville transforms the democratic revolution into the secret consolidation of a new American aristocratic power.

Pierre's own gesture of rebellion, including the burning of these fetishes, ought to involve some self-conscious rejection of the limitations of the family in favor of a larger social relation. But like most "young Americans," Pierre bids instead for radical individualism: "Henceforth, cast-out Pierre hath no paternity, and no past; and since the Future is one blank to all; therefore twice-disinherited Pierre stands untrammeledly his ever-present self!—free to do his own self-will and present fancy to whatever end!" (Pierre, 199). In his own will-to-power, Pierre hardly restores America to the *social revolution* in which it ought to have found its origin; Pierre merely repeats that illusory revolution by which his ancestors supplanted the authority of others with that of their own family name.

The truth of descendedness, Melville argues, involves an infinite regression: "For as the breath in all our lungs is hereditary, and my present breath at this moment, is further descended than the body of the present High Priest of the Jews, so far as he can assuredly trace it; so mere names, which are also but air, do likewise revel in this endless descendedness" (Pierre, 9). As radical breaks with the past, his ancestors' militarism and Pierre's rebellion against his family repudiate the *history* that is carried in every "name." Even as Pierre destroys the fetishes of the past, he begins to reproduce the rhetoric of such fetishism—of the Oriental despot, the English aristocrat, the Dutch Patroon—in his vainglorious self-reliance. For Melville, the only genuine nobility derives from our involvement in the process of constructing a human community, rather than from those apparently ahistorical "images" that monumentalize the family or the self. Our shared air, which circulates in the very breath of our speech, is the guarantee of a shared humanity, whose only proper labor is the construction of a social habitation—that is, a *history*—for such being.

For the American, such historical labor (labor *as history*) ought to involve the production of a *new* relation to Europe, rather than a simple break with that inescapable past. This, I take it, is the function of the recognition scene near the end of *Pierre*, when Isabel and Pierre encounter "another portrait of a complete stranger—a European," which "was as much the father of Isabel as the original of the chair-portrait" (Pierre, 353). This scene is actually a crucial scene of *méconnaissance*, insofar as it seems to plunge Pierre into despair regarding his folly in assuming a *portrait* to be *evidence* of actual bloodlines. On the other hand, the portrait of the stranger is used by Melville not merely to mystify absolutely family origins for the sake of plot reversal or some philosophical quandary; the portrait of the European stranger reminds us how every origin, every tradition, every *history* is the product of our social labor—whether such labor be imaginative or material: "But perhaps there was no original at all to this second portrait; it might have been a pure fancy piece; to which conceit, indeed, the uncharacterizing style of the filling-up seemed to furnish no small testimony" (Pierre, 353). As "a pure fancy piece," the portrait serves to expose the unconscious of Pierre's determination to legitimate Isabel through his own artistic labor. Yet, as the coordinated work of the historical and social imagination, the portrait may serve as a figure for the relation to Europe that American democracy ought to be working to produce.

What inhibits this historical labor is thus not just the family, oppressive as it is represented in the lineage and fortunes of the Glendinnings, but also individualism and its contemporary cant for Melville: Emersonian self-reliance.[27] Hegel's philosophical labor and Marx's more material labor both insist that the individual can realize himself only in and through an otherness that he works to produce, transform, and ultimately internalize as his own social bond. Social history is just this perpetual process of self-transcendence as the means of self-realization. In capitalism, however, the dialectic of self and other is transformed into a dualism between worker and owner, wages and capital, change and repetition, materiality and idealism, other and self: horologicals and chronomentricals. Marx's theory of surplus value describes the ways that the capitalist steals the labor-power of the worker by manipulating the working-day or mystifying the amount of capital actually consumed in production. The aim of surplus value in capitalism is for Marx, however, considerably more significant than the simple accumulation and expansion of capital. The first aim is to establish the most elementary class distinction: the laborer stakes his being on his physical body, which is successively "used up" in the production process; the owner finds his being in capital, whose very accumulation is a psychic defense against his fear of illegitimacy, a constant reminder that he has a material identity that grows in time rather than shrinking (as does the laborer's labor-power). And because it grows without the capitalist's labor, surplus value assumes the appearance of a *natural organicism*, a simulation of the Nature that industrial capitalism displaces. This chimerical organicism finds its precapitalist precedent in the peculiar pastoralism of Saddle-Meadows and the special brand of American aristocracy enshrined there.

In *Pierre*, physical labor is always at odds with individual identity, with an ideal of self-reliance. Isabel's romantic imagination equates self-consciousness with productive labor, but Isabel *experiences* only the alienating effects of her own labor. Indeed, the nearly mystical art of her guitar seems to be a compensation for the failure of her daily labor to produce the identity (spirit) she desires. Charlie Millthorpe's father, "a very respectable farmer," illustrates this discrepancy between what Henry James, Sr. called "doing" and "being:" "Pierre well remembered old farmer Millthorpe—the handsome, melancholy, calm-tempered, mute, old man; in whose countenance—refinedly ennobled by nature, and yet coarsely tanned and attenuated by many a prolonged day's work in the harvest—rusticity and classicalness were strangely united. The delicate profile of his face, bespoke the loftiest aristocracy; his knobbed and bony hands resembled a beggar's" (Pierre, 275). Melville uses farmer Millthorpe to illustrate the general observation that: "The political and social levelings and confoundings of all manner of human elements in America, produce many striking individual anomalies unknown in other lands" (275). These "anomalies," of course, ought to be the signs of an authentic American revolution, which would transform the illegitimate family of the aristocrat into a genuine democracy. But in this context, the signifier of poverty is *labor*; the signifier of wealth is idleness. The wear and tear of honest farming are considered *unnatural*, already hints of incipient death: "knobbed and bony hands." The "undiluted" transmission, the sheer repetition, of genetic traits is assumed to be the result of a mere inheritance that is more properly the *work of nature*: a "countenance . . . refinedly ennobled by nature."

The Millthorpes, themselves dependent on the aristocratic and feudal authority of Saddle-Meadows, "loosely and unostentatiously traced their origin to an emigrating English Knight, who had crossed the sea in the time of the elder Charles" (Pierre, 275). Thus farmer Millthorpe's labor is considered a degradation of such ancestry, and it is little wonder that his poverty and death are rumored to be consequences of drunken dissipation. Insofar as the wear and tear of human labor results in nothing but the apparently enduring identity of the aristocrat, then labor is quite literally dissipation and effectively "unnatural"— *other* than itself. Given these circumstances, then, it is hardly surprising that Charlie Millthorpe aspires "to be either an orator, or a poet; at any rate, a great genius of one sort or other. He recalled the ancestral Knight, and indignantly spurned the plow" (Pierre, 279).

Oratory, poetry, "great genius of one sort or other," we know involve Pierre's own project to "gospelize anew," to write the infernal book that would both declare his rebellion against the Glendinnings' hypocrisy and assure his fortune and reputation. Indeed, the labor of writing is given considerable attention by Melville, both in his representation of Pierre's anguished struggle at the Church of the Apostles and in his general observations on the differences between physical and intellectual labor. Even before he rebels against his family and departs Saddle-Meadows for New York, Pierre himself has worked and earned, after a fashion, by virtue of his trivial lyrics: "The Tropical Summer: a Sonnet," "The Weather: a Thought," "Life: an Impromptu," "The late Reverend Mark Graceman: an Obituary," etc. Like the "heir-looms" he burns, Pierre's poems are mere fetishes for his poetic self. Both literary formalism (a sonnet) and philosophical idealism (a thought) reify nature and thus speak only of the death of spiritual grace that they have helped to produce ("The late Reverend Mark Graceman: an Obituary"). The name of "Reverend Mark Graceman" seems to anticipate "Mark Winsome" in *The Confidence-Man*, who quite clearly is a caricature of Emerson. The actual products of Pierre's juvenile imagination parody the idealizations of nature and death that characterize literary transcendentalism. More specifically, Pierre's poetizing may indicate that the labor of idealism often produces the *death* of the spirit that the poet and scholar hope to *realize* in their works.

Emerson repeatedly affirms the dignity of labor that unites intellectual and manual work: "I hear therefore with joy whatever is beginning to be said of the dignity and necessity of labor to every citizen. There is virtue yet in the hoe and the spade, for the learned as well as for unlearned hands." Yet what unites different kinds of labor for Emerson is their mutual concern with the production of a spiritual self. Emerson is quick to warn us that work performed without regard for the soul it serves may well be enslaved by other temporal masters: convention and fashion: "And labor is everywhere welcome; always we are invited to work; only be this limitation observed, that a man shall not for the sake of wider activity sacrifice any opinion to the popular judgments and modes of action."[28] Emerson characteristically gives heavier weight to the work of *man* than to the work of the world. Because the "dignity of labor" requires a spiritual understanding of man's role in a natural economy, then the labors of idealists— "of the poet, the priest, the lawgiver, and men of study generally"—have special authority in Emerson's division of labor. In "Man the Reformer," his address to the Mechanics' Apprentices' Library Association of Boston in 1841, Emerson seems to take perverse pleasure before such an audience in distinguishing between "intellectual exertion" and "the downright drudgery of the farmer and the smith": "I would not quite forget the venerable counsel of the Egyptian mysteries, which declared that 'there were two pairs of eyes in man, and it is requisite that the pair which are beneath should be closed, when the pair that are above them perceive, and that when the pair above are closed, those which are beneath should be opened.' "[29] The manual laborer is all too quickly deceived by the apparent reality of the products of his labor and thus lured to accumulate and possess objects that ought to be mere symbols of the soul. The genius of the poet and scholar finds its wealth in its own activity; when genius confuses earthly and transcendental rewards, then it falls as Bellerophon did:

> He may leave to others the costly conveniences of housekeeping, and large hospitality, and the possession of works of art. Let him feel that genius is a hospitality, and that he who can create works of art needs not collect them. He must live in a chamber, and postpone his self-indulgence, forewarned and forearmed against that frequent misfortune of men of genius,—the taste for luxury. This is the tragedy of genius;—attempting to drive along the ecliptic with one horse of the heavens and one horse of the earth, there is only discord and ruin and downfall to chariot and charioteer.[30]

Emerson's description of the discipline and worldly privation of the man of genius is parodied in Melville's description of Pierre at work in his bare, cold room in the Church of the Apostles. And Emerson's warning that genius must not confuse the "horse of the heavens" with the "horse of the earth" or the eyes that "are above" with the eyes that "are beneath" is caricatured in Plotinus Plinlimmon's pamphlet, "Chronometricals and Horologicals."[31]

Melville criticizes Emerson's idealist foundations for human labor by suggesting that the special work of the intellect may serve merely to preserve us from the more difficult and concrete labor of producing a workable society. Emerson's labor of and for the self might require privation and "unworldliness" precisely because such alienation is its secret product. Transcendental idealism thus may be viewed as an elaborate system of psychological defense against the alienating consequences of more material labor in capitalist America. Until he faces the exigencies of earning a living for his own "family" in the city, Pierre has spent all of his literary earnings on cigars, "so that the puffs which indirectly brought him his dollars were again returned, but as perfumed puffs; perfumed with the sweet leaf of Havanna" (Pierre, 262). Melville parodies romantic idealism by transforming the spiritual activity of Emerson's genius or the human desire for transcendence in Wordsworth's image of "wreaths of smoke/ Sent up, in silence, from among the trees" into the ephemeral vapors of self-reliant man—what T. E. Hulme terms the "circumambient gas" of romanticism.[32]

"This towering celebrity," Melville writes, "—there he would sit smoking, and smoking, mild and self-festooned as a vapory mountain" (Pierre, 263). This ironic identification of Pierre as juvenile author with the Memnon Stone suggests that *this* formalist conception of poetic spiritualization is designed principally to obscure the self, to give it a protective outer wrapping (literally, a "white jacket" of smoke) that would protect it from the mob. Unlike the music of Isabel's guitar, the smoke from Pierre's poems and cigars protects and isolates the self, rather than serving as its virtual embodiment and medium for communication: its externalization, in Hegelian terms, in and for sociohistorical circulations.

In its own way, this figuration of Pierre as poet is the equivalent of the chair-portrait of his father. Both conceal a secret of illegitimacy that is related to their equally false claims to authority. His father's adultery is discovered in his mysterious smile in the portrait in the same way Pierre's plagiarism from other authors is revealed in his own ambitious work. Melville's description of Pierre as a "vapory mountain" also helps explain his paradoxical act of burning the chair-portrait. What Pierre intends as an act of rebellion serves as the means of protecting his father from exposure, insofar as Pierre finds in the portrait some family resemblance with Isabel:

> Painted before the daughter was conceived or born, like a dumb seer, the portrait still seemed leveling its prophetic finger at that empty air, from which Isabel did finally emerge. There seemed to lurk some mystical intelligence and vitality in the picture; because, since in his own memory of his

father, Pierre could not recall any distinct lineament transmitted to Isabel, but vaguely saw such in the portrait; therefore, not Pierre's parent, as any way rememberable by him, but the portrait's painted *self* seemed the real father of Isabel; for, so far as all sense went, Isabel had inherited one peculiar trait nowither traceable but to it.   (Pierre, 197)

The curiously prophetic quality of the chair-portrait, whether it be an effect of the painter's genius or merely Pierre's excited imagination, suggests a different artistic function than the defenses of Emersonian idealism or Pierre's protective veil of poetic smoke. The portrait of the father brings together both the aristocrat's conscious desire for authority and the unconscious illegitimacy that fuels such desire.

Like his ancestors, Pierre wants to turn himself into an enduring figure in the landscape, precisely by protecting himself from the "mob" (such as the one that assaults Delly, Isabel, and Pierre in that infernal first night they spend in the city) and at the same time rebelling against his predecessors by willfully authoring his own unnatural family of Isabel, Delly, and, ultimately, Lucy. It is a family composed of nothing but "sisters" and a "brother," we are quick to notice, recalling our earlier remarks about the relation of brothers and sisters in the metaphorics of the Hegelian family. Contemptuous of the various efforts of vanity presses and journals to exploit his minor celebrity, Pierre himself merely reproduces, even in his haughty denial of their overtures, the cult of authorial personality these publishers *labor* to produce. Like the aristocrat and capitalist, he vainly tries to father himself and a family to render honorable such imaginative incest.

Melville's representation of Pierre as some "vapory mountain" also associates him with the natural landmark at Saddle-Meadows, Terror Rock or the Memnon Stone, which later in the narrative will come to mythic life in Pierre's dream of Enceladus, the earthbound Titan. Earlier, I interpreted the Memnon Stone as a version of those colossal monuments Hegel and Marx associated with the despotism of Asiatic and Egyptian rulers. Although a natural formation, the Memnon Stone is discovered by Pierre, "the first known publishing discoverer of this stone, which he had thereupon fancifully christened the Memnon Stone" (Pierre, 132). The stone becomes Pierre's colossus, his monument to the *natural* surplus the genius ought to have in reserve. The cavity at the base of the rock and its general phallic suggestiveness make the Memnon Stone a figure for a hermaphroditism that is particularly appropriate either to the false self-sufficiency of the Glendinnings or Emerson's self-reliant genius: American aristocrat or radical individual.[33] It is interesting to note that the Church of the Apostles' architecture is the urban equivalent of the rock, insofar as the new tower where

Pierre has his rooms rises out of the courtyard of the old church. The hermaphroditism of the rural and urban forms—the former associated with the aristocracy of the Glendinnings and the latter either with Pierre's writing or the law and commerce in the buildings below—suggests the self-generative powers of the "original character" in *The Confidence-Man*: "The original character, essentially such, is like a revolving Drummond light, raying away from itself all round it—everything is lit by it, everything starts up to it (mark how it is with Hamlet), so that, in certain minds, there follows upon the adequate conception of such a character, an effect, in its way, akin to that which in Genesis attends upon the beginning of things."[34]

Yet, such an "Original" in both *Pierre* and *The Confidence-Man*, whether literary character turned author or citizen turned despot, remains Melville's grandest illusion—the secret passion of the idealist not merely to *participate* in nature's economy but to *originate* and thus *dominate* that economy.[35] Such self-procreative and ahistorical formalism belongs only to the impossible realm of the "chronometrical," and as such it is as "self-consuming" as "self-producing." It is, in a word, an *incestuous* form of artistic production that merely produces its own obscurity, weakness, and ultimate death. By the same token, it obscures its actual origins, which in the case of Pierre's writing must be termed the historical conditions—necessities and exigencies—under which he must work. The unified religious authority of the old Church of the Apostles has been replaced by the apparent dualism of material vs. ideal, utilitarian vs. transcendental. The lawyers and shopkeepers in the renovated church exercise their very real powers over the workers in the city by maintaining the *illusion* of freedom represented by the dreamers and free-thinkers occupying the tower. The "freedom" of such idealism (of Emerson's self-reliant genius) is, in Melville's closer scrutiny, merely a double of the servitude it hopes to escape; it is a *reflection* of the poverty and alienation of those who work to preserve such masters.

Such an interpretation of Pierre's art as the idealist version of the Oriental despot's colossal monuments—testaments to his arbitrary power, accumulated economic surpluses, and exploitation of labor—revises considerably the conventional reading of Melville's oft-quoted glimpse into the pyramid of the human soul:

> The old mummy lies buried in cloth on cloth; it takes time to unwrap this Egyptian king. Yet now, forsooth, because Pierre began to see through the first superficiality of the world, he fondly weens he has come to the unlayered substance. But, far as any geologist has yet gone down into the world, it is found to consist of nothing but surface stratified on surface. To its axis, the world being nothing but superinduced superficies. By vast pains we

mine into the pyramid; by horrible gropings we come to the central room; with joy we espy the sarcophagus; but we lift the lid—and no body is there!—appallingly vacant as vast is the soul of man! (Pierre, 285)

Generally interpreted in the context of Melville's nihilism or as his existential affirmation of the groundlessness of being, this passage deals less with man's essential nature (his "geology," as it were) than with the "nothingness" he produces by way of his labor to idealize the world in the service of very material interests. In this passage, Melville indicts not just transcendental idealism for offering us an absolutely elusive notion of spirit or soul, he also connects such idealism with those idealizing arts of political rulers who would mask their illegitimate power and their exploitation of workers in the form of majestic symbols of their supernatural authority. This political mystification initiates an historical process of labor through which we quite literally *unmake* ourselves and transform the natural energies of our bodies into alien, unnatural objects. "Nothingness" is not for Melville the essential condition for being that it would become for the twentieth-century existentialist; the vacancy in Melville's pyramid is the consequence of very specific historical acts of social labor made to serve perverse gods. [36]

Melville distinguishes Pierre's labor from that of farmer Millthorpe and even Isabel when he writes:

> The mechanic, the day-laborer, has but one way to live; his body must provide for his body. But not only could Pierre in some sort, do that; he could do the other; and letting his body stay lazily at home, send off his soul to labor, and his soul would come faithfully back and pay his body her wages. So, some unprofessional gentlemen of the aristocratic South, who happen to own slaves, give those slaves liberty to go and seek work, and every night return with their wages, which constitute those idle gentlemen's income. Both ambidexter and quadruple-armed is that man, who in a day-laborer's body, possesses a day-laboring soul. (Pierre, 261)

The spiritual slavery that Melville describes here connects Pierre's life-denying artistic idealism with the institutions of Southern slavery, just as the feudalism of the Dutch Patroons is associated with Oriental despotism. The passage suggests that the "division of labor" in modern bourgeois culture more subtly replicates the explicit exploitation of labor in slave-holding societies. Carolyn Porter considers the mythic oppositions of country and city, pastoralism and industrialism, to be characteristically American means of forgetting capitalism's deep roots in the feudalism of aristocratic class structures: "Perhaps it is partly due to a long-standing confusion in the minds of Americans over the difference between capitalist and aristocrat that they have never really been able to resist altogether the plantation myth's attractions."[37]

In particular, the transcendentalist's rejection of economic materialism often results in the substitution of an ideal economy of the self that comes dangerously close to the values and customs of the landed gentry. By explicitly *feminizing* Pierre's "soul" ("pay his body her wages"), Melville also returns this reflection on art and everyday labor to the psychosexual themes centering on Pierre's incestuous relation with Isabel, whose guitar plays as he writes. The mystical communion of Isabel and Pierre, like the spiritual friendship so prized by Emerson and Thoreau, is for Melville an inadequate substitute for the social product that ought to result from the coordinated labor of politically committed citizens. Recalling that the young Frederick Douglass worked for wages in Baltimore under just such an arrangement with Hugh Auld and that many African-Americans in Harriet Jacobs' Edenton, North Carolina had similar working arrangements with their slaveowners, we should conclude with Melville that the leisure of any citizen is always at the expense and often indenture of others.[38] In this passage, Melville makes clear his indictment of an aestheticism that relies parasitically on maintenance by others, effectively reversing the conventional master/servant relations between ideal and manual workers asserted by Emerson in "Man the Reformer."

Melville's association of Pierre's labor as a writer with the master-slave relation of Southern slavery begins with the Emersonian cliché: writing transcends ordinary labor by coordinating physical and spiritual functions. But Melville then suggests that the very function of writing may be to protect its author from the physical depletion of ordinary labor. In this regard, authorship is explicitly related to the ownership of slaves and the idleness of the aristocrat, but with the interesting qualification that such a relation of master and slave gives the slave the *illusion* of "liberty to go and seek work." That this exploitation of the slave's desire for freedom also involves the slave's desire to do his/her own labor is important for Melville's parable of writing. The illusion that the soul can work independently ("freely") from the body, which stays "lazily at home," is fundamental to Emersonian idealism: "Nature is the incarnation of a thought, and turns to thought again, as ice becomes water and gas. The world is mind precipitated, and the volatile essence is forever escaping again into the state of free thought. . . . Man imprisoned, man crystallized, man vegetative, speaks to man impersonated."[39] Melville effectively reverses the terms of Emerson's triumphant transcendentalist vision, transforming the essentially free mind into a *slave* to the *physical master*, who after all *still speaks to*, or governs, this presumptively free spirit.

The separation of the self from its labor and the separation of physical from spiritual production is the fundamental alienation operative in aristocratic families and in the romantic arts designed to naturalize such aristocracy. In Southern plantation feudalism, myths of the "extended" family of white owners and infantilized African-American slaves, the melodrama of white male "honor" and white female "virtue," and countless other social fictions sustained by a wide variety of arts helped achieve this naturalization and mystification of the family. As the white family was so celebrated, of course, in Southern mythology, systematic efforts were made to break up the African-American family, precisely because the family remains in this romantic ethos the crucial mediation between public and private, nature and culture. For this reason, among others, Douglass and Jacobs would reconstruct the African-American family by identifying the internal contradictions of the slave-holding family and revealing its parasitic function, substituting in its place their concept of the African-American family as socially constructed and politically effective—that is, socially *productive*.

In the purely abstract idealist terms that Melville both parodies and elaborates in *Pierre*, the family does nothing but project the concept of a remote, external law of authority, which cannot be internalized but merely reproduced as alien and external. In this sense, the family produces nothing other than alienation itself, that pure *negation* (*Verneinung*) that Hegel himself equated with the death of the Spirit. The move from family to society, from the Law of the Father to the internal law of self-governance, is the negation of negation, the transformation of stony externality into the self-moving principle of *Geist* as its historical movement: the *Bildungsweg* of Hegel's social theory that Marx could appropriate from an otherwise bourgeois apologist.

Pierre's labor in writing his "infernal book," his new gospel, is designed to reproduce this portrait of the stony self, of the Self as distinct from man's social dependency and the labor required to maintain the historical relation of self and society. We read little directly of Pierre's grand work, except those quotes from "the last sheet from his hand" and the slips he has cast to the floor. Still, we learn enough of "his apparent author-hero, Vivia" to recognize that Pierre has "directly plagiarized from his own experiences" (Pierre, 302). These fragments do not speak of self-consciousness as self-knowledge, as we would expect from this romantic author. Instead, Vivia speaks only of his contradiction and despair, of his hatred of life and his impotence—what Nietzsche would term his *ressentiment*: "Yet that knowing his fatal condition does not one whit enable him to change or better his condition. Conclusive proof that he has no power over his condition" (Pierre, 303). What Pierre/Vivia cannot know is that he has merely given objective form to a soul, a suffering self, produced by those contradictions in his family history that are also the disabling contradictions of a promised social democracy based upon radical individualism, whether such individualism assumes the form of the Father, the military leader, the mythic hero, the Dutch Patroon, the capitalist, or the visionary author. As Emory Elliott has noted, commenting on Pierre's conscious avoidance of comedy in his great work, "Pierre . . . . takes himself and his American heritage too seriously. He has believed so fervently in the myth of the greatness of the fathers and the glory of their achievement that he misses the human comedy in his own past."[40] His rebellion against these national forefathers, even when it is directed explicitly against their sins, is designed to venerate the revolutionary traditions they have come to represent. Pierre and Vivia are, as Elliott points out, "locked in prison"—the prison of a national ideology they know to be false.[41]

In this regard, then, Pierre/*Pierre* reproduces the aristocratic law of the Father by means of one of those arts that capitalism employs for similar purposes of naturalizing and legitimating its own founding contradictions: between self and society, owner and laborer, ideal and historical, chronometrical and horological. The art of the novel gives us a labor that *we as readers* perform only to *use up* our bodies (and our time) in the service of reproducing the "genius" of the author: Herman Melville or Pierre Glendinning. That always absent author governs and controls our labors in order to take the place of the social and communal relations our work of reading ought to yield.

In *Capital* Marx argues that it is the *identity* of the capitalist that is the true *fetish*, an alienated metonymy for the labor-power stolen from his workers in the form of surplus value. In this ontic theft, the capitalist shares the basic sin of the aristocratic slave-owner, who more flagrantly steals his very being from the labor of others. Indeed, the growth of surplus value, the incessant drive for accumulation, seems some desperate desire on the part of the capitalist to disguise what he recognizes to be the inauthenticity of his identity: that which represents him is never he himself. In a similar sense, Pierre's book is "filched" from those "vile atheists," Lucan and Voltaire, among others, who ought to remind Pierre of the impossibility of authoring anything outside the complex genealogy of literary and social forces. The infinite regress of *literature* and the infinite regress of *descendedness* that Melville uses to subvert aristocratic pretensions are both the preconditions for negating myths of self-reliant man and aristocratic authority in favor of that more enduring and integrated product: a social collective sustained by the labors of men and women.

Neither aristocratic ruler nor the American capitalist wants *that* dispersed, displaced, collective authority. In *Pierre*, Melville attempted to *kill* romance, to take it to its ultimate extreme as a formalist prop for the ideology of America's secret aristocracy of the Spirit: economic capitalism and philosophical transcendentalism. Rogin concludes that the "self-referentiality that takes over *Pierre* brings the book's narrative to a halt" and "explains its own failure, for it is the appropriate literary form for the claustrophobic family. *Pierre* is the victim of the domestic relationship which brings both storytelling and therefore life itself to an end."[42] In this regard, we can judge Pierre's swerve back into the chivalric action of the duel and the melodrama it stages to be merely the proper ending for the novel he has written, the "infernal" "new" gospel of capitalist individuation as sustained by the rhetoric of literary authority. It is altogether fitting that melodrama should be Pierre's choice in the face of his literary failure. Pierre's final actions, however, by no means compromise his own conception of literature; such action is perfectly consistent with Pierre's literary project: the realization of romance in experience, the substitution of the author's self for the worker's active labor. Such realization—life imitating art at last—merely enables Pierre to succumb to the "romance of the real" that is told by the authors of capitalism and enacted by their characters, whether intellectual or manual laborers.

Yet just as the chair-portrait of Pierre's father *reveals* his kinship with Isabel and thus the very secret the portrait artist attempted to conceal with the conventional nobility of his subject (and the conventions of the portrait genre), so *Pierre* represents its own unconscious and thus *escapes* fleetingly its identification with Pierre and his fragmentary monument, his unfinished colossus. By so ruthlessly connecting his own craft of fiction and his own will to literary authority with the political wills of despots, aristocrats, and capitalists, Melville completes his book by undoing his own claim to legitimacy and by *characterizing* himself in his parody of an author, Pierre. Insofar as Melville accepts the social anarchy he finds at the heart of the Glendinnings' and the Gansevoorts' conceptions of democracy, then Melville must be humiliated by a literary vocation that merely serves that ideology's effort to rationalize its contradictions. Melville does not accept these conditions for labor; his rebellion is exemplified by his refusal of the customary alternatives of philosophical idealism or the "world elsewhere" of art. The unconscious of *Pierre* is, like the unconscious of the chair-portrait, no mystical effect of artistic intuition; it is the ideological analysis that results from deconstructing those apparently self-evident distinctions we assume govern our everyday reality: ideal and material, self and other, author and reader, owner and worker, master and servant, state and family. That Melville understands these distinctions to have special roles to play in reconciling social democracy with radical individualism makes his labor in *Pierre* especially pertinent to Jacksonian America.

Rogin and others have judged *Pierre* to be symptomatic of Melville's ultimate self-referentiality as an author, his resignation to the delusions that later would define twentieth-century modernism. Emory Elliott warns us, however, not to confuse Melville with Pierre as Pierre deliberately conflates himself with his fictional Vivia. What the reader able to distinguish Melville's personal disappointments and commercial failures (including *Pierre*) from Pierre will find is "a searing cultural critique."[43] Melville deconstructs in *Pierre* the democratic pretensions of American capitalism by exposing the relation of radical individualism to the incestuous and claustrophobic closure of the aristocratic family and its demonic other, the Southern plantation forced labor camp. Melville further deconstructs the new authority of Emerson's expressive self, both subject and object of its own labor, by revealing how literary authority participates in the naturalization of capitalist contradictions. Given his own complicity with the principal subjects of his critique, Melville can hardly be said to have mastered the problems his narrative uncovers; there is, in short, a point at which the attentive reader must reconnect Pierre's problems with Melville's concerns about his writing. Parody, irony, and satire—mere literary terms, after all—hardly begin to address the force of Melville's critique in *Pierre*. Elliott argues that Melville protested in *Pierre* against the popular literature of his day—sentimental romances and verses—that mythologized America's flawed history of racial violence and class warfare. For Elliott, Melville struggled thereby to find a mode of expression that would "go beyond the sayings of the Revolutionary or the Puritan fathers" and that would therefore require an "intellectual flexibility and artistic power" few American writers "had been able to manifest."[44]

In my view, *Pierre* is Melville's farewell to the romance and the novel—to literature as he had attempted to practice it in his previous works. After *Pierre*, especially in works like *Benito Cereno* and *The Confidence-Man*, philosophical idealism works consistently in league with ideology, either by way of the transcendentalist's overt detachment from history and politics or by way of his active interest in political power and control. Captain Amasa Delano may be an actual, historical New Englander, but this is a convenience for Melville in *Benito Cereno*, because Delano's avowed innocence regarding events is also a measure of his blindness regarding his treatment of his own seamen on board the *Bachelor's Delight*. The "Philosophical Intelligence Officer" in *The Confidence-Man* is not simply a parody of New England abolitionists; he is another version of the numerous figures in the text intent upon cheating others by discursive sleight-of-hand.

Pierre is by no means the expression of incipient madness, despair, or nihilism. Quite the contrary, the book raises those questions about the ideological consequences of literary production that motivate his subsequent writings. Bercovitch describes *Pierre* as "a story about the rhetoric of Apocalypse," by which he means the ultimate revelation promised by apocalyptic judgment.[45] Melville's critique of literary production may have devastating consequences for his own sense of vocation, but it also makes possible the active study of the genealogy of social values that Melville's Ishmael futilely attempts to understand from his detached vantage and by means of his very romantic "negative capabil-ity" in *Moby-Dick*. By means of the deconstructive "failure" of *Pierre* as *literature*, Melville could make the *leap* from Ishmael to the confidence-men, whose agita-tions and subversions enter the social drama, provoking the labor of their inter-locutors, of their *readers*, either to *reproduce* the Wall Street World—America as the tomb of its past—or *produce* the carnival of an authentically democratic soci-ety. In *Pierre*, *Benito Cereno*, and *The Confidence-Man*, Melville developed a mode of writing that left behind "literature" as an idealist discourse and anticipated the cultural criticism of our own present moment.

Between Politics and Poetics:
Frederick Douglass' *Narrative of the
Life of Frederick Douglass, An American Slave,
Written by Himself*

> Douglass has subverted the terms of the code he was meant to mediate: He has been a trickster.
>
> — Henry Louis Gates, Jr.

Frederick Douglass' 1845 *Narrative* still occupies a curious position in U.S. literature and culture. Frequently taught from high school to college, it is indisputably a classic work of American literature and autobiography. By any standard, the rhetorical power and symbolic economy of the *Narrative*, especially when complemented by its impact on the major political·debates of the 1840s, ought to have earned it a position with the other great American autobiographies—Franklin's *Autobiography* and Adams' *Education*, for example—as well as the works of the great tradition of American self-reliance—Emerson's essays, Hawthorne's *The Scarlet Letter*, Thoreau's *Walden*, Whitman's *Song of Myself*, to mention only the prototypes of what has often been considered *the* American literary tradition. Yet, Douglass' 1845 *Narrative* has rarely been treated as a central text in the several "literary traditions" twentieth-century scholars have developed to define American culture. As a literary classic, the 1845 *Narrative* has been praised in isolation and singled out as an exemplary work, as in Carolyn Porter's assessment of it as "the finest example" of the "slave narrative."[1]

In the African-American literary tradition, of course, the 1845 *Narrative* is an undeniably central text, not merely because scholars frequently interpret it but more importantly for its defining role in establishing African-American literary genealogies. Whether it is celebrated as a literary and cultural model or criticized as blind to its patriarchal assumptions or free-enterprise ideology,

Douglass' *Narrative* is the central African-American literary text.[2] Just this glaring difference between the centrality of the 1845 *Narrative* in the African-American literary tradition and its continued marginalization by the schools claiming to define the dominant American literary tradition would seem to be readily explained by the racist aesthetics of modern American literary criticism. Indeed, the exclusion of major African-American writers from "American literature" as it was defined from the 1920s to the New Critics was one of the primary motivations for scholars to establish an African-American literary tradition with its own aesthetic and cultural criteria.

True as it is, I think, to say that American literary study well into the 1970s followed the racial divisions and exclusions that had provoked the Civil Rights' movement, this aesthetic racism hardly accounts for the continuing exclusion of Douglass' *Narrative* from the new traditions of American literature that have been developed in the past thirty years. Whatever the differences among post-structuralist, feminist, New Historicist, and cultural studies' approaches to American literature, they have shared a common concern to bring the insights of women's and ethnic literary studies to the work of reshaping the American literary tradition, even if this latter work has meant for many the substitution of several different traditions for an integrated, consensually established cultural tradition. It is almost as if Douglass' *Narrative* achieved canonical status too late for proper recognition and influence, at the moment when literary canons were so profoundly challenged as to make the *Narrative*'s belated canonization a problem rather than a virtue.

Less than a decade ago, Russell Reising claimed with some confidence that "Douglass' place in the American canon has, over the past decade, grown increasingly more secure," even if he could also worry: "Less certain . . . is just *how* Douglass' *Narrative* is to be situated in American literary history."[3] Reising's final chapter of *The Unusable Past*, "Conclusion: The Significance of Frederick Douglass," is one of the rare efforts to use the 1845 *Narrative* to revise the American literary canon, beginning with the canonical status of the work and then using what is best in it to challenge the limitations of previous definitions of a common American literary heritage.[4] Reising does not merely argue for including Douglass "among the major writers of the American Renaissance," he contends that Douglass *transforms* the very political and aesthetic concerns of these major writers that have been traditionally valued in American culture. Of particular interest to Reising is Douglass' rethinking of "an individual's relationship with his community" as a challenge to liberal democratic reflections on this important cultural theme in the mid-nineteenth century (Reising, 257). In other words, the familiar problem of how to reconcile individual rights and identity with the common good—a conflict that at times may be said to have become a national schizophrenia—is worked out in Douglass' writings as an important revision of its characteristic treatment by the writers of the American Renaissance.

In particular, Reising stresses Douglass' insistence in the 1845 *Narrative* on the social and economic construction of human identity, in both the best and worst senses, both of which he knows from his experiences of slavery and his relative freedom in the North. Rather than treating the "themes of isolation, orphanage, and alienation that pervade so many texts of the American Renaissance" as parts of "an existential given," Douglass takes this attenuation of the self as "the point from which he begins to construct an identity" (Reising, 257). In place of the metaphysical anguish and philosophical reflection often considered so proto-modern in the works of the major writers of the American Renaissance, Douglass substitutes concrete actions that will enable the African American robbed of proper identity by slavery to constitute identity in a reformed, post-slavery society. Just because identity is socially constructed, then it can be socially reconstituted, even if this means that the quest for individual agency ought always already be a struggle for greater social justice.

Although Reising recognizes this as a fundamentally *political* message in Douglass' writings, he also considers it essentially literary. Borrowing the terminology of modernism, Reising argues that Douglass repeatedly "defamiliarizes" slavery's claims to "natural" hierarchies of master and slave, white and black, as well as to the "naturalness" of plantation life in general. In a similar fashion, Douglass challenges conventional notions of liberal democracy by pointing out repeatedly the inequities, contradictions, and hypocrisies resulting not merely from Southern slavery but also from Northern racism: "Douglass forces us to recognize . . . that any self is a social construct, not a natural integer, and it is in that sense of human sociability and in Douglass' ability to render the institution of slavery as an ideological construct subject to change that provides the *Narrative* with its final act of defamiliarization, and, perhaps, its finest moment of literary and historical power" (Reising, 271). On this basis, Reising contends that "Douglass' life, his works, the institution of slavery, and the struggle against slavery waged by black and white alike are the material, social, and political basis on which the works of other major writers of the American Renaissance are founded. The dynamics of slavery made the less specific . . . meditations of Emerson, Thoreau, Hawthorne, Melville, Stowe, and others *possible*" (271). In Reising's argument, the 1845 *Narrative* occupies an especially important position in Douglass' life and writings, both because of its symbolic economy and because it antedates the traditional flourishing of the American Renaissance.[5]

Reising's conclusion was remarkable for the mid-1980s, especially insofar as it has still not been taken seriously by scholars, despite a work of such enduring importance in this regard as Eric Sundquist's *To Wake the Nations: Race in the Making of American Literature*. In his effort to acknowledge the unique contributions of African-American culture to American literary culture, Sundquist finds troubling the 1845 *Narrative*'s proximity to the main themes of the American Renaissance. He recognizes the problems posed by recent criticism of the *Narrative* for its reproduction of the values of the dominant ideology— Northern capitalism, patriarchy, and liberal individualism —and for its reproduction of the aesthetic ideology that sustained such values in the conventional *Bildungsroman* journey and narrative of triumphant self-discovery, even as he wants to grant the *Narrative* its historical importance in the political cause of Abolition. Sundquist solves this problem in an interesting way by judging Douglass' 1855 "revision" of his autobiography, *My Bondage and My Freedom*, a work that represents better than the 1845 *Narrative* just this internal conflict between Douglass' call for sweeping social reform and his unwitting complicity in the ideology of an unreformed liberal democracy: "The doubleness of Frederick Douglass' constructed persona and his narrative, his uneasy reconciliation of American and African American traditions, came from several sources: his preservation of the materials and memories of slave life within a narrative devoted to public action in predominantly white intellectual and political circles; his own notable ambivalence about his unknown but almost certainly white father and his subsequent fascination with the theme of genealogy; and his acute understanding that, whether in the South or the North, he was still a black man in nineteenth-century America and liable everywhere to discrimination and violent treatment."[6]

In his extraordinary interpretation of *My Bondage and My Freedom*, Sundquist demonstrates convincingly the historical and literary value of this relatively neglected work. Yet Sundquist's treatment of the 1845 *Narrative* for the sake of refocusing critical attention on *My Bondage and My Freedom* has several troubling consequences. Insisting that Douglass refined his understanding of the ideology of slavery and racism in the decade separating the *Narrative* from *My Bondage and My Freedom*, Sundquist undervalues the literary qualities of the *Narrative*: "No doubt the *Narrative* made a more decided contribution to rallying public support for black abolition, and it more resembles the spontaneous diary or memoir of a man suddenly asked to account for his life. . . . In its brevity and skeletal narrative structure the *Narrative* may create the greater illusion of immediacy. . . . Nonetheless, any careful comparison of the texts quickly reveals that *My Bondage and My Freedom* tells us far more about Douglass as a slave, and about slave culture generally, than does the *Narrative*, whose main virtue now, as in Douglass' own day, is pedagogical: it is easily absorbed and taught."[7] When he does praise the *Narrative* for its literary value, Sundquist does so in terms of how it "summed up the purpose of testimony by former slaves," thus reinforcing the critical tendency to exclude the 1845 *Narrative* from the canon of the American Renaissance by identifying it exclusively with the genre of the "slave narrative."

Sundquist's almost studied avoidance of the 1845 *Narrative* is understandable when we consider how often it has been used to relegitimate the American Renaissance, rather than to read critically and thus reconstitute that tradition. In the concluding chapter to *The Rites of Assent*, Sacvan Bercovitch chooses "two unlikely examples" to discuss classic American literature's relation to ideology in contemporary criticism: Stowe's *Uncle Tom's Cabin* and Douglass' 1845 *Narrative*.[8] These are "unlikely examples," because they are meant to *represent* "classic American texts," especially of the American Renaissance, and their complex relation to American ideology. On the one hand, Bercovitch chooses two texts traditionally marginal to the tradition of classic American literature, because he wants to show how even the most overtly political work is also prone, as are our more "literary" classics, to cooptation by American ideology. On the other hand, Stowe and Douglass are used by Bercovitch to relegitimate the political and literary value of classic American literature. Recognizing the 1845 *Narrative* as an undisputed "classic," Bercovitch acknowledges that its reputation is due "largely to the work underway in black studies," and then points out how Douglass appeals in the *Narrative* to the terms of the old democratic consensus that is so fundamental to the ideology of the American Self: "I refer to the *liberating* appeal for Douglass of free-enterprise ideology. On some level, certainly, he manipulated the ideology—the rhetoric of equal opportunity, contract society, upward mobility, free trade, and the sanctity of private property— to justify his flight to freedom. But it seems just as certain (to judge by his subsequent life and work) that on another level he was being manipulated in turn by those cultural key words *and energized by them*. Freedom for Douglass means self-possessive individualism. It takes the form of a movement from absolute injustice (represented by the slave system) to absolute justice, represented by the tenets of American liberalism" (370–371).

Bercovitch uses the 1845 *Narrative* to exemplify, or more precisely to *represent*, what he has elsewhere considered the essence of American literature: its capacity to call attention to American ideology, because our greatest writers are aware of their complicity in reproducing that ideology: "Precisely by laying claim to the values, ideals, and myths (as well as the economic benefits) of the dominant culture, *The Narrative of . . . An American Slave, Written by Himself* highlights the historical, contingent realities behind the symbology at large" (371). Bercovitch's conclusion is troubling, albeit instructive, especially because he buries it in a long footnote that is the proper conclusion to his discussion of the 1845 *Narrative*'s status as a representative or "classic" American literary text. The

fundamental contradictions in Douglass' text between social critique and cooptation by ideology are made by Bercovitch to represent the "dissensus" that is his
substitute for the failed American "consensus" and also his neologism for a new
kind of literary *dissent*.

Not surprisingly, Bercovitch's long footnote traces such a special literary
function to Emerson. Quoting Douglass' reflection in the 1845 *Narrative* on his
arrival in the North as "a glorious resurrection," embodied in the curious objective correlative of "the warehouses of Jacksonian New Bedford," Bercovitch
reads closely Douglass' rhetoric as an unattributable echo of Emerson's: "The
parallels to Emerson are remarkable, both in phrasing and in concept ('Uniters
absolutely isolated'; all 'work done in concert, though no man spoke'). But in
Douglass' case, the narrative 'I' remains alien, adversarial—not because *he* is
black, but because his blackness reveals the ideological limitations—the con-
structedness—of *their* utopia" (372). From the African-American identity he has
won with such difficulty in the 1845 *Narrative*, Douglass is "revised" to become
a version of Emersonian Man, whose "blackness" is now something like a transcendentalist concept or critical vantage, rather than a subject-position that
derives from both experience and political resistance of the most concrete sorts.

Sundquist's reasons for substituting *My Bondage and My Freedom* for the
classic 1845 *Narrative* is thus understandable, insofar as he hopes to avoid incorporating Douglass into the traditions of American literature initiated by the
major works of the American Renaissance. Bercovitch has been careful not to
repeat the mistake of previous critics who in their zeal to canonize the 1845
Narrative have read it closely in terms of the influences of New England
Transcendentalism on it.[9] Nevertheless, Bercovitch subordinates the *Narrative*
to literary traditions that by 1845 are well established, a point reinforced by
Bercovitch's citation in the footnote discussed above of an Emerson *Journal*
entry dated 1842 and discussed in close detail in Bercovitch's preceding chapter (372). Both scholars acknowledge that Douglass works in the 1845 *Narrative*
to use the rhetoric of the dominant culture to overturn it, but both scholars differently conclude that the force of this rhetorical transcoding is considerably
less than the obvious political impact of the 1845 *Narrative* in its own time.
Bercovitch responds to Reising's challenge that the 1845 *Narrative* (and the
African-American literary tradition it establishes) be used to politicize and
socialize our ideas of American literature by arguing that our classic literature
has always done just this cultural work. We need only add the *Narrative* to this
list of classics. Sundquist argues that such aesthetic cooptation is just the danger
of treating the 1845 *Narrative* in the context of classic American writing that is,
with few exceptions, so ideologically overdetermined as to be impossible to
reconstruct.

The debate I have staged among three important critics' reassessments of the 1845 *Narrative*'s position in literary culture expresses some of the problems confronting any scholar hoping to challenge literary traditions with works that are conversant with that tradition and yet highly critical of its assumptions. The exclusion of Frederick Douglass and his 1845 *Narrative* (as well as *My Bondage and My Freedom* and his other writings, including his journalism for *The Liberator* and his own newspaper, *The North Star*) from the American literary tradition was initially a consequence of what I have termed an "aesthetics of racism," but the recent marginalization of the 1845 *Narrative*, at a time when it has much to tell us about our formation of cultural values and traditions, represents the deep antipathy in American culture to the "confusion" of politics and aesthetics. What Douglass' 1845 *Narrative* uncannily achieves is a combination of political function with literary performance that has continued to trouble our definitions of what literature at its best should do. What Sundquist considers the "brevity," "spontaneity," and "pedagogical" qualities of the *Narrative* ought instead to be understood as its extraordinary economy of expression, the aesthetic *immediacy* or *urgency* of its narrator's concerns, and its didactic purposiveness. What Bercovitch considers the "dissensus" it exemplifies and yet reproduces in the same manner as other "great" American literature should be understood as Douglass' brilliant transcoding of the chief terms of the "American Symbology" to serve the purpose of a reformed democracy, transformed by the abolition of slavery into the freedom originally promised Americans but not yet properly realized.

In this regard, Douglass' 1845 *Narrative*, as well as other literary works challenging the traditions of American "aesthetic dissent," cannot be interpreted solely in terms of their responses to large cultural themes, as Reising has argued for Douglass, or even their explicit political agendas. The utopian dimensions of such works must be taken into account, especially insofar as they challenge the traditional emancipatory promise of liberal democracy. Abolition is unquestionably the political end of the 1845 *Narrative*, but increased freedom and human agency are the utopian ends of the reformed social vision implicit in this work. In much classic American literature, especially in the American Renaissance, such freedom and subjectivity are the rewards of the literary work itself, effects of poetic authority or the critical vantage provided by literary form and language. In Douglass—and this is consistent in both the 1845 *Narrative* and *My Bondage and My Freedom*—economic self-determination is far more central, virtually *grounding* any claims to literary and, in some cases, even political authority.

Nineteenth-century African-American writing is considerably more attentive to economic issues than classic American literature in the same period. As I shall argue in this chapter and the following chapter on Harriet Jacobs' *Incidents*

in the Life of a Slave Girl, African-American writers' close attention to the economy only begins with the pragmatics of escaping slavery—controlling one's
labor-power is a crucial step toward freedom—and in many works is elaborated
into a complex reconsideration of just what is meant by authority for one's own
work, including the labor of *self-representation*.[10] Further, such reflections on
labor-power, purchasing-power, and self-representation should not be dismissed
as mystified or ideologically coopted merely because such writers end up
endorsing (usually in highly qualified ways) the "opportunities" of free-enterprise capitalism. As I hope my readings of Douglass and Jacobs' important
American literary works will indicate, an endorsement of such opportunities
must be contextualized in the larger narrative struggle for African-American
identity and arguments *for* African-American community (often offered as a
reformed model for the white slaveholding or Northern white communities).

The economic aspects of nineteenth-century African-American writings
about slavery have generally been marginalized in critical accounts, despite
obligatory references to slavery as based on theft of African-American labor-
power and the systematic rape of African-American women by white owners or
their representatives. In her contribution to the *Columbia Literary History of the
United States* (1988), "Social Discourse and Nonfictional Prose," Carolyn Porter
calls attention to the central concern in African-American writing of the period
on economic questions: "Countless narratives testify to a fact that white abolitionists refused to acknowledge—that the path from slavery to freedom lay
through the cash nexus."[11] Porter barely touches upon an issue that ought to be
central not only in our revisionary histories of the slave narrative and antebellum writing in general, but also in that other history that is the real object of
study in any historical activity: that is, the history of our own contemporary
political situation. What is missing in Porter's brief reference to "the cash nexus"
is the far more complex history of the U.S. economy as it develops from the
Jacksonian period to our own postmodern, postindustrial era. Douglass' 1845
Narrative speaks with passion and canny knowledge of the various economic factors maintaining the system of slavery both in the South and the North; we know
that these factors are considerably more complex in 1845 than the mere "cash
nexus." It is not just the legal definition of the Southern slave as the owner's chattel that is criticized by Douglass. The rape of African-American women by white
masters and overseers, the division of African-American families, the exile of
elderly slaves served both practical economic purposes and the less tangible end
of maintaining the white master's power. By the end of the 1845 *Narrative*, we
also know that the authority of the individual over his or her actions will depend
in large measure on the degree to which this authority includes economic means
of self-maintenance.

In our own age, the economy is no longer concerned with either cash or even material products, whether those products be agrarian cotton or urban steel. In this age, the product is information, and it is the control of information that defines our "cash nexus." In *The Liberator* for September 22, 1848, Douglass published his justly famous letter, "Letter to His Old Master," to his former master, Thomas Auld. The date is the anniversary of Douglass' emancipation, itself the result of another powerful act of rhetoric: the purchase of his freedom that announced to every Southern slaveowner the contradiction of the system of slavery: that "property" could purchase itself, that those excluded from the protection of the law could *use* the law to expose its contradictoriness, and that the very *act* of "self-purchase" was in its own performance a symbolic abolition of the system of slavery.[12] It is, of course, not the cash that makes this act by Douglass so significant; it is the rhetorical authority of the act. In his letter of 1848, Douglass writes:

> Three out of the ten years since I left you, I spent as a common laborer on the wharves of New Bedford, Massachusetts. It was there I earned my first free dollar. It was mine, I could spend it as I pleased. I could buy hams or herring with it, without asking any odds of any body. That was a precious dollar to me. You remember when I used to make seven or eight, or even nine dollars a week in Baltimore, you would take every cent of it from me every Saturday night, saying that I belonged to you, and my earnings also. . . . I would not have served you so. But let that pass.

Freedom as a function of purchasing power seems obvious enough in this passage, requiring little comment, except to note rather conventionally what is so often ignored, as Porter observes, in the discussions of abolition: the importance of earning-power in the struggle for freedom. In *The Mind of Frederick Douglass*, Waldo Martin, Jr. shows how vigorously Douglass worked throughout his career to demonstrate "the dynamic interplay between capitalism and racism to obfuscate class antagonisms," even though Martin concludes that "Douglass opposed socialism, communism, or any attempt to abolish capitalism as chimerical."[13] But Douglass is hardly as anti-socialist or anti-communist as Martin has argued. In 1845, Douglass is not able to draw upon the more systematic Marxian economic analyses that might have provided him with a model for analyzing what he had experienced in both the Maryland countryside and the city of Baltimore, but he is clearly developing his own understanding of the complicity of Northern capitalism and Southern slaveholding in the 1845 *Narrative*. In his 1848 letter, he does not conclude with the optimism and Christian forgiveness with which he began; he has merely indulged certain sentiments of his white readers:

> I was a little awkward about counting money in New England fashion when I first landed in New Bedford. I like to have betrayed myself several

times. I caught myself saying phip, for fourpence; and at one time a man actually charged me with being a runaway, whereupon I was silly enough to become one by running away from him, for I was greatly afraid he might adopt measures to give me again into slavery.[14]

Wages and purchasing power are far more than simply cash; they are crucially related to language. "Counting money" in "New England fashion" means commanding the idiom of money. To use the wrong expression is to risk exposure as a runaway. The discussion of money as its representation—phip or fourpence—quickly becomes a commentary on the relation between language and freedom, which is, of course, the great theme of the 1845 *Narrative*. The performative "phip" is equated with the "silliness" of "running away" when charged with being "a runaway." By running away, Douglass gives reality to the perfectly nominal concept of "the runaway." In his telling of this story, of course, Douglass turns it from his own performance of slaveholding attitudes into an anecdote that exposes the purely nominal basis for slavery. The proper referent for money is one's own labor-power, as Douglass constantly reminds us in the *Narrative*; "phip" and "fourpence" are utterly trivial referents when compared to the "name"—freedom—that Douglass gives to his "money."

Such rhetorical turning of the ideologies of both Northern capitalism and Southern feudal slavery is characteristic of Douglass' writing, not only in the 1845 *Narrative* but also in his journalism for *The Liberator* and his own *North Star*. Indeed, his very project for the *North Star*, in itself one of the causes for his celebrated break with William Lloyd Garrison and the Garrisonians, was motivated by his conviction that a weekly newspaper under African-American editorial management "would be a *telling* fact against the American doctrine of natural inferiority, and the inveterate prejudice which so universally prevails in this country against the colored race," as Douglass put it in the *Boston Daily Whig* in 1847.[15] Douglass italicizes "telling" in the phrase *telling fact*, as if to call attention to the wordplay that equates the mere idiom for "significant fact" with the *activity of telling* as the significant labor of freed blacks.

"I soon, however, learned to count money, as well as to make it, and got on swimmingly," Douglass writes in his "Letter to His Old Master." The verbal conceit is transcendental in its doubleness: to "count" money is the same as "making" it, insofar as purchasing power in this economy is not so much the possession of cash" as the power to command what cash merely represents: authority over language.

At this moment, you are probably the guilty holder of at least three of my own dear sisters, and my only brother in bondage. These you regard as your property. They are recorded in your ledger, or perhaps have been sold to human flesh mongers, with a view to filling your own ever-hungry purse. Sir, I desire to know how and where these dear sisters are. . . . And my dear old grand-mother, whom you turned out like an old horse, to die in the woods—is she still alive? *Write and let me know all about them. . . . Send me my grandmother! that I may watch over and take care of her in her old age. And my sisters, let me know all about them. I would write to them, and learn all I want to know of them, without disturbing you in any way, but that, through your unright-eous conduct, they have been entirely deprived of the power to read and write."*

("Letter," p. 417)

Against his former master's ownership of these family members on his "ledger," Douglass pits the "ownership" of the very writing that is dramatized ironically in this "personal" letter, published in Garrison's Abolitionist paper. Douglass' imperatives are the consequences of his purchasing power: the psychologically complex language that exceeds mere names—phip or fourpence—for the sake of genuine human relations. The passage is full of references to the 1845 *Narrative*, and it constitutes a virtual sequel, especially for those readers moved by the exile of the grandmother to the woods: that counter-Sublime of New England Transcendentalism.[16] And yet the reader of the 1845 *Narrative* knows well enough that Douglass' family is in doubt from the very first page, by virtue of a slave-scheme that renders even the simplest facts of a man's life radically ambiguous: his parentage, the date and place of his birth, his brothers and sisters.

Eric Sundquist prefers *My Bondage and My Freedom* in part because it develops at greater length than the 1845 *Narrative* Douglass' obsession with his " 'lost patrimony' " that was likely the result of his father's white identity.[17] For Sundquist, Douglass treats this fact equally as a rhetorical resource, suggesting that the hint of "incestuous violence" in his own family history is part of every African-American's confused heritage under slavery. Yet, the 1845 *Narrative*'s emphasis on the narrator's ignorance about his paternity serves an equally important rhetorical purpose. Bereft of their proper family history, African-Americans under slavery must constitute the family anew, often through acts of political resistance that create the terms for social relations. In this sense, Douglass' narrator exemplifies the sort of resistance that helps "father" an African-American tradition.[18] In the 1848 letter, Douglass virtually constitutes a family, which is, of course, the considerably extended family of all his brothers, sisters, and grandmothers in bondage in the South. "I intend to make use of you as a weapon with which to assail the system of slavery . . . . I shall make use of you as a means of exposing the character of the American church and clergy—and as a means of bringing a guilty nation with yourself to repentance."

Like the money he learns to "use" by learning how to "count" it, so Douglass learns to use his former master by making him count in the fight against slavery. He has rendered Thomas Auld an exemplary figure, a character in Douglass' own narrative, but hardly for the customary literary purposes.

It is not the "cash nexus" that Douglass reveals to us as one of the distinctive issues of the slave narrative as a special genre of American literature. There is no "slave narrative" as a genre, except as it has been invented by white Abolitionists, liberal literary critics and historians, and compulsive classifiers of literary kinds. The "slave narrative" is never anything other than political writing, and it must be understood in terms of the other forms and kinds of political pamphleteering, speech-making, political demonstration, and even revolutionary actions that belong to political reform. And yet what is distinctive about the economic theme in antebellum African-American political writing is just what these passages from Douglass indicate: that the economy of antebellum America was changing from the "cash nexus" to a market economy, in which the power over language would be the real *capital*.

As hard as Douglass works to trivialize the *language* of his oppressors, he knows well enough that slavery—and its historical successor, urban capitalism—is maintained primarily by the power of words and the subtle manipulations by which slaves are not only forbidden to read and write but kept in positions of perpetual uncertainty regarding the authority of the Master. H. Bruce Franklin has argued that the seminal moment of revolutionary awakening in the 1845 *Narrative* is Douglass' fight with Covey, in which Douglass discovers in himself the power of physical rebellion: "To be reborn as a human being, to shed his animal identity imposed upon him by the white man, this Black slave must commit the most forbidden crime of all: he must strike the white man who oppresses him."[19] It would be foolish of me to debate with Franklin which passage in the *Narrative* is the central one in determining the young man's conscious rebellion. Indeed, the fight with Covey may do as well as any other, except that the physical struggle with Covey is in itself a relatively powerless act in terms of the larger revolutionary aims of Abolition. It is satisfying to the young Douglass, because it gives him an illusory *contact* with his oppressor, a sense that he has finally come to grips with the enemy. Douglass himself characterizes his battle with Covey as "the turning-point in my career as a slave," because it "revived within me a sense of my own manhood" and thus as "a glorious resurrection, from the tomb of slavery, to the heaven of freedom."[20] But the enemy is not exclusively Covey; it is the language—indeed, the entire representational system—of slavery itself, which is why the truly central "moment" in the *Narrative* is the ongoing drama of Douglass' education of himself in the ways of reading and writing.

Often sentimentalized as some version of the white novel's narrative of education, Douglass' education is much misunderstood. There can be little comparison, of course, between the urgency and danger involved in Douglass' very composition and publication of the 1845 *Narrative* and most novels and autobiographies. Wendell Phillips advised Douglass to burn the manuscript before publication, lest the book identify him to his slaveowner.[21] In addition, the *Narrative* risked confirming what many Northern abolitionists often claimed for such works: a demonstration of the "enlightenment" and "education" the abolitionist movement *gave* "embruted" runaway slaves. Indeed, the modern critical reading of the *Narrative* as a version of the novel of education is simply a later version of this liberal racism.[22] Douglass' *Narrative*, despite the legitimating preface by Garrison and letter from Phillips, demonstrates quite consistently how Douglass learned to read and write under slavery and already in active rebellion against it. And insofar as the *Narrative* exposes the secret complicity among sexism, capitalist exploitation, and slaveholding, it presumes to enlighten Garrison and Phillips. Douglass' literary power, like his celebrated power as an orator, is clearly the accomplishment of a cultural critic who has learned from the urgency of his situation how to comprehend the complex means by which people are held in bondage. The rhetorical turns of Douglass' 1848 letter in *The Liberator* are excellent examples of this strategic education into language, and they are complements to the pervasive style of the 1845 *Narrative*—a style that has still remained largely unread in terms of its rhetorical complexity.

Douglass' real instruction in revolutionary practice occurs in those moments when Douglass recognizes the subtle arts by which the slave master works to maintain the appearance of his power:

> Mr. Covey was one of the few slaveholders who could and did work with his hands. He was a hard-working man. He knew by himself just what a man or a boy could do. There was no deceiving him. His work went on in his absence almost as well as in his presence, and he had the faculty of making us feel that he was ever present with us. This he did by surprising us. He seldom approached the spot where we were at work openly, if he could do it secretly. He always aimed at taking us by surprise. Such was his cunning, that we used to call him, among ourselves, "the snake." When we were at work in the cornfield, he would sometimes crawl on his hands and knees to avoid detection, and all at once he would rise nearly in our midst, and scream out, "Ha, ha! Come, come! Dash on, dash on!" This being his mode of attack, it was never safe to stop a single minute. His comings were like a thief in the night. He appeared to us as being ever at hand. He was

under every tree, behind every stump, in every bush, and at every window, on the plantation. (Narrative, 103)

Douglass subtly transforms the "hard work" of Edward Covey from that of field hand to that of a supernatural devil. What at first appears to be his "manual labor" is quickly turned into crawling "on his hands and knees to avoid detection" in the cornfield, and this labor into that of "a thief in the night." It is, of course, a commonplace to speak of the deceptions and tricks played by the slavemaster to maintain his authority on the plantation, but Douglass' association of this illusory authority with *hard work* is hardly conventional. The plantation romance had certainly led antebellum readers to expect the slavemaster to be a gentleman enjoying his leisure at the expense of his slaves' drudging labor, and yet such a stereotype not only tended to idealize the slavemaster but to caricature the power of the slaveholding system. Understood as a complex rhetoric, a system of representation penetrating every aspect of everyday life, agrarian slavery would not be overthrown exclusively by hand-to-hand combat, unless hands were put to different purposes. In the narrative order of the 1845 *Narrative*, it is especially important that Douglass' exposure of Covey's rhetorical simulation of diabolical omnipotence precedes (by ten pages or so) his hand-to-hand combat with Covey. Indeed, the passages are rhetorically connected in a manner typical of the general style of the *Narrative*. In the earlier passage, Covey is named collectively by the fieldworkers as "the snake," thus providing an apt theological context for the struggle between Covey and Douglass ten pages later. Douglass' "victory" and "resurrection," of course, are not won conventionally over "temptation," but in the novel figuration of the slave's struggle for freedom as the defeat of a recognized evil—an evil now understandable as one achieved not so much by physical force as by means of semiotic trickery.

To speak of antebellum Southern slavery as an ideology operating principally through language (and other related semiotic means, including architecture, boundary lines, laws, and other aspects of everyday life) is hardly a great revelation to readers of Douglass' political writings. Indeed, the idea is the virtual precondition for understanding the significance of the Southern taboo against slaves learning to read and write. What is revealing, however, is the extent to which these arts of the ideology of slaveholding are shown not only to be Douglass' principal antagonists (and motives for his own metaphors), but also the common ground the feudal South shares with the expanding economy of the North.

In the 1845 *Narrative*, Douglass learns to read and write not only through Sophia Auld's initially kind efforts, then later by secretly practicing in Tommy

Auld's copybook, but also by watching the ships' carpenters make the parts of the ships they build in the Baltimore shipyards of Durgin and Bailey: "When a piece of timber was intended for the larboard side, it would be marked thus— 'L.' When a piece was for the starboard side, it would be marked thus—'S.' . . . I soon learned the names of these letters, and for what they were intended when placed upon a piece of timber in the ship-yard" (Narrative, 87). This has often been considered an indication of how brilliantly Douglass relates knowledge to its practical uses. What Douglass learns from watching these ships' carpenters, however, goes considerably beyond a narrow pragmatism in the use of language. Douglass' literary ships differ significantly from those of the white ships' carpenters. The ships he builds are hardly simple "material objects," but vehicles for "transport and use," as Emerson would define poetic metaphor in "The Poet."[23] The ships he "builds" in this rhetorical manner cannot be dissociated from the "sails" of freedom he romantically views on the Chesapeake:

> Those beautiful vessels, robed in purest white, so delightful to the eye of freemen, were to me so many shrouded ghosts, to terrify and torment me with thoughts of my wretched condition. I have often, in the deep stillness of a summer's Sabbath, stood all alone upon the lofty banks of that noble bay, and traced, with saddened heart and tearful eye, the countless number of sails moving off to the mighty ocean. (Narrative, 106)

This sentimental vision of freedom cannot be separated from its unconscious for the young Douglass, an unconscious that Douglass, the author, seems clearly to manipulate in his reference to those ships of "purest white" as "so many shrouded ghosts": the pirate ships that arrived, like thieves in the night, on the shores of Africa to begin abducted Africans' terrible Middle Passage (106). That similar ships would become the means of Northern commerce in Jacksonian America is hardly lost on Douglass, who comprehends the figurative mobility of this apparently material product.[24] From the opening pages, we know that his first master and probable father, "Captain Anthony," acquired his "title . . . by sailing a craft on the Chesapeake Bay" (50). If at first the young Douglass merely copies the letters of the ships' carpenters, the author of the 1845 *Narrative* writes *upon* those ships another message, which runs counter to the commercial purposes of trade in the North and the South in Douglass' lifetime. The romantic vision of freedom is a consequence of Douglass' rhetorical deconstruction of the "white" metaphor of the ship as freedom only for some.

 After Hugh Auld forbids his wife, Sophia, from teaching the young Frederick to read and write, Douglass tells us that he nevertheless "succeeded in learning to read and write" by "resort to various stratagems" (81). One of his stratagems is to trade bread for literacy with the "little white boys whom I met in the street": "As many of these as I could, I converted into teachers" (82). Douglass makes clear that even as a slave he was "much better off" than "many of the poor white children in our neighborhood." As he gives bread "to the hungry little urchins" in exchange for "that more valuable bread of knowledge," he also "used to talk this matter of slavery over with them" (83). This is, of course, the important moment in which the young Douglass discovers his vocation as orator; in the very next paragraph, he tells us of his reading in *The Columbian Orator*. Which comes first, his early ventures in oratory as he exhorts his "poor white" friends or his lessons from that book, is deliberately left unclear by Douglass. But Douglass suggests here that the purpose of such oratory is not only to declaim to any and all the evils of Southern slavery but also to suggest that those "poor white children" and the African-American slave have some common cause. When he contrasts himself with them, the young Douglass protests, " 'You will be free as soon as you are twenty-one, *but I am a slave for life*! Have I not as good a right to be free as you have?' These words used to trouble them; they would express for me the liveliest sympathy, and console me with the hope that something would occur by which I might be made free" (83). Douglass tells us that these "dear little fellows . . . lived on Philpot Street, very near Durgin and Bailey's ship-yard," where he learns to connect writing and making in his observation of the ships' carpenters (83).

For Douglass, labor and the utopian cooperation among workers is generally related to language in ways that are extraordinary for the nineteenth century. The children's "more valuable bread of knowledge" about reading and writing has for the young Douglass an obvious use-value: he is quite literally nourished by that knowledge. "Freedom" assumes sentient and material qualities for Douglass as he learns more about it and how he has been deprived of it: "Freedom now appeared, to disappear no more forever. It was heard in every sound, and seen in every thing. . . . I saw nothing without seeing it, I heard nothing without hearing it, and felt nothing without feeling it" (85). Even as what he has read "materializes" in this marvelous way, bringing him into the region of freedom, so language also continues to be linked with deception. In the same chapter he claims solidarity with the "poor white" children of Philpot Street and learns from the ships' carpenters at Durgin and Bailey's, he offers "unasked" to help "two Irishmen unloading a scow of stone" (86). Talking while they work, the Irishmen learn that Douglass is "a slave for life," and "both advised me to run away to the north; that I should find friends there, and that I should be free" (86). If this scene promises yet another solidarity between working-men and African-American slaves, especially as they work together, Douglass cautions the reader: "I feared they might be treacherous. White men have been known to encourage slaves to escape, and then, to get the reward, catch them and return them to their masters. I was afraid that these seemingly good men might use me so; but I nevertheless remembered their advice, and from that time I resolved to run away" (86).

When he expresses his determination to "learn how to write," Douglass specifies his purpose: "as I might have occasion to write my own pass" (86). What he learns from the ships' carpenters and the boys on Philpot Street he learns by copying on the walls and pavements of Baltimore: "During this time, my copy-book was the board fence, brick wall, and pavement; my pen and ink was a lump of chalk" (87). In the context of realism, of course, the young Douglass writing his letters on the pavements of the city seems little more than a variation on a child at play; in the context of Douglass' symbolic action in the 1845 *Narrative*, the African-American author writing his message upon the face of Baltimore, that infamous border city, has even more power than Whitman's egotistical sublime when taking poetic "possession" of his symbolic cities and countries.[25] What distinguishes Douglass from Whitman, however, is Douglass' insistence that the most sweeping symbolic claim, the grandest poetic metaphor, be linked explicitly to the practical purposes of emancipation: in this case, to his ability to forge his own pass and thereby attempt his escape north. Rather than splitting the material and immaterial, physical labor and poetic figuration, realism and romantic idealism, Douglass interrelates them in ways that register a silent reproach to American transcendentalism.

Later in the *Narrative*, as a caulker in the Fell's Point Shipyard, Douglass is badly beaten by his white coworkers, who view "free colored carpenters" as threats to the "employment" of "poor white men" (132). As he makes clear in his brief encounter with the working Irishmen on Waters' Wharf, the solidarity he easily achieves with the "poor white children" of Philpot Street has been fractured by the language of racism and the symbolic system of slavery in the adult world. The fight with Covey now may be read retrospectively as the beginning of a struggle that will embrace both Southern slaves and free blacks confronting the economic racism of Northern capitalism. The workers' in the Fells' Point shipyard object to "free" African Americans competing with them for wages. Just as the young Douglass lectured the white children, so Douglass the author must enlighten white workers regarding the exploitation of their labor and the theft of their labor-power. The shipyard is thus at once a site of reading and writing, just as it is a site of political instruction regarding the secret relation between racism and class-conflict.

The economy of Douglass' America is an economy of language that quite perversely finds some of its subtlest artists, its grandest stylists among the ruling classes, either North or South. In order to combat such language, Douglass may well work hard to develop a style of his own, but he knows that this literary voice is far less important than the subversive act of writing by which ideology is revealed in all its complexity as a moving army of tropes and metaphors, a system of deception and control. At the same time, Douglass' style is never *merely* ironic, *simply* the exposure of the perversely impressive power of slaveholding and capitalist ideologies to maintain control over their exploited workers. Douglass teaches his readers how crucially such subversion depends upon the collective and decidedly political alignments virtually necessitated by such an understanding of ideology. Tempted as readers may be to admire Douglass' rhetorical tours de force, the *Narrative* never lets us forget that the triumph of its style is to be achieved only in the new political alignments it helps those readers recognize as necessary consequences of its ideological critique. Waldo Martin has stressed Douglass' enthusiasm for Emersonian doctrines of self-reliance, even for the Emersonian hero, but the voice of the 1845 *Narrative* appeals for its realization through the writings and political actions of its others, its committed readers.[26] This authorial humility often has encouraged critics to conclude that the *Narrative* is primarily *realistic* and that the power of its story is that of the representative anecdote. Without minimizing the emotional power of the *Narrative* to evoke the terrors of everyday life under slavery, I would still contend that the text's power derives from its rhetorical efforts to turn the discourse of the ruling class in the direction of a utopian emancipation—not just of African Americans, but of workers and women as well.

In the 1845 *Narrative*, Douglass links the rights of African Americans, of workers, and of women in subtle rhetorical ways, even though they are always related in terms of an explicit politics of Abolition. The "slavery" of the worker and the white woman is never made equivalent to that of the legally and physically enslaved African American, but the analogies are subtly reinforced throughout the *Narrative*. In this regard, Eric Sundquist is right to argue that *My Bondage and My Freedom* provides considerably greater detail not only about Southern plantation life but also about the rights of workers, both African American and white, to control their own labor-power.[27] Returning to the fight in the shipyard in *My Bondage and My Freedom* (1855), Douglass states the issue with what he terms "some minuteness":

> The facts, leading to this barbarous outrage upon me, illustrate a phase of slavery destined to become an important element in the overthrow of the slave system . . . . That phase is this: *the conflict of slavery with the interests of the white mechanics and laborers of the south.* . . . The slaveholders, with a craftiness peculiar to themselves, by encouraging the enmity of the poor, laboring white man against the blacks, succeed in making the said white man almost as much a slave as the black slave himself. . . . The white slave

has taken from him, by indirection, what the black slave has taken from him, directly, and without ceremony. Both are plundered, and by the same plunderers.[28]

Douglass does not explicitly discuss here the implications of this Southern economy in the more industrialized North or even in the relatively immediate future of a desired abolition of slavery as an institution, but even so the solidarity that white and African-American laborers must recognize is predicated on the equally important awareness that their competition with each other is achieved by means of "a craftiness peculiar to" Southern slaveholders. The passage, when coupled with those dealing with the economic racism Douglass faced in urban Baltimore (and, of course, in his life in the North in all three of his autobiographies), serves as a warning to his readers that the "craftiness peculiar to" industrial capitalism will require not just ideological criticism comparable to Douglass' in the 1845 *Narrative* and his journalism, but political coalitions based on the knowledge and thus active power shared by those who have recognized the false divisions and specious competition between African-American and white workers.

The cooperation between rhetorical subversion and political action is equally effective in the 1845 *Narrative* in achieving a working relation between abolition and women's rights. I shall not here recount what is well-known: Douglass' vigorous struggle on behalf of women's rights throughout his career, and his consistent alignment of women's rights with the political and economic agenda for African-American rights. Unfortunately, Douglass' well-deserved reputation as advocate of women's rights has suffered from what his biographer, William McFeely, terms "one of the saddest divorces in American history": the split between African-American rights and women's rights activists in the post-Civil War fight for African-American and women's voting rights.[29] In his fine historical account of the complex rivalries that emerged between previously allied women's rights' and African-American rights' activists, like Susan B. Anthony and Douglass, McFeely makes it clear that the apparent call of political pragmatism caused both groups to make strategic mistakes that probably cost African Americans and women civil and legal rights that could have been won more quickly in close alliance.[30] The victory of the passage of the Fifteenth Amendment, guaranteeing African-American (male) voting rights, by no means belies Douglass' lifelong commitments to women's rights and his consistent integration of women's and African-American rights into his public positions from his earliest to his last writings. In the period of the 1845 *Narrative*, Douglass' position in favor of women's rights is clear; as Eric Sundquist writes: "Douglass was . . . a constant supporter of women's rights and other reform causes. He attended the Seneca Falls conference in 1848 as an advocate of women's suffrage and frequently spoke in favor of women's political rights both within and beyond the antislavery movement."[31] Douglass' work on behalf of women's rights is well documented in Philip Foner's useful collection, *Frederick Douglass on Women's Rights* (1976), although Foner includes none of the relevant selections from Douglass' three autobiographies. Of the most famous episode concerning women's rights in the 1845 *Narrative*, the whipping of Aunt Hester before the terrified young Douglass, Foner comments only in his "Introduction": "Douglass grew to detest slavery. He saw slaves brutally whipped."[32]

Yet the whipping of Aunt Hester exemplifies not only the especially perverse servitude of African-American women in the slaveholding South—victims of economic exploitation and sexual rape by white masters, but it refigures the episode in ways that cause the graphic realism of the whipping to serve a more profound critique of the Christian clichés used by slaveholders to legitimate the most brutal practices of sexual and economic domination. Concluding as it does the very first chapter of the 1845 *Narrative*, the whipping of Aunt Hester serves as "the blood-stained gate, the entrance to the hell of slavery," through which not only the young Douglass but the reader is forced "to pass" (Narrative, 51). Stunned as the reader is by the brutal whipping Captain Anthony's overseer, Plummer, gives Aunt Hester, he or she is tempted to conclude that the episode serves merely the most self-evident realist purpose: to reveal the physical brutality of slavery in a manner that is emotionally powerful. Douglass himself begins the episode by claiming, "I wish I could commit to paper the feelings with which I beheld it" (51). But this episode in no way is exhausted simply in the emotional pathos of its drama, in the sheer vulgarity of the overseer's epithet, "damned bitch," in the terrible brutality of tying Aunt Hester, naked to the waist, to "a large hook in the [kitchen] joist," as he "commenced to lay on the heavy cowskin," as "the warm, red blood (amid heart-rending shrieks from her, and horrid oaths from him) came dripping to the floor." Turning from the ugliness of the scene, the reader virtually follows the child, who was "so terrified and horror-stricken at the sight, that I hid myself in a closet, and dared not venture out till long after the bloody transaction was over. I expected it was my turn next. It was all new to me. I had never seen anything like it before" (52). Recalling as we must that the 1845 *Narrative* was written primarily for white readers, the episode renders the terrified black child and the naive white reader isomorphic at this moment, but not without reversing effectively racist clichés about "childlike" slaves and "rational," educated white readers.[33]

Cowering in the closet, still witness to the terrible scene, afraid that *we* would be next, we reproduce an archetypal biblical scene of perverse instruction: Ham witnessing his father, Noah, naked and drunken in his tent. Although

Douglass leaves ambiguous his paternity in the 1845 *Narrative*, he also makes clear that "my father was a white man" and speculates that "the opinion was whispered that my master was my father" (Narrative, p. 48). Since his "first master" is Captain Anthony, Douglass' paternity in the 1845 *Narrative* accords fairly well with what is still the best scholarly speculation about it, and Douglass manages to introduce such information into his narrative without losing the valuable rhetorical claim that the African-American under slavery often knew nothing precisely of his or her father or date or place of birth. Eric Sundquist writes: "Douglass' probable father, his first master, Aaron Anthony, was employed by Colonel Lloyd and was known to be a harsh and capricious man who raised himself from poverty to middling success as the owner of Holme Hill Farm on Tuckahoe Creek."[34] Although it is clearly Plummer, Captain Anthony's overseer—"a miserable drunkard, a profane swearer, and a savage monster," who carries out Captain Anthony's orders, Douglass brilliantly confuses the pronomial antecedents in this episode to confuse the reader about just who is wielding the whip: the overseer or the master.[35]

Frequently as this episode has been interpreted by scholars and because of the controversy surrounding these interpretations, there is still much that has been overlooked in it. Sundquist terms the "whipping of his Aunt Esther by Aaron Anthony" "a primal scene," and so it is.[36] It echoes an archetypal biblical scene of perverse instruction: Ham witnessing his father, Noah, naked and drunken in his tent, having intercourse with his wife. It was, of course, a popular biblical story in the antebellum South, precisely because it was Ham's "iniquity" that caused Noah to curse him and his son, Canaan, "Cursed be Canaan! / The meanest of slaves shall he be to his brothers," so that slavery itself might find one of its many perverse biblical warrants.[37] The nineteenth-century reader of the Bible hardly needed Freud to explain what otherwise seems such a cruel punishment for an otherwise modest curiosity: spying upon the father's nakedness and drunkenness threatens the patriarch's authority.

In the account in Genesis, Noah's wife is not even mentioned; this is a biblical family-romance only between fathers and sons. How different the episode when translated into Douglass' terrifying realism. The nakedness the child witnesses is that of the African-American woman, violently "stripped" by the enraged overseer, Plummer, and then not in the domestic privacy of the biblical tent, but in that curious crossing of the public and private in the Southern plantation house, the kitchen. We must recall that Captain Anthony's rage against Aunt Hester, "a woman of noble form, and of graceful proportions," focuses on her disobedience in seeing a young man, Edward Roberts: "Why master was so careful of her," Douglass writes, "may be safely left to conjecture" (51). The slaveowner's jealous rage focuses on the "property" of her body as both a sexual and economic possession. As the "warm, red blood" drips to the floor, Aunt Hester's sexual and economic violation are unavoidably connected, encouraged by Douglass' reference to "the innocence of my aunt" only a few lines earlier.

This double violation of the African-American woman is, of course, not unusual in itself in African-American and white abolitionist writings of the time. In the biblical context, however, the child and the reader's voyeuristic terror at witnessing this punishment powerfully undoes the authority predicated on "The Curse of Canaan." What mythically initiates slavery is not simply the irrational "curse" Noah hurls at his son, Ham, for having witnessed him in a moment of weakness. The biblical story, even as it ignores Noah's wife, includes the implication that what Ham has witnessed is his parents' sexual intercourse. Oedipal taboos in a Freudian reading of this biblical scene only obscure the archetypal significance that the Bible itself cannot command, but that Douglass' text skillfully uses. An oedipal reading would merely normalize the perversity of the scriptural scene, in which the son's and mother's bondage to the Law-that-is-the-name-of-the-Father is enacted. In Douglass' interpretation, Ham's "iniquity" is transformed into the knowledge the child and reader fearfully share that the relation between master and servant begins with the violent rape of woman by man. No distinction is made between economic and sexual rape: they are the same. Aunt Hester's servitude as domestic slave in the kitchen is identical with the rape she and other African-American women regularly experienced on the plantation; both forms of exploitation served the economic interests of the slaveowner. And it is, of course, Aunt Hester's rebellion against just such servitude that we must understand motivates her refusal to obey the command *not* to see Ned Roberts.

The historical Aunt Hester's choice of Ned Roberts in defiance of the perverse law of the master is, of course, not sufficient to identify her as a revolutionary. As Douglass turns this graphically realistic scene in the direction of its truly fantastic infrastructure—the myths of gender and slavery often based on scriptural warrants, he tropes "Aunt Hester" ("Aunt Esther" in *Life and Times of Frederick Douglass*) into her Old Testament namesake, Esther. Chosen by King Ahasuerus as his queen, Esther keeps her Judaism secret on the advice of her uncle, Mordecai, until Haman plots to destroy all the Jews in the kingdom. Using her power to plead the cause of her people with Ahasuerus, Esther saves her uncle Mordecai and her people, and Haman is hung on the gallows intended for Mordecai.

The Old Testament tale is only a hint and cannot be said to fit Douglass' purposes with perfect accuracy. The biblical Esther saves her uncle, Mordecai; in Douglass, the frightened nephew, prompted to flee and to write in part by her terrible punishment, eventually saves his aunt. The analogies are sufficiently accurate to achieve rhetorical effect: child saves elder, weaker redeems stronger. But the "family" constituted by this narrative of the generational transmission of power—from servitude to freedom, from submission to rebellion—is not for Douglass narrowly tied to blood. Like the biblical story echoed and appropriated, Douglass' 1845 *Narrative* conflates "family" and "people," just as it has used the young Douglass to represent the archetype of the African-American striving for freedom.

By weaving a complex biblical commentary into a putatively realist scene conventional in many fugitive slave narratives—the sexual or physical violation of African-American slave women, Douglass has done much more than merely shock us with an anecdote from modern American slaveholding society. "I expected it would be my turn next," Douglass recalls, reminding us how the patriarchal power of a biblical figure like Noah is achieved both by dominating the wife and the son, the woman and the slave. Indeed, Douglass' suggestion that Captain Anthony is his father gives the young Douglass' fear an even more powerful tie to its primal scriptural source: the young Douglass anticipates, without recognizing the scriptural antecedent, the sort of punishment meted out to Ham and Canaan. The master's fear that his arbitrary power as patriarch will be so revealed is at least one of the motives for slavery, a social institution that thereby grounds its power in its manipulation of the most elementary domestic psychology. The abolition of slavery will thus depend upon not only an understanding of how insidiously slaveholding rhetoric works to maintain its social and economic power, but how it constructs the most elementary master-servant relations between the sexes.

Douglass does not restrict his criticism of gender hierarchies to those established by white slaveholders over African-American women. In his famous account of Sophia Auld's response to her husband's insistence that she stop teaching the young Frederick how to read and write, Douglass not only shows how Sophia is morally corrupted by her husband's perverse command but also how she has missed her own opportunity for rebellion and thus feminine emancipation. In her initial relations with the young Frederick, Sophia "did not seem to perceive that I sustained to her the relation of a mere chattel, and that for her to treat me as a human being was not only wrong, but dangerously so. Slavery proved as injurious to her as it did to me" (*Narrative*, 81). This introduction of Sophia Auld suggests a potential bond of solidarity between the woman and the African American, even as Douglass carefully distinguishes between free woman and enslaved African American. Yet as she obeys her husband's command not to instruct Frederick, both her compassion and her intelligence are perverted by slavery:

There was no sorrow or suffering for which she had not a tear. She had bread for the hungry, clothes for the naked, and comfort for every mourner that came within her reach. Slavery soon proved its ability to divest her of these heavenly qualities. Under its influence, the tender heart became stone, and the lamblike disposition gave way to one of tiger-like fierceness. The first step in her downward course was in her ceasing to instruct me. She now commenced to practise her husband's precepts. She finally became even more violent in her opposition than her husband himself.   (Narrative, 82)

As Douglass does at virtually every didactic crisis in this narrative, he employs biblical rhetoric not only to assert his own authority (and that of the African-American Church) but also to stress that abolition is a moral crusade intent on saving not only African Americans but also white slaveholders corrupted by the system. Nowhere is this clearer than in the corruption of women, like Sophia Auld and Mrs. Flint in Jacobs' *Incidents*, both of whom project their own oppression by men onto their African-American servants. Interestingly, Douglass does not attribute Sophia Auld's initial kindness toward him to her maternal affections, as Stowe would account for white and African-American women's emotional rebellion against slavery in *Uncle Tom's Cabin*. Instead, Douglass points out that Sophia "was by trade a weaver; and by constant application to her business, she had been in a good degree preserved from the blighting and dehumanizing effects of slavery" (77).[38]

Douglass describes Sophia's turn from "lamb" to tiger under the influence of slavery in the paragraphs just preceding his account of the solidarity he achieves with the "poor white children of our neighborhood" (83). In my earlier reading, I stressed how Douglass turns the bread he trades for the children's lessons in literacy into "that more valuable bread of knowledge." Just two paragraphs earlier, he refers to Sophia's charity in terms of having "bread for the hungry, clothes for the naked." It is *Douglass* who replaces Sophia Auld as he carries her bread to the hungry children in the form of his lectures to them on the evils of slavery. It is just such knowledge that Sophia misses: her lack of self-consciousness regarding her own bondage to her husband's immoral rule.

Such an analysis of Douglass' canny understanding of the complicity between racism and sexism, between social and psychological economies, helps clarify his repeated insistence upon the importance of the family in the work of gender and racial equality. Douglass often appears to sentimentalize the family, understandably enough given the common division of slave families by white masters for the sake of profit and control. But for Douglass, the utopian family is never a natural fact, a mere biological given perverted by Southern feudalism.

Douglass' utopian family—like the one whose return he demands in his 1848 "Letter to His Old Master"—is always connected quite self-consciously with its social and political purposes, so that the domestic privacy of family psychologies might never again be the means of mystifying a more pervasive sociopolitical will-to-power.

Several critics have pointed out that the family so constituted in Douglass' 1845 *Narrative* is decidedly patriarchal and that Douglass' freedom depends significantly on his reproduction of the dominant white ideology of his time.[39] Such criticism applies as well to the scene of Aunt Hester's whipping, which has been judged representative of Douglass' general tendency to *silence* women, especially African-American women, in the 1845 *Narrative* and to *use* them as objective correlatives of his own, decidedly male, quest for freedom.[40] This argument is strengthened by the ways Douglass replaces a "fallen" Sophia Auld as nurturer and teacher of the "poor white children" of Baltimore in chapter 7. Douglass' women in the 1845 *Narrative* do not speak; Douglass speaks *for them*. In the case of Aunt Hester, I do not think Douglass' transformation of her brutalization into his triumphant resistance to and flight from slavery relies upon the eroticized scenes of African-American women's violation that so attracted white readers in other fugitive slave narratives of the period.[41] Douglass so focuses that scene of punishment upon his own youthful response (and that of the reader) that voyeurism is not so much the issue as Douglass' consistent displacement of the feminine with his masculine perspective.

Yet, Douglass' perspective is by no means exclusively masculine, even if there are parts of the 1845 *Narrative* that do follow the masculine rhetoric of heroic struggle and mythic conquest. Rather than simply analyzing the codes at work in the rape/punishment of Aunt Hester, Douglass turns those codes in the direction of that solidarity the reader feels with the African-American child and the violated African-American woman. The kitchen, as Jane Tompkins has argued in another context regarding the Quaker Settlement kitchen in *Uncle Tom's Cabin*, has become a site of empowerment for African-American men and women, as well as the white abolitionist.[42] In a similar sense, Douglass can imitate the kindness Sophia Auld showed him by bringing bread to his hungry playmates in Philpot Street. The narrator of the 1845 *Narrative* is capable both of nurture and furious resistance, clever stratagems and sympathy for racial, sexual, and class oppression.

Nevertheless, there remains a profound limitation in Douglass' thinking about gender and thus about class and race in the 1845 *Narrative*. Nowhere is this more evident than in his representation of his wife, Anna Murray Douglass, in this narrative. Scholars critical of Douglass' representation of gender in the 1845 *Narrative* have rightly focused on his virtual erasure of Anna Murray from the dramatic action of his emancipation, reserving her for the barest reference in the concluding chapter and then framed in the marriage certificate of which Douglass gives "an exact copy" (Narrative, 145). In this respect, Douglass conveniently forgets to mention the help Anna Murray gave the young Frederick in his flight north, as well as the considerable risk she ran as a free African-American woman aiding a runaway slave.[43] Both McFeely and Sundquist defend Douglass on this score on the grounds that his refusal to mention Anna Murray until they are married is his way of protecting his family from public abuse of the sort to which he would have to grow accustomed.[44] McFeely puts the matter in more practical terms, suggesting that Douglass was protecting his wife from the likely speculation that their premarital friendship in Baltimore "had not been chaste."[45]

In the barest rhetorical touch following his "copy" of the marriage certificate in the 1845 *Narrative*, Douglass hints at just what he has shared with his new wife: "Upon receiving this certificate, and a five-dollar bill from Mr. Ruggles, I shouldered one part of our baggage, and Anna took up the other, and we set out forthwith to take passage . . . for Newport, on our way to New Bedford" (Narrative, 145–46). Such symbolic action, quotidian as it also is intended to appear, is insufficient to take the place of Anna Murray's actual contributions to the young Frederick's emancipation, just as Douglass' revoicing of Aunt Hester's rebellion and Sophia Auld's compassion is an unsatisfactory substitute for their self-representations as nineteenth-century women. This limitation in the 1845 *Narrative* remains, however, one that the logic of the narrative has brought into view and thus called for its criticism and revision. If Douglass was unable to control in his own life the women's rights' movement he had initially worked to join with the cause of abolition, so he was unable to contain rhetorically the feminine agency in which he discovered a sympathetic attraction in many of his writings.

In the 1845 *Narrative*, he achieves an imaginative identification with other oppressed peoples in antebellum America—workers, immigrants, children, and women—that works rhetorically by means of narrative contiguities, analogies, and condensations that match the poetic economy of our greatest literary masterpieces. What Douglass accomplishes in a work the length of *The Scarlet Letter* or *Benito Cereno* is astonishing for its symbolic immediacy and thus the necessity of the reader, especially the white reader, to interpret with care the rhetorical and moral issues at stake. In this regard, the 1845 *Narrative is* Frederick Douglass' masterpiece. By the same token, the 1845 *Narrative* is no less *political* for its literary qualities, which is just what makes it such an extraordinary work in American literature. The reader never for a moment forgets the specific *cause* the *Narrative* and Douglass serve, a claim that can be made neither for *The Scarlet Letter* nor even for a work more overtly compatible with the *Narrative*, Melville's *Benito Cereno*. The political coalitions that Douglass believed were necessary to defeat not only Southern slavery but also American racism are emblematically enacted in the 1845 *Narrative*, often in literary ways that complement the more overt political organization that Douglass still realizes must be done.

When Mary Howitt wrote from England to Douglass about his interest in founding what would become *The North Star*, he answered:

> You speak of the printing press, and ask shall I like to have it? I answer, yes, yes! The very best instrumentalities are not too good for the cause; I should feel it quite improper to express myself thus, if the proposed present were merely an expression of personal consideration. I look upon it as an aid to a great cause, and I cannot but accept the best gifts which may be offered to it. . . . I hope to be able to do a good work in behalf of my race with it.[46]

In a similar manner, the 1845 *Narrative* is not simply a personal and auto-biographical account of the real terrors of slavery for the political purposes of acquainting its readers with representative abuses of the slaveholding system. Like that printing press and the paper it would help found, the 1845 *Narrative* "is a *telling* fact," which poetically makes alignments among African-American slaves, freed Northern African Americans, African-American and white women, and workers both North and South in terms of shared social, economic, and psychological situations in America that enslaved them all, albeit in ways manifestly different.

We have mistakenly characterized Douglass' writing either as literary (or autobiographical) realism or political journalism. Douglass exposes the rhetorical subtleties of slaveholding and capitalist ideologies not merely by insisting on their unnatural origins, but by demonstrating how such perversity assumes the appearance of normality. Yet, even as Douglass pits the natural rights of human beings against the unnaturalness of slavery and urban capitalism, he develops a utopian vision that is profoundly social and political. Revealing the common purposes behind Southern and Northern economies and ruling classes, Douglass can argue for political coalitions among apparently different, often competitive, interest groups. Although Douglass makes the appeal commonly enough to our "shared humanity," the political power he offers by way of such coalitions is achieved in response to the historical conditions these groups share. Political action against these oppressive conditions thus becomes the rediscovery of a utopian democracy, in which diverse groups recognize a collective and complementary social purpose. That the "real conditions" of oppression of African Americans, women, and workers in nineteenth-century America depend crucially upon the *fantastic* narrative of American ideology changes considerably what we have customarily understood as literary realism. The arbitrary, unnatural, fantastic will-to-power of slaveowners and capitalists is exposed in the interests of a utopian vision of cooperative labor that includes the work of cultural self-representation as much as it embraces the production of useful goods. What is realist in Douglass is what I would rename "political writing," rather than slave narrative or autobiography or even the novel, and it thus includes the whole range of Douglass' activities as writer, orator, and political figure.

Douglass' great accomplishment was not simply to recognize that such servitude relied on prejudices fundamental to the everyday use of language; many other American writers of the same period had come to the same conclusion. Douglass' great achievement was to discover the means of turning the very terms of such ideological mystification in the direction of new coalitions and social alignments that promised some measure of human emancipation. That such work can be understood as a collaboration among poetic style, formal innovation, journalism, oratory, and political organization should encourage us today as we attempt to find the clew that will lead us out of our narrow and forbidding poetic labyrinth.

6 Reconstructing the Family: Harriet Jacobs' *Incidents in the Life of a Slave Girl*

> Because they appear almost always in conjunction with representations of black or Africanist people who are dead, impotent, or under complete control, these images of blinding whiteness seem to function as both antidote for and meditation on the shadow that is companion to this whiteness—a dark and abiding presence that moves the hearts and texts of American literature with fear and longing.
>
> —Toni Morrison, *Playing in the Dark: Whiteness and the Literary Imagination*

> It has been painful to me, in many ways, to recall the dreary years I passed in bondage. I would gladly forget them if I could. Yet the retrospection is not altogether without solace; for with those gloomy recollections come tender memories of my good old grandmother, like light, fleecy clouds floating over a dark and troubled sea.
>
> —Harriet Jacobs, *Incidents in the Life of a Slave Girl*

The final sentence of Jacobs' extraordinary literary account of an African-American woman's rebellion against slavery, patriarchy, and capitalism in mid-nineteenth-century America echoes strangely with Toni Morrison's interpretation of the conclusion of Poe's *Narrative of Arthur Gordon Pym*. In her final simile, Jacobs' Linda Brent recalls the good works of her grandmother and then figures those "tender memories" as "light, fleecy clouds floating over a dark and troubled sea" of American slavery. That "dark and troubled sea" has also come to include in the course of Brent's narrative the economic, political, and psychological racism of the North, which Linda experiences far more extensively than Frederick Douglass does in the 1845 *Narrative*. Although Brent's suffering under slavery and so-called "freedom" is sometimes relieved by white women, it is more often extended and deepened by Southern and Northern white women who subscribe to the ideology of white womanhood. Nothing could be "whiter" than this ideology, which Hazel Carby has characterized in terms of feminine "modesty, meekness, and chastity," as well as the ideal woman's behavior as "appropriately delicate, an outward manifestation of an inner sensitivity and refinement."[1]

Brent's concluding figuration of her memories of her grandmother as "light, fleecy clouds" confuses the "memories" with the "grandmother," threatening to associate both with the conventions of nineteenth-century white femininity. In the first case, the figuration would add to evidence supporting the argument that *Incidents* borrows heavily from the sentimental romance.[2] Insofar as Linda Brent's "tender memories" refer specifically to "incidents" in her narrative relating to her grandmother, then the sentimental convention risks identifying the grandmother with the traditions of white womanhood. It is possible, of course, that Brent is confusing the value system that oppressed her with the hard-won values that come from her struggle for freedom both for herself and her own children. Without an adequate language to express the authority, intelligence, and resourcefulness of herself and other African-American women, especially her grandmother, Brent may lapse into an otherwise despised rhetoric of white femininity in order for Jacobs to expose the rhetorical and moral dilemma facing the African-American woman attempting to speak or write in her own voice.[3] To make matters worse, the ethereal clouds with which her memories of her grandmother are compared invoke nineteenth-century conventions of feminine spirituality and its Christian ethos of transcending the historical and material realms of Southern slavery and Northern capitalism. Most readers have recognized Jacobs' use of the conventions of nineteenth-century sentimentalism, but most scholars agree that Jacobs works hard to refunction these conventions. As Dana Nelson puts it: "The text reformulates sympathy so that it can recognize common bonds of humanity while acknowledging and respecting differences among people, and offers this model as a more viable means for real social change."[4]

Reread in the terms of Morrison's interpretation of the pervasiveness of the "closed white images" that conclude so many works of classic American literature, however, Jacobs' figuration of her memories of her grandmother takes on new meanings. What Brent is now able to remember is the family tradition that she and her grandmother have significantly saved from the systematic efforts of the slave system and Northern capitalism either to fragment or surrogate. The "light, fleecy clouds" represent Brent's emancipation of her family by virtue of her hard work and canny understanding of the rhetoric of slavery (and later Northern capitalism). Rather than subordinating her narrative to the sentimental conventions of white femininity, Jacobs dramatizes how her character, Linda Brent, translates such conventions into a new rhetorical register where they signify differently. That semiotic difference is fundamental to what Carby terms "a framework in which to discuss the social, political, and economic consequences of black womanhood" (Carby, 61). It is also the necessary precondition of an African-American women's *literary* tradition, because it establishes the terms by which such a tradition can distinguish itself from non-literary genres (the fugitive slave narrative) and established literary forms often in service of the dominant ideology (sentimental romance, autobiography, novel).[5]

Brent's "tender memories" need to be contextualized further if I am to place this much emphasis on her concluding figure of them as "light, fleecy clouds." Consistent as Linda is in praise of her grandmother's goodness, she often suffers terribly when caught between the authority of her grandmother and that of her white masters. When Mrs. Flint comes to the grandmother's house to falsely accuse Linda of carrying Dr. Flint's child, her grandmother believes Mrs. Flint and drives Linda away: "'You are a disgrace to your dead mother.' She tore from my fingers my mother's wedding ring and her silver thimble. 'Go away! . . . and never come to my house, again.'"[6] Despite her efforts to help Linda, the grandmother remains a freewoman whose freedom remains very much at the whim of the local slave-holders, and she is often used by Jacobs to represent how even the free African-American must live out the contradictions of the slave system while her freedom derives from such a perverse economy. Good as Linda's grandmother is, she remains relatively powerless to change the circumstances of Linda or Linda's children.

The specific context of Linda Brent's concluding figuration of her "tender memories" as "light, fleecy clouds" is the occasion of Mrs. Bruce's successful purchase of Linda and her children's freedom. And it is precisely Linda's memory of family members attempting, albeit unsuccessfully, to buy her freedom and that of her children that is sparked by Mrs. Bruce's tearful embrace of Linda as a free woman:

> When I reached home, the arms of my benefactress were thrown round me, and our tears mingled. As soon as she could speak, she said, "O Linda, I'm so glad it's all over!" . . .
>
> My heart was exceedingly full. I remembered how my poor father had tried to buy me, when I was a small child, and how he had been disappointed. I hoped his spirit was rejoicing over me now. I remembered how my good old grandmother had laid up her earnings to purchase me in later years, and how often her plans had been frustrated. How that faithful, loving old heart would leap for joy, if she could look on me and my children now that we were free! (Incidents, p. 200)

At the crucial, concluding moment of Linda Brent's narrative, Mrs. Bruce threatens to become yet another example of what Morrison terms the "closed white images" found so "frequently . . . at the end of the narrative" of classic American literature. Mr. and Mrs. Bruce are based on Mr. and Mrs. Nathaniel P. Willis. As Carby points out: "Unlike either his first or second wife, Nathaniel Willis was proslavery. Against Jacobs' wishes but to protect her from the fugitive slave law, the second Mrs. Willis persuaded her husband that Jacobs should be purchased from her owners and manumitted by the family" (Carby, 47). Just as Douglass' "self-purchase" posed problems for Abolitionists, like Garrison, so Jacobs' purchase and manumission by the Bruces poses problems for Jacobs' narrative of emancipation in *Incidents*. For Linda Brent to be finally "emancipated" by the Northern family for which she works threatens to transform her narrative of self-empowerment into one of white paternalism. As Dana Nelson recognizes, "Mrs. Bruce acts sympathetically in purchasing Linda's freedom," but "her action prohibits Linda from achieving the *quality* of freedom that she wants most."[7]

What Jacobs does rhetorically is testament to the literariness of *Incidents*, and it is consistent with similar rhetorical transcoding throughout the narrative. Rather than ignoring the historical fact of her emancipation by the Bruces' charity, Jacobs includes it in the scene of tearful celebration between Linda and her benefactress in the passage quoted above. Their "tears mingled" are clearly tears of joy, and they anticipate the renewal promised by the "light, fleecy clouds" that pass over the "dark and troubled sea" of slavery in the final sentence of the text. Yet, such renewal is also *resurrection*, in one Christian connotation of "clouds" as the path to heaven, and it is the resurrection of her father and grandmother that Linda enacts as she "remembered how my poor father had tried to buy me" and "how my good old grandmother had laid up her earnings to purchase me in later years." Both memories lead her to conclude: "I hoped his spirit was rejoicing over me now" and "how that faithful, loving old heart would leap for joy, if she could look on me and my children now that we were free!" (200). In this rhetorical transaction, Mrs. Bruce is not forgotten, but incorporated into the end of this paragraph in Linda's paean to true friendship: "My relatives had been foiled in all their efforts, but God had raised me up a friend among strangers, who had bestowed on me the precious, long-desired boon. Friend! It is a common word, often lightly used. Like other good and beautiful things, it may be tarnished by careless handling; but when I speak of Mrs. Bruce as my friend, the word is sacred" (200).

What emerges from this rhetorical play is an effective collectivity of the African-American family and Northern abolitionists as an ideal of social action. Of course, such solidarity is often lacking in Linda's actual experience, as it was in Jacobs' own life, but it becomes the ideal toward which the narrative leads its predominantly white women readers. It is an ideal, however, complicated by the other rightly celebrated part of Linda's conclusion, when she addresses the reader: "Reader, my story ends with freedom; not in the usual way, with marriage. I and my children are now free! We are as free from the power of slaveholders as are the white people of the north; and though that, according to my ideas, is not saying a great deal, it is a vast improvement in *my* condition. The dream of my life is not yet realized. I do not sit with my children in a home of my own. But God so orders circumstances as to keep me with my friend Mrs. Bruce. Love, duty, gratitude, also bind me to her side" (201). As a consequence of her experiences and their narration, Linda is able to recognize that the vaunted freedom of Northern whites is not as complete as some would think. By connecting her freedom with that of Northern whites, Jacobs appeals to a collectivity that is performed in her act of narration. By transcoding the conventions of the sentimental romance, of which the "light, fleecy clouds floating over a dark and troubled sea" is only one significant example, Jacobs engages her white readers in the process of abolition both by enlisting their sympathies and by changing the rhetoric through which their sympathies are conventionally expressed.

In the course of this emotional transformation, Jacobs has also criticized the assumed universality of those emotions. In Dana Nelson's interpretation, Jacobs subtly distinguishes African-American women's emotional histories from those of Northern white women even as Jacobs appeals for "sisterhood" with such Northern women as Mrs. Bruce represents. Pointing to the many places in *Incidents* where Jacobs reminds the reader that "if you have never been a slave, you cannot imagine" how Linda Brent responds emotionally to the abuse she experiences under slavery, Nelson concludes that Jacobs wants to teach the reader that: "Sympathy should contribute to an active strategy of social reform, but it cannot accomplish its goal of community based on equality until it is able to *acknowledge* and *value* the different perspective of the slave 'sister'—her different experiences in, and hence different knowledge of, the world."[8] In my view, much of the literariness of *Incidents* may be found in just those moments where Jacobs must negotiate carefully the rhetoric of sentimentalism, with its appeal to the white Northern reader, and the rhetoric of African-American women's experience, with its fidelity to the special emotional trauma of slavery.

As Carby and Yellin have pointed out, Linda's address to the reader in this context sets her achievement of freedom in contrast with the "usual way" sentimental romances end, "with marriage" and domestic submission.[9] Jacobs concludes Linda's narrative in political, rather than melodramatic, suspense: not yet entirely in charge of her home and family nor entirely certain of Mrs. Bruce as "mistress" or "benefactress" nor thoroughly able to claim the legacy of her grandmother as "matriarch" of the extended Brent family. Much as this creates an urgency for African-American emancipation, such a conclusion also leaves the fictional character, Linda Brent, in a narrative position relatively invulnerable to the overdeterminations by the stereotyped heroines of the fugitive slave narrative or the sentimental romance. Such narrative suspense functions to enable the construction of African-American woman's identity at a historical moment when such identity was virtually impossible to distinguish from contemporary stereotypes of the African-American woman as "tragic mulatto," "mammy," "demon lover," and a host of other racist constructions.

Before turning to other ways in which Jacobs uses rhetorical and narrative structures to achieve political ends, I want to address a potentially serious objection to this method of interpreting the text. My close attention to the concluding paragraphs and rhetorical figurations of *Incidents*, as well as my insistence on distinguishing Jacobs, the author, from her character, Linda Brent, are intended to stress the *literariness* of a narrative still treated generally as a "slave narrative." In the previous chapter, I have argued why the genre "slave narrative" continues to marginalize literary works that we ought to consider centrally in our reinterpretation of how literature (especially American literature) can function politically. Too often treated primarily as autobiographical testaments and thus rendered evidence for social histories, narratives like Douglass' 1845 *Narrative* and Jacobs' *Incidents* are misread in ways that separate literary function and political action. Because both Douglass and Jacobs self-consciously connect the problem of representation with the political end of freedom, they have much to teach us about how literature can work politically. But there is an equal danger in *aestheticizing* these narratives and thereby forgetting the real human urgencies that produced them. Valerie Smith points out that "Afro-American writers traditionally have attached great significance to the acts of reading and writing," not only because "antebellum laws privileged the acquisition of letters by explicitly prohibiting slaves from being taught to read and write," but also because "in our literate culture success is in large measure linked to one's ability to read and write the official language." Insofar as "literacy has been a tool of social organization and control," Smith continues, it often inspires "in the learner a respect for authority," even when such authority has been shown to be arbitrary and perverse, as both Southern and Northern white masters were.[10] Is, then, the demonstration of Jacobs' rhetorical sophistication another way of re-enslaving her body and voice by subordinating her to the "great tradition" of the representative works of American literacy—that is, including her in the American literary canon? If the interpretation of this rhetorical complexity were done to the neglect of the real urgencies of the African-American woman under slavery (and the quasi-slavery of domestic servitude in the North), then Smith's warning ought to be heeded. Smith herself, however, offers another approach, which I attempt to follow in my reading: "If, however, we take as our point of departure the textual status of a work and examine the way it engages with, challenges, and transforms narrative conventions and the politics they enshrine, we can arrive at a fuller understanding of its rhetorical achievement and the complexity of its ideology" (Smith, 7).

Such rhetorical reading must also take into account alternative forms of representation from those traditionally associated with literate culture, as Smith understands by connecting slave narratives to the oral traditions of nineteenth-century African-Americans.[11] I would argue that such alternative forms ought to include a wide range of social activities, including family organization and what might be termed "body-language"—the ways a particular body can be (or is forbidden from being) represented in a culture. All of these practices are not just constructions of language; they are themselves modes of discursive *situation* whereby subject-positions are manifested. Rather than simply *effects of language*, such practices often constitute *another language*, especially in cases when some social groups are excluded from or have relatively less access than others to the powers of the dominant discourse.[12] Because nineteenth-century African-American narrators, whether telling slave narratives or novels or poems, always *begin* with the problematic of how to speak when legally or conventionally deprived of voice and identity, they effectively problematize literary and onto-logical authority in their very address to the reader. Douglass' 1845 *Narrative* and Jacobs' *Incidents* are celebrated in part because they make this *donnée* of nine-teenth-century African-American narrative central to their social criticism and their different modes of self-discovery.

In *Incidents*, Linda Brent achieves her freedom through a wide range of social practices that differ from conventional reading and writing, but are nonetheless fundamentally discursive. As the 1845 *Narrative* makes clear, Douglass learns early in his life how the white slave-owner uses language to con-trol his slaves, both by forbidding African-Americans access to the powers of written English and by creating an elaborate symbology that rationalizes the contradictions of the slave economy. Linda Brent learns just as early in her life that slave-owners control and violate African-Americans by way of language, as well as the more obvious forms of physical abuse. In his persistent efforts to seduce Linda, Dr. Flint evades his wife's detection by using signs: "What he could not find an opportunity to say in words he manifested in signs. He invented more than were ever thought of in a deaf and dumb asylum. I let them pass, as if I did not understand what he meant." And rather than *forbidding* Linda from learning to read and write, Dr. Flint tries to use this secret as yet another means of seduc-ing her: "One day he caught me teaching myself to write. He frowned, as if he was not well pleased; but I suppose he came to the conclusion that such an accomplishment might help to advance his favorite scheme. Before long, notes were often slipped into my hand. I would return them, saying, 'I can't read them, sir.' 'Can't you?' he replied; 'then I must read them to you' " (31).In both instances, Linda plays the illiterate slave, deliberately refusing the use of signs to protect herself from abuse.

If Linda appears to repudiate conventional literacy as a means of escape in her early rebellion against slavery, she nevertheless finds other ways of signifying that rebellion. The most important in the narrative, apart from Linda's narration of *Incidents* itself, is her choice to become Sands' mistress in a conscious effort to defeat Dr. Flint's plan to make her his concubine. Linda's "deliberate calculation" is designed to help her take control of her own body back from a slavocracy that defines the African American as property. Valerie Smith argues that Linda knows that by "becoming Sands' mistress she will compromise her virtue and reputation," but it is equally clear that she understands how much more potentially powerful this decision makes her in her community than either her marriage to the free African American she loves (whom she is forbidden to marry) or her victimization by Dr. Flint (Smith, 32). Linda analyzes the difference between choosing Sands and being raped by Dr. Flint in terms that express her ambivalence: "There is something akin to freedom in having a lover who has no control over you, except that which he gains by kindness and attachment. A master may treat you as rudely as he pleases, and you dare not speak; moreover, the wrong does not seem so great with an unmarried man, as with one who has a wife to be made unhappy" (55).

Linda's sense that her choice is only "akin to freedom" is not, however, matched by the language in which she describes "A Perilous Passage in the Slave Girl's Life" (chapter 10). Her moral ambivalence about her decision is understandable, because Linda is "only fifteen years old" at the time, but the rhetorical emphasis of this passage is on the affirmative conviction that such decisions are absolutely crucial for what they signify of the contradictions of the slave economy and the authority they grant to the otherwise powerless, "poor slave girl." In effect, *Jacobs* writes beneath her narrator's account in this important episode, and she does so in a manner that links the language of the body with the language of the text. Even before interpreting Jacobs' rhetorical performance in this chapter, I want to underscore the importance of Linda's conscious *choice* of Sands as the father of her children. In Stowe's *Uncle Tom's Cabin* (1852), feminine authority is often set against masculine authority and aligned with the abolitionist cause. It is, however, a feminine authority that is tied closely to maternal "instincts" displayed both by white and African-American women characters. Just such "natural maternity" is often the warrant for Stowe's appeal to sentiments and thus a literary sentimentalism as alternatives to the perverse "logic" of the slave economy.[13] As Hazel Carby has pointed out, the stereotype of "independent black women" as "black matriarchs" has been as pervasive and problematic as the stereotype of the white woman finding strength in her "maternal instincts" (Carby, 39). What Jacobs accomplishes quite simply by stressing Linda's "choice" of Sands as the father of her children is a subversion of "natural maternity."

By demonstrating that Linda's choice of motherhood is part of her rebellion against the slave system and its inherent patriarchy, Jacobs prepares us for the ways Linda will consciously construct her immediate and extended family in the course of the narrative. This is one reason I began at the end of *Incidents* to stress the solidarity of African-American and white characters that Linda affirms as the ideal of abolition and implicitly women's rights' movements. Jacobs works from the beginning of her narrative to establish the terms by which the family can be extended to the community, and she does this explicitly in terms of the political functions of both groups. Whatever the understandable ambivalences of a fifteen-year-old desperate to avoid systematic rape by her slave-master, the language of chapter 10 is overwhelmingly that of a woman consciously choosing the one means of rebellion available to her: her body as it is interpreted within the slave economy. Beginning with the slave-woman's body as her primary means of creating value, Jacobs turns that same body into an effective weapon against slavery. To distinguish at this point between the "work" of the body (progeny) and "work" of language (the rhetoric of these passages) is likely to diminish Jacobs' point, which depends crucially on the degree to which a woman's body is already a system of representation capable of producing a variety of signs.

/ Linda's rebellion begins in fact with her overt rejection of the perverse fantasy of domestic bliss that Dr. Flint offers her: "He told me that he was going to build a small house for me, in a secluded place, four miles away from town. I shuddered; but I was constrained to listen, while he talked of his intention to give me a home of my own, and to make a lady of me. Hitherto, I had escaped my dreaded fate, by being in the midst of people" (Incidents, 53). The appeal Linda makes to the protection afforded by society is, of course, double-edged for African Americans under slavery. In the next sentence, she refers to "my grandmother," who "had already had high words with my master about me," but Linda recalls at the beginning of this paragraph Mrs. Flint's fierce jealousy, which is both a source of Linda's suffering and a partial protection from Dr. Flint's rape. The "small house" in a "secluded place" represents for Linda a "living death," which embodies for her how "the master, whom I so hated and loathed, . . . had blighted the prospects of my youth, and made my life a desert" (53). Anticipating Orlando Patterson's theory of the social psychology of slavery as experienced by the African American as "social death," Jacobs here represents Dr. Flint's effort to take absolute possession of Linda as an emptying of her self, stripping her both of social relations (however painful) and control of her own body.[14]

Linda's famous confession of her "sin" in the next paragraph of chapter 10 is often treated as her desperate act of self-reliance as well as her full acceptance of responsibility for her actions in taking "a white gentleman" for her lover. It is an extraordinary moment of literary self-consciousness, rhetorically equivalent to even more celebrated moments of "heightened self-consciousness" in American literature, such as Hester Prynne's reflections in chapter 13 ("Another View of Hester") of *The Scarlet Letter* or Isabel's Archer's "vigil of searching criticism" in chapter 42 of *The Portrait of a Lady*. In recalling this "period in my unhappy life," Linda rhetorically constitutes her identity in a manner that *embodies* her in contrast with the "desert" Dr. Flint has made of her life:

> The remembrance fills me with sorrow and shame. It pains me to tell you of it; but I have promised to tell you the truth, and I will do it honestly, let it cost me what it may. I will not try to screen myself behind the plea of compulsion from a master; for it was not so. Neither can I plead ignorance nor thoughtlessness. . . . I knew what I did, and I did it with deliberate calculation.   (Incidents, 53–54).

Having hitherto recounted what was done to her, Linda begins here to *remember* what *she has done*, even as she recognizes the moral problems her choice involves. Knowledge and design are now linked by a mode of action that is virtually identical with the act of representation, both in the calculation to "give" herself to a "white unmarried gentleman" and her narration of this story.

As she develops her reasons for this choice, Linda uses a language of *sensibility*, rather than sentimentalism, that testifies to a different affective experience from the "pain and fear" to which the cruelties of slavery have accustomed her since she came to the Flints at the age of six:

> Of a man who was not my master I could ask to have my children well supported; and in this case, I felt confident I should obtain the boon. I also felt quite sure that they would be made free. With these thoughts revolving in my mind, and seeing no other way of escaping the doom I so much dreaded, I made a headlong plunge. . . . I know I did wrong. No one can feel it more sensibly than I do. The painful and humiliating memory will haunt me to my dying day. Still, in looking back, calmly, on the events of my life, I feel that the slave woman ought not to be judged by the same standard as others.   (Incidents, 55–56)

The pain and humiliation that Linda here accepts belong to her own complex psychology, which she is able for the first time to acknowledge *as her own* precisely because she has chosen what is at once a practical and symbolic mode of rebellion. Valerie Smith stresses the practical advantages of Linda's relation with Sands: "Out of his consideration for her, he purchases her children and her brother from Flint. William, her brother, eventually escapes from slavery on his own, but Sands frees the children in accordance with their mother's wishes" (Smith, 33). Smith considers these advantages to be only sufficient to grant

Linda "a measure of power," but in the context of the totalizing system of slavery such gains for a fifteen-year-old are considerable measures of power. When the reader recalls that Sands ends up doing virtually what Linda has anticipated even before any children are born of their relationship, then the power she gains from this choice is greater yet.

Equally important is the power over herself that Linda gains as a consequence of choices that, despite the "pain and humiliation," grant her a sense of control over both her body and psychology. Like Douglass recognizing in his fight with Covey the emotional experience of freedom that comes from *action*, as opposed to the slave's characteristic experience of *self-negation*, so in this crucial episode Linda begins the process of personal emancipation by making conscious choices in opposition to the slave system. As Dana Nelson points out, Linda's rebellion involves more than just a personal and emotional choice; to act in this way, Linda "levels a critique against the epistemological structure of the system which denies her."[15] Earlier, Linda can only refuse the sexual advances of Dr. Flint, and such negation is her characteristic response to the domination of slavery.

Recognizing the jealousy her relation with Sands inspires in Dr. Flint, Linda plays upon that jealousy to take her revenge upon the cruel slave-owner: "I knew nothing would enrage Dr. Flint so much as to know that I favored another; and it was something to triumph over my tyrant even in that small way." Even in her indulgence of such feelings of revenge, Linda considers the possible practical advantages: "I thought he would revenge himself by selling me, and I was sure my friend, Mr. Sands, would buy me" (Incidents, 55). In fact, Linda's plan backfires in this regard, because Flint's jealousy seems to fuel his obsession with repossessing her after she has run away from his son's plantation. Yet, Linda's calculation of both the material and psychological advantages of her choice reflects not only her achievement of self-consciousness through one of the few rebellions available to African-American women under slavery, it also indicates the degree to which she understands her family relations as socially constructed.

Like Douglass, Linda discovers how socially determined lives are from the distortions of everyday life wrought by slavery. Everywhere the white lies of ownership, religious faith, racial purity, domestic bliss and marital fidelity are revealed in the daily lives of African-Americans who do the work of the economy, are barred from the white churches, yet often resemble their masters, and for all that inspire the violent rages of white men and women whenever these lies are made public. The contradictions of the slavocracy do, of course, empower Linda and others in *Incidents*; her recognition of the contrived fictions required by white society to preserve slavery enables her to find her own "loophole" of escape. She frequently wonders why Dr. Flint does not take her by force or kill her, as she has witnessed friends murdered for even less provocation.[16]

She also knows, however, that the jealousy of Mrs. Flint serves to check Dr. Flint, and that both are restrained in their actions by their common concern for social propriety.[17] But Linda also learns about how socially constructed otherwise natural relations are, such as those of the family and to one's self, in her developing relations with her own extended family, especially as this family is increasingly represented by her in terms of its political agency.

Valerie Smith judges the chapters following chapter 10, in which Linda makes her fateful choice of Sands, to distract us from the embarrassing fact that she has continued her relationship with Sands after the birth of her first child: "Her continued relationship with Sands and her own response to her second pregnancy are submerged in the subtext" of these chapters, which otherwise deal with "slave religion and the local response to the Nat Turner rebellion" (Smith, 42). But the chapters 12 ("Fear of Insurrection") and 13 ("The Church and Slavery") to which Smith refers actually connect Linda's individual rebellion with the specific political action of Nat Turner's Southampton Rebellion, especially as the messianic and millennial aims of that rebellion provide the spirituality the white Southern church has systematically kept from Southern slaves.[18]

Although the chapter on "The Church and Slavery" deals primarily with the exclusion of African Americans from the white Southern church, Linda offers two anecdotes that are little parables of Christianity's proper role in abolition. In the first, she describes the good works of a new clergyman, who admits African Americans to his church and whose wife teaches them "to read and write." When his wife dies, in her will she frees their five slaves and leaves them "with funds to establish them comfortably" (72). When the widowed clergyman returns to town after several years to preach a sermon to his congregation, he preaches an antiracist sermon that shocks the local slaveowners: "Try to live according to the word of God, my friends. Your skin is darker than mine; but God judges men by their hearts, not by the color of their skins" (72). In the second anecdote, Linda describes "an old black man . . . uncle Fred," who "joined the Baptist church" and had "a most earnest desire to learn to read," primarily to "serve God better" by reading the Bible. Linda gladly teaches Uncle Fred, who learns very quickly, despite the fact that both know of the laws forbidding them to learn how to read and write. Both anecdotes speak to the ways rebellion begins with individual acts, like Linda's decision to defy Dr. Flint, and grows through Christian acts of necessary defiance, like teaching Uncle Fred to read his Bible, into the rebellion that will sweep slavery and its hypocrisy away.

Although the style of Jacobs' narrative seems to be a curious mixture of sentimental conventions and autobiographical realism, otherwise unremarkable episodes are often remembered in ways that give them unexpected narrative significance. Linda's decision to escape Dr. Flint's son's plantation and ultimately seek her freedom and that of her children recalls the "leap" into sin she has taken in chapter 10: "I raised the window very softly and jumped out" (96). Yet this apparently impulsive act is carefully planned by Linda.

Among other preparations Linda makes for her flight, perhaps the most important is her visit to the graves of her parents "in the burying-grounds of the slaves." There she vows formally to save her baby from slavery "or perish in the attempt." Her parents' graves are nearly unmarked when she visits—"a black stump, at the head of my mother's grave, was all that remained of a tree my father had planted" and "his grave was marked by a small wooden board . . . the letters of which were nearly obliterated." Many of Linda's memories reconnect her with her nuclear and extended family, but Linda's vow in the graveyard virtually re-marks her parents' graves, thereby rending the site sacred: "For more than ten years I had frequented this spot, but never had it seemed to me so sacred as now" (90). And as she leaves the graveyard, passing "the wreck of the old meeting house," she is reminded of how "before Nat Turner's time, the slaves had been allowed to meet" there "for worship."[19] In this moment, the nuclear family, the brothers and sisters of all slaves whose sufferings she shares, and the political and religious zeal of Nat Turner are brought together in a figure that rhetorically opens the graves: "I seemed to hear my father's voice come from [the old meeting house], bidding me not to tarry till I reached freedom or the grave. I rushed on with renovated hopes. My trust in God had been strengthened by that prayer among the graves" (91). Hardly digressions, the chapters following her choice of Sands connect what appears to be the desperate, individual choice of a fifteen-year-old to the larger political purposes of abolition and building African-American community.

There are still other sacred moments in Linda's narrative that both give coherence to the otherwise episodic character of the slave narrative and connect the isolated narrator with the larger purposes of emancipation. After fleeing the young Flint's plantation, Linda is protected by a "kind lady" of the town who has known Linda's grandmother "from childhood" (99). Linda is hidden in a store-house above the lady's bedroom, a hiding-place that anticipates Linda's "loophole of retreat" in the garret of her grandmother's house. While Linda hides, Dr. Flint jails her brother, William, and her two children, Benny and Ellen, as well as an aunt, "as a means of compelling my relatives to give some information about me" (101). In the meantime, Dr. Flint travels to New York searching for the runaway Linda, spending "considerable money" and returning home "disheartened."[20] In her hiding places (at one point she is hidden beneath the floor of the kitchen out-building), Linda receives only occasional news, usually in the form of written notes from her grandmother or her brother, William, but in all cases the news counsels patience, as her discovery would bring even greater punishments to all concerned (and likely her death).

In his angry desire for revenge against Linda, Dr. Flint finally sells William, Benny, and Ellen to a "speculator," who has been commissioned by Sands to "work on" Dr. Flint's "discouraged feelings." In effect, Linda's choice of Sands as father of her children and her decision to flee Mr. Flint's plantation have both had the intended result, despite unexpected events leading to such a fortuitous end. Hidden away, Linda is unaware of the great rejoicing in her grandmother's house when Linda's two children and William secretly return to her house. Even "the father," Sands, "was present for a while" at this celebration, even though Linda qualifies "such a 'parental relation'" as one that "takes slight hold of the hearts or consciences of slaveholders" (107).[21]

Unaware of the good news of her family's emancipation and reunion, Linda nonetheless has a vision in her hiding-place:

> And now I will tell you something that happened to me; though you will, perhaps, think it illustrates the superstition of slaves. I sat in my usual place on the floor near the window, where I could hear much that was said in the street without being seen. . . . I sat there thinking of my children, when I heard a low strain of music. A band of serenaders were under the window, playing "Home, sweet home." I listened till the sounds did not seem like music, but like the moaning of children. It seemed as if my heart would burst. I rose from my sitting posture, and knelt. A streak of moonlight was on the floor before me, and in the midst of it appeared the forms of my two children. They vanished; but I had seen them distinctly. . . . and I felt certain something had happened to my little ones.   (Incidents, 107–8)

Linda's vision does seem derivative of the conventions of the sentimental romance, especially with the gratuitous strains of "Home, Sweet Home" from John Howard Payne's *Clari; or, the Maid of Milan* (1823) turning into the moans of her abused children and then their visual forms.[22] Dependent as her family is on the willingness of Sands to buy William, Benny, and Ellen, as well as on the unexpected kindness of the slave speculator chosen by Sands and Linda's narrow escapes from Dr. Flint's vigilance, there is an aura of romantic sentimentalism in this crucial episode.

Yet, the vision of her children appearing to Linda in hiding as another kind of message sent to her by her family is by no means the work of either African-American "superstition" or white "romance." Even after the briefest respite from the constant oppression of slavery, Linda is capable of *imagining* a better future for herself and her children. It is an imagination that has been made possible by the collective work of her extended family, which includes those sympathetic white women, like the "kind lady" who offers Linda her first hiding place, as well as good friends sharing the common suffering of slavery, like Fanny, the daughter of her grandmother's tenant, Aggie. This power to imagine a future that is not yet materially real is, of course, one of the traditional justifications of literature, both for the author and the reader. As Linda works with her extended family to manipulate the brutal ideological narrative of slavery for the sake of the emancipation of the enslaved members of that family—and thus the reunion in freedom of this family, she is already "telling" a story in the alternative means of narration I have only partially described here: her "choice" of Sands and its transgression of moral codes; her vow on her parents' graves and subsequent flight; her rescue of her brother and children from the cruel slaveowner, Dr. Flint. The "visionary" moments in this story—the voice of her father speaking to her from beyond the grave, the appearance of her children to her—are products of this mode of telling and reminders that her bid for freedom is a collective project.

Even as we keep in mind Dana Nelson's careful reading of Jacobs' distinction between the sentimental sympathies of white Northern women, like the fictional Mrs. Bruce or the historical Lydia Maria Child, and the different emotional experiences of African-American women oppressed by slavery, we must also acknowledge Jacobs' desire to construct moments of potential understanding through which a genuine sisterhood of women can be imagined.[23] Despite the differences of their experiences, white women and African-American women do achieve such moments, and they lend credibility to Jacobs' frequent appeal for the political ideal of a women's collectivity.

Valerie Smith argues that the male slave narrative, like Douglass' 1845 *Narrative*, reproduces the dominant ideology by following the formal logic of the *Bildungsroman*, especially in its emphasis on "the hero's stalwart individuality." I have argued in the previous chapter that Douglass revises this convention of heroism by developing an autobiographical voice that frequently reminds us that he merely represents the collective aims of emancipation shared by his "brothers and sisters" still in slavery. Smith is nevertheless right in pointing out that "Jacobs' tale is not the classic story of the triumph of the individual will; rather it is more a story of a triumphant self-in-relation" (Smith, 33). These relations include her extended family, friends, and even whites willing to help her escape the brutality of the Flints. It is the latter group that makes Jacobs' account of political collectivity troublesome, especially when *Incidents* is read primarily as an African-American feminist response to the limitations of the male slave narrative.

Tempting as it has been for some critics to conclude that *Incidents* describes the collectivity of African-American women, joined occasionally by sympathetic white women, Jacobs makes it clear that African-American and even some white men are crucial to Linda's eventual freedom.[24] Linda's Uncle Phillip, whose freedom was purchased by his mother, Aunt Marthy (Linda's kind grandmother), is primarily responsible for arranging Linda's and Fanny's safe passage from Edenton to Philadelphia. In countless ways, Uncle Phillip uses his intelligence and earning power to care for Linda, his sister, Aunt Nancy, his mother, Aunt Marthy, and even their family friend, Fanny. Phillip chooses the captain and ship that will take Linda and Fanny north, and the captain turns out to be a "friendly and respectful man," even though he is a Southerner: "He told us he was a Southerner by birth, and had spent the greater part of his life in the Slave States, and that he had recently lost a brother who traded in slaves. 'But,' said he, 'it is a pitiable and degrading business, and I always felt ashamed to acknowledge my brother in connection with it" (158). Sands' "kindness" to Linda may be at best qualified by his sexual desire for her, and when he "gives" her daughter, Ellen, to his cousins (the Hobbses) in Brooklyn to serve as their "maid-servant," he betrays Linda and their daughter.

White women range from the sympathetic friend of Linda's grandmother, who hides Linda in the storehouse above her bedroom, to the viciously jealous, Mrs. Flint. Obviously, African-Americans like Linda intent on freedom must choose their friends with great care, especially when they are white, but they must also avoid stereotyping these whites, some of whom become essential allies in the cause of freedom. There is not even solidarity among African-American women in their willingness to defy the slaveowners in *Incidents*. Linda and her relatives can only trust some of the other servants in town and on Mr. Flint's plantation. The kind white woman in town warns the grandmother: " 'No one in my house must know of it, except the cook. She is so faithful that I would trust my own life with her. . . . I will send the housemaids on errands, and Betty shall go to meet Linda" (99).

The uneven ways characters fit their designated class, gender, and regional identities is yet another characteristic that distinguishes *Incidents* from conventional slave-narratives that work through popular stereotypes of slaveowners, hunters, plantation ladies, and African-American men and women under slavery. There are several ways to interpret Jacobs' emphasis on such ideological disparities in the behavior of individuals. First, it may well be simply part of Jacobs' realism to give an accurate account of the many different interests and complex social psychologies at work both in the maintenance and anticipated dismantling of Southern slavery. Second, Jacobs shows us how as early as the 1830s the development of towns, their commercial economies, professional classes, and the consequent greater diversity of free and enslaved African-Americans in the South were changing social conditions in ways that complicated the political issues involved in abolition.[25] On the one hand, the relative degrees of freedom of some family members, such as the grandmother and Uncle Phillip, are crucial means of enabling Linda and her children ultimately to escape the Flints. As

Valerie Smith observes, "Jacobs was fortunate enough to have been born into a stable family at once nuclear and stable," and it is a family that is held together in part because such family members as Linda's grandmother and Uncle Phillip have achieved some measure of social and economic independence in the town, a far more difficult task even for free African-Americans in a strictly rural economy (Smith, 36). These very social conditions, however, made the flight of individuals from the oppression of slavery considerably more complicated, because punishments of family members suspected of harboring relatives fleeing slavery might cost those family members both their earning powers and freedom. Dr. Flint jails Linda's brother, William, and her children, Ellen and Benny, and her Aunt when she runs away, releasing them only when he and Mrs. Flint decide they cannot do without their slave-labor. But the free grandmother and Uncle Phillip are far more vulnerable to such punishments, since it is their *own* labor-power and small earnings they would lose were they charged with the usual fines and imprisonment for harboring runaways in North Carolina.[26]

There is yet another reason for the ideological "unevenness" I have described above and that is to expose the fictionality of the boundaries drawn between master and slave, public and private, finally even the distinctions between relative and friend (or, for that matter, friend and enemy). I began this chapter by reading closely how Jacobs rhetorically displaces Mrs. Bruce's generous but paternalistic act of buying Linda's freedom by having Linda recall her family genealogy, especially the efforts of her grandmother and uncle to "buy me."[27] The secondary effect of this rhetoric is to fold Mrs. Bruce back into the family, insofar as Mrs. Bruce is capable of rising above her own paternalistic feelings for African Americans. When the Brents help Fanny to leave her hiding place in her mother's house and seek freedom in the North, they use the passage they have booked in Linda's name when Linda's grandmother decides it is too dangerous at that moment for Linda to try to head north. But when her grandmother fears she has given away Linda's hiding-place to the "mischievous housemaid," Jenny, the grandmother insists that Linda join Fanny on the ship heading north. When the sympathetic captain is asked to take *another* "Linda" north, it takes all the talents of their friend, Peter, to convince the captain that he is not about to be betrayed. When Linda meets "Linda" (Fanny) in their "little box of a cabin" on shipboard, Fanny "started as if she had seen a spectre. She gazed on me in utter astonishment, and exclaimed, 'Linda, can this be *you*? Or is it your ghost?' When we were locked in each other's arms, my overwrought feelings could no longer be restrained" (156–57). This sentimental reunion anticipates the final embrace of Linda with Mrs. Bruce. In this case, the two victimized African-American women recognize each other as doubles in both name and purpose, but their sisterhood is the result of common suffering and determination:

Fanny and I now talked by ourselves, low and quietly, in our little cabin. She told me of the sufferings she had gone through in making her escape, and of her terrors while she was concealed in her mother's house. Above all, she dwelt on the agony of separation from all her children on that dreadful auction day. She could scarcely credit me, when I told her of the place where I had passed nearly seven years. (Incidents, 157)

The "sisters" and "brothers" made through the common suffering of slavery and equal determination for freedom only make explicit the false hierarchies that have fractured not only many African-American families under slavery and perverted white families complicit in the slavocracy but that also have worked to keep secret the family relations connecting white and African-American families in the antebellum South. Most nineteenth-century slave narratives expose at some point the miscegenation that slaveowners hid behind the elaborate taboos—some legal and others conventional—forbidding miscegenation. Jacobs, however, is unusually attentive to the family resemblances that link slaves with their owners' physical features as well as to the neglected family obligations whites owe to the African Americans with whom they live and work. When the reader is reminded on several occasions that Linda's grandmother had to stop breast-feeding Linda's mother to nurse the baby who would grow up to become Mrs. Flint, we are impressed not only with white cruelty to African-American families but also by how such cruelty is redoubled by someone like Mrs. Flint who owes such a debt of nurture to her nurse. When asked by Dr. Flint to "be kind" to his son in memory of the love her daughter, Aunt Nancy, felt for the son, the grandmother tells Flint: "'Your wife was my foster-child, Dr. Flint, the foster-sister of my poor Nancy, and you little know me if you think I can feel any thing but good will for her children'" (145).

Jacobs effectively captures this double-bind of slavery's impact on the family in her account of Aunt Nancy's life and death. Claudia Tate points out that "Aunt Nancy is [Linda's] dead mother's twin; thus she is Jacobs' ideal surrogate mother. . . . Not only does Aunt Nancy attempt to nurture her motherless niece in the Flint household, but she also counters with steadfast encouragement her own mother's (and Jacobs' grandmother's) repeated expressions about the futility of trying to run away from slavery."[28] Aunt Nancy has spent her adult life sleeping on the floor outside Mrs. Flint's door, a position emblematic of the "incessant toil that 'completely broke down her constitution'" and caused the eight children she bore to die "shortly after birth" (Tate, 110). Childless, Aunt Nancy protects Linda as if she were her own, and Linda does not qualify her judgment that Aunt Nancy "had been slowly murdered" by the very woman the grandmother calls Nancy's "foster-sister," Mrs. Flint. Indeed, Mrs. Flint is so obsessed with *her* loss that she asks permission of the clergyman to bury Aunt Nancy "in the doctor's family burial-place" (146).

Jacobs does not sentimentalize these interracial relations; Linda makes it clear that Mrs. Flint's concern is not with Aunt Nancy or her family's feelings, but only with Mrs. Flint's sorrow at losing such a faithful servant: "It had never occurred to Mrs. Flint that slaves could have any feelings." And when the grandmother is consulted, she "at once said she wanted Nancy to lie with all the rest of her family, and where her own old body would be buried" (146). Nevertheless, the dispute over where Aunt Nancy will be buried is not just another comment on the strict formal segregation of white and African-American social practices; it also reminds us that such formal division only arbitrarily divides a community in which family relations are already fundamentally miscegenated. This may well be why Linda's choice of Sands as father of her children is so significant, not only for its practical consequences but also for the visibility it gives to the otherwise hidden, yet tacitly acknowledged, interracial relations of the antebellum South.

Thus far I have said little of the most extraordinary event in a narrative otherwise filled with quite astonishing "incidents": Linda's seven years' hiding in the tomblike garret above the storehouse in her grandmother's house. Like most of the other fantastic events, her living death is all the more perversely *real* to us when we recognize how slavery twisted reality into a daily nightmare for millions of African Americans. Hidden in her grandmother's house, "buried" beneath the kitchen floor in the "kind woman's" town house or secreted in that same woman's storehouse above her bedroom, Linda becomes the unconscious of slavery in Edenton, North Carolina—the ghost that *chooses* a living death over the death-in-life of slavery that was her Aunt Nancy's fate. In hiding, Linda also is the *absence* that lives in the memory of the community, even for those few who know just where she is, as the one who made visible the "color line" by breaking the silence and transgressing the propriety that even her grandmother sought to maintain regarding the inescapable family relations between whites and African-Americans in the antebellum South.

On the positive side, it is just the commonality of whites and African Americans in the Southern community that is recognized by those whites willing to help her hide, escape, and eventually win the freedom of her family. On the negative side, the unevenness of this work—the "kind woman" who hides Linda owns slaves; the captain who helps Linda and Fanny escape to the North acknowledges his brother was a slavehunter—expresses the complex repressions in the social psychology that resists democratic ideals. Because Jacobs understands slavery to be more than just a physical violation and domination, despite the constant reminder of just such physical suffering in *Incidents*, and analyzes the jealousies, compulsions for revenge, and desperate bids for power and control by which Southern whites *represented* slavery in their own distorted faces, she can anticipate how many of its worst features will remain visible in the North, as well as in the general racism of a United States that nominally proclaimed "emancipation" only two years after the publication of *Incidents*.

Full of righteous anger and indignation as Jacobs' story is, it nevertheless insists upon renewing the common democratic purpose that slavery and racism have obscured in her nineteenth century. Earlier, I argued that Linda's common cause for freedom allows her occasional visionary moments, such as when her children appear to her in a dream and her dead father's voice speaks to her in the graveyard. I have no doubt that the struggle for freedom earned Jacobs her own visions, perhaps identical with these, and the very literary text of her emancipation allows us to experience by elective affinity similar visions. A transcendentalist might claim them for his own sorts of gnostic experiences, especially as they are so often made possible by a particular way of telling her own story, but it should be quite clear by this point in my argument that we could never have seen such wonders alone. Even when Linda is in the loneliest depths of her suffering, psychically or physically buried, there are knocks on her walls, voices that penetrate her distance, arms that encircle and uplift. Jacobs' narrative makes it virtually impossible to ignore this appeal to the family feelings and commitments that are made through the common purpose of emancipation. In Douglass' 1845 *Narrative*, political reform is also represented by the constructed "family" of "brothers and sisters" united in the cause of abolition. In Douglass, the young Frederick heads this family by virtue of his powers of physical resistance, as in his fight with Covey, and his intelligence, as evidenced by his literacy and oratorical skills. That family is decidedly patriarchal, however much it resists the paternalism of Southern slavery. In *Incidents*, Linda Brent is the single "parent" of her political family, as evidenced by rhetorical skills equal to Douglass' and a willingness to resist that is no less vigorous and physical, even if different from young Frederick's open fight with Covey. Linda "fights" Dr. Flint and even Sands in her own way as she claims her body, its labor-power, and finally her children back from slavery.

Discussing how "intelligent slaves are aware they have many friends in the Free States," Linda recounts some of the folklore surrounding Southern African Americans' dreams of Northern freedom, including this fantasy of America liberated from the curse of slavery by an avenging Queen:

> One woman begged me to get a newspaper and read it over. She said her husband told her that the black people had sent word to the queen of 'Merica that they were all slaves; that she didn't believe it, and went to

Washington city to see the president about it. They quarrelled; she drew
her sword upon him, and swore that he should help her to make them all
free. . . . I wish the President was subordinate to Queen Justice.

(Incidents, 45)

In her note on this story, Yellin points out that the "reference suggests not
only Queen Victoria but also African traditions," such as the Ashanti custom of
"the Queen Mother" having the "most to say" in the choice of a new chief, or the
"armed 'Amazons' of the Dahomey" (Yellin, 267n4). In her allegorization of the
feminine figure as "Queen Justice," Jacobs makes clear that she is not simply
claiming her own personal authority from the several white men who have
abused her. Instead, she appeals to a political community that ought to draw
upon feminine power as much as military might to overturn slavery and return
America to its democratic promise.

7   The Body Poetic: Walt Whitman's *Drum-Taps*

Behold me—incarnate me as I have incarnated you!
—"City of Ships," *Drum-Taps*, 1865

Whitman's transcendental genius is best expressed in his extraordinary rhetoric of the body. He does not just faithfully represent nineteenth-century bodies; he makes possible the translation of the body into language, and convinces us that this is the American response to Wordsworth's claim that poetry ought to be the "language really spoken by men." What is really spoken by nineteenth-century Americans is still for Whitman the language of human labor, the basis for his visionary community. Repeatedly, he connects his own poetic activity to the everyday work of the nineteenth-century laborer, even though he knows how difficult it will be to convince his readers of this, accustomed as they are to the "pale poetling seated at a desk lisping cadenzas piano."[1] Human labor is sensuous, sexual, evocative, productive, and finally figurative. In this sense, the poet is merely one worker among many, "a strong man erect" with "sinewy limbs," but no more so than the smith or the mechanic.

In this spirit, Whitman's poetry implicitly criticizes Emerson's abstractness and the disembodied ideals that elude more ordinary, unphilosophical activities of daily life. Even in his best efforts to address directly the values expressed by the honest toil of the ordinary American or to protest loudly the violence slavery does to the body, Emerson consistently subordinates the materiality of human labor to what he had termed in *Nature* "man's power to connect his thought with its proper symbol, and so utter it."[2] However passionately Emerson insists that "Use, labor of each for all, is the health and virtue of all beings," he consistently subordinates such labor to "ideas," "nature," "morality," and other key concepts in his transcendentalism.[3] In the face of the mounting casualties in the Civil War and the continuation of slavery's violence to African Americans, Emerson was certainly chastened by the knowledge that "ideas must work through the brains and the arms of good and brave men, or they are no better than dreams" ("American Civilization," 289). But even the "good and brave men" dying on the battlefields of the Civil War, however necessary Emerson insists they are, remain abstractions for him: "Better the war should more dangerously threaten us,—should threaten fracture in what is still whole, and punish us with burned capitals and slaughtered regiments, and so exasperate the people to energy, exasperate our nationality. There are Scriptures written invisibly on men's hearts, whose letters do not come out until they are enraged. They can be read by war-fires, and by eyes in the last peril" (282–83).

We must recall that Emerson's poetic rage is inspired by the crisis of the War and the continuation of slavery as an institution. His appeal for "immediate Emancipation" is unquestionably courageous, but his transcendentalism still neglects the *fact* of the human body and its damage in both war and under slavery. What appeals to us in Whitman's poetic concern for the human body is his refusal of such mystifying sentiments and his insistence that whatever is good in his poetry merely speaks to the body in its everyday struggle to express itself in the toil of honest labor. In this regard, Whitman strikes me as an even more satisfactory revision of Emersonian transcendentalism than Thoreau.

Thoreau did attempt to give concrete particularity to Emerson's abstractions, to follow as literally as possible the disciplines of transcendental man, if only to discover thereby the visionary connection of spiritual and material life. This sense of concreteness is conveyed to the reader by way of Thoreau's sensuous rhetoric, and it satisfies a sort of hunger left by Emerson's philosophical essays. Thoreau's writing is always autobiography, and his demand of the reader is equivalent to what Thoreau has *done*: the production in writing of a body that is also a self. This is what Stanley Cavell understands as Thoreau's deliberate confusion of the book with his body, of the figura for the figure: "The boon of Walden is *Walden*. Its writer cups it in his hand, sees his reflection in it, and holds it out to us. It is his promise, in anticipation of his going, and the nation's, and Walden's. He is bequeathing it to us in his will, the place of the book and the book of the place."[4] The rhetorical chiasmus Cavell employs here effectively captures the "imbrication" of self and text, object and idea, spirit and place that distinguishes Thoreau's transcendentalism. Beautiful as this entanglement is, it confronts a fundamental problem when the circumstances are shifted from the contemplation of nature (either in Thoreau or Cavell) to the experience of war and physical injury. It is this problem I wish to explore in Whitman's *Drum-Taps*.

Thoreau's concreteness is an effect of his figurative language, not just of some naive realism, but it is composed primarily of what Eliot termed "objective correlatives." The inner world assumes the dimensions of a landscape or a scene or the simplest object, richly charged with its significance in Thoreau's auto-biographical purpose and thus with its careful placement in a narrative of self-representation. Thoreau's body is always there, but more often than not by implication, metonymically displaced by its proper extension—a hoe, an axe, the fields and woods, the pond itself. We see relatively little of Thoreau's actual body, even as he baptismally bathes in the pond each day; object-relations have replaced it, even if we are supposed to guess how that body has entered into those objects, extended itself, made itself by way of them. Near the end, in the famous spring thaw of *Walden*, it is the railroad bank that becomes the ultimate metonymy for the transcendental body, the streams and mud figuring the circulation of the blood. The Spring thaw is at once the birth of the poet, rebirth of nature, and the origin of language. Nevertheless, the "nature" of language still requires Thoreau as interpreter; for Whitman, it promises simply to be there in the figural presence of the body. The woodcutter still has much to learn from the author of *Walden*; the mechanic, the "strong man erect," with "well-gristled body and sunburnt face and hands," is greeted on the open road by Whitman, who carries his burden of words with the same apparent ease as his companion bears "the trowel, the jack-plane, the black-smith's hammer." The difference between Whitman's democracy and the idealism of Emerson and Thoreau is that Whitman's utopian vision comprehends the equality of the labor of the poet and the mechanic.

My bits and pieces from Whitman have been from *Drum-Taps* to suggest how Whitman's great revision of American romanticism persists even here in the midst of the War's perverse invocation of the body. Of all human labor, the work of war insistently requires the most strenuous and urgent exertion; even more explicitly than other kinds of labor, war requires of the body symbolic as well as material expenditure. For these reasons, the Civil War posed the ultimate philosophical, as well as political, challenge to our greatest poetic celebrant of the human body and that diverse labor in which coordinated bodies make a community. *Drum-Taps* marks a crucial turn in Whitman's poetry that I shall interpret as Whitman's ultimate failure to sustain the democratic vision of the poet as merely one worker among many.[5] It is nonetheless a great failure, because it genuinely risks the poet's authority as neither Emerson's nor Thoreau's safer, qualified transcendentalisms would.

What Whitman risked in *Drum-Taps* was a poetic voice that could not incorporate war, even a war as just as the Union's cause in the Civil War—that is, a voice that despaired of transforming human pain into poetic meaning. The best parts of *Drum-Taps* spring from this refusal to render war "poetic," but it is a strong denial that even Whitman could not sustain. *Sequel to Drum-Taps* (1865–66) charts the poet's return from the despair of ever transcending war and its suffering through rhetoric and song, resulting in the two poems for which he is best known, "When Lilacs Last in the Dooryard Bloom'd" and "O Captain! My Captain!" The irony of Whitman's struggle with the ethics of poetically representing war and the violence it does both to the sacred body and human community is that the assassination of President Lincoln provided Whitman just the symbolic event necessary to overcome his pain regarding the suffering of the common soldier. The poetic genius of both poems in the *Sequel* is a consequence of Whitman's renewed ability to affirm poetic authority in the face of the absence of political authority left by the assassination of Lincoln. Empowered by this new sense of urgent responsibility for the poet to take up the "song" of the nation, Whitman may forget the terrible lessons of the hospital wards he visited in New York and Washington in 1863. By "forget," I do not mean, of course, to repress utterly the everyday pain of those ordinary Americans addressed first and last by Whitman's democratic vision. I mean instead that Whitman rediscovers a poetic voice and authority in the *Sequel to Drum-Taps* that allows him to incorporate more easily and thus more transcendentally the damage to the body in war.

I propose, then, to look at the first edition of *Drum-Taps* as distinct from its *Sequel* for the sake of understanding the internal conflicts of the former collection *before* Whitman found a way to overcome these problems in his elegies for President Lincoln. *Drum-Taps* was printed and ready for distribution when Lincoln was shot, and the conjecture that Whitman withdrew the volume "because of Lincoln's death" seems confirmed by Whitman's organization of the *Sequel to Drum-Taps* around his two great memorials for the president.[6] Yet, I do not want this close focus on *Drum-Taps* to suggest some special authority for the original text beyond its expression of Whitman's struggle with the realities of war and his ideals as a poet. In fact, Whitman's subsequent revisions of *Drum-Taps*, beginning with his decision to bind *Drum-Taps* and *Sequel to Drum-Taps* together for the 1865–66 publication, support my thesis that Whitman was able to overcome the ethical problem of representing the physical suffering of individuals in the war by way of symbolic enactments that reaffirmed the authority of the poet and the value of his figurative language.

From the inclusion of the *Sequel* to his final arrangement of the poems in *Drum-Taps* and *Memories for President Lincoln* for the 1891–92 edition of *Leaves of Grass*, Whitman rearranged the narrative of his Civil War experiences into a kind of poetic *Bildungsroman*, proceeding from the poet's initial patriotism through his disillusionment over the suffering of individual soldiers to the reaffirmation of the

redemptive powers of the poet, both in his testament to the otherwise anonymous Union dead and his ecstatic substitution of his own authority for the dead
president in the two great elegies. These revisions of the last twenty-five years of
Whitman's life seem to confirm Timothy Sweet's thesis that the threat posed by
the Civil War to political union was understood by Whitman as equally a threat to
his democratic poem, *Leaves of Grass*, and that *Drum-Taps* "presents itself as a recu-
perative political-poetic response."[7] In effect, Whitman was reaffirming the ethics
and aesthetics of American romanticism in the course of these revisions. In doing
so, he produced one of the greatest poems of American nationalism, "When Lilacs
Last in the Dooryard Bloom'd" and thereby legitimated the romantic concept of
the poet as spokesman for a nation.[8] Whitman's rediscovery of his transcendentalist roots, however, was purchased at the expense of his earlier commitments to
the equality of material and intellectual labor in the building of community. The
renaissance of Whitman's idealism after the War also resulted in the vainglory of
the egotistical sublime expressed in poems like "Passage to India" and "Prayer of
Columbus"—works that helped legitimate culturally the emerging imperialism
of the United States in the Western Hemisphere and the Pacific.[9]

The narrative I wish to trace in *Drum-Taps* begins with the patriotic strains
that Whitman sings with only the most troubled voice. Beating the drum and fly-
ing the banner of the Union, he acknowledges the justice of the Union cause,
even as he recognizes how easily such sentiments transform the critical edge of
the poet into wartime clichés and propaganda. From the first, he is troubled by
the ineffectiveness of poetry to address History:

> Words! book-words! what are you?
> Words no more, for hearken and see,
> My song is there in the open air, and I must sing,
> With the banner and pennant a-flapping.
>> ("Song of the Banner at Day-Break," DT, 458)

Yet the image of the active, militant poet, some medieval troubadour leading his
troops in battle, singing defiance on the battlefield, is equally unacceptable, since
the poet in such circumstances must sing only the military general's command.
Despite the performatives, so often in the volitive mood, Whitman doubts the
capacity of his words to act, to carry the agency and urgency of the poet, rather
than the general or statesman:

> I'll pour the verse with streams of blood, full of volition, full of joy,
> Then loosen, launch forth, to go and compete,
> With the banner and pennant a-flapping.
>> ("Song of the Banner at Day-Break," DT, 458)

From the first poems of *Drum-Taps*, such lines ring false, and Whitman is intent upon reclaiming some natural or divine authority that will liberate him from mere service to the government's cause without forgetting his commitment to social justice.

The chief propaganda of the war poem has often been the rhetoric of sacrifice, that perverse appeal to mothers and fathers to surrender their children to the noble purposes of war. From the outset, Whitman identifies his poetic voice with the banner of the Union and the pennants of its military units. But already he claims for that poetic voice a *generative* power that both exceeds the parent's natural authority over the child and antedates the Union's leadership. The visionary authority of the poet does not simply gather together communally the labor of others; throughout *Drum-Taps*, it claims a superiority that stems from both Whitman's panoptic view of historical purpose and his prior knowledge of the inevitability of war. The opening lines of "Rise O Days from Your Fathomless Deeps," "probably composed in the early days of recruiting" for the War, suggest that the poet's entire career, especially the rhetorical travels of *Song of Myself*, has been simply preparation for the war:[10]

> Long for my soul hungering gymnastic I devour'd what the earth gave me,
> Long I roam'd the woods of the north, long I watch'd Niagara pouring, . . .
> I heard the wind piping, I saw the black clouds, . . .
> Noted the slender and jagged threads of lightning as sudden and fast
>   amid the din they chased
> each other across the sky;
> These, and such as these, I, elate, saw—saw with wonder, yet pensive
>   and masterful,
> All the menacing might of the globe uprisen around me,
> Yet there with my soul I fed, I fed content, supercilious.
>
> ("Rise O Days from Your Fathomless Deeps," 483–84)

In the concluding stanza of this same poem, the poet claims to have returned from his long preparation in the colder northern climates, where he had "waited the bursting forth of the pent fire—on the water and air I waited long," only to be satisfied now with the realization of his prophecy: "But now I no longer wait, I am fully satisfied, I am glutted, / I have witness'd the true lightning, I have witness'd my cities electric, / I have lived to behold man burst forth and warlike America rise" (DT, 485–86).[11]

Whitman's claim for foreknowledge of the war's necessity not only reaffirms his prophetic powers, it also becomes the occasion for recalling the historical purposes of revolutionary America.[12] *Drum-Taps*, like all serious poetry of war, is obsessed with the problem of memory, for it appears to be the hopeless task assigned the poet either to memorialize gloriously war or simply remind us of its pain. The "old man bending" who arrives "among new faces" in "The Wound-Dresser" is the poet reduced to failure, "To sit by the wounded and soothe them, or silently watch the dead," even as he is charged to "witness again, paint the mightiest armies of earth," and answer the question: "What stays with you latest and deepest? of curious panics, / Of hard-fought engagements or sieges tremendous what deepest remains?" ("The Wound-Dresser," DT, 479, 480). As Sweet argues, Whitman's questions in *Drum-Taps* reflect the self-doubt manifested both in Whitman's physical and emotional breakdowns while serving as a volunteer in Army hospitals and the poetic struggle in *Drum-Taps* to reaffirm the romantic self of his antebellum poetry.[13]

Neither the transcendental self nor the patriotic purpose of the Union quite serves the poet's effort to reaffirm his own voice and prophetic mission. As if searching for a more profound justification for the human damage he witnesses, Whitman returns to the original revolutionary purpose of the nation. To be sure, this is by no means unique to Whitman's Civil War poems; it was commonplace for abolitionists to make the call to arms in terms evocative of the Revolution, often insisting that the Civil War must complete the unfinished work of our first war against tyranny.[14] What distinguishes Whitman's appeal to the revolutionary past, however, is his claim that only poetic vision can turn that past and the present carnage of the war into an optimistic future. In "The Centenarian's Story," for example, the aged veteran of the Revolution is an alter-ego for the poet, who in "The Wound-Dresser" is reduced nearly to the feeble condition of the blind Centenarian. Both are left apparently with nothing more than their powerless memories, but in "The Centenarian's Story" this poetic recall is finally transformational. The veteran claims that "as I talk I remember all," and what he remembers for the sake of the "Volunteer of 1861–62," "assisting the Centenarian," is initially conventional war propaganda:

> I remember the Declaration,
> It was read here, the whole army paraded, it was read to us here,
> By his staff surrounded the General stood in the middle, he held up his
> unsheath'd sword,
> It glitter'd in the sun in full sight of the army.
>
> ("The Centenarian's Story," DT, 471)

Whitman's invocation of General Washington reading the troops the Declaration of Independence at the Battle of Long Island (August 27, 1776) is metamorphosed from patriotic lore into a resource for the poet himself, who concludes the poem abruptly and with surprising authority:

Enough, the Centenarian's story ends,
The two, the past and present, have interchanged,
I myself as the connecter, as chansonnier of a great future, am
    now speaking.
And is this the ground Washington trod?
And these waters I listlessly daily cross, are these the waters he cross'd,
As resolute in defeat as other generals in their proudest triumphs?
I must copy the story, and send it eastward and westward,
I must preserve that look as it beam'd on you rivers of Brooklyn.

("The Centenarian's Story," DT, 473–74)

Whitman has not quite displaced Washington, as he will attempt later to fill the absence left by the death of Lincoln in "Lilacs," but the active purpose of poetic memory to construct a positive future out of the chaos and damage of the present is clear enough.[15]

Whitman's entanglement of poetic and political *genii loci* is evident throughout *Drum-Taps*, as if he were struggling to take over the sites of the war, with both their verbal conventions and physical horrors, for the sake of some finer poetic vision. In "City of Ships," the Union's naval strength is quickly subordinated to the poet's imaginative powers, especially as the latter have been identified with Whitman's Brooklyn and New York throughout *Drum-Taps*. Once again, the rhetoric of *Song of Myself* is employed primarily for the sake of restoring to the poet his special authority to be more than a mere chronicler of war. This is also the poem in which Whitman makes his most direct, albeit still figuratively disguised, address to the true moral purpose of the War: the abolition of slavery. For all the patriotic enthusiasms of *Drum-Taps*, there is scant evidence of this issue in the collection, strangely since this issue seems the justification of the poet's claim to "prior knowledge" of the necessity of war. They are "black ships" and thus "fierce ships" in this "City of the world! (for all races are here, / All the lands of the earth make contributions here;)" ("City of Ships," DT, 490). It is above all, however, Whitman's poetic city: "City of the sea! city of hurried and glittering tides! / . . . Proud and passionate city—mettlesome, mad, extravagant city!" that is indistinguishable from the poet's imagination:

Spring up O city—not for peace alone, but be indeed yourself, warlike!
Fear not—submit to no models but your own O city!
Behold me—incarnate me as I have incarnated you!

("City of Ships," DT, 490)

This power of incarnation is achieved by way of imaginative identification with military power, the genius loci of the democratic Northern city, and the revolutionary history of the republic. It enables Whitman to substitute his own egotistical sublime for the conventional propaganda of war poetry. What emerges in *Drum-Taps* is Whitman's reaffirmation of the poet's ability to redeem what has been destroyed in war, thus answering those who ask: What has the poet to tell us of war? In effect, Whitman answers by insisting that the poet bring the indispensable vision of what will redeem the pain and damage of war.

In some poems, Whitman merely continues to compete with the generals and statesmen for authority. Even in those poems Matthiessen praised for their painterly impressionism, such as "Cavalry Crossing a Ford," "By the Bivouac's Fitful Flame," and "Bivouac on a Mountain Side," Whitman is doing more than merely poetically describing armies in the field.[16] In such poems, the process of perception itself is often problematized, suggesting some division between the military strategists and the poet, who in most instances subordinates the terrible practicalities of battle to his larger, often redemptive vision. The speaker in "By the Bivouac's Fitful Flame," for example, reviews his own troops while the real troops sleep, drawing on the rhetoric of that much-revised poem from *Leaves of Grass* whose final version was "The Sleepers" (1871, 1881):[17]

> A procession winding around me, solemn and sweet and slow—
>   but first I note,
> The tents of the sleeping army, the fields' and woods' dim outline, . . .
> Like a phantom fear or near an occasional figure moving, . . .
> While wind in procession thoughts, O tender and wondrous thoughts,
> Of life and death, of home and the past and loved, and of those that are
>   far away;
> A solemn and slow procession there as I sit on the ground,
> By the bivouac's fitful flame.
>
> ("By the Bivouac's Fitful Flame," DT, 466)

In keeping with the conventions of the dramatic monologue Whitman used so often, the reader is tempted to understand this poem (and others like it in *Drum-Taps*) as spoken merely by a soldier in the field.[18] Yet when connected with the rhetoric of poetic aspiration in the rest of *Drum-Taps*, the voice of even the most realistic war poems takes much of its resonance from that of the poet's distinctive identity. Indeed, the mark of Whitman's poetic genius is just such ventriloquism and subsequent confusion: Who is not a poet when the urgencies of history provoke significant speech? Thus the funereal procession that fades into the poet's own dreamy reflections marks the sort of transformation he desires: from a "solemn and slow procession" declaring death—just what the soldier of the field fears—to the respect paid the poet (whether he be Whitman or the soldier turned poet) for his "wondrous thoughts."

Whitman's appropriation of military and political authority reaches its romantic limit when the power of poetic incarnation quite literally becomes the power of parental generation and divine regeneration. Poems like "Come Up from the Fields Father" and "Vigil Strange I Kept on the Field One Night" complement the "Wound-Dresser" by claiming for the poet not simply the voice of mourning but also the power to resurrect the dead. The Ohio farming parents who receive the message that their son has been wounded read the official lie, "*At present low, but will soon be better*," which is not unlike the patriotic enthusiasm for war the poet himself expresses in poems such as "Pioneers! O Pioneers!" and even "Beat! Beat! Drums!" that immediately precedes "Come Up from the Fields Father" in the first edition of *Drum-Taps*.[19] The mother is stricken with grief and thus "catches the main words only, / Sentences broken," but the unpoetic character of the message is not just an effect of her emotion, but of the manner in which the official word betrays the natural affections of a family for its wounded son:

> O this is not our son's writing, yet his name is sign'd,
> O a strange hand writes for our dear son, O stricken mother's soul!
>> ("Come Up from the Fields Father," DT, 489)

Even as the daughter attempts to console her mother by repeating the official lie—"*Grieve not so, dear mother, . . . the letter says Pete will soon be better*," the poet answers honestly; "Alas poor boy, he will never be better. . ./ While they stand at home at the door he is dead already" (489). What appears to be Whitman's substitution of his own poetic truth for the official lie in sympathy with this family's grief turns quickly in the direction of poetic legitimation at the expense of the family. "While they stand at home at the door he is dead already" is concluded with: "The only son is dead." Sympathy gives way to poetic identification of this dead child with Christ, His "only son," and this "sacrifice" now serves not the war-effort but the visionary aim of the poet. In the final stanza, the mother wastes away, yearning "silent from life [to] escape and withdraw, / To follow, to seek, to be with her dear dead son" (489).[20]

Neither the farmer nor his wife can address the loss of their son, only the poet replaces the "strange hand" signing the official message with their son's "name" with the allusion to Christ that allows *Whitman* to substitute his forgery for that of the War Department. Such a perverse reading would be strained were it not for the development of this Christological imagery in the subsequent poem, "Vigil Strange I Kept on the Field One Night," in which the substitution now involves not the poet for the grieving parents but the poet for the corpse of a soldier. In the first edition of *Drum-Taps*, this poem is preceded by "Mother and Babe," a two-line lyric without apparent relevance for the war:

> I see the sleeping babe, nestling the breast of its mother;
> The sleeping mother and babe—hush'd, I study them long and long.
>
> ("Mother and Babe," DT, 491)

In later editions of *Leaves of Grass*, the poem was moved out of *Drum-Taps* to find its eventual place in *By the Roadside* in the 1881 edition, as if Whitman recognized that his invocation of mother and child could serve no other purpose in *Drum-Taps* than reinforce his own bid for authority as the redemptive father of a new, postbellum order of things.

Read in this way, "Vigil Strange" nearly provides the story behind the official message of "Pete's" wounding in the earlier poem, although it is clear enough that the two poems refer to different events and characters. Even so, "Vigil" substitutes an intensely personal account of a soldier's death in the field for the "Sentences broken" that announce Pete's wounding to his family in "Come Up from the Fields Father." And the "son" of this poem is also the poet's "comrade," allowing the poet to claim the special intimacy that only veterans of war have for each other:

> When you my son and my comrade dropt at my side that day,
> One look I but gave which your dear eyes return'd with a look I shall
>   never forget,
> One touch of your hand to mine O boy, reach'd up as you lay on
>   the ground
>
> ("Vigil Strange I Kept on the Field One Night," DT, 491)

The poet's vigil is earned as a consequence of shared battle, and the body he views so lovingly is inspired by his own sense of miraculous escape from death. As he contemplates this double, "leaning my chin in my hands," the poet has discovered the certain purpose that escaped the more emotional response of the parents in the previous poem:

> Passing sweet hours, immortal and mystic hours with you dearest
>   comrade—not a tear, not a word,
> Vigil of silence, love and death, vigil for you my son and my soldier,
>
> ("Vigil," DT, 492)

Even as the poet acknowledges the impotence of mere words before actual death, he does so only parenthetically and within the same aside recognizes what seems to contradict the claim that he cannot save this boy:

> (I could not save you, swift was your death,
> I faithfully loved you and cared for you living, I think we shall surely
>   meet again,)
>
> ("Vigil," DT, 492)

Ritually wrapping his comrade in his blanket, the poet "envelop'd well his form," and "bathed by the rising sun, my son in his grave, in his rude-dug grave I deposited, / Ending my vigil strange with that" (492). Sweet reads this poem in conjunction with others that invoke the father for the sake of recalling "the healing power of adhesiveness," including "Quicksand Years" and "The Wound-Dresser."[21]

"Vigil" is a strange combination of compassion and arrogant assertion through which "my son" quite literally becomes Christ buried by the poet/god just as the dawn announces not his son's resurrection, but that of the poet transfigured:

> I rose from the chill ground and folded my soldier well in his blanket,
> And buried him where he fell.
>
> ("Vigil," 492)

It is not, of course, Whitman's purpose to rationalize the carnage of the Civil War by invoking some vague reference to Original Sin and our collective fall, but rather to suggest how the poetic voice can redeem all those who have fallen in the War. It is the form of the poetry that will not simply chronicle the War but claim the memorializing function that will quite literally resurrect poetic vision from the terror of history. By the end of the poem, the fallen comrade has become "my soldier," and he marches for the sake of the poet's restored confidence in his vocation.[22]

For me to claim that Whitman's *Drum-Taps* has as its ultimate purpose the reaffirmation, even resurrection, of poetic power, rather than an address to the problem of remembrance occasioned by the bloodiest American war, tends to trivialize the compassion that his rediscovered poetic voice expresses. "Many a soldier's loving arms about this neck have cross'd and rested, / Many a soldier's kiss dwells on these bearded lips," Whitman writes in "The Wound-Dresser" (DT, 482). Few poems of any war are as powerful in their evocation of sheer human suffering, of the waste of the body occasioned by war. Even in the *Sequel to Drum-Taps*, written expressly to mourn Lincoln and to assert more forthrightly than *Drum-Taps* the regained voice of the romantic poet, the nightmare of war's injury to the body remains untranscended, as in "Old War-Dreams":

> In midnight sleep of many a face of anguish,
> Of the look at first of the mortally wounded, (of that indescribable look,)
> Of the dead on their backs with arms extended wide, I dream, I dream,
> I dream.
>
> ("Old War-Dreams," DT, 550)

Yet, there is still something disturbing in the poet's rediscovery of his voice, of his capacity to wander from the maimed to the dead to receive his blessing. Thus that troubling line at the end of "Long, Too Long America" is more than just the customary bravura of the poet who previously had taken into himself the whole of America. Now there is a note of a poetic voice that must remain always before and after the knowledge of fathers and mothers, of comrades and lovers, of sleepers and readers:

> But now, ah now, to learn from crises of anguish, advancing, grappling
>   with direst fate and recoiling not,
> And now to conceive and show to the world what your children en-masse
>   really are,
> (For who except myself has yet conceiv'd what your children en-masse
>   really are?)
>
> ("Long, Too Long America," DT, 495)

From the end of *Drum-Taps* to the end of his career, Whitman speaks of those "bodies" that can "make" themselves only in the redemptive language of *his poetry*. The egotistical sublime of "Passage to India" and "The Sleepers" may be the understandable consequence of this working-out of the problem of death in the face of war. What other answer could allow the poet to keep singing? How survive those hospital wards and witness such wounds without the consolation that poetry could redeem them? Sweet concludes that *Drum-Taps* performs rhetorically the "re-union" that War can only require but not itself achieve. Quoting "Reconciliation" from *Sequel to Drum-Taps*—"Beautiful that war and all its deeds of carnage, must in time be utterly lost" (*Sequel*, 555), Sweet claims: "Discourse itself is represented as possessing the aesthetic power to make war disappear."[23] In the back of our minds, heard with the compassion we feel for Whitman's struggle to preserve poetry in *Drum-Taps*, there is the other knowledge that the body poetic soon allows us to forget the body politic, which is perhaps why Whitman had repeated in the 1871 and 1876 editions the lines from "The Wound-Dresser" as an epigraph for the whole:

> But soon my fingers fail'd me, my face droop'd and I resign'd myself.
> To sit by the wounded and soothe them, or silently watch the dead.

As Whitman's romantic voice "rose from the chill ground" of the battle-field and the hospital, it arrived in time to sing the most extraordinary elegy of our nationality, "When Lilacs Last in the Dooryard Bloom'd." Whitman's fears that the political issues of the Civil War would subordinate his poetry to patriotic sentiment and propaganda are dispelled thoroughly by this poem, certainly one of the most poetically successful elegies for a public figure ever written. Whitman's undeniable achievement derives in large part, however, from his invocation of the voice and theme of his antebellum romanticism in poems like "Out of the Cradle Endlessly Rocking" (1859) and "Starting from Paumanok"

(1860). The visionary poet is able once again to commune with nature, "tallying" the dirge of the thrush with his poetic translation of its song and finding a companion in death:

> Then with the knowledge of death as walking one side of me,
> And the thought of death close-walking the other side of me,
> And I in the middle as with companions, and as holding the hands
> of companions,
> I fled forth to the hiding receiving night that talks not. . . .
>
> ("When Lilacs Last in the Dooryard Bloom'd," XIV)

Whitman's ambivalence in such oxymorons (or near oxymorons) as "fled forth" and "hiding receiving night" is a measure of his poetic capacity to encompass what otherwise appears baffling and contradictory to the reader. Unable to comprehend the carnage and suffering of the Civil War or the assassination of President Lincoln, the implied reader of the poem must be reminded that death is part of a natural renewal process.

Yet just what such a romantic convention has to do with the problems of political division left by the Civil War is unclear until the reader recognizes that the spring flowering in the poem figures that of the poet himself. In "The Wound-Dresser," Whitman doubted he could find the language to represent war; in "Lilacs," he confidently answers his own rhetorical question at the beginning of section 11, "O what shall I hang on the chamber walls?/ And what shall the pictures be that I hang on the walls,/ To adorn the burial-house of him I love?"

> Pictures of growing spring and farms and homes, . . .
> And the city at hand with dwellings so dense, and stacks of chimneys,
> And all the scenes of life and the workshops, and the workmen
> homeward returning.

Whitman's usually panoptic vision is here especially inflected with his desire to take poetic possession of the nation, especially now that his political alter-ego has died:

> Lo, body and soul—this land,
> My own Manhattan with spires, and the sparkling and hurrying tides,
> and the ships, . . .
> Lo, the most excellent sun so calm and haughty, . . .
> The coming eve delicious, the welcoming night and stars,
> Over my cities shining all, enveloping man and land.
>
> ("Lilacs," XII)

It is not just Whitman's use of the familiar possessive pronouns that renders these lines such excellent illustrations of his poetic will-to-power; the possession he takes of these now poetic cities and prairies is well-established by his allusiveness throughout "Lilacs" to his previous poems, including those in *Drum-Taps*.[24] What Whitman is able to see as a consequence of this rhetorically structured field of vision is just what he often complained he could *not* see in *Drum-Taps*: the purpose of the human suffering in the war:[25]

> And I saw askant the armies,
> I saw as in noiseless dreams hundreds of battle flags,
> Borne through the smoke of the battles and pierc'd with missiles . . .
> I saw battle-corpses, myriads of them,
> And the white skeletons of young men, I saw them,
> I saw the debris and debris of all the slain soldiers of the war,
> But I saw they were not as was thought,
> They themselves were fully at rest, they suffer'd not,
> The living remain'd and suffer'd, the mother suffer'd,
> And the wife and the child and the musing comrade suffer'd,
> And the armies that remain'd suffer'd.
>
> ("Lilacs," xv)

The poet turns the elegeaic strains of the poem from Lincoln and the war dead to the suffering of those who remain in a democracy still divided and in need of a leader to revivify its ideals. In the final section of "Lilacs," the poet leads us away from mourning the dead and toward the nation's expansive destiny in the West. Figuratively and literally the direction of Lincoln's passing, the West is also the site of his poetic annunciation as the Western Star, Venus:

> I cease from my song for thee,
> From my gaze on thee in the west, fronting the west, communing
>   with thee,
> O comrade lustrous with silver face in the night.
>
> ("Lilacs," xvi)

Whitman invokes the elegeiac convention of placing the dead in the visible heavens, but he makes clear that Lincoln's immortality is only possible if Americans follow his vision. Yet the vision Whitman sketches is that of *Whitman's romanticism*, not anything remotely recognizable as Lincoln's statesmanship:

> Yet each to keep and all, retrievements out of the night,
> The song, the wondrous chant of the gray-brown bird,
> And the tallying chant, the echo arous'd in my soul,

With the lustrous and drooping star with the countenance full of woe,
With the holders holding my hand nearing the call of the bird,
Comrades mine and I in the midst, and their memory ever to keep,
    for the dead I loved so well,
For the sweetest, wisest soul of all my days and lands—and this for
    his dear sake,
Lilac and star and bird twined with the chant of my soul,
There in the fragrant pines and the cedars dusk and dim.

                                                        ("Lilacs," XVI)

First weaving together his democratic "comrades" with the "memory" of
the Civil War dead by way of his own poetic centrality ("I in the midst"),
Whitman claims that we do this for the dead Lincoln's sake, but Whitman concludes the poem by transferring the poetic metaphors that have organized the
elegy—lilac, western star, and thrush—from Lincoln to the trinity he has just
constituted: the people, the poet, and those who have sacrificed for the survival
of the Union. The result is that Lincoln is displaced by Whitman—"I in the
midst"—and by the power of Whitman's metaphors. In the parallelism of the
metaphors and their referents in the final lines, "I in the midst" matches the "star"
of "Lilac and star and bird," so that the chief metaphor for Lincoln—"comrade
lustrous with silver face in the night"—becomes finally the visionary poet himself. To be sure, such technical symmetries are unnecessary to make this point,
because the concluding sentiments of "Lilacs" so clearly express Whitman's
romanticism in the place of some more programmatic democratic vision we
might expect from Lincoln.

Beautiful and moving as the concluding lines of "Lilacs" remain, I wonder
what has happened to Whitman's struggle in *Drum-Taps* to confront the true suffering of war, including such costs as Lincoln's assassination, without idealizing
the damage done to real bodies. The poet's pain, confusion, and deep sorrow in
Drum-Taps are uniquely powerful because poetry fails properly to express these
emotions. Such moments are by no means central to *Drum-Taps*; Whitman's
overall affirmation of his poetic capacity to "encompass all" is consistent in both
Drum-Taps and the *Sequel*. Yet in poems like "The Wound-Dresser," in which he
does dramatize the breakdown of poetry in the face of war, Whitman writes a
premodern "anti-poetry" that has never been equalled by other writers attempting to come to terms not just with war but with their aesthetic responsibilities.
The democratic collectivity that Whitman sees mocked in modern warfare—
coordinated killing rather than making—is rediscovered in *Sequel to Drum-Taps*
as merely another version of American transcendentalism. Brilliantly successful
as a poem, "When Lilacs Last in the Dooryard Bloom'd" reminds us of how dif-

ficult it is for poetry to represent someone else's suffering or to suspend its own figuration for the sake of true mourning. For all its beauty and pathos, it is also a poem that dehistoricizes and thus depoliticizes the great events the poet presumes to discuss: the disunion of America that must be healed in the post-war years, as evidenced clearly in the assassination of the President.[26] Instead of focusing our attention on these urgent questions, especially as they bear on issues of race in America (that topic barely mentioned in *Drum-Taps*), Whitman swerves away and casts his vision westward. The common work of Americans will be what Whitman reminds us throughout the poem lies before us in the West: the ever-expansive and presumably emancipatory song of American romanticism, whose unconscious was the expansionist policies of Manifest Destiny, our best nineteenth-century substitute for the violence of the Civil War.

Fatal Speculations—
Murder, Money, and Manners:
Mark Twain's *The Gilded Age*
and *Pudd'nhead Wilson*

"You can't do much with 'em," interrupted Col. Sellers. "They are a speculating race, sir, disinclined to work for white folks without security, planning how to live only by working for themselves. Idle, sir, there's my garden just a ruin of weeds. Nothing practical in 'em."

"There is some truth in your observation, Colonel, but you must educate them."

"You educate the niggro and you make him more speculating than he was before. If he won't stick to any industry except for himself now, what will he do then?"

"But, Colonel, the negro when educated will be more able to make his speculations fruitful."

—Charles Dudley Warner and Mark Twain, *The Gilded Age* (1873)

It is good to begin life poor; it is good to begin life rich—these are wholesome, but to begin it poor and *prospectively* rich! The man who has not experienced it cannot imagine the curse of it.

—*Mark Twain's Autobiography*

In the "Conclusion" of *Pudd'nhead Wilson*, Tom Driscoll is sentenced to "imprisonment for life," only to be claimed as the legal property of the creditors of the Percy Driscoll estate, who had been able to recover only "sixty per cent" of the indebtedness of the estate at the time of Percy's death in the fall of 1845. The final two paragraphs of this uncanny novel constitute Twain's most withering satire of slavery as a legal and economic institution. Claiming that "'Tom' was lawfully their property and had been so for eight years," the creditors claim that his imprisonment would deprive them further of their property and any return they might expect from its "investment."

Their arguments go well beyond, however, Twain's customary satire of the obvious absurdity involved in defining a human being as chattel. The creditors argue successfully that the violation of their rights occasioned by the mystery of Tom's origins is the real cause of the murder of Judge Driscoll: "[I]f he had been delivered up to them in the first place, they would have sold him and he could not have murdered Judge Driscoll, therefore it was not he that had really committed the murder, the guilt lay with the erroneous inventory. Everybody saw that there was reason in this."[1] The absurd attribution of a murder to an "erroneous inventory" is understood conventionally as Twain's satire of an antebellum legal system that in its worst moment would throw out Dred Scott's suit for liberty on the grounds that as a slave he had none of the legal rights of a U.S. citizen. Indeed, the conflict between property rights and civil rights is such a common theme in Twain's writings that this final turn in the already labyrinthine legalities of *Pudd'nhead Wilson* seems merely to underscore a familiar issue.

Yet by 1894, the surreal legal and existential situation of the antebellum slave must have seemed an increasingly anachronistic issue for the contemporary reader, even if the social and economic fates of African Americans were recognized by many to be as hard as ever.[2] Twain's historical romances, as I think such works as *Huckleberry Finn*, *Pudd'nhead Wilson*, *A Connecticut Yankee*, and *The Prince and the Pauper* deserve to be called, employ historical distance to suggest how little the contemporary reader's society has progressed from the serfdom of either medieval England or antebellum America. In each of these works, Twain suggests that apparent—and often very dramatic—social changes merely have reinstated rigid social and class hierarchies; hints and foreshadowings of how such social transformations will effectively repeat the past quite often are incorporated in the dramatic action of the historical romance. Thus the fate of Jim at the end of *Huckleberry Finn*—a free African American with nowhere to go—or that of the educated and free African American ("a p'fessor in a college") scoffed by Pap Finn (in chapter 6) foreshadow accurately the plight of emancipated African Americans under reconstruction.[3] More obviously, the technological marvels that Hank Morgan brings to Arthurian England merely intensify the violent power struggles of the ruling class. In *Pudd'nhead Wilson*, the arbitrariness and irrationality of the law will survive the Civil War and Emancipation without substantial reform.

Despite the thematic continuities Twain may establish between the preindustrial societies in which his historical romances are set and modern, industrial America of the Gilded Age, he often subscribes to his own special "history" of an America divided strategically by the Civil War. The rural, settled, slow-paced Midwest of "Old Times on the Mississippi" is forever changed by the railroads, land development, and westward expansion that accompanied—both as causes and effects—the political upheaval of the Civil War. I need not quote here those familiar passages from *Life on the Mississippi* in which Twain contrasts the romance of the steamboat and the near-transcendentalist qualities of its pilots with the brute realism of the railroad and the aggressive enterprise of its agents. Even when charged with the sins of the slave-scheme, Twain's frontier Missouri often assumes the guise of a more innocent and manageable world than the openly corrupt cities of post-Civil War, industrial America. Within this mythology, then, slavery is a cruel institution of rural America whose passing is replaced by the more insidious forms of social and economic domination that would be faced by the immigrant, the emancipated African American, and virtually any man or woman with only the means of honest labor. In this context, Twain serves well those myth-critics who would maintain a sharp distinction between rural and industrial economies in America and thus, of course, the distinction between their social values.

Despite Twain's understandable sentimentality about an older, rural America, works like *The Gilded Age* and *Pudd'nhead Wilson* suggest that the sources of modern, postbellum, industrial corruption are to be found in rural America. A vigorous, albeit equivocal, even hypocritical satirist of modern technology, Twain understands slavery itself as not just a provincial agrarian institution but the basis for the speculative economy that would fuel industrial expansion, Manifest Destiny, and laissez-faire capitalism. The slave is, after all, the ultimate "speculation," insofar as the buyer invests a relatively small amount of money— for purchase and maintenance—in hopes of watching that capital grow into the accumulated labor-power of a healthy, long-lived worker. And insofar as the slave may be forced to multiply her owner's wealth, the speculation promises an enormous and virtually endless return for a very modest investment. All of this is accomplished by means of virtually no labor invested by the owner, whose claim to a high return on his venture-capital must be based on the risks that he is willing to run: the unpredictable losses that may be occasioned by mistreatment, illness, flight, or infertility of his slaves. In short, the slave-owner stakes his claim to authority on his "business acumen," his ability to tell a "good" property from a "bad," in virtually the same manner that a speculator stakes his claim by *predicting* how a particular property will rise or fall in the market place. Slaveowners commonly counted their slaves as capital assets, but the market value of such assets depended upon speculation regarding future productivity of both crops and children. Indeed, such speculations might well be improved by development, much as land speculators attempted to improve a particular property by subdivision, cultivation, or even the improvement of natural features (dredging rivers, draining marshes, clearing forests). One of the motives behind the taboo against miscegenation, other than the obvious motive of maintaining clear distinctions between rulers and ruled, may well have been the fear that publicity regarding "mixed progeny" might jeopardize the legal standing of the slave as chattel. Slaveholders raped African-American women not merely for their perverse pleasure or for the willful exercise of power, but with the hope of producing assets, of increasing the promise of their original investments.[4]

In *The Gilded Age*, Warner and Twain represent virtually every aspect of post-Civil War American business and social life as infected with the disease of speculation. Colonel Beriah Sellers was immensely popular with nineteenth-century readers, thanks to the gaudy splendor of his speculative rhetoric. A darling of contemporary theater-goers, Colonel Sellers inflates everything from turnips and water to his own name: "When we first came here [Washington,

D.C.], I was *Mr.* Sellers, and *Major* Sellers, and *Captain* Sellers, but nobody could get it right, somehow; but the minute our bill went through the House, I was *Colonel* Sellers every time. And nobody could do enough for me; and whatever I said was wonderful. . . . Yes, sir, to-morrow it will be General, let me congratulate you, sir; General, you've done a great work, sir,—you've done a great work for the niggro; Gentlemen, allow me the honor to introduce my friend General Sellers, the humane friend of the niggro."[5] In *The Gilded Age*, parents have more children than they can care for, husbands are bigamists, and people speculate in the most unexpected futures: social reputation, political speeches, congressional votes, literature, genius, the imagination, a university.

The very notion of "speculation" in *The Gilded Age* is expanded from mere investment in the future of a marketable commodity to include the venture of psychic, social, or financial capital in something that has only a potential future value. The value of such speculation depends, of course, on the inverse proportion of investment to return: the less work, money, or human energy committed to a project, the greater its potential value. In the place of hard work and capital, the speculator spends *words* profligately on his projects—in brochures, speeches, conversation. Words, it would seem, especially those that require no thought (*conventional* words), are *free*. Speculation in postbellum America is criticized by Warner and Twain quite simply because it discourages honest labor and increasingly alienates economic and moral value from labor. Great fortunes are made and lost overnight, as Colonel Sellers never tires of telling his disciples; steady, dedicated labor seems sheer folly in an economy in which the value of a manufactured item or agricultural product might change dramatically as a consequence of market conditions fuelled by unpredictable speculators. To refuse to play the speculative game is merely to become a victim of the system; most of the honest laborers in *The Gilded Age* end up losing their earnings to some boss whose speculative scheme fails or being cheated of their wages by the real bosses, the accountants.[6] To play the game puts you in precisely the situation of the gambler, who has only an illusory authority over an intentionally arbitrary system.

The town of Dawson's Landing in *Pudd'nhead Wilson* begins as a sleepy "slave-holding town, with a rich slave-worked grain and pork country back of it. . . . It was fifty years old, and was growing slowly—very slowly, in fact, but it was still growing" (4). Twain describes a town in 1830 (Tom and Chambers are born on February 1, 1830), which is, like most of his fictional Missouri towns, virtually indistinguishable from Hannibal or a host of other riverfront towns at the eastern edge of the American frontier. By 1853, however, Dawson's Landing has elected a Mayor, incorporating itself as Hannibal had done in 1845, and otherwise shows signs of adapting to the economic ferment that helped

Jacksonian America enter the modern industrial age. Like St. Petersburg in *Huckleberry Finn* or Hawkeye, where Colonel Sellers has his "mansion" in *The Gilded Age*, Dawson's Landing is Twain's touchstone for the changes coming to rural, agrarian, slaveholding America.

The transitional quality of Dawson's Landing during the twenty-three years covered by the narrative is often noted, but primarily to indicate how modern America brings into relief the antiquated values of antebellum feudalism. Twain provides certain details, however, that make *Pudd'nhead Wilson* a commentary on the shared economics of slavery and the new speculative economy that would carry us through the Civil War into the Gilded Age. When read in light of these economic details, David Wilson becomes an even more problematic character than he has been for previous critics, because it is Wilson who helps adjust the law to this new economy, vindicates the murdered Judge Driscoll and his venerable descent from the First Families of Virginia (F.F.V.), and lends scientific credibility to speculations in commodities as diverse as dogs, mothers, babies, slaves, signatures, fingerprints, and birthrights.

Critics often forget Percy Driscoll, younger brother of Judge Driscoll, actual father of Chambers and assumed father of Tom. This neglect is hardly surprising, since Percy Driscoll's funeral is announced at the end of chapter 4; his role seems to provide merely the means for Twain to help Roxy cover the tracks of her deception in switching the infants. Percy appears to be little more than a guywire in the general stage machinery of the drama. In customary fashion, Twain quickly makes Tom an orphan, whose adoption by his uncle and aunt helps emphasize his marginal familial status. In general, the unnatural bonds between children and nominal parents (aunts and uncles are customary) in Twain's fiction remind us that parent-child relations in such an artificial society are more conventional than natural. In *Huckleberry Finn*, parents repeatedly are exposed as inadequate for the most elementary tasks of child-rearing, as Huck's stories of abandoned, mistreated, and orphaned children attest.[7]

In *Pudd'nhead Wilson*, the distance between parents and children is made even more explicit. Raised by slaves, ignored by their white parents, the children of slaveowners have more in common with the slaves than their own parents. Given the long history of unacknowledged miscegenation, slaves like Roxy may be as little as "one-sixteenth black," so that her own child is "thirty-one parts white," even though he remains "by a fiction of law and custom a negro" (PW, 9). In view of such circumstances, it is hardly surprising that Percy Driscoll might have difficulty telling his own child apart from Roxy's, but Twain adds that Percy is also easily tricked because he has little familiarity with his own child. Describing Roxy's child, Twain notes: "He had blue eyes and flaxen curls, like his white comrade, but even the father of the white child was able to tell the children apart—little as he had commerce with them—by their clothes: for the white babe wore ruffled soft muslin and a coral necklace, while the other wore merely a coarse tow-linen shirt which barely reached to its knees and no jewelry" (9)

It is common enough to comment that the only difference between these two children is their dress, signifying class in the perfectly conventional manner so likely to be satirized by Twain. Yet, there are two other observations worth making at this point. First, the close resemblance between Tom and Chambers, especially in a novel so obsessed with twins and doubles, encourages us to think at this early stage in the narrative that they share the same father. This expectation is only partially frustrated by Roxy's confession to Tom that his father was Colonel Cecil Burleigh Essex, another F.F.V. in Dawson's Landing. By chapter 9, when Roxy tells Tom who his father was, we are not likely to trust much of what Roxy says; indeed, the pride with which she tells Tom suggests at least delusions of grandeur if not outright deception on her part. Percy Driscoll and Colonel Cecil Burleigh Essex die conveniently in the same season and paragraph: "There were two grand funerals in Dawson's Landing that fall—the fall of 1845. One was that of Colonel Cecil Burleigh Essex, the other that of Percy Driscoll" (22).

The only other mention of the Colonel is made in Twain's introduction of the chief citizens of Dawson's Landing in chapter 1: "Then there was Colonel Cecil Burleigh Essex, another F.F.V. of formidable calibre—however, with him we have no concern" (PW, 4). This mysterious character often has troubled critics. Why introduce him, if he is to play no other role in the narrative than to provide the name of Tom's white father? And why dismiss him so hastily, if the entire plot depends on family origins? On the other hand, his name, title, and convenient death in the same season as Percy Driscoll's provide Roxy with an excellent means of protecting herself. If we assume that Tom is the natural son of Percy Driscoll and Roxy, then we might conclude that Tom would have less to fear were Roxy to expose his true identity to Judge Driscoll. Mindful of the scandal such miscegenation in his own family might cause, Judge Driscoll would be likely to reach a settlement with Tom, albeit hardly one comparable to the inheritance that Tom expects from his uncle. On the other hand, exposed as the bastard child of Cecil Burleigh Essex and Roxy, Tom could expect little from Judge Driscoll other than prompt sale down the river.

Assuming that Tom is at least possibly the illegitimate son of Percy Driscoll, we may also suggest that he is but one part of Percy's general speculations. The younger brother of Judge Driscoll has little commerce with his only surviving heir, leaving him to the care of Roxy, not only because Mrs. Percy Driscoll dies "within the week" of the child's birth, but also because "Mr. Driscoll soon absorbed himself in his speculations" and left Roxy "to her own devices" with the children (PW, 5). Percy Driscoll's financial speculations have a central part to play in the plot, even though they are mentioned so early in the narrative as to be forgotten by the end. Roxy's plan to switch the babies is motivated principally by the fear inspired by her master's threat to sell all his slaves "down the river," unless the one who has stolen a "small sum of money" confesses to the theft (9). As Twain points out, "all were guilty but Roxana," and Twain goes on to explain the unwritten custom by which Southern servants were entitled to take small items—generally food or supplies—without punishment. Such informal servants' "rights" (sometimes called "smouching rights") are still in effect in the South, so Percy Driscoll's anger over that missing money seems extreme, if not indecorous. It is possible that his anxiety reflects the urgent circumstances of his own finances. Once Roxy has switched the babies, she is saved from the risk of the master's close attention to such domestic matters by his preoccupation with business: "For one of his speculations was in jeopardy, and his mind was so occupied that he hardly saw the children when he looked at them, and all Roxy had to do was to get them both into a gale of laughter when he came about them; then their faces were mainly cavities exposing gums" (16).

Further problems with this speculation force Percy and Judge Driscoll to leave Dawson's Landing for seven weeks, further assuring the success of Roxy's deception: "Within a few days the fate of the speculation became so dubious that Mr. Percy went away with his brother the Judge, to see what could be done with it. It was a land speculation, as usual, and it had gotten complicated with a lawsuit. The men were gone seven weeks. Before they got back, Roxy paid her visit to Wilson and was satisfied" (16). By the time he dies in 1845, "Percy Driscoll had worn himself out in trying to save his great speculative landed estate, and had died without succeeding. He was hardly in his grave before the boom collapsed and left his hitherto envied young devil of an heir a pauper" (PW, 22).

Percy Driscoll's speculations in real estate recall, of course, John Clemens' bequest to his family of 100,000 acres in the Knobs of Tennessee (for which he paid $400.00), as well as his financial failure in Hannibal. The legendary "Tennessee land," with its fabled natural resources and excellent location, haunted the Clemens' family for many years after the father's death. It is the same land that Squire Hawkins buys at the beginning of *The Gilded Age* and becomes the focus of the plot in Warner's and Twain's ruthless satire of the speculative economy of postbellum America. Twain's mother and his brother, Orion, floated any number of grandiose schemes on the promise of that Tennessee land, most of which was sold off in small parcels over the years to meet the family's urgent needs. In *The Gilded Age*, the Hawkins' land in the Knobs of East Tennessee becomes the center of an elaborate congressional swindle, engineered by two of the Hawkins' children, Colonel Sellers, and Senator Dilworthy. The Senator sponsors a bill for the government purchase of the land as the site for the "Knobs Industrial University," which would be "open to all persons without distinction of sex, color or religion," and whose principal purpose would be the educational emancipation of African-American men and women (GA, 311, 312). That this colossal swindle trades on public sentiments for the improvement of the educational and economic opportunities of emancipated African Americans in postbellum America is obvious enough; that slaves and free African Americans share the common fate of being commodities in speculative America is somewhat less obvious.

What finally caused Judge Clemens' financial ruin remains somewhat unclear, although Twain refers in his *Autobiography* and the sketch, "The Villagers," to the debt on which Ira Stout defaulted and which Judge Clemens had co-signed as guarantor. Dixon Wecter notes that there is no surviving record of any default by Stout that also involved Judge Clemens.[8] Nevertheless, one of the several subplots of *The Gilded Age* concerns the romance between Philip Sterling and Ruth Bolton, whose father, despite being a Quaker and a lawyer, is ruined several times by his friend, Bigler, who repeatedly talks him into providing surety for Bigler's many speculative schemes.

Judge Clemens' financial plight was so extreme by 1841 that he and Jane had to sell their interest in their home and lot; in the same period, "the Clemenses parted with their slave girl Jennie, . . . whom the Judge had once whipped, but who had served as 'mammy' to Sam and the other young children."[9] This was the same domestic slave that Twain recalls his father selling to his business associate, Beebe, who subsequently sold her down the river. In "The Villagers," Twain writes: "Was seen years later, ch[ambermaid] on a steamboat. Cried and lamented."[10] At least in some sense, Roxy, Percy Driscoll, and Judge Driscoll have biographical origins in Twain's recollections of his personal family circumstances in Florida and Hannibal, Missouri in the 1830s and 1840s, just as the "Tennessee Land" and various speculative schemes in *The Gilded Age* explicitly satirize his father's cursed bequest to his family.[11]

Besides Ira Stout's financial irresponsibility, what most likely wrecked Judge Clemens' speculations in vacant land and "rental properties along Hill and Main" in Hannibal was the ten-year depression that followed the Panic of 1837. Most of the speculative ferment in the United States in the 1830s was sparked by the promise of the vast frontier, so that speculators invested heavily in canal projects, early rail and other transportation ventures, as well as in land that would be in the path of westward expansion. Andrew Jackson attempted to control land speculation by issuing the "Specie Circular" of 1836, which required "specie payment for public land." The economic consequences of this act were declining prices for land, pressures on banks holding government funds, and subsequent bank failures in many states.[12] Missouri was still primarily an undeveloped part of the frontier in 1837, and it consequently suffered less than eastern states committed to ambitious canal and railroad developments. Even so, the Panic of 1837 and the depression that followed it had national consequences, severest for those who had staked their fortunes to speculative enterprises. The Panic of 1837 falls precisely between the births of Tom and Chambers in 1830 and the death of Percy Driscoll, who is ruined by his land speculation, in 1845.

Roxy's switching of the babies is itself a speculative venture, a gamble against the chances of being discovered and thus "sold down the river" for her sins. What prompts her rebellious action is the master's threat to sell all his slaves down the river, a threat that we have suggested may well be caused more by his own financial reverses than mere arbitrariness. Roxy's "venture" with such modest human "capital" is little more than an imitation of what white masters do with humans treated as commodities under slavery, risking that the African-American child will grow to become a valuable property from a relatively small investment. Virtually "born" (born *again*?) of this speculative enterprise, which like most of Roxy's actions imitates white men's behavior, Tom would seem to have the proper background for a gambler.

Twain is careful to tell us, however, that Tom learns to gamble at Yale, because he wants the reader to be certain not to associate Tom's vices with his African-American heritage. His gambling is his "inheritance" from his white father, whether "Cecil Burleigh Essex" or Percy Driscoll. Land speculation and gambling go hand-in-hand, of course, and the Western folk-myth of the Mississippi gambler has its origins in the gamblers and speculators who did business on the steamboats that were so crucial to the commercial development of Missouri from 1820 to 1865.[13] Tom's gambling is part of his effort to play the role of the Southern aristocrat with disposable income and leisure time, but it also associates him with the new economy fuelled by speculators and get-rich-quick artists from Eastern urban centers of banking and finance.

That Tom learns to gamble at Yale should not surprise readers of *The Gilded Age*, in which the two most naive speculators, Philip Sterling and Henry Brierly, were classmates at Yale. Henry's first words are, "Oh, it's easy enough to make a fortune," and he sends them both on the road to ruin by vaguely asking Philip, "Well, why don't you go into something? You'll never dig it out of the Astor Library" (GA, 95). As a couple of Eastern swells, Philip and Henry epitomize "the young American," to whom "the paths to fortune are innumerable and all open; there is invitation in the air and success in all his wide horizon" (GA, 95). Although Warner and Twain make their own capital out of Senator Dilworthy's fraudulent scheme for the "Knobs Technical University," they repeatedly compare its innovative technical curriculum with models in Switzerland and Germany. Indeed, part of the cleverness of the plan for this university is that it *does* propose the sort of educational institution that Twain and Warner would consider enlightened. By contrast, the liberal arts education offered at nineteenth-century Yale would seem to encourage nothing other than the vague expectations and romantic ideals of young fops like Henry Brierly and Philip Sterling, each of whom learns ultimately the hard realities of this speculative economy.[14] Like Percy Driscoll's land speculation, Tom's gambling jeopardizes his estate and thus the Driscolls' social authority. All of Tom's criminal actions are designed to cover his debts and thus assure his inheritance from Judge Driscoll. The child of speculating parents and of a speculative era and region, Tom fulfills that destiny by repeating in his own character the economic failures that punctuated the American economy from the Panic of 1837 to the Panics of 1873 and 1893.

Indeed, *Pudd'nhead Wilson* was written on the verge of the Panic of 1893 (and rewritten and proofed during the Panic), which was the final blow to Twain's publishing company, Webster and Company, and his dreams for the commercial success of the Paige Typesetter. Twain returned from Europe in the middle of the Panic, and he "couldn't borrow a penny."[15] Everything that he and Warner had predicted in *The Gilded Age* had come to pass with a vengeance, so it is hardly surprising that the legal servitude of the African American in antebellum America should be confused so brilliantly with the economic servitude of Tom to the speculative interests of the new age. $80,000 in debt as a consequence of the failure of Webster and Company and the Paige Typesetter, Twain would work his way back to solvency only by repeating his father's own honorable payment of "a hundred cents on the dollar" of the debts he had collected half a century earlier.[16] As familiar as the story of Twain's business failure and moral triumph may be, its relevance to the economic themes in *Pudd'nhead Wilson* remains untold. That he *did* follow his father's example reveals more than just Twain's integrity; that repetition may well have suggested to him the perverse continuity between antebellum and postbellum America. The gulf separating "Old Times on the Mississippi" from the new, progressive America must have appeared much narrower than it once had seemed to Twain. Writing his early drafts of *Pudd'nhead Wilson* in Italy, where he had "exiled" himself and his family to try to "economize," Twain responded to the Panic of 1893 as if it were some perverse fate sent specifically to punish him. The agrarian institution of slavery had been replaced by the urban servitude of those victimized by a speculative economy. The fact that Twain was no mere innocent victim, but himself an active figure in the very speculative enterprises that Warner and he had so viciously criticized in the year of the last major American panic—the Panic of 1873— must have weighed heavily upon the writer's conscience. In this regard, Tom Driscoll and Percy Driscoll might be read allegorically as versions of Mark Twain and Judge John Clemens.[17]

Such an autobiographical allegory, however, is less interesting than the more general consequences of a narrative designed to reflect the continuity between an older slavery and the new slavery of urban economics. Tom and Percy are not the only characters affected by this speculative economy. Freed in Percy Driscoll's will, Roxy works for eight years (1845–1853) on a Mississippi steamboat, saving her money to provide herself with a modest income when she is too infirm (at 43!) to work any longer: "She had lived a steady life, and had banked four dollars every month in New Orleans as a provision for her old age. She said in the start that she had 'put shoes on one bar'footed nigger to tromple on her with', and that one mistake like that was enough; she would be independent of the human race thenceforth forevermore if hard work and economy could accomplish it" (PW, 33). As every reader will recall, she bids goodbye to her "comrades on the *Grand Mogul*," only to discover that the "bank had gone smash and carried her four hundred dollars with it" (33).

Had Roxy's modest savings remained safely in that New Orleans bank to pay her a poor return in interest as retirement income, she never would have returned to beg and threaten her natural son, Tom. Without the support of Roxy's intelligence and rage, Tom undoubtedly would have even more quickly caused his own financial ruin. Nevertheless, it is unlikely that he would have murdered his uncle or had his curious origins exposed. Quite obviously, both Roxy's vengeful authority and the rage inspired in Tom by her revelation of his black origins fuel his subsequent crimes in *Pudd'nhead Wilson*.[18] Giving quite so much weight to the economic "deus ex machina" of this New Orleans bank failure would, of course, be excessive, were it not that *Pudd'nhead Wilson* incorporates so many equally minor details regarding speculation, each of which has a rather significant effect on the plot.

Critics have often noticed that Roxy's character, as powerfully vengeful as it becomes in the narrative, is nonetheless governed consistently by the values of the white ruling class. Roxy's pride regarding Tom's high birth, her attendance at the duel between Judge Driscoll and Luigi, her hard work and economy while a chambermaid on the *Grand Mogul*, and her maternal sentiments for Tom—all of these somewhat questionable "virtues" identify her self-reliance as well as her criminal potential with white values. Writing in a period when white America addressed the "negro question" by calling in various ways for the religious, educational, and economic "reformation" of emancipated African Americans, Twain ruthlessly satirizes the ways in which the African American who would follow the customs of white America would end up victimized yet again, trapped in a new economic servitude that would continue to our own day. The free African American would share with the European immigrant and the naive young white American the fantastic promise of speculative, expanding America, only to become the agent of the same old thieving powers of the Eastern bankers and urban tycoons.

Such a gloomy scenario for the reconstruction of racial relations in the South and throughout postbellum America may also be said to carry its own racist undertone. At the moment that emancipation has been achieved by virtue of the sacrifices and struggles of white and African-American abolitionists and the military conflict of the Civil War, Twain suggests that it is all for naught, that African Americans will be quickly coopted to yet another system of bondage. Insightful as Twain's criticism of early modern American capitalism remains, it cannot be separated finally from Twain's assumption that African Americans would be passive victims of that economy.

Percy Driscoll dies in 1845, the year in which John L. O'Sullivan "coined the phrase Manifest Destiny . . . to promote the annexation of Texas."[19] As Michael Rogin reminds us, Manifest Destiny became the rallying cry of a short-lived group sponsored by O'Sullivan, "Young America," which "was militantly expansionist and Anglophobic," as well as in favor of "universal democracy, equality, and the overthrow of European kings."[20] In *Pudd'nhead Wilson*, the political enthusiasms of groups like "Young America" are satirized by the anti-temperance "Sons of Liberty," whose only rallying cry seems to be a drinking song. Even so, the liberal movements that supported Manifest Destiny and opposed slavery often claimed that the encouragement of Northern industrial interests in the course of westward expansion might provide the "answer" to slavery. Abolitionists knew that mere emancipation by law would not grant social and economic liberty to African Americans born and raised in slavery. New land and ambitious speculative ventures, including the railroads that would open the frontier, were often promoted on humanitarian grounds as promising employment and opportunity for freed slaves and other oppressed minorities. Roxy's hard-earned $400 is a small measure of the economic promise that Manifest Destiny might offer the freed slave; its loss in the bank's failure is Twain's satire of the economic realities that would disillusion free African Americans as well as European immigrants with the economic promise of American expansionism.

Roxy, Tom, and Percy are not the only speculators in *Pudd'nhead Wilson*. David Wilson, "a young fellow of Scotch parentage . . . had wandered to this remote region from his birth-place in the interior State of New York, to seek his fortune. He was twenty-five years old, college-bred, and had finished a post-college course in an eastern law school a couple of years before" (5). Like Philip Sterling in *The Gilded Age*, David Wilson lacks the obvious trappings of the fortune-hunter; Philip's friend Henry Brierly, in contrast, spends with virtual abandon others' money on hotel rooms and fancy dinners. Brierly is a youthful Colonel Sellers, whereas Sterling and Wilson have the modest qualities and potential virtues of the honest laborers Twain admires. Even so, both Sterling and Wilson are lured to the frontier of Missouri by the promise of fortune. It is only as a consequence of Wilson's apparently casual remark about the dog that he is condemned to hang out a shingle and try the practice of law, then the more modest professions of surveying and accounting.[21]

Even so, all of the three professions Wilson attempts to practice in Dawson's Landing are dependent upon the speculative economy of the region. Like the Kentuckians who came to Missouri in the 1820s and 1830s with capital and slaves, David Wilson, who is from New York state, "had a trifle of money when he arrived, and he bought a small house on the extreme western verge of the town" (PW, 6). That this "small house" is next-door to Judge Driscoll's house suggests that Wilson's "trifle of money" is somewhat greater than Twain leads us to believe. Arriving in Dawson's Landing to profit from the modest development boom of the years following the admission of Missouri to the Union (1821), Wilson virtually announces himself as a speculator and fortune-hunter in his "deadly remark": " 'I wish I owned half of that dog' " (5). Only a fool or a speculator would think in terms of "half-interest" in a dog, and the townfolks' judgment of Wilson's certain folly reflects their reliance on the customs of an older, landed economy.

Unable to practice law on account of this foolish remark, Wilson does occasional surveying and accounting, occupying his "rich abundance of idle time" with the "universe of ideas," notably his experiments in palmistry (PW, 7). In *The Gilded Age*, Colonel Sellers always has some new invention underway, ranging from eye-drops to stoves. Scientific experimentation and speculation go hand-in-hand for Twain, whose own experiences with the Paige Typesetter and fascination with inventions of all sorts are notorious features of his biography. Although Twain respected inventiveness and the technology it promoted, he had good reason to be suspicious of the inflated expectations that the scientific spirit brought to America. Wilson and Judge Driscoll are both "free-thinkers," by which we assume they are mild agnostics, but "free thinking" in general is mercilessly indicted in *The Gilded Age* as one of the sources for the unchecked speculative "instinct" (as Twain and Warner call it) in modern industrial America.

David Wilson and Tom Driscoll are frequently contrasted by critics, who follow Twain's own lead in calling attention to Wilson's rise at the expense of Tom's fall. Because Wilson attracts our sympathies with the satiric humor of his "calendar" and his generally marginal status in Dawson's Landing, modern readers have been quick to associate him with Twain's own views. Thus George Spangler suggests that Tom's greed anticipates the rampant materialism of the Gilded Age, whereas Wilson's "disinterestedness and immaterialism" are tokens of an alternative that we ought to associate with Twain's ideal.[22] Such interpretations have always foundered on the simple fact that David Wilson uses his experiments in fingerprinting not merely to "solve" the murder of Judge Driscoll and save the innocent Luigi from hanging, but that these same experiments are given legal status in a case that allows the townspeople to attribute such criminality to Tom's African-American heredity. David Wilson's "triumph," as the new mayor of the newly-chartered city of Dawson's Landing, as courtroom lawyer and expert witness, even as amateur sleuth, is perhaps the most perverse heroic conclusion in modern literature.

Tom twice associates Wilson's forensic work with his fingerprints as "his palace-window decorations," and Wilson himself declares in court that he knows these "signatures . . . as well as the bank cashier knows the autograph of his oldest customer" (105, 109–10). Wilson's idle "speculation" in "paw prints" clearly assumes more than just *economic* value by the time he has solved the crime; his scientific "knowledge" of the origins and identity of any man so recorded is comparable to that of the absolute authorities of the European monarch or the American judge. In the speculative economy of the Gilded Age, no one's identity will be subject to the customary tests—the property, social habits and company, and local history that had given a man reputation and thus identity in older, small-town America. In this new world of changeable roles, ever-new schemes, and both geographical and social mobility, men and women will be known only in their styles and fashions. Only a Colonel Sellers, whose "absolute" is paradoxically his infinitely malleable rhetoric (his only enduring capital), will have a character, but the word will thus assume its idiomatic meaning: "Oh, *what a character!*"

At the dawn of such an era, Wilson's idle speculation in fingerprints, an avocation that is until the trial apparently useless, becomes the capital of the law, the scientific basis for judging human actions and relating those actions to larger sociohistorical forces. When Tom murders the Judge, Tom is disguised as an African American (he has blackened his face with charcoal); when he flees the scene, he is disguised as a girl. These masks are the proper murderers, who take their revenge against the master who has stolen both the African-American's man's liberty and exploited both white and African-American women. These exploited "halves" of the slave, especially as they are prompted by the justifiable rage of Roxy, are the avenging angels of Tom's apparently individual and criminal act. It is worth noting at this point, that Twain's literary style enables us to make such connections between individual characters and their socially symbolic acts, in ways that are distinctly different from the "writing" of David Wilson's dramatic pantographs. Wilson introduces a "scientific" measurement of personality that extends the commodification of human beings under slavery to the general economy of America; it has rightly been compared with the pseudo-scientific theories of race that were developed in late-nineteenth-century

America. Aware of the writer's complicity in the corruptions of the new economy (Philip Sterling, for example, initially wants to be a writer), Twain is at some pains to distinguish his own tall tales from the inflated rhetoric of Colonel Sellers or the courtroom histrionics of David Wilson.

A reasonable objection to this argument is that Wilson does indeed save Luigi from conviction for Judge Driscoll's murder, but the fact that Luigi is held legally responsible for this murder depends upon another of the many hypocrisies of Dawson's Landing. We must remember that while Wilson runs for mayor, the Italian twins are running for seats as aldermen. Judge Driscoll and Tom are reconciled as father and son during the campaign by virtue of their "election labors" to defeat the twins. What Twain calls twice their "hard work" includes spending "money . . . to persuade voters" and the Judge's "closing speech of the campaign," which is notable for the inflated rhetoric by which it offers a "character assassination" of the twins. Previously associated with the new speculative economy only in the help he gives his brother, the Judge is in this context directly linked with what Warner and Twain consider two of the most insidious effects of the "speculative instinct": exaggerated, romantic rhetoric (hyperbole) and vote-buying.[23] Having "scoffed at them as adventurers, mountebanks, side-show riff-raff, dime-museum freaks," the Judge closes by claiming that "the reward offered for the lost knife was humbug and buncombe, and that its owner would know where to find it whenever he should have the occasion *to assassinate somebody*" (83). The Judge's accusation invokes the *code duello* of the region, and it is the *Judge* who refuses Count Luigi's challenge, declining "to fight with an assassin—'that is . . . in the field of honor' " (PW, 92). Wilson then explains the significance of the Judge's refusal to Count Luigi: "The unwritten law of this region requires you to kill Judge Driscoll on sight, and he and the community will expect that attention at your hands—though of course your own death by his bullet will answer every purpose. Look out for him! Are you heeled—that is, fixed?" (93). Nothing could be stranger, of course, than the newly elected mayor explaining the murderous intent of the town's judge to his intended victim! But even granting the absurdity of this "unwritten law of the region" and the circumstances of its narration, we are bound to wonder why Luigi is at risk for his life in the trial from which Wilson nominally "saves" him. Given the circumstances of such an "unwritten law," Luigi certainly has the reasonable argument of "self-defense," whether Tom's criminality is revealed or not.

Unfortunately, Twain provides no explicit motivation for Wilson's defense of Luigi other than his immediate perception that "neither of the Twins" made the marks on the knife handle (97). The motives for Wilson's triumphant revelation of Tom's identity in the courtroom, however, have often been interpreted as part of Wilson's bid for legitimacy with the townspeople of Dawson's

Landing. Until his murder, Judge Driscoll was Wilson's protector and guarantor of his rights in town. In fact, the Judge's paternal concern for Wilson, this aspiring lawyer, perversely doubles the Judge's relation to his stepson and nephew, Tom. Without this surrogate father, Wilson must legitimate his new role as mayor, which he does not only by assuming legal authority in the courtroom but also by "saving" Luigi. Luigi is, of course, no more saved by Wilson than Jim is saved by Tom and Huck at the end of *Huckleberry Finn*, but the irony of this salvation is that it causes Luigi and Angelo to "weary of Western adventure" and return "straightaway . . . to Europe" (114). Although Wilson and the twins run for different civic positions, Twain announces the results of the election in terms that suggest syntactically their competition: "Wilson was elected, the twins were defeated—crushed, in fact, and left forlorn and substantially friendless" (84). That the Judge would suspect these two foreigners of being charlatans, all the while being surrounded by a society based on fraud—whether that of slavery or the new speculative economy—fits perfectly Twain's satiric purposes. The fact that Wilson's hard work—the first he performs in the narrative—in saving Luigi, revealing Tom as a slave, and turning the hapless "Chambers" into a white heir helps restore order in this small community remains far more troublesome.

For Wilson is no "mysterious stranger" sent to Dawson's Landing to reveal its own unconscious lie. What Wilson helps accomplish is hardly that familiar "disturbance" in Twain's other small towns that provokes some searching re-examination of their social values and contracts. Wilson proves himself to be not only a proper gentleman but also a leader, who will carry this town into its urban era in the wake of the new economics that would sweep America in the course of the Civil War and its aftermath. In this sense, Wilson is the appropriate heir to the arbitrary authority represented by Judge Driscoll and the F.F.V.s. Wilson is the accountant who helps make possible the correct accounting of Percy Driscoll's mortgaged and speculative estate. Wilson's palmistry is a new "science" of human accounting that promises the effective translation of the chattel of slavery into the commodity of labor manipulated by the urban speculator. Roxy, that wily imitator of the white man's slickest tricks, convinces her son to sell her down the river on the basis of a *forged bill of sale*. Tom's *signature* turns Roxy back into a salable commodity. Wilson melodramatically concludes his courtroom speech by commanding: "Valet de Chambre, negro and slave—falsely called Thomas à Becket Driscoll—make upon the window the finger-prints that will hang you!" (112).

For a second time, then, Tom's "signature' turns a human being into capital, which will in fact circulate by way of Percy Driscoll's creditors. Tom's forgery of his signature on his mother's bill of sale is, of course, doubly forged. Every signature of ownership on a slave deed must be a base forgery for Twain.

Industrial, speculative America would transform that "forged ownership" into the captial *naturally* authorized by the very body of its workers. In America of the Gilded Age, there will be yet other forgeries by means of which the fact of slavery will be transformed into the broken promises and elusive opportunities that would become the wages of the freed black and European immigrant. The profit earned from such a speculative accounting as David Wilson's is neither property nor cash; like the antebellum slaveowner, David Wilson plays for power and authority. The last we hear from Colonel Sellers in *The Gilded Age*, he is embarking on yet a new and even more vainglorious venture than any before it: "I've seen enough to show me where my mistake was. The law is what I was born for. I shall begin the study of the law . . . . There's worlds of money in it! whole worlds of money! . . . Climb, and climb, and climb—and wind up on the Supreme bench. . . . A made man for all time and eternity!" (GA, 426). In the character of David Wilson, Colonel Sellers finds at last the profession and personality to which the speculator is born: philosopher, scientist, humorist, detective, lawyer, and mayor—America's Renaissance Man.

What, then, of "Pudd'nhead Wilson's Calendar" with its evocations of Twain's familiar skepticism and irony? The aphorisms still serve the purposes of Twain's general satire of Dawson's Landing, its slaveholding values, and the modern economy that it is entering. As David Wilson's "scratchings," such social and human criticism have become merely the "decorations" of a popular calendar, witty "saws" like the wisecrack about that dog. That his own skepticism and social criticism would become merely the "idle" pastimes of "freethinking" hypocrites like Judge Driscoll and David Wilson may well be Twain's deepest fear—and one realized in part in our postmodern economy, whose stock in trade may be the "wisecrack."

9 The Politics of Innocence: Henry James' *The American*

> Knowledge works as a tool of power. Hence it is plain that it increases with every increase of power—
>
> —Nietzsche, *The Will to Power*

> The Republic will now be in republican hands (till now it has been managed altogether by conservatives) and we shall see how it will behave. I hope for the best. I see none but ardent monarchists and hear everything vile said about the Republic but I incline to believe in it, nevertheless.
>
> —Henry James to Alice James, February 22, 1876

Henry James' *The American* incorporates so many conventions of the novel and the romance in such a bewildering manner that critics have been understandably preoccupied with assessing the formal consequences. The international theme has remained just that—a "theme" that helps critics organize the otherwise disparate parts of a work that begins realistically only to end with a flurry of melodramatic events. Yet, the political and historical aspects of the international theme were of considerable importance to Henry James as he began work on *The American* in the winter of 1875–1876. Having ventured to become recognized as an international writer, James was personally concerned with exploring the national constraints that he would have to overcome.[1]

Choosing to live in Europe, James was attempting to overcome the narrow provincialism that he imagined had limited Hawthorne's achievement.[2] Hawthorne typified for James the tendency of American romantics to substitute airy fancies and vague speculations for more substantial historical subjects and themes. In this regard, we may say that James in his turn typified a late nineteenth-century cosmopolitanism assumed by American intellectuals to declare their independence from their unworldly forebears. James belonged to the generation that would originate the myth of "New England Puritanism" as a legacy of passionless reflection and stubborn provincialism that extended from the early Bay colonists to the American transcendentalists. In his 1887 review of James Elliot Cabot's *A Memoir of Ralph Waldo Emerson*, James refers to "the white tint of Emerson's career," by which he means that: "Passions, alternations, affairs, adventures had absolutely no part in it. It stretched itself out in enviable quiet—a quiet in which we hear the jotting of the pencil in the notebook." Of course, it is the New England son who recoils in fear from this "life of New England fifty years ago" and the "achromatic picture" it paints "without particular intensifications."[3] James' oedipal anxieties about repeating the sober past of his New England forebears is at the heart of his caricatures of them.

By the same token, James did not want to surrender those American qualities he considered necessary for the development of a truly international outlook. Christopher Newman is the original type of the American businessman, who is so often criticized by James for his lack of artistic sensitivity, his blunt pragmatism, and his ignorance of the psychological complexity of human relations. Nevertheless, James does not systematically criticize American capitalism in his writings, and he seems especially sympathetic to certain features of the entrepreneur in his early works. In particular, James favors Newman with a vague republicanism and a respect for work of all kinds. I am tempted to add that James also admires the ignorance of class distinctions that allows Newman to threaten the stability of such closed societies as the legitimist aristocrats of the Bellegardes' circle. Yet, it is not the *ignorance* that James admires in Newman and the American modernity he promises; indeed, it is just this *ignorance* that James identifies as Newman's fatal flaw. What James himself hopes to achieve as an international writer is precisely what Newman fails to achieve in Europe: the *conscious* subversion of those provincial societies (in Europe and America) that legitimate the most unnatural and arbitrary systems of class distinctions. Such an ambition, James knows well enough, requires a thorough knowledge of both social forms and the political realities in which they are involved. Newman's innocence is not the same as the "white tint" of Emerson's New England, which has on its side a history of keen intelligences, however tied they might have been to home. Nevertheless, Newman's innocence may be for James a modern version of Emerson's: "Hawthorne's vision was all for the evil and sin of the world; a side of life as to which Emerson's eyes were thickly bandaged. There were points as to which the latter's conception of right could be violated, but he had no great sense of wrong—a strangely limited one, indeed, for a moralist—no sense of the dark, the foul, the base. There were certain complications in life which he never suspected."[4]

Critical discussions of *The American* customarily begin by equating Newman's innocence with his ignorance of the complex arts of European high society. Much of James' irony and social criticism focuses on the ambiguous distinction between ignorance and innocence, although the moral dimensions of this problem generally are better served in his writings by characters young enough to give some credibility to their innocence. Newman is thirty-six years old, has served in the army in the Civil War, has made a great fortune, and has experiences as vast the American West from which he comes.[5] Roderick Hudson, Isabel Archer, Hyacinth Robinson, the Governess in *The Turn of the Screw*, Milly Theale, Maggie Verver—these characters are much younger than Newman, both chronologically and in terms of experience. Like Lambert Strether in *The Ambassadors*, Newman is old enough to know better, which is to say that his innocence always appears to us as a slightly absurd naïveté.

Nevertheless, we are tempted to excuse Newman's ignorance on the grounds that he is in a foreign country. James introduces us to Newman as a caricature of the American tourist, exhausted by his efforts to comprehend the artistic sublimity of the Louvre. Marking his Baedeker, buying bad copies of masterpieces, counting the churches he has visited (he tells Valentin de Bellegarde that he has examined "some four hundred and seventy churches" in a single summer [83]), Newman is a clever parody of the tourist type. For that very reason, however, he is rather endearing and sympathetic to the reader, who undoubtedly has done something similar in one country or another.

Newman's ignorance of European customs is at least initially qualified by his eagerness to "get to know the people," in the old cliché of the guidebooks. Unlike his later avatar, Adam Verver, who ships crates of European art home for his museum in American City, Newman is not a mere collector and commodifier of experiences. Strictly speaking, Newman buys very little on his tour. In the first chapter, he buys Noémie Nioche's poor copy of Murillo's Madonna and then commissions her to paint an impossible number of other masterpieces, but he does so primarily to satisfy his curiosity regarding this young woman and her strange father. He also buys "a grotesque little statuette in ivory, of the sixteenth century" of "a gaunt, ascetic-looking monk" with "a fat capon hung round the monk's waist" (73). As a perverse present for the morally scrupulous (and very Emersonian) Benjamin Babcock, Newman's former travelling companion, the purchase gives substance to Newman's thought. In his first appearance in the Salon de Carré of the Louvre, Newman seems destined to be caricatured as a gross sensualist, bent on turning every experience into a possession, with his hand always reaching for his purse. Yet, as the drama unfolds, Newman seems to use his money in subtler ways to involve himself in the lives of others: "He liked doing things which involved his paying for people; the vulgar truth is that he enjoyed 'treating' them. This was not because he was what is called purse-proud; handling money in public was on the contrary positively disagreeable to him . . . . But just as it was a gratification to him to be handsomely dressed, just so it was a private satisfaction to him (he enjoyed it very clandestinely) to have interposed, pecuniarily, in a scheme of pleasure" (197). The confusion of selfishness and generosity in this passage says a good deal about Newman's difficulties with the Bellegardes and European society in general, but it refers to a man who is by no means a vulgar tourist intent on shipping his experiences home in a trunk.

We are encouraged, then, to understand Newman's naïveté as his unfamiliarity with European society, rather than the mere vulgarity of an acquisitive tourist or the inexperience of a raw youth. By "society," James customarily means all the inherited forms and styles, subtle codes and postures by which a particular group maintains its authority and coherence. For the Jamesian character to enter such a group, he must first study the complicated rules of inclusion and exclusion, then attempt to imitate the behavior prerequisite to initiation.[6] In the cases of those who subscribe to such artful customs, the cost of initiation is generally the loss of individual character and surrender to a prescribed role. Those who refuse to play by the rules and violate deliberately or unwittingly the necessary proprieties are generally exiled, killed, or otherwise sacrificed. Characters like Daisy Miller, Hyacinth Robinson, Milly Theale, or Charlotte Stant serve James primarily to expose the deadly formalism of these closed worlds. Innocent or stupid, deluded or misadvised, these characters are ultimately devices James employs to expose the hidden laws by which such societies maintain their exclusive authority.

Christopher Newman's innocence is far more complicated, however, than that of those victims sacrificed in the cause of James' social anatomies. For one thing, Newman is central to the dramatic action; he cannot be understood merely as a device to expose the Bellegardes. Unlike other relatively powerless innocents in James' fiction, Newman acts powerfully to change destinies, tempt characters with money and jobs, and offer them seemingly endless possibilities. He is not ignorant of the supersubtle psychologies of the other characters, even when he doesn't quite understand the motivations behind their behavior. Although James reminds us frequently that Newman has missed a deprecating look or a whispered joke at his expense, Newman still is conscious of significant glances, implied insults, and patronizing smiles.

As much as James' narrative depends upon the interplay between what *we* are allowed to see and Newman's much more limited, subjective views and opinions, we still understand Newman to be considerably more penetrating in his psychological judgments than the conventional Jamesian naif. He misjudges Noémie Nioche, for example, but he subsequently revises his opinion on the evidence of her actions and the advice of Valentin. Although he often stereotypes other characters (M. Nioche, Valentin, the younger marquise, Lord Deepmere, and others), he is also capable of remarkably accurate first impressions of such characters as the Marquis and his mother. In fact, James gives Newman a sort of uncanny prescience that often seems a function of his intuitive understanding of other characters. Shortly after he has been accepted as Claire's suitor, Newman judges the Marquis and his mother for Mrs. Tristram: "I shouldn't wonder if she had murdered some one—all from a sense of duty, of course" (151) and "If he has never committed murder, he has at least turned his back and looked the other way while someone else was committing it" (152). To be sure, Newman commits many errors in judging others and misses much of what goes on around him, but he is hardly the "great Western Barbarian" Mrs. Tristram knights him (42).

Nevertheless, Christopher Newman is profoundly naive, primarily because he remains so fatally ignorant of the forces governing the European social circle he wishes to enter. William Stowe claims that Newman's innocence is a consequence of his failure to understand "the importance of active social interpretation for the success of his project. [Balzac's] Rastignac knows that he must fathom the secret workings of Parisian society. Newman, by contrast, is content to sit back and be amused by the antics of his foreign friends, whom he sees as performers in a great comedy of manners, actors speaking lines learned by heart and hiding their 'true selves' beneath conventional masks."[7]

This strikes me as a very accurate assessment of Newman's failure, but it is just the sort of judgment that encourages readers to develop very abstract theories about appearance and reality, detachment and involvement, active understanding and passive resignation as central *themes* in James' fiction. I want to give particular concreteness to Stowe's insight by arguing that Newman's superficial observation of the Bellegardes is a consequence of his ignorance of the special role played by this family in French history and politics. Further, I shall argue that Newman's studied detachment from what the Bellegardes represent is finally part of an elaborate system of psychological defense by which Newman avoids recognizing in their aristocratic pretensions the distorted reflection of his own American identity. Newman serves James as a particular reminder that the great republican promise of the self-reliant American might end up merely repeating the rigid hierarchies of the European aristocracy. James Tuttleton succinctly describes the familiar problem James explored repeatedly in his international novels: "Instead of exploiting the freedom of a unique social experience to create beautiful, new, and distinctive social forms, Americans sought both to impose on the democratic New World an aristocratic social pattern developed in the Old World and, returning to the Old, to beat the Europeans on their own ground."[8] James makes it clear that such a repetition is directly proportionate to our ignorance of the political consequences of our ordinary acts. Finally, James recognizes in the secret alliances that bind together the legitimist and Ultramontanist families of the Bellegardes' circle that there are several kinds of "internationalism," not all of which encourage the liberal and republican values that James himself hoped to achieve in his own project as international modern.

Newman's ignorance of the particular psychological, cultural, and political forces governing the Bellegardes' social behavior is simply astounding when we consider how much Newman prides himself on being current. Other than his Baedeker, "the newspapers form" Newman's "principal reading."[9] Repeatedly, James tells us of Newman's fascination with "how things were done" (55). M. Nioche combs the bookstalls for almanacs and "began to frequent another *café*, where more newspapers were taken . . . to con the tattered sheets for curious anecdotes, freaks of nature, and strange coincidences," in order to fill the French lessons he is giving Newman with the kind of timely material Newman desires: "Newman was fond of statistics . . . it gratified him to learn what taxes were paid, what profits were gathered, what commercial habits prevailed, how the battle of life was fought" (55). During his courtship of Claire, Newman "explained to her, in talking of the United States, the working of various local institutions and mercantile customs" (150–51). Yet, for all of Newman's practical American "curiosity" about how everything works, he remains absurdly ignorant of the political situation of the family into which he plans to marry.

At the most elementary level, Newman pays little attention to the Bellegardes' religion: "He had never let the fact of her Catholicism trouble him; Catholicism to him was nothing but a name, and to express a mistrust of the form in which her religious feelings had moulded themselves would have seemed to him on his own part a rather pretentious affectation of Protestant zeal" (246). Even after Claire has entered the Carmelite convent in the rue de Messine, Newman cannot accept the reality of a strong, committed religious vocation: "It was like a page torn out of a romance, with no context in his own experience" (276). Yet, what American traveling in Europe in 1868–1869 would be so utterly ignorant of French history as not to understand the significance of religion in any proposal of marriage into an aristocratic family like the Bellegardes?

It is not until Newman's second visit to Madame de Cintré that he asks her: "Are you a Roman Catholic, madam?" (83), even though Mrs. Tristram already has given him a very precise account of Claire's religious and social backgrounds and associations (46–47). He asks this question rather idly, in the context of what appears a chatty conversation about the age of the house. Valentin has shown Newman the "sort of shield" above the chimney-piece that records the date 1627, and Valentin says: "That is old or new according to your point of view." Newman responds, "Well, over here . . . one's point of view gets shifted round considerably" (83). Valentin is speaking quite specifically of different political interests that might variously find their origins or ends in the date 1627. At the very least, Newman ought to make some connection between this date and the early years of the Puritan Bay Colony, but even more important than this American connection are the historical events of the war waged between 1624 and 1629 by Cardinal Richelieu against the Huguenots. Richelieu attempted to exterminate the Huguenots not simply as the major Protestant opposition to Catholicism in seventeenth-century France, but also as the religious basis for republican sympathies opposed to the monarchy.

Much later, Newman learns "from a guide-book of the province" that the Bellegardes' chateau at Fleurières "dated from the time of Henry IV" (237). Even so, the chateau strikes Newman as utterly "melancholy" and foreign, "like a Chinese penitentiary" (237). The date of the chateau further connects the Bellegardes with the Catholic and monarchical struggle against Protestantism and republicanism—a struggle that has particular relevance for Parisians on the eve of the Franco-Prussian War (1870–1871). Henry IV protected the civil rights of the Huguenots by issuing the Edict of Nantes in 1598, but Henry's assassination in 1610 brought Cardinal Richelieu to power during the regency of Louis XIII and virtually ended all hopes of a peaceful political settlement between the Catholic monarchists and the Huguenots. Some hint of these events is given in the architecture of the Bellegardes' chateau, which has "an immense facade of dark time-stained brick, flanked by two low wings, each of which terminated in a little Dutch-looking pavilion, capped with a fantastic roof" (237). These "ugly little cupolas" suggest Henry IV's futile effort to reconcile Catholics and Protestants, because it was to Holland that many of the 400,000 Huguenots fled when they were driven out of France on the revocation of the Edict of Nantes in 1685. From Holland, of course, many persecuted Huguenots emigrated to America, where they would find sympathy with other Puritans persecuted politically and religiously in Europe.

In another sense, the "little cupolas" are "ugly" because they don't "fit" the architecture of the Bellegardes' Catholic stronghold. Perhaps these architectural additions are meant to recall how the Catholics forced the Huguenots to surrender their fortified towns under the Peace of Alais in 1629. In any case, the mixed architecture of the chateau tells the story of the Catholic monarchists' claims to power in the stormy years of the seventeenth-century French religious wars. In her final interview with Newman, Claire explains herself only by saying, "Mr. Newman, it's like a religion. I can't tell you—I can't! . . . It's like a religion" (242). Try as he subsequently does to understand what Claire has said, Newman hasn't the vaguest idea that the connections established among religious beliefs, political positions, familial duties, and personal feelings could have any bearing on Claire's ultimate refusal of him.

When these old issues of seventeenth-century French history are discussed by critics, they are often used to associate the Bellegardes with a common theme in James' representation of the Old World. Even a critic as astute to historical details as John Antush places the greatest emphasis on a familiar but very general thesis about the "rise of the bourgeoisie."[10] Living in an impossibly remote past, bound tightly by anachronistic duties and obligations, the Bellegardes seem to anticipate such grotesques as Juliana and Tina Aspern, who repudiate the modern age only for the sake of entombment in a dead past. Thematizing the Bellegardes in this manner, critics quickly stereotype them and neglect the immediate relevance of seventeenth-century French religious and monarchical struggles for the conflicts between monarchists and republicans, Catholics and Protestants, clericals and anticlericals at the time James was writing the novel. Like Prince Casamassima, the Marquis and old Marquise are associated with reflex Catholicism, which in James' other works becomes a convenient tag for an old, impoverished, and powerless aristocracy.

The Bellegardes are by no means represented as powerless or impoverished, and they would appear to be intimately involved in the contemporary political scene, even if such involvement may be defined simply in the precise forms they maintain as the signs of their particular political affiliations. The Bellegardes are not simply aristocratic Catholics; they are monarchists who resist vigorously not just the modern age, but the specific politics of the republicans in the aftermath of the 1848 revolution. Their association with monarchists is even more specific: they are legitimists and Ultramontanes, as Mrs. Tristram clearly informs Newman in her first description of Claire and her ancestry (46–47). Shortly after the Marquis and his mother have accepted Newman as a suitor, Newman tries to establish a more personal relation with Claire's older brother by discussing politics: "Newman was far from being versed in European politics, but he liked to have a general idea of what was going on about him, and he accordingly asked M. de Bellegarde several times what he thought about public affairs. M. de Bellegarde answered with suave concision that he thought as ill of them as possible, that they were going from bad to worse, and that the age was rotten to its core" (153). As an important representative of his class and its specific politics, the Marquis is not so much offering an opinion as a formal statement.

Newman's elaborate rooms overlook the Boulevard Haussmann, but Newman seems unaware of the great transformation of Paris that Haussmann directed in the ten years following Louis Napoleon Bonaparte's seizure of power from the Second Republic in 1851. The modernization of Paris was not merely a grand public works' project; it was an effort to consolidate Louis Napoleon Bonaparte's authority in the aftermath of the republican uprisings of 1848. The broad, straight boulevards that Haussmann designed afforded more than the long perspectives admired by Newman; they made possible much more rapid mobilization of troops in the case of popular demonstrations. Modern Paris reveals in its very architecture and urban planning the general division of classes in mid-nineteenth-century France.[11] Apparently oblivious to all of this, Newman tries to call the Marquis' "attention to some of the brilliant features of the time," without realizing that such brilliance more likely than not would only sharpen the Marquis' sense of his embattled position as a monarchist of the old school.

On the evidence of Newman's apparent innocence of the political issues involved, the Marquis makes a very direct statement: "The marquis presently replied that he had but a single political conviction, which was enough for him: he believed in the divine right of Henry of Bourbon, Fifth of his name, to the throne of France" (153). Newman is neither "horrified nor scandalised, he was not even amused" by this declaration, but "after this he ceased to talk politics with M. de Bellegarde." James makes it clear that Newman judges such views the quaint reminders of a distant past with no relevance for the present: "He felt as he should have felt if he had discovered in M. de Bellegarde a taste for certain oddities of diet; an appetite, for instance, of fishbones and nutshells. Under these circumstances, of course, he would never have broached dietary questions with him" (153). What is particularly remarkable is the degree to which Newman judges such views to be peculiar personal idiosyncrasies, like dietary habits.

Nevertheless, the Bellegardes belong to a very well-defined and active political minority in nineteenth-century France. As *legitimists*, the Bellegardes support the royal claims of Henri Charles Ferdinand (1820–1883), who styled himself "Henry V" and was the legitimist pretender until his death. The younger Bourbon line of the House of Orléans had come to power during the Revolution of 1830 when Louis Philippe (1773–1850) was named King by the revolutionaries after Charles X had been deposed. Louis Philippe was himself deposed in the Revolution of 1848, but Orléanists' claims to power were maintained by a succession of pretenders between 1848 and 1873, when Louis Philippe Albert (1838–1894), the grandson of King Louis Philippe, relinquished his claim to the throne in favor of the legitimist pretender, Henri Charles Ferdinand, known as the Comte de Chambord as well as "Henry V." The controversies between the legitimists and Orléanists in the period following 1848 turned primarily on the more general disputes between clericals and anticlericals in the nineteenth century. The Orléanists had already made a shaky alliance with republicans in the Revolution of 1830, but the legitimists remained stubbornly opposed to any reconciliation with republican or liberal politics. Unlike the Orléanists, the legitimists worked to build an international power-base centered in the pope's temporal and spiritual authority in Rome. They aligned themselves (and were often the same as) those *Ultramontanes* ("beyond the mountains"—referring to Rome as their ultimate authority) who worked in the nineteenth century to protect the temporal power of the papacy and dreamed of a Europe united along the lines of the ancient Holy Roman Empire and under the papacy's absolute sovereignty.

Although there is no specific evidence associating the Tristrams with Orléanist circles, there is a strong sense in the novel that the Tristrams and Bellegardes belong to very different social sets. Customarily, this social distance, especially between the old school friends, Claire and Lizzie, is explained in terms of the extremely exclusive aristocratic order of the Bellegardes, and the relative modesty of the Tristrams' social connections. Tom Tristram is so self-indulgent as to make any attempt to connect him with politics seem ludicrous. Nevertheless, he fits almost perfectly the "type" of American expatriate James describes in several contemporary letters in the following manner: "A type I have little esteem for is the American Orléanist of whom I have seen several specimen [sic]. Of all the superfluous and ridiculous mixtures it is the most so."[11] There is at least the hint, then, that the Tristrams are associated with those Orléanists who sought alliances with French republicans and foreign democrats. Needless to say, the Bellegardes would hold the frivolity of such allies in considerable contempt and rightly so in James' view.

The French republican revolution of 1848 spread liberal, anti-Bourbon sympathies to Germany, Austria, and Italy. The ducal line of Bourbon-Parma and the royal line of the Two Sicilies connected the French Bourbon legitimists with imperial claims in Spain and Italy as well as with the Holy See. The Italian Risorgimento focused republican antagonism against the Church and the Bourbons, notably in the famous expedition of Garibaldi's One Thousand that overthrew the Bourbon government of Sicily and Naples in 1860. Between 1860 and 1870, Pope Pius IX (r. 1846–1878) was continually under siege from republican Italian troops intent on reclaiming Papal territories in Italy. Only French troops sent to Rome by Napoleon III prevented Pius from being stripped utterly of his temporal power until 1870, when France's losses in the Franco-Prussian War (notably the Battle of Sedan) forced the withdrawal of its troops from Rome.

Valentin tells Newman early in the novel: "The only thing I could do was to go and fight for the pope. That I did, punctiliously, and received an apostolic flesh-wound at Castelfidardo. It did neither the Holy Father nor me any good, that I could see. . . . I passed three years in the Castle of St. Angelo, and then came back to secular life" (93). Valentin's bitter irony says a good deal more about the political situation in Europe than Newman comprehends. In the first place, Valentin served the pope as a Zouave, mercenaries recruited from French soldiers in Rome in 1860, under General L. C. Léon Juchault de Lamoricière, to serve as personal defenders of the pope. On August 28, 1860, Italian republican ambassadors requested Napoleon III's permission to invade the Papal States, which separated the northern states, unified in April as "Victor Emmanuel's kingdom," and the Kingdom of Naples to the south, where Garibaldi's forces were fighting the Bourbons. "*Bonne chance, mais faites vites*," Napoleon III was reputed to have told them, acknowledging that his permission was a betrayal of legitimist interests in France. Only a quick Italian victory might save the French emperor from the possibility of growing opposition at home. The Piedmontese army moved south, encountering only pockets of resistance from the papal army. The only significant clash in this first advance occurred in the small village of Castelfidardo on the Adriatic coast. The military annexation of the Papal States, together with Garibaldi's military successes in the South, marked the beginning of a genuinely unified Italy and the virtual end of the pope's temporal authority in Europe.[13]

It is little wonder that the Duchess and others in the Bellegardes' circle trade stories about snubs or insults given to "the great Napoleon" (290). Undoubtedly Napoleon III of the Second Empire is the object of their abuse, since he had helped precipitate the collapse of Bourbon and papal power in one swift decision. Only a year after the end of the action of *The American*, in 1870, the Zouaves in Rome would be overrun by Italian troops, thus concluding formally the pope's rule of any political territory in Europe, except for the one square mile granted him as "Vatican City." Mobilized for action in the Franco-Prussian War, the Zouaves were disbanded after the French surrender to the Germans in 1871. Thus Valentin is associated not merely with the "battlefield" and a "dying aristocracy," as critics have been fond of noting; he is associated with the sharp reverses to legitimist hopes that accompanied the Italian Risorgimento. The embattled position of French legitimists is in some measure reflected by the situation of the Catholic Church. While the republican troops invaded Rome, the ecumenical council was meeting to issue that monument to the Church's defensive position in the nineteenth century: the Dogma of Papal Infallibility issued in 1870.

I cannot fully reconstruct here the complex history of the legitimist supporters of the Bourbon line in the stormy years of European history following the Revolution of 1848, but these familiar details of that history should suggest that the legitimists' concerns about their vanishing political power in France, their stubborn resistance to alliances with republicans (variously negotiated in the same period by Orléanists), and their vain hopes of establishing an international power-base that would restore Papal rule of Europe has considerable relevance for Newman's little romance in the winter of 1868–1869. Only one year later, France would go to war with Germany primarily over the threat of a Hohenzollern assuming the Spanish Crown and thus surrounding France to the east *and* the south with Prussian rule. Yet, the political concerns fueling the Franco-Prussian War went considerably beyond the military jeopardy posed to France by a Prussian's accession to the Spanish throne. In the minds of many Frenchmen, the idea behind this political maneuvering was the Austro-Germanic dream of reviving the old Holy Roman Empire under German and *Protestant* authority.

In the midst of these ongoing power struggles and on the eve of open hostilities between France and Germany, the Bellegardes represent an embattled political force in contemporary France. In the letters Henry James wrote for the New York *Tribune* between 1875–1876, while he was working on *The American*, he pays special attention to the effects of political life in Paris on the arts and high society. As Leon Edel notes, the *Tribune* "was not relying upon James for its French news coverage; for that it had the seasoned William H. Huntington, and for political stories it could also call upon the services of John Paul. James was free to deal with whatever struck his fancy in the Parisian scene."[14] Even so, James begins many of his letters (especially the first nine or so) with fairly detailed accounts of political events. Familiar with legitimist opposition to the newly elected republican majority, he calls repeatedly for liberal toleration of this and other conservative minorities in France. The abortive republican commune of 1870, provoked by Napoleon III's disastrous losses in the first stages of the Franco-Prussian War, had resulted in a conservative backlash at the end of the War. The National Assembly of 1871 was Catholic and royalist, and the Bourbon pretender, Henry V, was very nearly restored to power.

The return of republicans to political power during James' year in Paris brought with it a particularly vehement liberal anticlericalism. The rapid changes in the political revenge drama acted out in France after the Franco-Prussian War has certain similarities with the cycles of revenge that organize the plot of *The American*.[15] Throughout the nineteenth century, Catholics had struggled to maintain the freedom of their schools; freedom of primary teaching had been granted them in 1833, and freedom of secondary teaching with the Failloux Act of 1850. But republican fears of a legitimist restoration of the Bourbon monarchy in the 1870s fueled an anticlericalism that focused on the freedom of Catholic education in France.

Léon Gambetta (1838–1882) was a political moderate, except in his vigorous opposition to the Ultramontanes and legitimists. In his letters for the *Tribune*, James criticizes Gambetta's opposition to the Catholic University— that is, opposition to the toleration of Catholic education at the university level. We ought to recall that the Hotel de Bellegarde is located in the rue de l'Université. It *is* an important street in the aristocratic neighborhood of the Faubourg St.-Germain, but James' selection of it may well be intended to evoke the current clerical and legitimist claims for freedom of Catholic universities. In his letter of March 4, 1876, James writes:

> M. Gambetta has just been making an eloquent speech at Lille . . . . It is all very reasonable as well as eloquent, save in so far as it commits the liberal program to antagonism to the new Catholic University. M. Gambetta denounces in violent terms the admission of the Church to a share in the superior instruction. This is a point on which many sagacious Republicans distinctly differ with him. . . . If I were a Frenchman I am inclined to think that I should feel more at my ease in a republic in which the Catholic party was allowed to carry on, in competition with the Sorbonne and the Collège de France, as successful and satisfactory a university as it could, than in a republic in which it was silenced and muzzled and forced to disseminate its instruction through private channels. It is hard to imagine a Catholic university, with the full light of our current audacity of opinion beating down upon it, proving very dangerous. (PS, 75)

Leon Edel suggests that James' "typically American point of view" in this passage prevented him from fully understanding "how much more difficult such a question was in a context of European politics than of American" (PS, 177). In particular, Edel notes how the Catholic University issue is linked with the larger claims by legitimists and Ultramontanes for an authority outside France: "The Church was not only competing in the matter of education, but was trying to make France the defender of papal interests against the new Italian kingdom and against Bismarck's *Kulturkampf* in Germany" (PS, 177). James' proposal for republican toleration of Catholic legitimists is not as self-evidently naive as Edel suggests, although it certainly betrays a rather idealistic faith in the model of American democracy at this early stage in James' career. James confidently assumes that a free democracy defends itself best by granting freedom of speech to those minority views that challenge the ruling government. James concludes that such a free exchange in France would prove the superiority of the republicans' liberalism over the Catholic legitimists' narrower concerns. It is also possible that James understood how much more dangerous repressed minorities can be to a government than those openly tolerated. Republican persecution of the legitimists and clericals *did* drive them into foreign alliances that were not in the best interests of the French nation. Indeed, the secrecy and exclusiveness of the legitimists have some affinity with the secrecy and privacy of the Bellegardes in *The American*. James' position regarding the Catholic university issue expressed his commitments to open political debate and the citizen's right to be informed of all conflicting views, in order to make intelligent political choices.

Above all, James shows his knowledge of the contemporary political situation in France and Europe in his letters for the New York *Tribune*. Newman remains blithely unaware of the effects of these historical and political events on his own personal destiny. Newman never understands that his proposal to Claire de Cintré is from the beginning a political act. When Newman proposes a fête in his apartments on the Boulevard Haussmann to celebrate his engagement, he is attempting to force the Bellegardes to acknowledge publicly his acceptance into the family. Newman attributes their reluctance to publicize the engagement merely to their personal snobbery; he never reflects upon the political significance that would naturally attend the announcement by an important legitimist family of its alliance by marriage with an American democrat. Coerced by Newman's political blundering into hosting the party at the Hôtel de Bellegarde, Madame de Bellegarde must realize that she is publicizing and giving social credibility to the marriage of a vaguely Protestant American to the daughter of committed Catholic legitimists. Valentin remains sufficient evidence that a number of legitimists, especially those who had fought for the pope in Italy, were disillusioned with the ultraconservativism of their kin and inclined to reach some accord with the republicans. As the Risorgimento reduced the Bourbon and papal powers between 1860–1870, many legitimists must have given up their international cause for more practical alliances.

Deprived of power as a younger son, unrewarded for his military service, the dilettantish Valentin is a likely candidate for reconciliation with the republicans. Valentin seems merely "curious" to see what Newman's proposal to Claire will bring about, much in the manner of Mrs. Tristram's personal curiosity. Nevertheless, he is careful to warn Newman about the family's history—"we are eight hundred years old" (109)—and to insist that Newman's "success will be precisely in being to her mind, unusual, unexpected, original" (108). When Valentin does agree to accept Newman's suit, he seems at first to do so according to Newman's very commercial habit of making a verbal contract. Yet, Valentin's offer of his hand to Newman has much more the character of a political or military alliance: "*Touchez-là*, then,' said Bellegarde, putting out his hand. 'It's a bargain: I accept you; I espouse your cause" (109). He adds that he does so not only because he likes Newman personally, but because: "I am in the Opposition. I dislike someone else" (109). There is no reason to assume that Newman's guess, "Your brother?" isn't correct, but it might just as well be Henry V or Pope Pius IX or virtually any other significant representative of legitimist and Ultramontanist claims to authority. Understood in that political context, Valentin's brother might certainly be hateful in terms of the frustration his party has caused Valentin.

There is considerable evidence to support the speculation that the Bellegardes have agreed to Newman's suit as much for its political significance as for the financial advantages he brings. This hypothesis admittedly does not bear the scrutiny of James' remarks on the Bellegardes in his 1907 Preface for the New York Edition of *The American*. In a less romantic version, in a thoroughly realistic mode, the Bellegardes "would positively have jumped then . . . at my rich and easy American, and not have 'minded' in the least any drawback" (12). Nevertheless, the older and more skeptical James of 1907 concludes that "such accommodation of the theory of noble indifference to the practice of deep avidity is the real note of policy in forlorn aristocracies—and I meant of course that the Bellegardes should be virtually forlorn" (12). Yet in this judgment, James in 1907 simply may not be recalling very well his own youthful idealism. The Bellegardes are hardly represented in the 1877 edition of the novel as "virtually forlorn," either in terms of financial means or political influence. They may have lost much of their ancestral authority, but their behavior betrays little of the desperation of those later aristocrats in James' fiction who preserve only the scantest tokens and ribbons of nobility.

Perhaps James' more skeptical twentieth-century views of the European aristocracy reflect something of his own development as a social critic as well as the changes in European history since 1875. In any case, the difference between James' representation of the Bellegardes' dignity, to say nothing of their relatively comfortable circumstances, in the first edition of the novel and his more evident contempt for "forlorn" aristocrats in 1907 may account for the substantial revisions he made in the version prepared for the New York Edition. This change in James' views—and biographical matters would seem to support such a change—gives further warrant to those critics who contend that the two editions constitute two different novels.[16] In any case, the argument for the political allegory in *The American* shows to its best advantage in the first edition, which remains the closest to the particulars of Parisian politics that James was observing first-hand.

When Newman approaches the old Marquise to receive her approval of his marriage suit, he finds her in the company of the old Comte and Comtesse de la Rochefidèle. Indeed, a reading of *The American* as political allegory gains considerable support from the tag names James uses for the legitimist aristocrats: Rochefidèle, Grosjoyaux, d'Outreville, Lord Deepmere, et al. Many of their names refer to natural objects or places that would give some tonal legitimacy to their rights to rule. Madame de Bellegarde introduces Newman by saying: "I have been telling Madame de la Rochefidèle that you are an American. . . . It interests her greatly. Her father went over with the French troops to help you in your battles in the last century, and she has always, in consequence, wanted greatly to see an American" (145). The Comte tells Newman: "Monsieur is by no means the first American that I have seen. . . . Almost the first person I ever saw . . . . was

the great Dr. Franklin. . . . He was received very well in our *monde*" (146).
Newman responds in no way to these remarks, which he apparently takes for idle
social chatter. Yet, the very presence of the Rochefidèles on the planned occasion
of the Bellegardes' acceptance of Newman's suit argues for some premeditation
and design. On the one hand, we might speculate that the Rochefidèles are
merely speaking defensively and thus justifying their tolerance of democrats like
Franklin. On the other hand, they may be suggesting much more significantly
that an alliance of legitimists and Ultramontanes with American republicans
might help these embattled aristocrats gain even more international support for
their battles within France. Indeed, an alliance with that paradoxical democratic
type, the American millionaire, might well be viewed by some legitimists as a
gain in financial and political power that would offer an acceptable compromise
to those urging reconciliation with the proletarian republicans of 1848.

Critics intent on viewing *The American* as James' first major transformation
of the romance into his own brand of realism are fond of discussing Newman's
"education" from innocence to disillusioned knowledge. R. W. Butterfield's
argument is representative: "It should be noted that *The American* changes character, as Newman's vulnerable naïveté develops into a self-protective awareness.
It begins as a novel that is 'realistic' in its social observation and narrative material, yet one that is seen chiefly through the eyes of a man who has a 'romantic'
(and thus, in some sense, false) vision of Europe, a vision altogether too benign
and 'innocent.' It concludes as a novel in which melodramatic and 'romantic'
events (duels, dark secrets, devilish glances, murders, flights into convents)
expose the 'reality' of Europe, which Newman now sees, in all its thickness and
complexity of history and evil, beneath the deceptive surface of appearances."[17]
Yet, Newman's consistent ignorance of French politics and history supports
another view: that Newman's fatality is his utter failure to turn his experience
into any kind of instructive or useful knowledge.

Even the fortune Newman has amassed confirms this judgment of his lack
of education. Critics hunt about for clues to the real basis for Newman's fortune:
wash-tubs, leather, copper, railroads, the stock market? Newman is as much a
dabbler in these commercial fields as Tristram is a social dilettante; neither
respects the material he works and the product he makes. No idea transcending
his immediate appetites takes any firm hold in either man's mind. This helps
explain why Newman's desire for some such idea results in nothing more significant than his romantic idealization of himself, projected onto the screen of a
twenty-four-year-old French woman, who is in herself neither particularly beautiful nor accomplished. Newman's "idea" is as childishly selfish as the story Claire
reads to her niece, Blanche, "Florabella and the Land of the Pink Sky." To the bitter end, Newman remains convinced of his goodness, generosity, and honesty,

just as Tom Tristram maintains his buoyant good nature in all weathers. There are many different, often deceptive ideas that will wreck James' subsequent characters, but the idea that Newman lacks still has some attractions for the young James. *The* idea that transvalues selfishness into self-consciousness always involves some conception of involvement in a larger and more enduring community. There can be no proper marriage between Claire and Newman until there is some idea of a social responsibility that will transcend the self and the family.

In his zeal for revenge against the Bellegardes, Newman visits the Duchess, Madame d'Outreville, that planted presence who attracts such worshipful attentions from the aristocrats at the Bellegardes' fateful ball. In her conversation with Newman, she "talked to him about flowers and books, . . . about the theatres, about the peculiar institutions of his native country, about the humidity of Paris" in what strikes Newman as nothing so much as the idle twaddle of a powerless leisure class. By the same token, we might speculate that the tangle of social subjects in the Duchess' conversation reflects James' own conviction that social, personal, political, and philosophical issues are all part of the same conversation, but such an insight is lost on Newman: "And then as the duchess went on relating a *mot* with which her mother had snubbed the great Napoleon, it occurred to Newman that her evasion of a chapter of French history more interesting to himself might possibly be the result of an extreme consideration for his feelings" (290).

Interrupted by the arrival of an Italian Prince, Newman is asked by the Duchess to remain. The Duchess' conversation with this Prince is quite explicitly political and thus more difficult for Newman to personalize:

> She made a fresh series of *mots*, characterised with great felicity the Italian intellect and the taste of the figs at Sorrento, predicted the ultimate future of the Italian kingdom (disgust with the brutal Sardinian rule and complete reversion, throughout the peninsula, to the sacred sway of the Holy Father), and, finally, gave a history of the love affairs of Princess X –. . . . The sentimental vicissitudes of the Princess X – led to a discussion of the heart-history of Florentine nobility in general; . . . and at last declared that for her the Italians were a people of ice. (290–91)

Newman senses "a sudden sense of the folly of his errand. . . . The duchess . . . had built up between them a wall of polite conversation in which she evidently flattered herself that he would never find a gate" (291). The Duchess and the Italian Prince are engaging in a polite but nevertheless significant discussion of European politics. The "sentimental vicissitudes of the Princess X – " have as much to do with the Bourbon claims to European rule as Italian military exploits against the Bourbons in Sicily and their annexation of Papal territories. Given the entanglement of noble family genealogies and political issues in European history, there is every reason to suppose that the flirtations of a princess may have as much political significance as a military coup. Newman, together with many modern critics, assumes that Urbain de Bellegarde's work on his history of "The Princesses of France Who never Married" simply represents the ascetic ideals of a dying aristocracy. Yet, the aristocrat's obsession with family genealogies had very specific political importance. Any political group supporting a pretender to the throne, particularly one who claims his divine right to rule, has some special interest in royal families' genealogies. The barrier that separates Newman from the Duchess and the Prince is certainly determined by different hereditary classes and cultures, and we have no reason to suppose that James finds these ultraconservative aristocrats any more attractive for all Newman's ignorance. It is also a wall that continues to divide the personal from the social, the subjective impression from historical event for Newman. The Duchess may well be putting Newman off with her endless banter, perhaps in deference to her friends and allies, the Bellegardes. On the other hand, it is possible that she is teaching Newman a little lesson about the necessary entanglements of social and political concerns in her *monde*.

To the end of his story Newman continues to ignore or repress the political realities of European aristocratic society. The romance and melodrama that he composes out of the unacceptable fact of his rejection by these legitimists is quite evidently a defensive effort to contain and neutralize the power they have wielded over him. He treats the Bellegardes in much the same manner as he treats Urbain's apparently frivolous wife, the young Marquise, and as he treats Claire and Valentin: helpless children in need of his paternal care. Yet, in this paternal role, he is blinder to the power these "children" wield over him than M. Nioche is of the machinations of his daughter, Noémie. Indeed, the curious crossing of the apparently farcical subplot of the Nioches with the larger drama involving Newman and the Bellegardes suggests something of Newman's enduring ignorance of the bare events of the world into which he has entered. Repeatedly, Newman tells Claire that he will make her "safe," be a "father" to her, and thus paradoxically give her complete "freedom" (163–164). Yet, James understands democratic freedom comes only from a full awareness of the different and often conflicting political choices that citizens are required to make. Thus James endorses the rights of the Catholic legitimists to be represented in a free democracy such as he hopes will come from the republican majority in the Assembly of 1875–1876. All of Newman's patronizing sexism and patriarchal condescension to women is involved in his utter ignorance of contemporary European politics and past history. Having divided polite society from commercial and political concerns, Newman imagines a woman's ambition to reach no further than maternal care and a wife's duty to her husband. His attitudes toward women are at least as reactionary as those of the Old World Bellegardes.

Newman's paternalism is, of course, linked with his naive understanding of self-reliance as an individualism that carries with it obligations only to one's self and the immediate family that is merely an extension of such a patriarchal self. It is little wonder that Newman so disturbs Benjamin Babcock, because Newman transforms the ideals of New England transcendentalism into a kind of Epicureanism. Never does Newman wonder about the political responsibilities of the self, in its various manifestations as son, daughter, businessman, aristocrat, father. He views poor old M. Nioche as a deluded and hypocritical man, manipulated against his shattered will by a daughter who uses her arts to rise in the world. The story that the Bellegardes circulate about Valentin's death in his sordid duel with Mr. Stanislas Kapp is explained by Lord Deepmere: "They got up some story about its being for the Pope; about the other man having said something against the Pope's morals. . . . They put it on the Pope because Bellegarde was once in the Zouaves. But it was about *her* morals—*she* was the Pope!" (300). By the same token, *Claire* is the pope, especially in her withdrawal into the Carmelite convent in the rue d'Enfer. The story told by the Bellegardes about Valentin may be strictly "false," but it suggests how every social relation carries with it significant political consequences.

Valentin dies in a duel with Mr. Stanislas Kapp, the son of a German brewer, in a way that seems to speak only of the disappearance of an anachronistic class, incapable of changing to meet the new age. Prompted by a trivial romantic triangle, the duel farcically anticipates the absurd national honor for which France nominally entered the Franco-Prussian War.[18] But Valentin's absurd gesture seems preferable to James to Newman's utter ignorance of how politics and high society work together. Valentin *chooses* consciously his vain destiny, even down to the second shot he fires deliberately wide of its mark. Newman chooses nothing but ignorance, willfully repressing the larger political issues that might well have caused the Bellegardes to command Claire to break her engagement with Newman. The "romance" that Newman finally "closes" as he stares at the blank walls of the Convent in the rue d'Enfer has been constructed by Newman out of this willful blindness.[19]

Yet, it is not just Newman's ignorance of history and politics that frightens James in his treatment of the modern American. Above all, James recognizes how easily this New Man might serve the old causes. Ignorance is always an obedient servant. Properly tutored by Babcock, of course, Newman might withdraw to his own religious retreat in some revival of Emersonian scholarly detachment. James' real concern, however, is that the American "new man" might well become just another version of the arbitrary European ruler, all the while professing the most democratic sentiments and in full confidence of his own good will. It is just Newman's paradoxical combination of aristocratic "self-reliance" and democratic appearance that might make him a reasonable candidate for marriage into a French legitimist family.

Throughout *The American*, Newman's political ignorance serves as a measure of his failure to recognize *himself* in any of the characters he encounters, including the imaginary "Claire" he constructs in his own image. The superficiality of his *perceptions* and *impressions* involves not only his political ignorance— that is, the extent to which history underlies every apparently direct impression or observation. It also involves his studied refusal to recognize his own paternalism in the Bellegardes' imperious authority over Claire, his own hypocrisy in M. Nioche's surrender to his daughter's ambitions (are these any worse than Newman's prospective service in the political ambitions of the Bellegardes?), his own passions for revenge and violence in the Bellegardes' implied murder of the old Marquis. It is in this final respect that Newman's supposed education is so utterly deficient by Jamesian standards.

In this last regard, we must recall what drove Newman to Europe in the first place: "I had come on to New York on some important business. . . a question of getting ahead of another party, in a certain particular way, in the stock-market. This other party had once played me a very mean trick. I owed him a grudge, I felt awfully savage at the time" (34). Newman's ride in his "immortal, historical hack" provokes that "sleep" or "reverie," from which: "I woke up suddenly . . . with the most extraordinary feeling in the world—a mortal disgust for the thing I was going to do" (34). Many critics speculate that Newman repeats this gesture of cathartic renunciation when he burns the incriminating note and gives up his revenge against the Bellegardes. As I have argued, however, Newman's first decision to throw revenge over occurs not when he dramatically burns the note in Mrs. Tristram's grate, but on his visit to the Duchess. There he surrenders before the impenetrable "wall" of her conversation. It is the same figurative wall Newman will contemplate much later in the rue d'Enfer—not just the "blank wall" of Claire's withdrawal from the world, but the wall of Newman's ignorance of those political realities—those larger ideas—that bind the Duchess, Italian Prince, and Carmelite Sisters to the same social will.

For after all, when faced with "mortal disgust," Newman flees both the situation and himself. Those who would contend that Newman maintains his integrity from the beginning to the end of the romance need to be reminded that repetition is proportionate to repression. Newman has never come to terms with that mortal disgust he could experience only involuntarily in his sleep or reverie, but that tells only part of his final story. The doubling of these two significant moments of renunciation help bring America and Europe closer together, insofar as both New World capitalism and Old World aristocratic politics may have more in common than first meets the eye. In a similar manner, James links the asceticism of his New England forebears with the sacrificial gestures of these European Catholics, suggesting a secret bond between Protestants and Catholics when they have been socially disenfranchised.

The political interpretation of the Bellegardes' willingness to marry Claire to Newman adds an interesting perspective to this argument. Perhaps the international aims of American capitalism are for James potentially more kin to the internationalism of French legitimists and Ultramontanes than to James' own republican ideals. *The American* may well be a subtle warning to James' readers as well as to James' own literary ambitions that the international destiny of the self-reliant American may have more in common with those imperial claimants in France (the Bellegardes), England (Lord Deepmere), and Italy (the ducal line of Bourbon-Parma; the pope) than we are willing to admit in our democratic enthusiasm. Given the intense concentration in his subsequent works on the special consciousnesses of imaginative and willful characters, James was right to express some concern that such fine consciences not be mistaken for a new aristocracy, as intent upon securing its power by international means as today's heads of multinational corporations.

10 The Economics of the Body: Kate Chopin's *The Awakening*

In families that I know, some little girls like to saw wood, others to use carpenters' tools. Where these tastes are indulged, cheerfulness and good-humor are promoted. Where they are forbidden, because "such things are not proper for girls," they grow sullen and mischievous. Fourier had observed these wants of women, as no one can fail to do who watches the desires of little girls, or knows the ennui that haunts grown women, except where they make to themselves a serene little world by art of some kind.

—— Margaret Fuller, *Woman in the Nineteenth Century* (1845)

Of the many awakenings Edna Pontellier experiences in Chopin's novel, each involves centrally her sense of her body. In the little side room of Madame Antoine's cottage on *Chênière Caminada*, Edna touches and looks at her body as if for the first time: "She ran her fingers through her loosened hair for a while. She looked at her round arms as she held them straight up and rubbed them one after the other, observing closely, as if it were something she saw for the first time, the fine, firm quality and texture of her flesh. She clasped her hands easily above her head, and it was thus she fell asleep."[1] This is, of course, only one among many moments in which Edna seems to recognize herself by feeling the texture, form, and complexity of her biological body. Utterly unlike Dreiser's Carrie Meeber, whose body is nothing but her clothes or the gazes of others in which she assumes form, Edna experiences her body in scenes that are remarkable for their refusal of the reader's own gaze. As many critics have noted, Edna's special experience of the materiality of her own body occurs in moments of intense privacy, whether indoors or out. In public, her husband and her lovers possess her body, treating it as "a valuable piece of personal property," the intentional object of masculine desire.

It thus appears that the mere sentience of Edna's body is a site of rebellion against such possession, a refusal of the gaze or touch of the masculine *other* that so defines this closed Creole world. Significantly, it is the surfaces of Edna's body that suggest most powerfully to her some inner, private, governing self. Her act of shedding her bathing suit as she heads for her concluding swim in the Gulf is foreshadowed repeatedly in the novel. Not only does she strip away the confining clothing in the little side room at Mme. Antoine's, she repeatedly loosens her clothing or replaces a stiff costume with a looser peignoir just before her most significant moments of self-recognition. Hidden within the fabric is another surface, alive to touch and its own sentience.[2]

Apart from its construction by the masculine gaze and independent of the roles Edna is expected to assume (most often figured in her clothing), the stylistic postulation of Edna's body rescues Edna's claims for some essential, still indefinable self from evaporating into transcendentalist sentiment and cliché: "Edna had once told Madame Ratignolle that she would never sacrifice herself for her children, or for any one. . . . 'I would give up the inessential; I would give my money, I would give my life for my children; but I wouldn't give myself. I can't make it more clear; it's only something which I am beginning to comprehend, which is revealing itself to me' " (KCA, 48). From beginning to end, this essential self is associated not only with Edna's physical body but also with the submersion of that body in the ocean, the medium in which the wholeness of the body can be sensed. As Chopin writes on the verge of Edna's final swim: "The touch of the sea is sensuous, enfolding the body in its soft, close embrace" (KCA, 113).

Sandra Gilbert's important reading of *The Awakening* as a modern retelling of the "second coming" of Aphrodite, to develop a feminine mythology for the otherwise alienated Edna and Chopin's women readers, depends crucially on the mythic body of Aphrodite as an incarnation of the oceanic medium.[3] In Greek, *aphros* means "sea foam," making Aphrodite's associations with generative power explicit. The magic in Ovid or Hesiod derives from such extreme transformations—the formlessness of the sea into animated, individualized form of a divine being, in this case the personification of natural energy in the erotics of the goddess's body. And ancient conventions of the human being carrying within its bodily form traces of its primal origins—the oceanic circulation of the blood, as well as a woman's body as microcosm for the ocean's vital fluid—support Gilbert's reading of the fantastic, mythic metamorphosis that Chopin effects in an otherwise ostensibly naturalist narrative.[4] If the myth of Aphrodite works in *The Awakening*, however, it does so only by incorporating into our thinking about the body its essential power of transformation. Just this sense of the body as an act, as unthinkable apart from what it can do, however, including the most elementary recognition of the body as such, escapes Edna, even as Chopin uses this knowledge to explore woman's problematic relation to the new economics of speculative capitalism in the concept of the New Woman.

From Emerson's "transparent eyeball," "bathed by the blithe air and uplifted into infinite space," through which "the currents of the Universal Being circulate," to Thoreau's longing to stand "neck-deep" in a swamp, to Whitman's oceanic sublimes, the idea of discovering the body by surrendering it to some natural element that figures spirituality (air, water, earth, fire) is a recognizable transcendentalist convention.[5] For Chopin, however, the moment of total immersion, in which the body experiences itself at once as self and natural other, marks the distance separating her narrative from those of the great romantics. For Edna, her body can be experienced only in its profound alienation from any natural context, denying absurdly the self-evidence of natural health and vitality of this twenty-eight-year-old woman's body. The body as such, free from what is done to it or what it is capable of doing, is simply unpresentable: it cannot be made to appear in its own self-evidence in any way that will provide Edna with the confidence to leave her tedious husband, trivial lovers, bonbon-hungry sons.

Listening to Mlle. Reisz play in Mme. Lebrun's parlor, Edna imagines "the figure of a man standing beside a desolate rock on the seashore. He was naked. His attitude was one of hopeless resignation as he looked toward a distant bird winging its flight away from him" (KCA, 26–27). The imaginary figure is erotically charged with Robert Lebrun's presence, and as such it is the best image Edna can give to her own body, at once naked and resigned yet full of desire. In sum, even at the moment of imagining a body for "Solitude" (the name she gives the musical piece), a rather conventional imaginary object, this metaphoric body is already marked by its distance from the free activity of "a distant bird winging its flight away from him." Erotically charged as the naked figure is, it is physically barred by Edna from the desire that ought to inspire it. His "hopeless resignation" is quite the opposite of desire, and it is the taboo on erotic desire that is strangely bound up with Edna's unformulated sense that she has been forbidden the sheer experience of the whole and natural body figured in "a distant bird winging its flight."

What does it mean to have a body? For Edna and for Mme. Ratignolle, it is always someone else who *possesses* your body, and such possession already signifies something other than your body: a wife, a lover, a white sunshade, sons, heirs. In short, the body is exchangeable for something else, has been transformed into something else, has entered into an *economy* in which it can be so changed. What troubles Edna so profoundly is that her body no longer belongs to her, and she thus can find no natural ground or purely transcendental experience of herself in and through her body (as Emerson, Thoreau, and Whitman claim to do). Even in that apparently primal moment of naked submersion in the sea, her body experiences itself as such only by means of an activity, a making, that may be as simple as the motions of the body swimming, either in a Kentucky meadow or off Grand Isle.

I do not mean to be metaphysical in offering some fundamental phenomenology of the body as its own activity of transformation; instead, I want to connect these sentiments to the late-nineteenth-century context of Kate Chopin's novel. Swimming in the sea, even standing naked by a rock to gaze longingly after the spiritual token of the natural scene, that soulful bird, might have sufficed for Emerson, Thoreau, and Whitman. For Chopin, the "swimming" motions of the child in her father's meadow in Kentucky disguise just what Edna would like to but can never genuinely do: cut and harvest, till the soil, grow and make something that would be a proper expression of her own bodily activity. Sharing with Edna that significant recollection of her childhood in Kentucky, Adèle asks, "Where were you going that day in Kentucky, walking through the grass?" Edna answers, "I don't remember now. I was just walking diagonally across a big field. My sunbonnet obstructed the view. I could see only the stretch of green before me, and I felt as I must walk on forever, without coming to the end of it. . . . Likely as not it was Sunday . . . . and I was running away from prayers, from the Presbyterian service, read in a spirit of gloom by my father that chills me yet to think of" (KCA, 17–18).

The romantic promise of that meadow's grasses and the wind in her face will give Edna some sense of her independent body as she passes, as a scythe passes, diagonally across the meadow, but it is quickly barred from her as she recalls that "my sunbonnet obstructed the view" and then that "I was running away from prayers" and the gloom of her stern Presbyterian, military, cocktail-mixing father.[6] Only a few pages earlier, at the end of chapter 5, as Robert urges Edna to come down to the shore for her bath, "the water must be delicious; it will not hurt you. Come," he reaches "up for her big, rough straw hat that hung on a peg outside the door, and put it on her head" (KCA, 14). Much as we would like to read this earlier scene as an invitation to the sea, the erotic dalliance with Robert, and thus as a certain liberation, Edna's memory reminds us that the sunbonnet of Kentucky or Grand Isle always belongs to the father, to the world of feminine decoration, to the masculine lover, and thus to a certain blindness, an incapacity to see as a woman. It is, after all, Robert who teaches Edna to swim and the "spurs of the cavalry officer" on the "porch" that she remembers in her final swim (KCA, 114). The rough straw hat and Edna's rejected bathing suit in her final swim both hang from a phallic "peg." She has learned something at least at the very last in her rejection of the bathing suit, whereas here she allows Robert to place that hat on her head. Even so, a woman's rebellion will involve much more for Chopin than merely the assertion of her naked self; that rebellion will require a thorough transvaluation of the modes of production that govern both the psyche and the economy of late-nineteenth-century capitalism.

But for the body to experience itself as such, it must feel itself making some thing in the particular process of making that allows the body to recognize itself in and through an *other*. In *The Body in Pain*, Elaine Scarry reads with care Marx's philosophical conception of human labor as the fundamental act of self-consciousness, which makes the alienation of the laborer from her product as psychically as it is materially impoverishing under capitalism. Focusing on "making," rather than "thinking" and "seeing," Marx and Engels' specific motives in focusing on bodily labor as the site of human self-consciousness are clear enough in *The German Ideology* (1846), and Chopin seems to agree with them insofar as she too stresses Edna's physical body, especially its arms and hands and legs, rather than her eyes, head, or even speech.[7] As Scarry argues:

> That sentient beings move around in an external space where their sentience is objectified means their bodies themselves are changed. . . . Perhaps the single most striking formulation occurs in Frederick Engels' essay, "The Part Played by Labour in the Transition from Ape to Man." . . . Engels' speculation that the crucial location of the transition from ape to man had been in the hand, the organ of making, rather than in the skull, the attendant organ of thinking, has after many years been confirmed by the discoveries of anthropologists. . . . Engels also introduces into the essay the idea that the hand is itself an artifact, gradually altered by its own activity of altering its external work.[8]

Engels' principal examples of the hand as agent of human self-making—paintings and lacemaking—are both conventional enough indications of how the hand produces design out of materials (paint and thread) lacking any inherent disposition to such designs. As Scarry demonstrates, Engels' point is that the complex anatomy of the hand—the "intricate weave of tendons, ligaments, muscles, and bones"—is quite literally transferred to the painting or the lace: "It is this interior disposition that is made visible and celebrated in the paintings or the lace; whatever the specific subject matter, part of what makes it available to the viewer, is the shape of the interior complexities and precisions of the sentient tissue that held the brush." The "remaking of the human body" is at once the ultimate philosophical aim of human labor—and thus of society—for Marx and Engels, even as this phrase carries with it all the horror felt by the late-nineteenth-century intellectual about the increasingly palpable threat that industrialism would transform nature, including the human body, into the artifices of commodity capitalism.[9]

Léonce Pontellier represents much more than the conventional dangers of industrial capitalism to factory and domestic workers. In *The Awakening*, we have moved a step beyond the reflection of capitalist values in family relations (*i.e.,* gender relations determined by class and property) that Engels develops in *The Origin of the Family, Private Property and the State* (1884).[10] Léonce is not a "cotton broker" in the old sense but a commodities broker who deals primarily in futures. Reversing one of the sexist conventions of the domestic romance, Chopin stresses Edna's concern regarding her husband's extravagances. But Léonce reminds Edna of the basic law of the speculator: "The way to become rich is to make money, my dear Edna, not to save it" (KCA, 53).

Léonce places his emphasis on the making of money as if it were an organic product, like the cotton he undoubtedly never sees. He refers to a kind of making that occurs apart from any expenditure of bodily energy and that has only the most illusory relation to the substance of the actual object or product to which it refers. As Walter Michaels has pointed out, successful dealing in futures depends in large part on *not* owning the actual goods.[11] The recurrent nightmare of the commodities speculator is that he might have to take delivery of all those soybeans for which he has purchased future contracts. By deferring ownership to some future and finally fictional date of delivery, the speculator concentrates on the increasingly independent game (or fictional story) of money (risk capital) that appears to grow without any labor on the part of the investor.

This Wall Street magic was a matter of considerable concern to agrarian interests in the later nineteenth century, since the farmer's production depended absolutely on the size of the crop, whereas the knowledgeable speculator could profit from either abundance or scarcity of the actual product. The fact is that this speculative economy and its fantastic narrative of money growing without human labor has come to define our postindustrial age, to the extent that farm subsidies and other efforts to control natural growth according to the conditions of the market are now accepted, even necessary practices.

Thus for Edna's domestic relations with her husband and her relation to her body as a productive agency, the very property that Engels insisted was the sole determinant of family (and thus sexual) relations has changed dramatically from the accumulated capital of the middle-class industrialist to the power to sustain the illusion of this new "commodity form" that is the speculator's crucial fiction. As Engels stresses, "The supremacy of the man in marriage is the simple consequence of his economic supremacy, and with the abolition of the latter will disappear of itself. The indissolubility of marriage is partly a consequence of the economic situation in which monogamy arose, partly tradition from the period when the connection between this economic situation and monogamy was not yet fully understood and was carried to extremes under religious form."[12]

The important scenes of gambling in *The Awakening*—Léonce playing cards at Klein's Hotel and Edna winning big on the horse races at the Jockey Club in New Orleans—are meant to refer to this new speculative economy, which substitutes the entertainment (even the romantic adventure) of the game, its chance and risk, for the productivity of the farmer, wife, or industrial laborer. Léonce's patronizing attitude toward Edna as he patiently explains the way to become rich is supposed to remind us how thoroughly unfamiliar Edna is with any of these changes in the commodity from manufactured object to money that may grow fantastically on its own.

Thus my initial claim that Edna's body can be known only in and through its own activity, its own "self-making," is complicated by the fact that bodies in this new speculative economy may be nothing more than the effects (rather than causes) of certain economic practices that have dispensed quite neatly with the need for any particular product or any particular labor. The perverse beauty of a speculative economy is that it virtually liberates itself from the domain of bodily labor, both on the part of the speculator and the workers he nominally employs. The labor of the farmer (or manufacturer) in producing the object of speculation has little significance for the speculator as long as that speculator has reliable information regarding that labor. Good horses or bad, the experienced gambler knows how to wager and win.

The crucial difference between Marx and Engels' lingering Hegelian conception of the human being as a maker of his or her self-image, and thus of his or her conception of the body as visible and familiar, and the relentless capitalist production of a fantastic world of consumer commodities radically detached from their means of production underlies Edna Pontellier's ambivalence regarding her body. Much of this depends on the complex processes Georg Lukács analyzes in *History and Class Consciousness* (1923) as *reification*, a term that draws significantly on ideas in one of Chopin's most important contemporaries, Thostein Veblen, whose *Theory of the Leisure Class* is generally considered a crucial part of the intellectual history required to read *The Awakening*.[13] Veblen and Lukács expanded Marx's "commodity fetishism" as the alienation of the worker from his own labor power to include what Carolyn Porter has termed "the consciousness of everyone living in a society driven by capitalist growth." Reification "generates, on the one hand, a 'new objectivity,' a 'second nature,' in which people's own productive activity is obscured, so that what they have made appears to them as a given, an external and objective reality, operating according to its own immutable laws." On the other hand, according to Porter, it generates people who assume a passive and "contemplative" stance in face of that objectified and rationalized reality: people who seem to themselves to stand outside that reality because their participation in producing it is mystified.[14]

The speculator, of course, *works* that "second nature," which itself is constituted exclusively by the disembodied circulation of exchange values that we call the market. I say "disembodied" because the market's definition in and through exchange value subordinates the discreteness of the commodity to its variable rate of exchange. The only sentience involved in such a market economy is the simulated excitement or thrill that the investor experiences when he risks his capital. Such excitement is, I think, often conflated in *The Awakening* with the sort of erotic titillation that Edna experiences with Robert and Alcée, mere doubles of her husband, and that provides her with an illusory sense of the erotics—that is, the productivity—of her body. The passive and contemplative stance of the alienated worker is analogous to the oppressive languor and torpor that so often overcome Edna and are objective correlatives of her imaginary figure's "hopeless resignation."[15] These moments of physical exhaustion are worth analyzing in some detail, because they appear to have a certain structural regularity that organizes Chopin's overall narrative.

Before analyzing some of these moments, however, let me suggest their importance in terms of the Marxian thesis that the human body is presentable only in and through its productive labor, in terms of some representation that is a product of that labor. I want to begin by drawing an analogy between the physical exhaustion of the laborer—the using up of the body and even the shortening of life—and the psychic torpor of Edna Pontellier. For Marx and Engels this exhaustion of the laborer has practical consequences in their arguments, especially in *Capital* where careful economic analyses demonstrate the inefficiency of capitalism insofar as it fails to provide for its workers' basic needs to renew their abilities to produce the product. Poor working conditions are extended in *Capital* to include inadequate living conditions and salaries insufficient to provide nourishment for the human body to perform required tasks. These practical arguments are equally philosophical since the "theft" that constitutes the capitalist's surplus value is quite literally stolen from the body of the worker.[16] Taken too literally, of course, the concept of the human body employed in *Capital* could be termed narrowly mechanistic since not all labor wears away the body. Physical exercise strengthens the body, extends the life cycle, and so forth.

Marx and Engels are equally concerned with the quality of life in psychic terms, and the exclusively *physical* exhaustion of the worker's body is more accurately understood as a psychical despair and resignation before the futility of labor.[17] What is produced by such labor never returns to the worker as such, especially in assembly-line production where the finished product may never be seen by the worker. Such alienation of labor is what makes possible the more "developed" practices of the speculator, because industrial capitalism enacted a literal diminution of the significance of the worker's body. The next phase, often hopefully termed "late capitalism" by optimistic Marxians, is part of that industrial logic: capitalism's ability to dispense completely with the human body as a meaningful agent, a productive subjectivity.

Edna's moments of "exhaustion" express a certain despair regarding the value and integrity of her labor, which helps align her anxieties regarding the reproductive powers of a woman with the comparable frustration of the industrial worker. Like Jacobs' Linda Brent, Edna reminds the reader that problems in the public and private spheres are profoundly interrelated, especially when hierarchies of gender are involved. Edna's sense of futility is rendered even more problematic when we consider how the new speculative economy represented by Léonce, Robert Lebrun, and Alcée Arobin has transformed even that physical labor into a sort of phantom of the speculative game. In its furthest reach, *The Awakening* aligns the exhaustion of the body in labor with the absolute extinction of the body enacted in this new speculative economy. Along with the death of the body, then, goes any concept of self as the making of a representation of the body. In the place of such material selfhood, which is just what Edna desires throughout the narrative, the new economy offers us nothing but roles or personae. Thus Edna's final swim may be read in two contradictory ways that nonetheless describe quite adequately the two economies that Chopin wants to represent.

In one sense, Edna's final swim enacts the ultimate extinction of the body as its own activity, its own labor. Reduced to nothing more than roles assigned to her by male others—her father, her husband, her lovers—Edna moves like some automaton to the Gulf and symbolically drowns a body that has lost its use value. Its skeleton goes to join the submarine world that figures the unconscious of speculative capitalism, that watery grave in which the stolen booty of pirates like Jean Laffite lies buried. In another reading, compatible with Sandra Gilbert's, Edna rejects the roles of this economy of simulation by stripping herself naked, exposing the phallic peg that has kept her discarded swimsuit "ready" for her all along, and heads for the Gulf to discover the value of her active body. In this context, Edna's final swim is a rebellion against this fantastic world of speculation for the sake of the undeniable productivity of the body itself, not simply as a biology ("Remember the children!") but as the organ of self-representation. In this latter reading, the myth of Aphrodite is quite relevant since a symbolic renewal is performed by Edna, a rebirth of those values of productivity that industrial and then speculative capitalism have caused us to repress.

Edna's first experience of physical torpor occurs at the center of chapter 3, just after Léonce has returned late from gambling at Klein's Hotel and awakened her to attend to Raoul, who the father is certain has "a high fever" and needs "looking after" (KCA, 7). When Edna answers sleepily that she is quite sure Raoul has no fever, Léonce reproaches "his wife with her inattention, her habitual neglect of the children" and lectures her on the domestic duties she has assumed as a wife. It is a scene of patriarchal authority that will be repeated again in New Orleans when Léonce complains about the cook's scorched fish, and in this instance it clearly identifies Edna as her husband's servant.

Although she obeys his command in this instance, Edna finds herself crying as her husband sleeps soundly: "An indescribable oppression, which seems to generate in some unfamiliar part of her consciousness, filled her whole being with a vague anguish. It was like a shadow, like a mist passing across her soul's summer day. It was strange and unfamiliar; it was a mood. . . . The mosquitoes made merry over her, biting her firm, round arms and nipping at her bare insteps" (KCA, 8). This scene hardly requires much analysis since it self-evidently expresses the dependence of the wife's labor on her husband's command. Awakened to her duties by her husband, she is oppressed by an anguish that virtually immobilizes her, were it not for the mosquitoes recalling her to her body: "The little stinging, buzzing imps succeeded in dispelling a mood which might have held her there in the darkness half a night longer" (KCA, 8).

Just as Edna refuses "to answer her husband when he questioned her," so Chopin refuses to tell the reader anything about the health or sickness of Raoul. In fact, the sleeping children exist in this scene only in Léonce's words, just as Edna's body is subject to his commands (quite literally, the sleeping body is ironically awakened by the patriarchal command). Only a few pages later, at the end of chapter 11, Edna withholds her body from Léonce's desire in a scene explicitly designed to echo that in chapter 3. Léonce tries to convince her to come into the cottage and his bed by arguing, "The mosquitoes will devour you." From her reply, "There are no mosquitoes," to her command, "Léonce, go to bed," and her refusal to be bullied, "Don't speak to me like that again; I shall not answer you," Edna finds strength and voice in denial (KCA, 32).[18]

Both scenes are necessary stages in Edna's awareness of her own body, but both turn upon the denial of what the body can do, on the limited labor available to Edna at these stages in the narrative: childbirth and the satisfaction of her husband's sexual desire. In this scene, too, the work of denial, of rebellion, provokes a sort of languor: "The physical need for sleep began to overtake her; the exuberance which had sustained and exalted her spirit left her helpless and yielding to the conditions which crowded her in" (KCA, 32). In these two scenes Edna's frustration and rebellion are analogous to the industrial worker's recognition of the alienation of her labor power, an alienation by means of which the capitalist affirms his power to rule.

Dale Bauer and Andrew Lakritz have argued that "Edna's alienation is necessary to her awakening because it forces her to confront the values of her culture and to articulate her own. . . . Only by articulating her own stance, by bringing into the open what is her own ambivalence toward her culture, can she overcome both her self-imposed isolation and the repressive demands made on

her by society. Edna's gradual awareness of her voice, her burgeoning consciousness, is crucial to her resistance . . . . Edna awakens to her cultural alienation rather than to sexual passion."[19] Bauer and Lakritz distinguish significantly
between Edna's cultural and sexual awakenings, perhaps because previous critics have placed so much stress on the erotics of her body to the neglect of the
political imperatives of her awakenings.

Much as I agree with Bauer and Lakritz that the fundamental question for
Chopin is a woman's awareness of her cultural situation, her participation for
better or worse with the modes of production that extend from the factory and
brokerage to the bedroom and the parlor, I think that Chopin wants for these
very reasons to entangle Edna's erotic sense of her body with more general economic questions of human production. For women in the United States at the
end of the nineteenth century, Chopin argues, these domains cannot be easily
distinguished. Sexual ennui, like the fatigue of the industrial laborer, is not
exclusively a physical consequence of exertion but a psychical effect of frustrated erotic and economic energies. As Engels reminds us, sexual production
follows the same laws as industrial production under capitalism: the alienation
of the mother and children is achieved by the patriarch's transformation of them
into his property (surplus value) and their obedience to his domestic law, including public laws against divorce and carefully regulating the transmission of property by inheritance.[20] This point is made explicit by Engels in his discussion of
the Athenian father's legal right to sell his children.[21]

Edna's status as her husband's property involves the translation of her
body into a masculine fetish. In the opening scene of *The Awakening*, Edna appears
quite literally through the haze of Mr. Pontellier's cigar smoke, figured in a succession of phallic metonymies that define decisively the masculine gaze: "Mr.
Pontellier finally lit a cigar and began to smoke, letting the [newspaper] drag idly
from his hand. He fixed his gaze upon a white sunshade that was advancing at a
snail's pace from the beach. . . . Beneath its pink-lined shelter were his wife, Mrs.
Pontellier, and young Robert Lebrun. When they reached the cottage, the two
seated themselves with some appearance of fatigue upon the upper step of the
porch, facing each other, each leaning against a supporting post" (KCA, 4). In
chapter 11, when Edna finally rises, full of physical exhaustion, to enter the cottage, she "tottered up the steps, clutching feebly at the post before passing into
the house," asking, "Are you coming in, Léonce?" (KCA, 33). Léonce has been
smoking cigars and drinking wine to dull his sexual desire, frustrated by Edna's
refusal of his overtures. We hardly need Freud to read the transference from
cigar to sunshade to post in the opening scene, cigar to post in chapter 11. In
chapter 1, Léonce reproaches Edna, "What folly! To bathe at such an hour in such
heat!" and concludes, "You are burnt beyond recognition,' looking at his wife as

one looks at a valuable piece of personal property which has suffered some damage" (KCA, 4). The burning of the cigar, its transference from the hand of Léonce to the body of Edna, is brilliantly accomplished by Chopin, for it makes possible the first bodily representation of Edna that we have in the novel: "She held up her hands, strong, shapely hands, and surveyed them critically, drawing up her lawn sleeves above the wrists. Looking at them reminded her of her rings, which she had given to her husband before leaving for the beach. She silently reached out to him, and he, understanding, took the rings from his vest pocket and dropped them into her open palm" (KCA, 4). In this moment, the capitalist's gaze and law come together. We see Léonce looking, whereas what we see of Edna is just what signifies her capacity to work: her hands. Under the masculine gaze of the husband-capitalist, Edna's hands become "ugly" and "damaged" rather than "strong, shapely" implements of production. Edna's dalliance with Robert Lebrun seems not to bother Léonce, as if such flirtation is understood by the husband to be part of the holiday behavior expected of a rich Creole's wife.

When Edna attempts to carry her rebellion further by way of Robert Lebrun and later Alcée Arobin, she merely encounters again and again the patriarchal structure of domination that binds her very conception of her body to the law of a masculine gaze that by the end of the narrative encompasses not only the various arts of society but also its economics. In these episodes physical exhaustion follows her failed efforts to represent her self beyond the mode of physical production that governs social and economic patriarchy. In chapter 12, just after she has withheld her body from Léonce in chapter 11, she sends Robert the command to join her on the excursion to the Chênière: "She had never sent for him before. She had never asked for him. She had never seemed to want him before" (KCA, 33). But the romantic voyage that she performatively commands turns out to be little more than a journey into her unconscious alienation: a retelling of the masculine narrative in which she is nothing but a disembodied character.

Even if we disregard the wharf crowded with the two lovers, the lady in black, old M. Farival, and one of Robert's other dalliances, the "Spanish girl," Mariequita, we cannot ignore the conventionality of the romance that Robert and Edna compose as they sail away. Robert proposes an excursion on the following day to Grande Terre where they will "climb up the hill to the old fort and look at the wriggling gold snakes, and watch the lizards sun themselves," and Edna "thought she would like to be alone there with Robert." Even more conventionally, Robert suggests, "I'll take you some night in the pirogue when the moon shines. Maybe your Gulf spirit will whisper to you in which of these islands the treasures are hidden" (KCA, 35). The history of Spanish colonialism—itself a version of its romantic other, the piracy and smuggling that flourished in the Gulf in the first decades of the nineteenth century—is merely a fantastic landscape for these lovers. Later, Mme. Antoine will tell Edna and Robert "legends of the Baratarians and the sea" she had been "gathering" "all her years" on the island (KCA, 39).

The stories of Jean Laffite are part of Gulf legend and history, especially in Barataria Bay where he and his brother Pierre created a community of pirates and smugglers between 1809 and 1817. It is not simply that piracy is capitalism's secret law; for Marx, piracy is one of capitalism's origins, as he makes clear in his efforts to account for the "primitive accumulation of capital" in *Capital*: "In actual history, it is a notorious fact that conquest, enslavement, robbery, murder, in short, force, play the greatest part [in the so-called primitive accumulation of capital]."[22] Just as Robert's flirtation with Mariequita and his subsequent combat with his brother, Victor, over her is strangely bound up with his neocolonial business in Mexico, so sexual and economic politics are entangled in his otherwise trivial romance of the Baratarian pirates and their spoils.

If the legendary hideout of the Laffites offers Edna a romantic glimpse into the idea of an alternative community that might wage war against the proprieties and conventions of lawful government, she was certain to know the rest of Laffite's story. Invited to join the English in their attack of New Orleans in the War of 1812, Laffite notified Louisiana officials of the impending attack. Despite Laffite's patriotism, Louisiana ordered an expedition to destroy the Baratarian community and capture the outlaws. Having escaped capture, Laffite offered the services of his imprisoned company in defense of New Orleans, an offer accepted by Governor William Charles Coles Claiborne in his proclamation of December 17, 1814. For their patriotism in defense of New Orleans the Baratarians were pardoned by President Madison on February 16, 1815.

The legends of Laffite seem to suggest for Chopin how easily rebellion may be co-opted. It is, after all, Robert who begins to tell these stories as just another part of his superficial flirtation, another effort to make his own pathetic bravura appear grander than it is. President Madison's pardon didn't do much to reform Jean Laffite, who subsequently set up a variety of other smuggling communities on the eastern coast of Mexico, which is also Robert Lebrun's destination when he leaves Grand Isle and Edna. I can't claim Chopin could have known of Jean Laffite's reputed interests in European communism and his trip to Europe to meet Karl Marx. This still-contested argument regarding Laffite's revolutionary purposes and interests was not made until 1952 in Stanley Clisby Arthur's *Jean Laffite, Gentleman Rover*.[23]

Robert Lebrun's own plan to seek his fortune in some undefined commercial project in Mexico, specifically Vera Cruz, has a different significance from the rebellious pirate communities Jean Laffite and his brother established on the east coast of Mexico following their pardon. As Eric Sundquist points out, proslavery interests in the antebellum South were often expressed in "glamorous visions of an empire that reached beyond the United States' continental borders. . . . Peculiar to the South's version of manifest destiny, of course, was the extension of slavery and the shift of national power geographically to the south." This imperial dream was predicated in part on the "presupposed decay of the Spanish empire and its replacement by an Anglo-Saxon empire in the western hemisphere."[24] As soon as Robert announces his plans to leave for Mexico, the assembled company begins to tell stories about Mexicans. Mme. Ratignolle, for example, warns Robert to "exercise extreme caution in dealing with the Mexicans, who, she considered were, a treacherous people, unscrupulous and revengeful. She trusted she did them no injustice in thus condemning them as a race" (KCA, 43). What Robert actually discovers in Mexico hardly lives up to the antebellum fantasy of a land ripe for a new Southern empire; in one of his letters to Edna, he complains that "the financial situation was no improvement over the one he had left in New Orleans" (KCA, 61). Nevertheless, Robert's little romance of Mexico is full of fantasies of commercial conquest that have certain homologies with the antebellum Southern version of manifest destiny. On the more local level, his venture in Mexico is equivalent to his desires to conquer Mariequita and Edna.

The stories of pirates and buried treasure frame Edna's next great moment of "oppression and drowsiness," which occurs predictably in the little "Gothic Church of Our Lady of Lourdes." Like conventional tales of romance, the church offers little relief to Edna, who must find reminders there of the strict Catholic taboos against adultery and divorce in Creole culture. It is not just the religious superego at work in this episode, however, it is the distance separating Edna's creative power from that figured in the miracle of Our Lady of Lourdes. The reference to Lourdes certainly connects the water imagery in *The Awakening* with the miraculous healing powers of the waters in the grotto where the Virgin Mary appeared to Bernadette Soubirous (1844–1879) in February 1858. Chopin was familiar with the various accounts of Bernadette's visions from Zola's 1894 novel, *Lourdes*, which she reviewed for *St. Louis Life*, on November 17, 1894.[25]

Given the mythic associations of women's creative powers with water and its powers of birth and miraculous revival, the allusion seems to give special credibility to Gilbert's argument that *The Awakening* promises a second coming of the Aphrodite myth. It remains, however, a profoundly ironic allusion since it refers Edna and the reader only to the means by which the history of the Catholic Church reinforces patriarchal authority. The peasant shepherdess Bernadette Soubirous, who has her vision while tending her sheep, is utterly subordinated to the spiritual ineffability of the Virgin Mary, who becomes the Church's proper Lady of Lourdes. Between 1858, the year of Bernadette's first visions, and 1901, when Pope Leo XIII consecrated the Church of the Rosary on the site of her visions, Bernadette of Lourdes was often an item in the Catholic news. Bernadette would not be canonized until 1933, however, a testament to the magical powers of Catholic patriarchy in virgin birth, of which the Church's miracles are simply lesser and historical repetitions. The humble but honest labor of Bernadette is nothing in contrast with the magic of the Church, virgin birth, miraculous cures.

The buried treasure of Gulf pirates and the secret powers of the Church share the same power to alienate Edna, just as later in New Orleans she will "drowse" over Emerson's essays. None of these idealist lures has any productive relation to her body; each is as alien as the wedding ring she vainly stamps with her boot heel in New Orleans. And yet Edna misses the shepherdess Bernadette Soubirous in her flight from the church, fails to recognize how the relation of one's body to nature depends upon the labor of that body, perhaps because she knows the apparent freedom of the Gulf is haunted by the ghostly treasures of pirates, the submerged depths of the sea filled with the wrecks of culture.

Throughout the narrative, Chopin gives us several modern versions of Bernadette Soubirous, modest instances of working women whose labor might perform miracles if it were dedicated to their ultimate social representation. Each is a servant: the African-American girl who "with her hands worked the treadle" of Mme. Lebrun's sewing machine (KCA, 22) and later delivers Edna's invitation to the Chênière to Robert; Mariequita, the "Spanish girl," who is probably Mexican-American, over whom Robert and Victor Lebrun have fought, who carries her bamboo basket of shrimps "covered with Spanish moss" on the boat trip Robert and Edna take to the Chênière (KCA, 34); the cook in New Orleans whose soup Léonce finds "impossible" and whose scorched fish he pronounces inedible (KCA, 51–52). Edna recognizes the black girl merely as a servant and Mariequita only as an unworthy rival. Only with the cook does she have some passing empathy since she is responsible for the domestic servants. With some conviction, however, we may conclude that she never directly addresses her sisterhood with these exploited women from others classes, races, and economic circumstances. Similar as the oppressive conditions of their labor are to her own, they never constitute an alternative community even fantastically glimpsed by Edna, whose awakenings remain specific to the class and thus psychic profile of her own confinement.

Thus her torpor and sense of oppression are understandable. Edna successively experiences the inadequacy of the modes of production available to her to express her body, to offer her any substantial and self-sufficient being. It is, of course, naive to forget the eroticism of these languors, the sexual reference of virtually every moment in which she encounters her ennui. We cannot speak as categorically as I have of the mere inadequacy of Edna's roles as wife, romantic lover, wife of a Catholic, since each of these moments is charged with sexual excitement, the affective tensions of desire withheld (from Léonce) or antici-pated (with Robert). Each alternative for Edna to this point in the narrative—wife, romantic, Catholic—betrays explicitly its failure to sublimate her vital sexual energy. This unrepresentable vitality exhausts her. At times, it is virtually postorgasmic, as when she emerges from her fitful nap at Mme. Antoine's rav-enously hungry, tosses an orange at Robert, as if to parody some more dramatic Christian moment of sin, and experiences momentary euphoria.[26]

Inextricable as such uncanny psychic awakenings are from sexuality, their very inadequacy, compounded by the successive references to Edna's natural will as an effect of her body, returns us with a certain perverse determinism to a woman's biological labor in birth. Thrown back endlessly on this alternative to a woman's social productivity, Edna is understandably horrified by the "torture" of Adèle's act of giving birth and by her friend's misguided advice, "Remember the children." The child is at once a living sign of the undeniable productivity of a woman's body, but Edna's children belong only to a patriarchal legal system that governs both the market and the home. No wonder that Edna experiences such ambivalence regarding her children and that those same children are the ultimate "antagonists who had overcome her; who had overpowered and sought to drag her into the soul's slavery for the rest of her days" (KCA, 113). In a novel cele-brated for its authenticity regarding a woman's natural sensations and affections, *The Awakening* represents a woman's nature in extraordinarily ambivalent ways. In fact, as Edna only dimly recognizes at the very end of the narrative but Chopin knows all too well, there can be *no* nature for a woman that is not always already shaped and determined, inscribed and charted, by the laws of the social order.

No wonder, then, that Edna turns to art as her only defense against such a contrived world in which her body is nothing but a character in the dramatic fic-tion of patriarchy. In this regard, Chopin remorselessly denies Edna such conso-lations, as if to warn subsequent moderns that art is not always a way out. Chopin decisively represents Edna as lacking any distinctive artistic or intellec-tual talents. Mlle. Reisz's music stirs Edna's desire no more than an ordinary lis-tener might be moved. Edna's drawings are either failed efforts at realism of the most autobiographical sort—sketches of Adèle, Edna's father the Kentucky Colonel—or of banal genre themes. "Surely, this Bavarian peasant is worthy of framing; and this basket of apples! Never have I seen anything more lifelike. One might almost be tempted to reach out a hand and take one," Mme. Ratignolle praises her, "Your talent is immense, dear!" (KCA, 56, 55).

If I were to venture any reading of these subjects beyond the sheer con-ventionality of Edna's art, I would suggest that both again refer us to the prob-lematic qualities of this new economy of speculation. The peasant's labor and the use value of the apples have been reduced by art to decorative images, such as one finds in the genre portrait or the still-life. Edna's drawings express nothing more than the listless yearning of the leisure-class wife. The literary moderns like Henry James, T. S. Eliot, Virginia Woolf, and Gertrude Stein, who offered woman her identity in and through the self-making of art, should have been required to read Chopin's *The Awakening*. Clarissa Dalloway may someday grow up to become Virginia Woolf, Isabel Archer aspire to the self-consciousness of Henry James, even Alice B. Toklas long for the rhetorical skill of Gertrude Stein. But what of the Edna Pontelliers, who have little more than their common sense, human sensitivity, health, and longing for a body, a being, of their own? What of those who write no books, paint no pictures, have only recourse to faculties and affections that they possess in no greater degree than their servants and their friends?

Even when Edna tries merely to improve herself, in accord with the values placed on education and culture by the bourgeoisie, she ends up dozing over Emerson: "Then Edna sat in the library after dinner and read Emerson until she grew sleepy. She realized that she had neglected her reading, and determined to start anew upon a course of improving studies, now that her time was completely her own to do with as she liked" (KCA, 73). Of course, her time is *not* "completely her own" as Chopin's wry selection of Emerson suggests. As we have seen in chapter 2, Emerson's position on the "woman question" was thoroughly meliorist, urging on the one hand full, even transcendental freedom for women and on the other hand arguing for women to "choose" to subordinate themselves to men. Edna has no inkling of this sort of critique of Emerson; he represents to her simply a cultivated intellectual, whose work ought to improve her mind. Whether or not his transcendentalism is invoked here by Chopin as an influence on her own work is less important than what Emerson fails to mean for Edna. When she does grow sleepy over Emerson in this scene, she "went to bed" but not before taking "a refreshing bath" (73). If this bath foreshadows Edna's final swim, it does so only by way of a certain *bathos*: the emancipatory gesture of Edna's final swim makes us reread this episode as one in which the arts merely contribute to idle pleasures of the leisure class, rather than the genuine freedom that comes from self-making.

When she does move out of Léonce's house, it is thanks only to a curious combination of resources: her winnings at the horse races with Alcée; income from her sketches, which she claims she is "beginning to sell"; and "a little money of my own from my mother's estate, which my father sends me by driblets" (KCA, 79). If they are selling, Chopin suggests, then those sketches are as bad as we are meant to think them, given the dilettantism of Edna's social companions. More significantly, these proceeds from her labor have the same status as her winnings at the track and her mother's small bequest. Each source of income, even as it helps Edna escape her husband's economic domination, derives from the patriarchy she flees. What connects the cotton speculator Léonce with the pirates of the Gulf is just what attracts him to gambling. The bonus of Edna's winnings at the Jockey Club is as sexually charged as the money Léonce divides with Edna the night after his late night of gambling at Klein's Hotel and his command that she attend the feverish Raoul. And her mother's bequest, itself the promise of some free transmission of property rights from mother to daughter, merely serves to sustain her father's authority over her since he sends it to her "by driblets." Long before she bids farewell to her husband's grand house, long before Alcée and his flowers invade the private world of her pigeon house, Edna's room of her own already belongs to another, can be named by her servant, Ellen, as just that which represents a site of domestication, the confinement of a yearning spirit.

At Edna's farewell birthday party, Chopin employs the same irony to suggest how Edna's best gestures at freedom merely betray their patriarchal animation. Sandra Gilbert argues that the dinner party Edna "gives in chapter 30 is her most authentic act of self-definition. Here, she actually plays the part of the person she has metaphorically become: 'the regal woman, the one who rules, who looks on, who stands alone.' . . . Edna's dinner party is in a sense a Last Supper, a final transformation of will and desire into bread and wine, flesh and blood, before the 'regal woman's' inevitable betrayal by a culture in which a regenerated Aphrodite has no meaningful role."[27] Gilbert is unquestionably right in claiming a certain serious drama, a decisive will to mythic truth, on the part of Edna in this episode. Certainly, her desire to constitute a pleasant and comfortable company, to create a meaningful, albeit microcosmic, social relation in which she might be said to have played a productive, even emancipatory role is essentially mythic. There can be no myth, after all, without culture, and it is just this mythopoetic role that both Chopin and Marx imagine every worker ought to assume in his or her everyday labors, at home or in the factory.

Yet from the outset of this party, the absent patriarchs, Edna's father and her husband, continue to direct the play. Although earlier she had refused to accompany her husband to select "new library fixtures," Edna here dresses splendidly to match the table settings: "The pale yellow satin under strips of lace-work" of the tablecloth matches "the golden shimmer of Edna's satin gown" covered by a "soft fall of lace encircling her shoulders" (KCA, 87–88). Is Edna's lace (and that of the tablecloth) Chopin's ironic reference to the legend that Aphrodite's husband, Hephaestus, catching her in bed with her lover, Ares, threw a delicate golden net of his own making over them and displayed their embarrassment to the other gods? If Edna's diamonds and lace are simply updated versions of

Hephaestus' net, her figuration of Aphrodite deflates the power of at least that myth to save women from the masculine conflation of erotic love, marriage, and phallic making. The crystal on the table "glittered like the gems which the women wore," in Edna's case arranged as a crown, "a magnificent cluster of diamonds that sparkled, almost sputtered, in Edna's hair," a birthday present from her absent husband. And in her opening toast, Edna seems unaware of how closely she remains tied to the patriarchal rituals of this confining social world: "I shall ask you to begin with this cocktail, composed . . . by my father in honor of Sister Janet's wedding" (KCA, 86).

Edna's party cannot live up to her dramatic, her mythic expectations, not simply because Chopin indulges the realist's propensity for mock epic and the fine art of sinking, or bathos, but because the quotidian realities of this frivolous evening are even more fantastic than myth. What is utterly phantasmagoric about this dinner party is the manner in which the father and husband speak, even in their absences, and thereby dictate by a kind of perverse table-turning the very terms of Edna's rebellion: "But as she sat there amid her guests, she felt the old ennui overtaking her; the hopelessness which so often assailed her, which came upon her like an obsession, like something extraneous, independent of volition. It was something which announced itself; a chill breath that seemed to issue from some vast cavern wherein discords wailed" (KCA, 88). It is desire for "the unattainable," but it appears, as desire most often does, in the absence of its object of satisfaction. Perhaps it is just his desire that a husband wants to encourage in his wife in accord with the inflationary laws of this new speculative economy.

Edna's desire is finally quite ordinary, simply realistic—*natural*, if that term still carries meaning in the *fin de siècle*. She wants to experience her body in the world around her, not simply in the private moments when she touches herself as if to confirm an existence so tenuous in public; she desires participation in the labor of socialization, a process ironically mimed in her little party. As Scarry writes:

> The socialization of sentience—which is itself as profound a change as if one were to open the body physically and redirect the path of neuronal flow, rearrange the small bones into a new pattern, remodel the ear drum—is one of Marx's major emphases. Sense organs, skin, and body tissue have themselves been recreated to experience themselves in terms of their own objectification. It is this now essentially altered biological being that, in going on to remake himself or herself in other ways, enters into that act of making as one whose sentience is socialized, fundamentally restructured to be relieved of its privacy.[28]

Because these modes of objectification can be shared by others, they enable us to extend our bodies, amplify our privacy (and thus our mortality) to encompass society (and thus an enduring history). In Scarry's reading of Marx's philosophy of the social commodity as an extension and amplification of the individual body, that commodity is not fetishized but endlessly productive: "For Marx, the more extended and sublimated sites of making should extend this attribute of shareability: the interaction made possible by a freestanding object is amplified as that object now becomes a 'commodity' interacting with other objects and so increasing the number of persons who are in contact with one another; the socialization of sentience should continue to be amplified as one moves to more extended economic (money, capital) and political artifacts."[29] Under capitalism such a socialist economy is detoured into the peculiar economy by which the amplification of the fabricated body (the capitalist's capital) depends upon the diminution of the natural body (the worker's physical body).

Put a simpler way, Edna's problem is also that of Chopin the writer: how to make the body *other*—an object, an artifact, a child, a novel—without losing that body. I have made Kate Chopin sound like a committed Marxist, which she was decidedly not, but she nevertheless understood her activity as a writer to involve a problematic sort of labor. As she writes in "In the Confidence of a Story-Writer," "The story completed, I was very, very weary; but I had the satisfaction of feeling that for once in my life I had worked hard, I had achieved something great, I had taken pains."[30] It seems simple enough to claim this painful satisfaction for literary creation until we recognize as Chopin does that such labor is meaningless without its circulation, without entrance into a market: "But the story failed to arouse enthusiasm among the editors. It is at present lying in my desk. Even my best friend declined to listen to it, when I offered to read it to her."[31] Scarry suggests that Marx's ideal socialist economy would depend upon commodities that serve functionally as verbal signs, that is, as points of contact between labor of sender and receiver rather than products belonging either to author or reader, capitalist or worker.

Perhaps Chopin's formal innovations in *The Awakening* demonstrate the utopian transformation of capitalist reification into a sharable social discourse. What begins as a naturalist novel concludes, as Gilbert argues, as a series of symbolic enactments subject to a wide range of interpretations. In reading the conclusion in terms of Edna's fate—does she sink or swim?—the reader merely affirms the laws of capitalism and their conventional reproduction in the naturalist novel. By observing the destiny of a fictional character intended to represent a class or group in an explicit social situation, the implied reader of the naturalist novel tacitly accepts the idea of sociohistorical determinism. To image a new history and economy in which the New Woman (and the New

Man) might share in the coordinated labor of social production requires a new literary form.[32]

Chopin's turn from naturalism to symbolism, from dreary realism to suggestive parable, offers the reader just such a gift. But we must be careful not to privilege any literary text lest we forget literature's conditions of production, its history. *The Awakening* marks the threshold between naturalism and modernism. Insofar as it offers its own symbolism as an alternative to the reification of capitalism, it is potentially a narrative of emancipation. But to the extent that this symbolism is produced only by sophisticated (and profoundly private) authors and readers, the novel merely anticipates the aesthetic utopias offered by the literary moderns. Symbols are, after all, an acquired taste and not very nourishing. As long as Chopin's literary economy excludes the labor of the young African-American woman and of the "Spanish girl" Mariequita in the racially divided postbellum South, then *The Awakening* remains an interesting contribution to the restricted economy of literary modernism.

There remains one other way a purely literary symbolism might suggest an ethical dimension relevant to ordinary life and practical human concerns. As I have argued, Chopin represents Edna's unsatisfied desire in art, philosophy, labor, and social relations in addition to her sexual and erotic desires. In the simplest sense, some expansive notion of love would be required to satisfy Edna's desire as it calls to her through these different areas of her everyday activities of painting, thinking and reading, working at various tasks, and talking with others. At times, Chopin seems to equate the special cognition of the literary symbol with the kind of communication between subjects that respects differences and thus might be said to exemplify a new understanding of love. In Edna's most intimate and erotic moments with her lovers, we might expect just some hint of a more comprehensive notion of love that would coordinate her conflicting desires. These moments, however, are marked either by her sudden exhaustion or her horror and loathing in the face of the violence that sexuality signifies in this patriarchal culture.

Alone with Edna, Arobin presses for intimacy by revealing a bit of his body, drawing up his cuff "to exhibit upon his wrist the scar from a saber cut which he had received in a duel outside of Paris when he was nineteen. . . . A quick impulse that was somewhat spasmodic impelled her fingers to close in a sort of clutch upon his hand. He felt the pressure of her pointed nails in the flesh of his palm" (KCA, 76). It is perhaps the most uncannily intimate moment Edna has with another in the text, precisely because it exposes how profoundly masculine aggression and power have shaped relations of intimacy and sharing. That Edna repeats in miniature the Parisian duel by pressing "her pointed nails into the flesh of his palm" only confirms how illusory her romantic escape with

Arobin actually is. " 'The sight of a wound or scar always agitates and sickens me,' she said, 'I shouldn't have looked at it' " (KCA, 76).

Edna experiences only the disgust occasioned by Chopin's recognition that "love" in this culture is simply another word for warfare. It is at the moment that she touches his wound, the damaged body of patriarchal capitalism, that Edna attempts to end her relation with Arobin by refusing to go to the races again, because: "I've got to work when the weather is bright, instead of—. . ." (KCA, 76). She is interrupted by him, who can hardly take the work of women with any seriousness. Like all capitalists, Arobin is cynical, not only regarding the value of women, but regarding *himself*. But it is also a sentence that Edna Pontellier cannot finish by herself; she is grateful for his interruption. Certainly Chopin's redefinition of love, suggested obliquely in Edna's brief moments of confidence with Mlle. Reisz and Adèle, must be understood in terms of Edna's (or any subject's) ability to work and thus contribute to social value. In no sense could such an idea of love be equated with the romantic love offered by Arobin.

Unfortunately, Chopin is also unable to finish Edna's sentence, cryptically writing "love" as productive communication in the margins of *The Awakening*. Such a conclusion is perfectly modern in its affirmation of the power of literary modernism to negate social corruptions even as it denies its own power to create livable alternatives. Chopin's accomplishment is to have forced us to look at these sites of bodily violation, of wounding, in order to understand how completely social and human intercourse have failed. As they re-enact the duel that Arobin fought in Paris when he was nineteen, Edna and Arobin merely reproduce the secret role of the individual in capitalism as soldier or pirate. Arobin's memory of Paris, of course, does not belong to him; it is something he has recollected from a cheap French romance.

The pathos of *The Awakening* is just this: that the self has become a character in a melodrama. As such, the self is based on nothing, lacks substance, and only haunts the reader and Edna with the more substantial powers of natural transformation and social communication that in our own fantastic postmodernity have become quaint memories. From our perspective, Chopin's undeveloped notion of social love seems merely sentimental. If we identify in that word Chopin's failure, then we must also recognize our own failure to be capable of such love.

11 The African-American Voice: William Faulkner's *Go Down, Moses*

> On a riverbank in the cool of a summer evening two women struggled under a shower of silvery blue. They never expected to see each other again in this world and at the moment couldn't care less. But there on a summer night surrounded by blue-fern they did something together appropriately and well.
>
> —Toni Morrison, *Beloved* (1987)

> Go down, Moses,
> 'Way down in Egypt land,
> Tell ole Pharaoh,
> Let my people go.
> —"Go Down, Moses"
> (African-American Spiritual)

Although I do not intend my argument in this book to constitute a comprehensive survey of American literature from Emerson to Faulkner, the historical gap separating Kate Chopin's *The Awakening* (1899) from William Faulkner's *Go Down, Moses* (1942) cannot be silently passed over. Were I to do so, then my readers might incorrectly conclude from my epigraph and my conclusion to this chapter that only Toni Morrison has responded adequately to the problem Faulkner's fiction, especially *Go Down, Moses*, poses: that African-American cultures cannot be satisfactorily represented by writers other than African Americans. As I argue in this chapter, Faulkner cannot speak for Southern African Americans, no matter how profoundly he claims to understand the history and social psychology of African-American disenfranchisement and disempowerment in the South. What makes *Go Down, Moses* such an important work of modern American literature is its dramatization of this conflict between the writer's desire to speak for others in the interests of their political and cultural rights and the reader's recognition that such aesthetic advocacy is still very much a part of the problem of cultural exclusion both in the political and literary domains.

There is, of course, a great tradition of African-American writing that addresses just such problems long before the publication of Faulkner's *Go Down, Moses*. W. E. B. Du Bois' writings and political and educational activism throughout his long career address centrally the need for African Americans to constitute their own cultural traditions, educational practices and institutions, and political agendas, even as Du Bois argues eloquently for African-American culture building on what it has borrowed from African, Caribbean, and Euroamerican cultures. Du Bois' *The Souls of Black Folk* (1903), for example, answers nearly forty years earlier the question posed by *Go Down, Moses*. Du Bois' answer is eloquently expressed in his epigraphs to the fourteen chapters of *The Souls of Black Folk*. Accompanying appropriate poetic epigraphs from the Euroamerican literary tradition—Symons, Swinburne, Elizabeth Barrett Browning, Schiller, Whittier, Byron, and others—there are fourteen musical extracts from the "sorrow songs" or spirituals analyzed and historicized by Du Bois in his final chapter. In only that final chapter does Du Bois change his pattern of choosing a poetic epigraph from the Western literary tradition and a musical epigraph from African-American spirituals. Chapter 14 quotes from the African-American song, "Lay This Body Down," and a musical extract from the spiritual "Wrestlin' Jacob."[1]

As many critics have noted, Du Bois' epigraphs express the "double consciousness" or "twoness" that he argues in chapter 1 is such a fundamental part of African-American epistemology and thus cultural experience in the United States:

> It is a peculiar sensation, this double-consciousness, this sense of always looking at one's soul by the tape of a world that looks on in amused contempt and pity. One ever feels his twoness,—an American, a Negro; two souls, two thoughts, two unreconciled strivings; two warring ideals in one dark body, whose dogged strength alone keeps it from being torn asunder.[2]

Given the neo-Hegelian cultural progressivism that Du Bois frequently invokes, it would seem that his aim in these epigraphs is to express finally some synthesis of the great Euroamerican and African-American cultural traditions: a blending of poetry and music that would transcend twoness and represent a distinctive American identity:

> The history of the American Negro is the history of this strife—this longing to attain self-conscious manhood, to merge his double self into a better and truer self. In this merging he wishes neither of the older selves to be lost. He would not Africanize America, for America has too much to teach the world and Africa. He would not bleach his Negro soul in a flood of white Americanism, for he knows that Negro blood has a message for the world. He simply wishes to make it possible for a man to be both a Negro and an American, without being cursed and spit upon by his fellows, without having the doors of Opportunity closed roughly in his face.
>
> (Souls, 5)

Yet this passage, like Du Bois' epigraphs to chapter 14, subtly rejects an assimilationist ideal for African Americans. What emerges in the course of Du Bois' *Souls* is the construction out of African-American and Euroamerican intellectual traditions just what the title promises: the *souls* of black folk. That ontology depends crucially for Du Bois on the African American's right, even *responsibility* in the case of the African-American intellectual, to know and use the "best that has been thought and written," including the traditions of Western civilization that have often excluded African Americans:

> I sit with Shakespeare and he winces not. Across the color line I move arm in arm with Balzac and Dumas, where smiling men and welcoming women glide in gilded halls. From out of the caves of evening that swing between the strong-limbed earth and the tracery of stars, I summon Aristotle and Aurelius and what soul I will, and they come all graciously with no scorn or condescension. So, wed with Truth, I dwell above the Veil.   (Souls, 90)

Du Bois' final chapter of *Souls*, in which he analyzes the history and forms of the "sorrow songs," seems to explain just what the purpose of such immersion in Western tradition ought to serve. The work of such education is decidedly not for African Americans to imitate Aristotle and Shakespeare, but rather find a way to make the history of African-American spirituals communicate with the history of Western culture. The first task in such a cultural project is to theorize an African-American voice, which is just what Du Bois does throughout *Souls* and then dramatizes in his final chapter. As Eric Sundquist writes: "The last chapter of *The Souls of Black Folk* brings text and music into their greatest antiphonal proximity. At the outset of 'The Sorrow Songs' the alternating epigraphs from the European tradition of 'high' literature has been replaced by the lyrics of a sorrow song, 'Lay This Body Down,' which does not just stand in juxtaposition to but virtually merges with the musical bars from 'Wrestling Jacob.' "[3]

Du Bois successfully gives voice to the African-American music that he at times patronizingly characterizes as the "naturally veiled and half articulate" "message" that "the slave spoke to the world" (Souls, 209). To be sure, Du Bois carefully constructs African-American history in *Souls* to situate himself at the forefront of a progressive development that virtually demands his intellectual leadership. Thus he may claim in the concluding chapter to give voice to the "half articulate" message of his forebears under slavery by making that message intelligible within the Western tradition. That he does so without subordinating African-American culture to Euroamerican tradition is clear from the systematic way he uses African-American traditions to criticize the failings of Western democracy—failings manifest in practices of slavery and policies of imperial conquest.

Du Bois' use of epigraphs is a brilliant rhetorical device, because the musical epigraphs leave most white readers, even those able to read the music, unable to comprehend allusions to a musical tradition nearly self-evident to African Americans. Just as the traditional poetic extracts constitute a code for educated white readers at the turn-of-the-century, so the musical quotations are intended to offer a similar code for the African-American reader. As Sundquist puts it: "The code of black America, although Du Bois was loath to reduce it to a separatist philosophy, was latent in those elements of the spirituals that had not been appropriated by the dominant culture."[4] When lyrics and music are brought together by way of the African-American tradition in what might be termed the musical "call and response" of "Lay This Body Down" and the musical extract from "Wrestlin' Jacob," Du Bois claims not to have forgotten or put aside his Aristotle and Shakespeare, but learned how to use them for the purposes of reading and thus constituting his own African-American heritage. Unquestionably, Aristotle and Shakespeare will "sound" differently in such a tradition, and it is just this difference that makes a work like *The Souls of Black Folk* central in any consideration of the representation of African-American culture.

My brief discussion of Du Bois is intended only to mark the difference between the modern African-American writer's effort to speak *for* African-American culture in the representative manner that we take for granted in literary writing, which is nonetheless one of the least theorized issues in literary study. When Faulkner speaks *about* the history of African-American suffering throughout Southern history, he may do so with a powerful commitment to the cause of African-American civil liberties and social justice. Nevertheless, the authorial voice he uses inevitably discovers its own limits as those Du Bois so clearly marks in *Souls*. Faulkner's African-American characters are silenced not so much by Faulkner's ascription to them of passivity and stoic endurance, but more by Faulkner's failure to understand that what he takes to be their *inability* to speak for themselves may well be a *refusal to speak* in the discourse of the tyrant. At just such a moment, Faulkner must confront the dilemma that his own style is inevitably trapped within a Western cultural tradition that is very much part of the social and human problems he wishes to remedy in his fiction.

Between Du Bois' *The Souls of Black Folk* and Faulkner's *Go Down, Moses*, the Harlem Renaissance offers a complex and diverse history of cultural and intellectual responses to what it means to "represent" African-American culture— that is, to *speak for* the several cultures composing African Americans' communities in the United States. No major figure of the Harlem Renaissance fails to address centrally just this problem of African-American "voice," but Zora Neale Hurston's efforts to think through the theoretical implications of how African-

American voices *refuse* their ideological containment by Euroamerican traditions may provide the best transition from Du Bois to Faulkner. In *Mules and Men* (1935), Hurston dramatizes the "double-consciousness" of African-American experience in an interesting variation on Du Bois' formulation of this identity. As Henry Louis Gates, Jr. has characterized her narrative voice, "she constantly shifts back and forth between her 'literate' narrator's voice and a highly idiomatic black voice found in wonderful passages of free indirect discourse."[5] As Gates recognizes, Hurston supplements Du Bois' "twoness" with her "double experiences as a woman," as well as an African-American urban intellectual trying to represent her Southern heritage and its strongly oral components in a text written avowedly as "anthropology."[6]

In *Mules and Men*, African-American folk culture is expressed in a wide range of media and social practices that have been subordinated to urban high cultural forms of literature, the arts, and scholarship. Hurston's persona finds it difficult and at times dangerous to try to rediscover just how conversation, dance, drinking and working songs, gossip, preaching, and hoodoo function as the semiotic infrastructure of Southern African-American culture. The data she is compiling for her book for her mentor, Franz Boas, and her patroness, Mrs. R. Osgood Mason, is constantly undercut by the oral practices and nonverbal modes of communication that constitute the cultures she visits. As she explains in her introduction:

> Folklore is not as easy to collect as it sounds. . . . And the Negro, in spite of his open-faced laughter, his seeming acquiescence, is particularly evasive. You see we are a polite people. . . . We smile and tell him or her something that satisfies the white person because, knowing so little about us, he doesn't know what he is missing. . . . The theory behind our tactics: "The white man is always trying to know into somebody else's business. All right, I'll set something outside the door of my mind for him to play with and handle. He can read my writing but he sho' can't read my mind. I'll put this toy in his hand, and he will seize it and go away. Then I'll say my say and sing my song." (Mules, 2–3)

The "lyin' " and "signifyin' " through which folk-culture communicates in *Mules and Men* constantly remind us of the communal character of any individual voice and the distance separating oral and oral-formulaic modes from print culture.

In one of the several tales Hurston includes in *Mules and Men* to comment explicitly on this problem, Jim Presley offers an origin myth for African-American labor. The story is a venerable part of African-American folklore, and it is cited by Emerson in his 1844 lecture, "Emancipation in the British West Indies," which I have discussed in chapter 2:

God let down two bundles 'bout five miles down de road. So de white man and de nigger raced to see who would git there first. Well, de nigger outrun de white man and grabbed de biggest bundle. . . . When de nigger opened up his bundle he found a pick and shovel and a hoe and a plow and chop-axe and then de white man opened up his bundle and found a writin'-pen and ink. So ever since then de nigger been out in de hot sun, usin' his tools and de white man been sittin' up figgerin', ought's a ought, figger's a figger; all for de white man, none for de nigger.   (Mules, 74–75)

This division of labor in Jim Presley's parable seems to give divine sanction to the assignment of material work to African Americans and rhetorical representation to whites. Of course, the "god" of folk culture in *Mules and Men* is a diverse and often contradictory figure who works more like a trickster than a Christian patriarchal authority. In Hurston's retelling of Jim's story, which is told amid a rapid succession of different folktales toward the end of chapter 4, African Americans are in charge not only of labor but also of their own telling. The white man in the parable is relegated merely to keeping the accounts ("oughts" and "figgers"), and thus the arbitrariness of his authority seems even more glaring in the context of a series of rich stories that display the communicative skills of African-American tellers. In declaring the ways the white man cheats the African American, Hurston's version of Presley's story offers such communal telling as one means of taking back the community's rightful authority over its own earnings. What Emerson judges to be the "very sad . . . negro tradition" expressed in this story is transformed by Jim Presley and Hurston into an account of African Americans taking charge of their own cultural narrative. Indeed, the *comedy* in Hurston's version is part and parcel of her utopian vision in which this retelling has its part to play. In other words, Hurston's version calls for African Americans to do their own accounts, which is what her narrative attempts to express in its effort to represent the diversity of discursive means traditionally used in rural African-American communities.

Hurston's version does go some distance toward reclaiming the work of cultural representation, even in the details of this parable. In the final chiasmus—"ought's a ought, figger's a figger; all for de white man, none for de nigger"—Hurston's Presley makes two suggestive points. First, the white man uses mathematical signs in his account, sharply distinguishing between "o" and "1," much in the manner slavery depended upon the exclusion of African Americans from identity under the law in order to constitute the Southern white's identity as such. Like the scientific racism of Schoolteacher in Toni Morrison's *Beloved*, the white man's "oughts" and "figgers" implicate enlightenment rationality in maintaining racial hierarchies Hurston, Presley, and the reader know to be social fictions. In the rhetorical chiasmus, "ought" (o) is apportioned to the African American and "figger" (value) to the white man. Yet in the folk rhyme, "figger" is associated with "nigger," and it is just this power to "figure" in the sense of making rhetorical meaning, rather than mathematical sums, that distinguishes African-American culture from the white man's culture in Hurston's and Jim Presley's interpretations. Finally, Jim Presley may reclaim "figgerin' " as equivalent to his own rhetorical *figuring* in the story (or "lyin' " or "signifyin' ") in ways that reconnect material labor "out in de hot sun" and the intellectual and managerial tasks of using signs to "account" for our labor either in strict account books (the ledgers of the slaveowner and later of the farmer who lets land to sharecroppers are invoked here) or in the more sophisticated "accounting" of labor that comes in the community's internal communication (what is occurring in Hurston's account of the "signifyin' " among tellers at the end of this chapter).

My brief examples from Du Bois and Hurston are meant to do no more than testify to what the African-American tradition has long been saying in music, song, dance, religion, politics, and literature: "We have been speaking for ourselves for a very long time; you just have not been listening." Just what constitutes "not listening," however, is what I want to investigate in Faulkner's *Go Down, Moses*, because it bears directly on the problems confronting American writers who want to respond to social issues affecting African Americans and other communities marginalized by the dominant ideology, especially when these American writers do not belong to these communities. Such writers are only now beginning to understand the complex ethical and aesthetic problems posed when they attempt to "speak for" other groups, and those writers who understand these problems often do so primarily because they have been challenged by writers and intellectuals from the communities they would represent. Yet when Faulkner wrote "for" African-American rights in his fiction, he did not realize how profoundly his own authorial position was contaminated by the will-to-power he criticized in Southern slaveowners and their tragic heirs. Twentieth-century African-American writing, especially in the work of the authors of the Harlem Renaissance and subsequent Black Arts' Movement, has constituted its own coherent literary and cultural tradition, much as women writers and intellectuals have constituted a literature and culture of their own.

Part of my argument in this book is that classic American writers from Emerson to Faulkner can only claim for their works emancipatory political potential if they learn from writers who have consciously worked in the great liberatory movements of modern America: abolition and civil rights; the women's rights', suffrage, and feminist movements. Part of this "learning" is, of course, our education as scholars and critics, which is why I attempt to assess in this book the political aims of mainstream American writers in terms of the political achievements of writers like Frederick Douglass, Harriet Jacobs, and Kate Chopin. *How* should we read literary texts to comprehend not only their overt political messages but their exclusions and blindnesses? Reading *Go Down, Moses* with the message of Du Bois, Hurston, and the modern African-American tradition in mind, we discover how deeply our own habits of professional reading imitate and thus redouble Faulkner's own tendency to repeat the will-to-power of the Southern white landed estate, even as this critical tradition spoke with apparent confidence about the "racial themes" in William Faulkner.

In *Playing in the Dark*, Morrison finds "interesting" but "not surprising" that "some powerful literary critics in the United States have never read, and are proud to say so, *any* African-American text;" she finds "surprising. . . that their refusal to read black texts—a refusal that makes no disturbance in their intellectual lives—repeats itself when they reread the traditional, established works of literature worthy of their attention."[7] At the end of a list of major American writers from Henry James to Flannery O'Connor whose works would benefit from interpretation by way of their representations of race, Morrison concludes: "With few exceptions, Faulkner criticism collapses the major themes of that writer into discursive 'mythologies' and treats the later works—whose focus is race and class—as minor, superficial, marked by decline."[8] *Go Down, Moses* is at the very center of those "discursive 'mythologies'" that have until only quite recently distracted Faulkner scholars from any adequate treatment of his struggle to come to terms with his ancestors' legacy of racial division. In order to reread Faulkner as Morrison suggests, we need to reconsider not only his neglected "later works" but also those works that have been used to build his modern American reputation by way of certain strategic mythologies that have reinforced the very racial hierarchies Faulkner wished to, but could not alone, dismantle.

Thirty years ago, in *The Achievement of William Faulkner*, Michael Millgate argued that the aesthetic unity of *Go Down, Moses* resulted from Faulkner's successful representation of "the white-Negro theme."[9] Like other literary formalists of his generation, Millgate focused on a theme notable for its tension and conflict, in order to show how the literary work effects "the conjunction, and in some measure the fusion, of a number of disparate ideas" (201). For Millgate, this aesthetic synthesis depends crucially on the character of Ike McCaslin, "whose combination of sensitivity and long life would afford scope for the two complementary strategies of innocent childhood and retrospective old age" (201). More than simply anchoring the thematic tensions of *Go Down, Moses*, Ike *embodies* them in a complex character that serves as an ironic patriarch for a new, redeemed South. Ike may never "father" the "new family" that would transform the conflicts of Southern whites and African Americans into an openly miscegenated family, but this is surely what Faulkner claims for himself as author in dramatizing the twinned fates of the whites and African Americans of the McCaslin family as the central action of *Go Down, Moses*.[10]

Ike is "father to no one" but "uncle to a county;" Faulkner creates what ought to be built in the moral space made possible by Ike's renunciation of his family's legacy: the sins of slavery. Like Eliot's Tiresias in *The Waste Land*, Faulkner's Ike can only bear witness to the sinful world he inhabits.[11] As a consequence, Faulkner is Ike's supplement, the patriarch who will cathartically purge the conflicts of the Old South in a new genealogy in which family secrets become the news of his literary narrative. Such a reading is, I think, extraordinarily close to Faulkner's own intentions, which explains how successful formalist interpretations of Faulkner have been long after their theoretical assumptions have been thoroughly deconstructed. As long as we continue to read *Go Down, Moses* as a "modern novel," we repeat the victimization of African Americans, in part by subordinating ourselves as readers to a literary authority often as paternalistic as that of the Southern patriarch.[12]

Even when the reader, the African American, the woman, and the child—all victims in Faulkner—are permitted by such a narrative to speak, their voices are already echoes or necessary functions within the larger purposes of this modernist's story. It is for this reason, I think, that the interpretation of *Go Down, Moses* according to the education of Ike McCaslin has been so successful and yet remains so profoundly dissatisfying, not only for the cultural critic but also for Faulkner. Whatever Faulkner's modernist intentions in novels like *The Sound and the Fury* and *Absalom, Absalom!*, both of which certainly shape the "unity and coherence" of the stories in *Go Down, Moses*, he still understood at some level beyond the purely aesthetic that the political arguments of his major works demanded an African-American voice at once more rebellious and utopian than any of the voices he ever projected in his fictions.

The organization of *Go Down, Moses* in terms of the central action of Ike McCaslin's renunciation both empowers Faulkner as the author required to complete Ike's unfinished story and further marginalizes the African-American characters who paradoxically appear to have more substantial fictional realities than in any of Faulkner's previous works. Faulkner seems caught by the contradiction of his own aesthetic and political logics: on the one hand, he emulates the white Southern patriarch in the responsibility he assumes for his extended family; on the other hand, he knows that the sins of such families can be redeemed only by publicizing the scandal of slavery *and* encouraging its victims to revolt against the social psychological habits that are as much the insidious legacy of slavery as the legal and economic bonds of postbellum racism.

As far as the formal definition of this famous "short-story cycle" is concerned, my thesis regarding the complex interplay between Faulkner's expression—the genealogy from Ike to Author—and repression—the subordination of African Americans to the moral authority of Ike or Faulkner—would seem best served by considering the seven-part work as characterized by its "disunity, discontinuity, and never-ending strife."[13] This is Susan Donaldson's argument in "Contending Narratives: *Go Down, Moses* and the Short Story Cycle," which convincingly demonstrates that Faulkner's equivocal descriptions of the collection "as a novel and as a short story collection" might be interpreted in terms of what theorists have often claimed are the inherent "conflicts and tensions" of the literary form itself. Appealing as such an approach is, it tends to reaffirm Faulkner's modernist and even formalist intentions, insofar as it concludes by a certain inevitability that "Faulkner" (that is, the author-function of this name) encompasses this conflict and struggle. As Donaldson concludes her essay, the tensions and discontinuities in *Go Down, Moses* finally achieve a "small measure of victory" in the literary effort to resist the monologic discourse of the McCaslin ledgers with "the unbending nature of" the literary struggle "to revise and transform" the ugly facts of those ledgers. Thus she may end her interpretation by recalling "Faulkner's definition of life as motion and motion in turn as a kind of revisionary triumph," modernist virtues we now identify closely with the ideology of modernism.[14]

While acknowledging the importance of Donaldson's approach in taking us beyond the obsession with the unity and coherence of *Go Down, Moses* in terms of Ike, "The Bear," and the related themes of the hunting stories, I want to propose a more radical disunity in this collection that focuses on Faulkner's ultimate inability to grant his African-American characters the independent voices he knows they must have in a truly New South. In this regard, Faulkner's text (and not just *Go Down, Moses*, but the Faulknerian text in general terms) must confront the fundamental limitation of the *family* as simulacrum for community, the public sphere, and the social relations of those who share the work of culture. It is the hypocrisy of the white Southern family that Faulkner criticizes so vigorously, exposing the violence and lies such families employ to maintain the illusion of racial "purity." Among the many consequences of the violence of slavery against African Americans, damage to the African-American family as a basis for community is one treated at length in Faulkner's fiction. Even in the face of his own literary critique of the violence done by slavery to Southern families, Faulkner insists upon reconstructing the family, offering another ideal that often finds its new genealogical basis in the relation of the literary author and reader.

Insofar as Ike McCaslin's story in "The Old People," "The Bear" and "Delta Autumn" works out the logic of Faulkner's previous novels, our attention to his education is likely to reproduce the values of the modern but still middle-class novel. There is, however, another narrative in *Go Down, Moses*, and it is one that must be read in conflict with the sentimental myth of Ike McCaslin's *imitatio Christi*. In the four other stories in *Go Down, Moses*, Faulkner attempts to give real voices, lives, and thus characters to African Americans, in ways that go far beyond his previous works.[15] Yet even as he tries to overcome the melodrama he recognizes in the nostalgia for nobility and sacrifice of an older Southern aristocracy represented by Ike in its passing, he also reaches what I consider a fatal limitation in his representations of these "other" voices—those African-American persons he knows must speak and write for themselves in order for any true redemption of the sins of slavery and racism to begin. In *Go Down, Moses*, Faulkner realizes the impasse of his own fictional project, even as he struggles impossibly to transcend imaginatively his own white Southern heritage.

Go Down, Moses is a sustained elegy for the disappearance of the Old South and the failure of the New South to overcome the moral ruin of a system built on slavery. But there is another kind of mourning organizing *Go Down, Moses* that works differently from the sentimentality shaped out of the tattered elegance of de Spains, Beauchamps, and Edmondses. From the opening story, "Was" to the concluding, title story, "Go Down, Moses," Faulkner's collection is unified and coherent in its sustained mourning less for what has been lost than for what has been killed. From the murder of a man (Tomey's Turl), who could be traded in a card game in "Was," to the return from Chicago of Butch Beauchamp's corpse, all decked out in the good will of Gavin Stevens' collection from the shamed townsfolk of Jefferson in "Go Down, Moses," the legacy of racial violence is consistent from the antebellum to postbellum South, both as a fact of African-American experience and as what white Southern culture represses. "Is you gonter put hit in de paper? I wants hit all in de paper. All of hit," Molly demands of Mr. Wilmoth, the city editor, while they are waiting at the station for Butch Beauchamp's body to arrive from Chicago.[16]

It is just such publication of what Molly expects to be published in the paper, but never will be, that Faulkner insists redeems his own work from hopeless elegy, desperate nostalgia. What Molly really wants to be published in the Jefferson newspaper is hardly the headline: "Butch Beauchamp Executed for Murder of a Chicago Policeman," but that other headline that only literature could publish: "Roth Edmonds Sold My Benjamin . . . . Sold Him to Pharaoh," which is not just Molly's refrain but intended to be that of the entire African-American community, as it tries to explain how emancipation has come to mean only another insidious sort of economic and psychological bondage for its children (GDM, 362–63).

"Go Down, Moses" ends in a curiously ambivalent way that underscores the conflict between the two narratives I find wrestling for dominance in *Go*

Down, Moses: Ike McCaslin's myth and the stories of the African Americans struggling to set themselves free. Molly's desire to publish "in de paper" what has happened to Butch Beauchamp is communicated to the reader in a final conversation between the two white men, Gavin Stevens and the newspaper editor, Wilmoth. Leaning out of his motor car, Wilmoth asks Stevens, "Do you know what she asked me this morning?" and Stevens knows enough to say, "Probably not" (GDM, 364). But even as both of them sense they cannot know the inner experience of the African American's oppression, each concludes Faulkner's narrative (the story and the collection) by trying to do so. Although both of them have "protected" her from the truth that Butch was executed for murdering a policeman, Wilmoth suspects that "if she had known what we know even, I believe she would have" still wanted it "all in de paper" (365). Gavin Stevens reads the grandmother's intentions more predictably, with all the benign paternalism of the white liberal: "*She just wanted him home, but she wanted him to come home right. She wanted that casket and those flowers and the hearse and she wanted to ride through town behind it in a car*" (365). As Millgate concludes, "nowhere in the whole of Faulkner's work is there a more persuasive dramatization of the gulf dividing the white man's mind from the Negro's than the scene in which Stevens, confronted by Molly's grief, flees from the house in a kind of terror" (212).

There is yet another reading that Faulkner leaves unwritten in the gap between Molly chanting her own version of the African-American spiritual— "Roth Edmonds . . . Sold my Benjamin"—and Mr. Wilmoth quoting her strange question to Gavin Stevens: "Is you gonter put hit in de paper?" In this implicit reading, what Molly wants published in the paper is just the "news" that Roth Edmonds, surviving representative of the sins of slavery, is responsible for the fates of African Americans who are as doomed by their migrations north, like Butch's flight to Chicago, as their ancestors were by their captivity in the slaveholding South. Gavin Stevens vainly imagines that "Aunt Mollie" wants only the imitation of propriety and respectability that she identifies with white culture— casket, flowers, hearse, car, published obituary. Faulkner knows better, even as he cannot quite bring Molly to say what the two white men quote without understanding: she wants the heritage of slavery to be "published" in "de paper."

So much for good intentions. Faulkner does publish that headline, again and again, in that curious literary repetition-compulsion that characterizes his genius and his special regionalism, but it is not enough, or perhaps it is simply too much. For like the town newspaper of this better, moral sort, Faulkner's *Go Down, Moses* offers to publicize the South's Original Sin for the sake of reform: a new and better community, full of knowledge of its sinful past. All the celebrated mythopoeia of "The Old People" and "The Bear" works not simply to mourn a vanished America, but to lend a myth to this new, reformed community. Much as we would like to think that *Go Down, Moses* deals with the ugly facts of the Southern past, it deals as much, if not more, with the utopian future beyond slavery, that remote future Ike McCaslin can imagine only at its remotest: "*Maybe in a thousand or two thousand years in America*" (GDM, 344).[17]

There is little need for Faulkner to repeat in *Go Down, Moses* the historical analyses of the tangled human motives that permitted chattel slavery, the systematic rape of African-American women by whites for power and profit, the entanglement of Southern agrarianism with postbellum capitalism, and the wrecks of families for the sake of the fiction of the taboo against miscegenation. These and many more historical issues are the essence of Faulkner's earlier works, such as *The Sound and the Fury* and *Absalom, Absalom!*. What is missing from those two great novels is just what *Go Down, Moses* attempts to add: a future for the South beyond the cynical and racist judgment of that foreigner, Shreve, in *Absalom* that "The Jim Bonds will inherit the earth" or the shooting (again and again) of Charles Bon as he crosses the shadow of the gate at Sutpen's Hundred or the endlessly repeated suicide of Quentin Compson in *The Sound and the Fury*.

This is elegy with a vengeance, like the revenge Molly Beauchamp would take on all the Edmonds and McCaslins and Compsons and de Spains for selling her Benjamin to Pharaoh. Yet such vengeance, insofar as it suggests an apocalyptic revelation of what the slaveowning South has destroyed in itself, is also intended to establish a new visionary community. It is in this that Faulkner stumbles, perhaps inevitably on the very elements in his own background that cannot be reformed, the white Southernness that can never be read entirely out of his fictional histories. It's clear enough that what is wrong with the New South (even before it was called such) is simply an elaboration of the sins of the Old South. The card game that Hubert Beauchamp plays first with Uncle Buck, then with Uncle Buddy, for the twinned wagers of Sophonsiba and Tomey's Turl, for ownership of a woman and a slave, is played again and again in these stories without regard for history. It's the same game that Lucas plays with the St. Louis drummer for the "divining machine" that will find the buried treasure in the Indian Mound in "The Fire and the Hearth," and the same game that informs Lucas' crazy quest for buried treasure. Just as the churn in which he discovers that $ 1,000 gold piece doubles perversely Hugh Beauchamp's bequest of the tin-pot stuffed with IOU's in "The Bear," so does the cheat of this game find itself revealed in the game of dice that the bereaved Rider exposes as he forces the white night watchman to open his hand to reveal the "miss-outs" with which he's cheated his workers for years in "Pantaloon in Black." Butch's game in Chicago was the numbers, "that people like him make money in," Gavin Stevens tells Miss Worsham, but the ghetto game was already learned at home from the white slaveowner or the white night watchman at the Lumber Mill, as Ike McCaslin learns surely enough from the numbers game of the ledgers in the Commissary (GDM, 357).

The numbers game is run in everyday Southern life before and after the Civil War. It's the numbers game that Nat Beauchamp runs on her father, Lucas, when she bargains for a new back porch, a stove, and that husband, George Wilkins, just as marriage becomes the equivalent of the same game to save Lucas and George from Patcham Penitentiary for their illegal stills. But the reader is supposed to know all this; the original Numbers Game began as white traders counted the slaves in the holds of their ships, white masters totted their profits in the children of rape, even paid those children, as Buddy and Buck did, with the paternal "legacy" that would "take care of them for life." That frivolous, most dangerous game structures the elegy of *Go Down, Moses*, but it takes us no further than the previous novels, gives no warrant for a collection of stories other than the customary repetition-compulsion that bespeaks most often repression. It is just such repression that encourages us to read the collection according to the three stories that shape the myth of the vanishing wilderness and its moral equivalent, Ike McCaslin, last individualist on the much diminished frontier.

But that narrative of Ike's unsuccessful sacrifice only distracts us from the other story of "What Is To Be Done?" for which Faulkner has often been reproached for his answers. Renunciation is, of course, disallowed from the outset, either for the sons and daughters of slaves or for the nominally legal heirs of white slavers. Ike's renunciation is no more Christological than Quentin's suicide, no more redemptive than Shreve's racist surrender to the "Jim Bonds" inheriting the earth in his outburst at the end of *Absalom, Absalom!*. Endurance, as in "they endured," is no redemption either, although Faulkner tries that here and there, but with a tired hand, knowing already in *Go Down, Moses* that the lifelong endurance of the African American has permitted only the same oppression and exploitation with a vengeance. The real sacrifice is the one recorded in Faulkner's somewhat stilted dedication of the volume:

To Mammy
CAROLINE BARR
Mississippi
[1840–1940]
Who was born in slavery and who gave to
my family a fidelity without stint or
calculation of recompense and to my
childhood an immeasurable devotion
and love

(Dedication, *Go Down, Moses*)

It is Caroline Barr's century that frames the narrative, even if Faulkner can only "name" her with the slave name, "Mammy," and the white paternalism inscribed in his testament to her "nobility" for "fidelity without . . . calculation of recompense."

It is "recompense" that the African Americans refuse when offered by Ike, again and again in the stories telling his side of the myth, but it is "recompense" that African Americans deserve and begin to demand in the other stories of the collection. "Recompense" not just for the lost wages, the lost land, the abused bodies, the broken families, but also for the voices and words stolen from them: the power to *represent themselves*. Lucas Beauchamp is as barred from the white law in "The Fire and the Hearth" as chained slaves were, spite of his $ 3,000 in the Jefferson Bank, his magical farming, his profitable still in the woods, his wariness of the drummer's swindle even in the midst of his own treasure madness. He may defy the law, as he does when he marches before the Chancellor to retrieve the paper of divorce filed by Molly, sick of his white man's craziness for treasure, or when he creeps into Edmonds' bedroom with his open razor to avenge his manhood (yes, it is his manhood, not Molly's honor, that he is saving as he wrestles Edmonds for the pistol, saved again by the pistol's misfire). He may defy the law, but Lucas never beats the law, because the true law sits on his head in that carefully tended beaver hat (or the worn vest or the watch-chain) given him by McCaslin fifty years' before.

It's that *beaver hat*, let's say, that Rider doesn't wear when he flashes his razor against the throat of the cheating night watchman in "Pantaloon in Black." Rider imitates Lucas when he "rented the cabin from Carothers McCaslin and built a fire on the hearth on their wedding night as the tale told how Uncle Lucas Beauchamp, Edmonds' oldest tenant, had done on his forty-five years ago and which had burned ever since," as if connecting his story with Lucas', "Fire and the Hearth" with its successor, "Pantaloon in Black" (GDM, 134). But Rider more consistently than Lucas tries to break the family bonds of obligation that continue to subordinate African Americans to their old slave masters. Rider insists upon paying for everything he uses with money that represents clearly his labor. He is a new kind of self-reliant man, who knows better than Ike (or his transcendentalist ancestors) *why* independence is so important. Lucas accepts the propriety of the law, respects its rituals and symbols; Rider refuses such legal conventions, speaking forthrightly when Maydew comes to arrest him, "Awright, white folks. Ah done it. Jest dont lock me up,"—"advising, instructing the sheriff," Faulkner adds, as if to remind us that Rider has his own voice, even though he is being quoted here (152). It's not the *law* of Jefferson that gets Rider—he tears the prison bed from its anchors, the bars of his cell from the wall. It is a wonderful scene, tragicomic in the way it renders trivial for just a moment the power of the white folks' law, now that Rider

> had done tore that iron cot clean out of the floor it was bolted to . . . and throws the cot against the wall and comes and grabs holt of that steel barred door and rips it out of the wall, bricks hinges and all, and walks out of the cell toting the door over his head like it was a gauze window-screen, hollering, "It's awright. It's awright. Ah aint trying to git away." (GDM, 153)

In the end, however, if the "law" can't hold him, the Birdsongs will, as the Deputy reminds us: "Of course Ketcham could have shot him right there, but like he said, if it wasn't going to be the law, then them Birdsong boys ought to have the first lick at him" (153). We are reminded here that the "white folks" still have the community of their families to crush even the most willful and furiously honorable self-reliance, like Rider's. The law won't even recognize properly Rider's family—"So we loaded him into the car, when here come the old woman—his ma or aunt or something," and it's true that the "old woman" can't do anything to save him from the Birdsongs (152).

What "saves" Rider in the moment he reveals the law to be powerless to contain him is in fact "them chain gang" African Americans who have come back to the jail, who obey Sheriff Ketcham's order, "Grab him! Throw him down!" Rider throws them off and out of the room "like they was rag dolls," reminding us, "Ah aint trying to git out," until at last they pulled him down—"a big mass of . . . heads and arms and legs boiling around on the floor" (GDM, 154). The Birdsongs are a *family*, but the group on the floor of Ketcham's jailhouse is "a big mass," a metonymy for that "old woman—his ma or aunt or something." And if they "save" Rider for the moment, it is only for Sheriff Ketcham's bullet or the Birdsongs' lynching (it's lynching, in fact, that murders him).

In moments such as these, Faulkner wants us to understand how crucial it is for African Americans to have a sense of community built from shared labor, just as the heritage of slavery was their shared violation, the theft of that labor. Yet in just such moments, it is the family that returns as Faulkner's model, as if he cannot quite see clearly what African Americans struggling against slavery generally understood so well: that the "family" and the "community" are synonyms in the common work of Abolition.[18] Nearly half a century later, Toni Morrison would rewrite in *Beloved* this ugly scene, in which the African American is condemned to dig his own grave, build his own prison, abandon her own child, witness her brother's whipping, crush his own spirit. In the prison in Alfred, Georgia, Paul D will join the other men in the "chain up" in their collective escape from the rain and mud rising in their cells, diving down beneath the mud and walls:

For one lost, all lost. The chain that held them would save all or none, and Hi Man was the Delivery. They talked through that chain like Sam Morse and, Great God, they all came up. Like the unshriven dead, zombies on the loose, holding the chains in their hands, they trusted the rain and the dark, yes, but mostly Hi Man and each other.[19]

Lucas Beauchamp is too dependent on white symbols in his bid for economic independence. He is still caught in the social psychology of the old and tangled genealogies. Rider is too insistent upon a complete and utter independence, not only from white culture but also from his own community, driven there no doubt by his experience of other workers' acceptance of the racial and economic hierarchies. In Morrison's rewriting, the chain-gang's escape is a consequence of the coordinated labor that is as much physical effort as communication, in that beautiful figuration in which the "chain" becomes the telegraph cable, and "they talked through that chain like Sam Morse." "Zombies on the loose," indeed, for they are "resurrected" by their own efforts, giving credence to the "hoodoo" of communal effort that defies ultimately the disciplined cruelty of white culture.[20] This is the new speech that Morrison roots in an African-American community forged in the resistance to slavery and consolidated by its history from Reconstruction to the Civil Rights movement.

"Blood relations," we know from "The Old People" and "The Bear," have nothing to do with family descent, inheritance, genealogical tables. That way, madness lies, again and again, not as a consequence of some perverse biological theory of secret incest, but simply as a result of the unnaturalness psychically and sociologically bred into the South by its power-hungry patriarchs. "Blood relations," family bonds, are born even more perversely of Thomas Sutpen's recognition and refrain, "Because I own this rifle," from which all else issues in the violent procreation that follows the scriptural model of the original white Southerner, Cain, that city-builder who murdered to create. The "blood relations" for Faulkner ought to be symbolized in the sweat and blood of shared labor, which ought to be the meaning of the blood that Sam Fathers daubs on the cheeks of the young Ike McCaslin following his first kill of deer in "The Old People." This is the "blood hot and strong for living, pleasuring, that has soaked back into" the earth of which Cass McCaslin tells Ike at the end of "The Old People" (GDM, 179). To be sure, this is part of the customary white rationalization of the sins brought on by slavery: "And even suffering and grieving is better than nothing," although Faulkner is careful to remind the reader: "There is only one thing worse than not being alive, and that's shame" (179). Above all, Cass naturalizes this economy of community, in which "the earth dont want to just keep things, hoard them; it wants to use them again" (179). "Using" the grief and suffering of the African American "again" may be what Faulkner at times appears to be doing with the sin of the South and all the melodrama of General Compsons and Major de Spains. But there is also a sense in which Faulkner wants to think *beyond* the natural family, wrecked as the very concept was by the violence of slavery, to some community beyond the biological family.

The distinctions among the "blood" shared by way of common violence (the blood that stains the hands of the children of white slaveowners), the "blood" earned in the common cause of the hunt, and the coordinated labor of building a community are finally very hard to make, since each version participates in the basic economy of the South, old and new, and desperate as he is to do so, Faulkner cannot quite identify the moral boundaries. Given the evasiveness of the law on just these issues—its tendency to slip from the defense of property to the justification of violence, both displacing the human concerns at stake, how could Faulkner do much more than merely worry about the new circulation of "blood" through the political, legal, economic, and familial "bodies"?

Presumably, Faulkner's utopian alternative is the "treasure" that Lucas hunts with the damnfool "divining machine," that falls on him in the form of a gold coin when the Indian Burial Mound collapses on him, that Rider furiously uncovers as he buries Mannie in the opening paragraph of "Pantaloon in Black," building anew the Indian Burial Mound disturbed first by Lucas, then by the sheriffs hunting for his still in "The Fire and the Hearth." Once again, it is Rider, who "speaks" in ways that Lucas cannot, with an eloquence of action independent of the "white folks:"

> Flinging the dirt with that effortless fury so that the mound seemed to be rising of its own volition, not built up from above but thrusting visibly upward out of the earth itself, until at last the grave, save for its rawness, resembled any other marked off without order about the barren plot by shards of pottery and broken bottles and old brick and other objects insignificant to sight but actually of a profound meaning and fatal to touch, which no white man could have read. (GDM, 131–32)

Faulkner and the reader, of course, are the exceptions, because they are meant to "read" the "profound meaning" of these shards of history as equivalents to the Southern history Faulkner is uncovering for a similar purpose of ritual mourning, only to build up again the Indian Mound for those willing to read unlike the "white man." It is little wonder that Rider concludes this little act of grave-digging art with his characteristic dignity and self-reliance: "Then he straightened up and with one hand flung the shovel quivering in the mound like a javelin and turned and began to walk away." And yet it is the moment in which the "old woman" the white folks can't identify *is* identified for us by the narrative, by Rider's actions and by her *own*: "An old woman came out of the meagre clump of his kin and friends and a few people who had known him and his dead wife both since they were born, and grasped his forearm. She was his aunt. She had raised him. He could not remember his parents at all" (GDM, 132).

All this and more is quite splendid, both stylistically and intellectually: the measure of Faulkner's genius. The sanctity of human labor is invoked at every turn as the redemption of mourning, hard work and discipline being the values that might transform a society based so foully on the theft of another person's treasure: his or her own productivity. The racist clerks, the red-neck sheriffs, the submissive Southern tenant farmers (white and African American) are simply dismissed to the margins of the landscape in *Go Down, Moses*; only those who recognize implicitly their responsibilities to the community are given any space, the fictional equivalent of a body. Faulkner vivifies them, whether they are proud and sure, like Lucas and Sam Fathers, or determinedly confused, like Boon Hogganbeck and George Wilkins, or transcendentally above any law other than the community established by such labor, like Molly and Rider.

Their labor is not some throwback to a fantastic georgic, not some celebration of agrarian delights "before" slavery, the lumber-mill, the city, the automobile. It is always a labor of symbolic relations, not to be confused with symbolic labor, but the real labor of establishing relations among men and women according to their shared needs. Those encompass the customary wants of hunger, thirst, shelter, and reproduction, but embraced more widely by the primal need of human exchange, of that *intercourse* through which the members of a community take responsibility for what they have made. Thus the horrid comedy of the entangled hunt for Tomey's Turl and for Miss Sibby's mate in "Was" is redeemed in part by Lucas and George and Carothers hunting for the runaway wife, Molly, fleeing her treasure-mad husband. The perversity of that opening comedy is rendered apparently charming by Lucas' ritual renunciation of the "divining machine" that he sets, all polished and clean, on Roth Edmonds' dining-room table, amid the landlord's lonely meal.

All of this is intended, I think, to redeem the mythic vision of Ike in "The Bear," not so much in the form of the primeval, which Faulkner reminds us has its dangers for man, else there would be no need for community in the first place, but more enduringly as the symbolic speech that is meant to communicate the tangled family fortunes of the McCaslins and the tenant Beauchamps in "The Fire and the Hearth." In many ways, this story would be the centerpiece of the collection, the hinge of the door that Faulkner hopes to open to a future, "*in a thousand or two thousand years in America*" (GDM, 344), rather than simply the lid he lifts repeatedly to expose the dead, as in "The Bear" and its satellites, "The Old People" and "Delta Autumn," which so generalize the Southern mythos in the *American* Quest as to render the genius loci a mere forest mist. It is much harder to read "The Fire and the Hearth" than "The Bear" outside its Mississippi context, harder yet to wrench it into a general narrative of American initiation. The regionalism of "The Fire and the Hearth" encompasses problems of race, gender, and class that have wider significance for modern America, but it is nonetheless a narrative that begins with the very specific socioeconomic problems facing African Americans in the New South.

Yet "The Fire and the Hearth" is still part of Faulkner's problem, because it achieves that fragile redemption of the racist and sexist comedy of "Was" only by reinstating subtly a class system as insidious for our own age as the slave system of the Old South. After all, the labors of this utopian community are delegated according to the responsibilities virtually determined by the history uncovered. Carothers "Roth" Edmonds is no innocent Ike, no preternaturally old child refusing his patrimony. In "The Fire and the Hearth," Roth accepts the necessary rule of the landlord, and he wields it generally with the compassion that comes from his knowledge of the heritage he shares with Lucas and Molly, with Nat and George Wilkins. Threatening his sharecroppers with the law, he always saves them for his more temperate and humane laws. Leveling ultimatums, threatening them with exile, Roth always surrenders before their weaknesses, in the most decidedly paternal manner. There is no need to detail this paternalism; others have related how benignly Roth tolerates the foibles of his tenants, only to expose his secret motivation: the purification of his own history through his hard-won right to rule. Alternatively, he appears at times intent on proving his authority by virtue of his hard work, even when that work involves little more than occasional work with the accounts, tolerance of his tenants' whims, and selective knowledge of the larger historical scheme.

Of course, he is Molly's child, but only as a consequence of being orphaned at birth by his mother and rejected by his father, Zack. Of course, he knows the history of miscegenation in the ledgers, which is why he is so often interrupted writing at his own accounts. His right to rule is never clearer than in those moments of compassionate and pained recognition of his own ancestry in the nobility of his African-American tenants, as when Lucas crosses the Square to buy Molly that nickel's worth of candy, the same candy Roth ritually brings her each month to remind himself and her of his debt:

> He stood beside the car and watched Lucas cross the Square, toward the stores, erect beneath the old, fine, well-cared-for hat, walking with that unswerving and dignified deliberation which every now and then, and with something sharp at the heart, Edmonds recognized as having come from his own ancestry too as the hat had come. (GDM, 125)

That damned, absurd beaver hat, with its presidential pretense, that reminder of every man's need for authority, leaves Lucas still comic, and allows Roth Edmonds and perhaps the reader to forget just what both are forced to recognize fleetingly: that the ancestry Roth shares with Lucas derives its real nobility from the African Americans' refusal to submit to the brutalizations of the white slaveowner and then the white landowner (or just the plain white owner).

The vision that Roth Edmonds has so fleetingly just a few paragraphs before the end of "The Fire and the Hearth" occurs in a sustained way at the beginning of this last chapter (that is, chapter 3). It interrupts yet another "solitary supper" that he "couldn't eat." It is a perfectly imaginary moment, close to the Faulknerian sublime, in which Roth:

> Could see Lucas standing there in the room before him . . . the face which was not at all a replica even in caricature of his grandfather McCaslin's but which had heired and now reproduced with absolute and shocking fidelity the old ancestor's entire generation and thought . . . and he thought with amazement and something very like horror: *He's more like old Carothers than all the rest of us put together, including old Carothers. He is both heir and prototype simultaneously of all the geography and climate and biology which sired old Carothers and all the rest of us and our kind, myriad, countless, faceless, even nameless now except himself who fathered himself, intact and complete, contemptuous, as old Carothers must have been, of all blood black white yellow or red, including his own.* (GDM, 114–15)

Roth's vision in *Go Down, Moses* is the closest, I think, that any character comes to imaginative identification with Faulkner, who is also amazed and very nearly horrified by the visible thought of that face, which declares that the African American is the proper ruler, has the only right to authority, is the proper redeemer of community. The antecedence is only nominally ambiguous, strategically confusing the "he" and "his" in the twinned destinies of white masters and African Americans, but there is no radical undecidability here. It is "Lucas" alone who is meant to gloss those pronouns, so that we see only *him* at the end of the long historical and syntactic labyrinth that is Faulkner's encounter with his invented Minotaur. Lucas is now Theseus, and Faulkner and Edmonds too noticeably versions of King Midas. Both Roth and Faulkner must repress the heroism of Lucas Beauchamp, *encouraging* us (at least, Faulkner) to drift from "The Fire and the Hearth" in the direction of "The Bear" and its more conventional wisdom. For the generative power of Lucas Beauchamp is transformed hastily into that of the *patriarch*, quite a different figure indeed, "impervious to time" as well as to different races, intent only upon the maintenance of his undeniable *selfhood*, his insistent self-reliance and self-generation.

That tames it, puts aside the vision that is "very like horror" for both Faulkner and Roth Edmonds, so that they can imagine the African-American community centered on the familiar ideal of the "white folks": the self-made man. Lucas is that alright, but only as we recognize the jaunty angle of that beaver-hat. The beaver-hat is not only presidential; it links Southern history with manifest destiny, with the "capital" trapped originally by those Astors, and all that links Northern capitalism with the violence of the South. Unlike Rider, whose last words are prophetic—"Hit look lack Ah just cant quit thinking. Look lack Ah just cant quit," Lucas knows when to stop thinking, knows when to repress the powers Faulkner is finally afraid to grant him (GDM, 154). Refusing Roth's offer to lend him the divining machine from time to time, Lucas commands him: "Get rid of it. I dont want to never see it again. Man has got three score and ten years on this earth, the Book says. He can want a heap in that time and a heap of what he can want is due to come to him, if he just starts in soon enough. I done waited too late to start" (126–27). Wiser than Boon Hogganbeck, Lucas renounces modern machinery, but thereby joins company again with the dependent Boon, in effect commanding Roth Edmonds to take care of him and his.

Rider, too, is finally caught by a system in which the work of community reproduces the authority of the "white folks" or their surrogates. He never would be caught dead in any Beaver hat nor fool with any divining machine, but he works in the mill, gambles with the foreman, and then not just with those dice. Nevertheless, Faulkner needs "Pantaloon in Black" between "The Fire and the Hearth" and the hunting stories, because he knows Lucas is too conventional, too much the "white folks' "African American, even when, perhaps especially when, Roth Edmonds acknowledges Lucas' superiority. Recalling the story of when Lucas entered Zack Edmonds' bedroom and put the pistol to his head, just the misfire saving them both, Roth grants: "*And by God Lucas beat him. . . . Edmonds.*" Even an African American "*McCaslin is a better man, better than all of us. . . . Yes, Lucas beat him, else Lucas wouldn't be here. If father had beat Lucas, he couldn't have let Lucas stay here even to forgive him. It will only be Lucas who could have stayed because Lucas is impervious to anybody, even to forgiving them, even to having to harm them*" (GDM, 112). For all Faulkner grants Lucas in this moment, he nonetheless makes him available for the "white folks' " imaginary, where he himself can begin to be mythified, not entirely unlike that bear. "Impervious," as in "they endured" and gave "immeasurable devotion and love" "without stint or calculation of recompense." But what is needed is what Faulkner cannot give: African-American identity that is no longer "impervious" and thus historical, that does earn some "recompense" for its "devotion and love" and work.[21]

In his interview with Gwynn and Blotner, Faulkner said of progress: "But if in the end [change] makes more education for more people, and more food for more people, more of the good things of life—I mean by that to give man leisure to use what's up here instead of just leisure to ride around in automobiles, then . . . it was worth destroying the wilderness."[22] The divining machine and Boon's shotgun are in themselves just versions of those automobiles—just for people "to ride around in," but they are also metaphors for the machinery of writing and publishing, for the "divining machine" that Faulkner uses to find the often terrible treasure in the Indian Mound. Roth offers to lend that machine to Lucas from time to time, but Faulkner makes sure that we know how much Lucas fears such writing (although he is careful to let us know that Lucas can read and write) and would rather leave it to Roth and Faulkner. Perhaps Molly knows better, for she wants the editor to put "it" in the paper. Not the bare facts of Butch's pathetic end in a Joliet prison, but the African American mourning that is also her right to rule: "Done sold my Benjamin. . . . Sold him in Egypt." Gavin Stevens may think that "It doesn't matter to her now," but Faulkner knows better and does publish her dirge. If it captures the sufferings of African Americans before and after slavery, then it does so only at the discretion of the Carothers and Faulkners. The real divining machine remains stored in their attic.

Of course, I am arguing that Faulkner created a fictional conflict in *Go Down, Moses* that demonized his own literary authority, indicting it as part of the history of white masters from cruel slaveowners to paternalistic landowners. If Faulkner forgets himself in "The Old People," "The Bear," and "Delta Autumn," purposively creating an alter-ego in Ike McCaslin, then he criticizes himself in "Was," "The Fire and the Hearth," "Pantaloon in Black," and "Go Down, Moses" as a double of Roth Edmonds or Gavin Stevens or even Mr. Wilmoth. Beyond this it would be unreasonable to expect any writer to go, even one as brilliantly divided between a corrupt past and utopian future as Faulkner.

Still captives of the white imaginary as constructed by Faulkner and enacted by Roth Edmonds or Ike McCaslin, African Americans in *Go Down, Moses* nevertheless begin to *speak* and *act* in ways that exceed the customary melodrama of Faulkner's grand narrative in the novels. To be sure, they "speak" primarily in quotations, even their Southern dialects imitated (and thus mimicked) by paternalistic landowners or racist sheriffs. Lucas is still not *really* the father of us all, and Rider never *really* escapes the law. But these symbolic actions remind us with our own horror of recognition how rarely African Americans speak or act in Faulkner's other narratives; how silent and impervious and enduring they are.

So it is not the "racial theme" that is explored in *Go Down, Moses* as much as it is the African-American voice that begins to challenge the sentimental romance of the Old White South. Faulkner does not control or command these conflicts; they begin to crack his own voice. This would be the case whether the stories were distinguished with separate titles or arranged merely as numbered chapters, as Random House proposed for a reissue of *Go Down, Moses*.[23] We can always read a "cycle of stories" as if it were a novel, as I have argued so many professional readers of Faulkner have done by emphasizing the hunting stories and the myth of Ike's *Bildung*. But one motivation for choosing a short-story cycle may well be the author's sense that its inevitable formal disparities—the seams and sutures of the different parts—may challenge assumed unities and tacit coherences.

Understood in this way, what I have interpreted in Faulkner's *Go Down, Moses* might be considered a way of reading literary narratives differently from novels. Although in the popular imagination, Toni Morrison will continue to be hailed as a novelist, she strikes me as a storyteller who understands the need for communal and collective tellings that will transcend the limitations and bourgeois ideology of the novel. Like *Go Down, Moses*, *Beloved* is not a novel, but a collection of stories, less separated than those in Faulkner's cycle, to be sure, but nonetheless stories that cannot be read apart from their disparities. The difference between *Beloved* and *Go Down, Moses*, however, is that the stories of *Beloved* belong to Sethe, Paul D, Sixo, Denver, Stamp Paid, the Cherokee, and that runaway servant, Miss Amy Denver of Boston, and other victims who are redeemed in part and in passing by their abilities to tell the stories of their oppression and thereby imagine alternatives to it.

> Sethe was looking at one mile of dark water, which would have to be split with one oar in a useless boat against a current dedicated to the Mississippi hundreds of miles away. It looked like home to her, and the baby (not dead in the least) must have thought so too. As soon as Sethe got close to the river her own water broke loose to join it. The break, followed by the redundant announcement of labor, arched her back. (Beloved, 83)

Craig Werner has argued that the African-American literary tradition substituted "call and response" for the "repetition and revenge" the characterizes Faulkner's narratives.[24] Between my epigraph and this closing quotation from Morrison, I am trying to invoke my own version of "call and response" to transfigure Faulkner, as I think Morrison herself has done so eloquently and consciously throughout her writings. I also want to suggest that "call and response" as both a rhetorical mode fundamental to African-American culture and integral to the polyvocal short-story cycle may help us understand why this form has played such an important part in African-American literary history, not only as it has offered an alternative to the novel but also as it has expressed and thus helped transcend Du Bois' "twoness," the "double-consciousness" that can be a measure of the African American's schizophrenic experience in racially divided societies but also can be the measure of the African American's visionary powers: "After the Egyptian and Indian, the Greek and the Roman, the Teuton and Mongolian, the Negro is a sort of seventh son, born with a veil, and gifted with second-sight in this American world" (*Souls*, 5).[25]

Put another way, Morrison put it in the paper, all of it, just as Molly wanted it, maybe even better.

12 Revivals

In the preceding chapters, I have reinterpreted classic American literature in terms of its attention to changing nineteenth-century attitudes toward race, class, and gender. I have not simply "added" Douglass, Jacobs, and Chopin to an established tradition of classic American literature; I have argued instead that our enduring literature must meet the demands of political reform. By this I do not mean *any sort* of political reform, as I indicate in my critique of Poe's deeply ideological work in chapter 3. The literary work that aspires to undo democratic principles and yearns nostalgically for the strict, albeit arbitrary, hierarchies of a vanished aristocracy, certainly does not belong to the tradition of American literature that ought to provide a cultural foundation for utopian ideals of equal justice and opportunity. Douglass, Jacobs, and Chopin teach us that our greatest literature has an obligation to these simple goals, even if we grant that there are many different ways to work for such democratic ends.

This broad definition of literature's political functionality is appropriate to the cultural, regional, and historical diversities that continue to inform America, and it thus takes central issue with more restricted definitions of what is distinctive about American life and letters. What I have termed Emersonianism in this book is one of those narrow conceptions of American Exceptionalism that has depoliticized our literary tradition, contrary to my understanding of

American letters as fundamentally political. I began this book by criticizing one version of this Emersonianism in Richard Poirier's *The Renewal of Literature: Emersonian Reflections*, in which Poirier insists that "Literature is not in itself an effective political form of action, except under the rather limited conditions described later in this book."[1] Those limited conditions turn out to be those that apply to the special rhetorical and cognitive performativities reserved for literary language and its experience—that "world elsewhere" that the general public does indeed assign to literary experience. Such an Emersonian conception of a limited political function for literature has done a great deal to diminish the fundamental political function of American writing. Too often this Emersonian idealism has served ideological purposes contrary to its own avowed liberalism, in large part because this artificial separation between literature and life has made the voice of the intellectual sound distant and hollow.

In the struggle for the abolition of slavery, for women's rights, and for civil and economic rights in nineteenth-century America, writers and intellectuals played important parts both in the political and legal activism required but also in the transformations of habitual attitudes necessary for social reform. When literature is understood as an independent discourse, a "world elsewhere," then it certainly is "not in itself an effective political form of action," but our most committed writers have rarely understood literature to be so detached from those other discourses that make up social reality. What Douglass, Jacobs, Twain, James, and Chopin remind us is that literature is deeply involved in the creation of the "imaginary relationship of individuals to their real conditions of existence."[2] Althusser seminally defined ideology by adding that ideology is a 'representation' " of that "imaginary relationship," and we may conclude that literature either contributes centrally to that prevailing ideological representation or it finds ways of connecting its mimetic practice with the representation of another, better, and fairer relationship of individuals to the real conditions of their existence.

Literature never does its representational work alone, then, no matter how rigorously the artist and the critic struggle to sever the balloon of romance from the world of experience. In periods of historical crisis, literature has joined other discourses in the complementary work of political and social reform. Emerson and Douglass together on the stage in 1844 speaking on behalf of abolition present a powerful image of the coalition that ought to have connected their literary interests and political commitments. Emerson reading "The Boston Hymn" at the Jubilee Concert in the Boston Music Hall to celebrate the Emancipation Proclamation is an equally significant image of literature and politics together accomplishing the work of history. In his biography of Emerson, John McAleer describes the charged political atmosphere on that day:

At the sight of William Lloyd Garrison making his way into the hall, a spontaneous ovation rose from the assembled throng. Maestro Zerrahn tapped to let the audience know the orchestra was ready to play. . . . The audience was jubilant. Emerson himself was ebullient. His nervous fingers fumbled the manuscript and some of the pages flew from his hand and fluttered out into the crowd. . . . He read his poem with a confidence that gave a thrill of emphasis to his words, especially the celebrated eighteenth stanza:

Pay ransom to the owner
And fill the bag to the brim.
Who is the owner? The slave is owner
And ever was. *Pay him.*

. . . . With the last stanza the crowd, among which mingled former slaves, rose to its feet, shouting and singing.[3]

I quote this important episode in Emerson's career not only for its high political drama, but also for the emphasis it gives to the change Emerson made in his own thinking. Having repeatedly endorsed compensation to slaveowners along the lines of the British model of emancipation in Jamaica, repeatedly calling in his essays from 1844 to 1851 for the "thousand millions" necessary, Emerson here reproaches himself for having ever thought to "pay" an improper "owner." The coalition Emerson made with abolitionists brought about an important and instructive change in his own thinking, albeit quite late in the struggle against slavery. Emerson's insistence that "The slave is owner/ And ever was" repeats just what Douglass and Jacobs had said in their own versions of literary activism, and the lines correct Emerson's own earlier misunderstanding of the relations among labor, human identity, and value.

Such changes in Emerson's political thought did not finally transform his transcendentalism into a philosophy compatible with social activism, even though Emerson tried variously to adapt his idealism to the changing social circumstances of mid-nineteenth-century America. In fact, Emerson's struggle to connect transcendentalism to the prevailing values of Northern industrialism actually made it easier for subsequent interpreters to use his thought to justify commercial interests. In short, the intellectual struggle by itself is not sufficient to grant thinkers like Emerson more than occasional credit for the work of social reform they often claim for their thought. Yet the fitful commitments, deficiencies, and frequent contradictions of the idealist tradition in regard to social activism are worth understanding in contexts that exceed the narrow histories of ideas or aesthetics through which we so often view our philosophers and artists. Emerson's failure identifies certain points of necessary revision in our understanding of intellectual functionality, and it is therefore a failure that calls for the necessary supplements I have found in the politics of abolition and women's rights.

Such an approach to Emerson's intellectual and political limitations differs considerably from the Emersonian tradition that has celebrated both his theory and exemplification of self-sufficient genius. For Poirier, transcendental genius is characterized in part by its ceaseless *futurity*, "this apparent obliviousness to the present circumstance, this living into the future," which at its furthest extreme expresses Kant's idealist notion of genius as that which gives the rule to a concept yet remains itself ungoverned by that rule.[4] Always beyond the reach of social and historical laws, such genius can be represented only in the singularity of its historical examples: that is, the pantheon of great writers, each of whom merely repeats the basic qualities of the others. The literary critical enterprise of testifying to the greatness of the "major author" has often been our substitute for a genuine literary *history*. In the idealist account, literature offers only the promise of utopia. Quoting Emerson's final sentence in "Experience"—"The true romance which the world exists to realize, will be the transformation of genius into practical power"—Poirier acknowledges the futility of such utopia: "It is impossible to say what this transformation will mean, or how in our present state we would even be able to recognize it. We would have to be there already, in a future that seems to recede as we approach it, thanks to Emerson's accumulated terms of postponement."[5]

In the place of such a mystified theory of "genius," which Poirier is quite right to identify with the Emersonian tradition, I have tried to argue in this study for an historical narrative of American writers struggling to connect intellectual and practical powers, aesthetic and social transformation. None can connect either domain on his or her own; each requires work with and by others, as well as communication through the several different media every historical urgency demands. No artist, writer, intellectual, or political activist considered in this book has the luxury of *living in* that "future" Poirier associates with Emersonian genius, even if Edgar Allan Poe tried desperately to do so. Each is profoundly shaped by conflicts that make his/her work a product of its time, even as many of these writers struggled for better and for worse to transform their times. What allows us to think of these writers as constituting a tradition, rather than a museum of distinguished and discrete worthies, is their mutual dependence on each other for a nuanced account of literature's contribution to political reform in nineteenth-century America.

Emerson must be understood in terms of the reactionary unconscious his idealism produced in Poe, in the transcendentalist impasses ironized by Melville, and in the entrepreneurial "good will" (and historical ignorance) of James' Christopher Newman. In a similar fashion, Melville's critique of transcendentalism should not stand alone, distinct from the efforts of Douglass and Jacobs to figure ways to transvalue a perverse cultural symbology both in the slaveholding South and the industrial North. Whitman should not be read exclusively for his representation of the pain and damage of the Civil War; the suffering of that war remembers the long oppression of African-Americans represented so well by Douglass and Jacobs just as it anticipates the failure to overcome such suffering in the post-Civil War urban societies criticized by Mark Twain. In many cases, I have read together in this fashion writers who may have historical and political proximity but who have nonetheless had too little to say to each other in their own times. Thus Emerson and Douglass are put into what I think is a productive conversation, in the same manner that Faulkner is framed by W. E. B. Du Bois' and Zora Neale Hurston's anticipatory "answers" to his questions about African-American self-representation.

Such readings and cross-readings are by design the work of such critical history, which is no less *historical* for its invention of connections, complementaries, and supplementarities that may in fact have not been imaginable across the borders of the racial and gender divisions of nineteenth-century America. Because history is, as I argued in chapter 1, as much the work of the present as it is the recovery of a past, then our critical readings of the nineteenth century ought to make clear just what sorts of political and cultural connections were missed in the past, especially if we might learn from this past. In that same chapter, I argued that our "classic" literature when read in rehistoricized and repoliticized contexts might take on a new significance, a wider political relevance, and thus a revived value for this generation of readers.

Today there is a revival of literature's political function in a wide range of writers who understand both the importance of the imagination in social reform and also the necessity of linking aesthetic experience with political praxis. Toni Morrison is the voice that becomes audible at the end of chapter 11, because she answers so powerfully and eloquently Faulkner's question about how African Americans should represent their own communities. In so doing, Morrison works by way of what can only be termed an extraordinary modesty about what her art can accomplish, because so much of what is represented in her fiction comes from the deep resources of folklife and storytelling that constitute African-American communities. In a similar manner, Maxine Hong Kingston often poses as a mere literary medium through which Chinese-American cultural reality passes for the sake of literary expression, even though any reader of *Woman Warrior* or *Tripmaster Monkey* knows how crucial Kingston's art is to the representation of Chinese-American history.

What Native American writers like Leslie Marmon Silko and Louise Erdrich, Chicana writers like Sandra Cisneros and Helena Viramontes, and Vietnamese-American writers like Le Ly Hayslip have demonstrated in the past fifteen years—perhaps the most remarkable "renaissance" in American literary history—is that literature may contribute significantly, albeit never exclusively, to the practical politics of the rights movements by women and minorities that continue to shape American social and cultural reality. Once upon a time, scholars might have read these contemporary writers in terms of their allusions to the tradition of classic American literature, as Ellison's *Invisible Man* was too narrowly interpreted by literary experts. Contemporary American literature, especially in the prominence of authors representing cultural and sexual diversity, is rich in its allusion to and reinterpretation of classic American literature. In a far more important sense, however, contemporary American writers have revived a political standard by which we ought to measure both their works and whatever we choose to include in the "tradition" of "classic" American literature. Today our best literature has interests, allies, purposes, and causes with which we are encouraged to identify it in order to realize better this literature's social and political functions. Read in this way, contemporary American literature has revived a literary tradition of political activism that has remained for too long unrecognized, lost in the Emersonian aura.

Notes

1. At Emerson's Tomb

1. John Carlos Rowe, *Through the Custom-House: Nineteenth-Century American Fiction and Modern Theory* (Baltimore: Johns Hopkins University Press, 1982).

2. Richard Poirier, *The Renewal of Literature: Emersonian Reflections* (New York: Random House, 1987), p. 11. Further references in text cited as: Renewal.

3. Poirier, *A World Elsewhere: The Place of Style in American Literature* (New York: Oxford University Press, 1966), p. 3.

4. Poirier, *The Renewal of Literature*, p. 11.

5. Carolyn Porter, *Seeing and Being: The Plight of the Participant Observer in Emerson, James, Adams, and Faulkner* (Middletown, Conn.: Wesleyan University Press, 1981); Maurice Gonnaud, *An Uneasy Solitude: Individual and Society in the Work of Ralph Waldo Emerson*, trans. Lawrence Rosenwald (Princeton: Princeton University Press, 1987); Barbara Packer, "The Transcendentalists," in *The Cambridge History of American Literature*, vol. 2, Prose Writing 1820–1865, eds. Sacvan Bercovitch and Cyrus Patell (New York: Cambridge University Press, 1995), pp. 329–604; Len Gougeon, *Virtue's Hero: Emerson, Antislavery, and Reform* (Athens: University of Georgia Press, 1990); Howard Horwitz, *By Law of Nature: Form and Value in Nineteenth-Century America* (New York: Oxford University Press, 1991).

6. Porter, *Seeing and Being*, p. 117: "As this identity of poet and capitalist suggests, beneath the level on which Emerson attempted to compensate for alienation by

adopting the idealist position—making man 'whole again in thought'—lay a fundamental alliance between transcendent vision and neutral observation."

7. See the discussions of this conflict in chapter 5.

8. Eric Sundquist, *To Wake the Nations: Race in the Making of American Literature* (Cambridge: Harvard University Press, 1993), p. 7.

9. Sundquist's work is also comparative in the traditional sense of treating different national literatures, because he includes substantial material from Caribbean, West African, and European cultures that inform African-American and Euroamerican literatures. But my point here is that Sundquist's method of reading canonical literature in terms of African-American traditions, in order to enrich the former and to recognize better the contributions of the latter, is the sort of comparatism that Paul Lauter advocates in "American Literature: A Comparative Discipline," in *Canons and Contexts* (New York: Oxford University Press, 1990) and I advocate somewhat differently in "A Future for American Studies: The Comparative American Cultures Model," in *American Studies in Germany: European Contexts and Intercultural Relations*, eds. Günter H. Lenz and Klaus J. Milich (New York: St. Martin's Press, 1995), pp. 262–78.

10. Sundquist, *To Wake the Nations*, p. 22.

11. I am relying on the Index to Frederick Douglass, *Autobiographies*, ed. Henry Louis Gates, Jr. (New York: Library of America, 1994).

12. Sundquist, *To Wake the Nations*, p. 19.

13. Sacvan Bercovitch, *The Rites of Assent: Transformations in the Symbolic Construction of America* (New York: Routledge, 1993), p. 363.

14. Sundquist, *To Wake the Nations*, pp. 102–3, 75–83. See also chapter 5 in this study.

15. Bercovitch, *The Rites of Assent*, p. 370. I treat Bercovitch's reading of Douglass by way of Emerson in greater detail in chapter 5.

16. Harriet Jacobs, *Incidents in the Life of a Slave Girl*, ed. Jean Fagan Yellin (Cambridge: Harvard University Press, 1987), p. 54.

17. One of the limitations of the political scope of my argument in this book is sexuality and sexual preference, which are not treated in any significant way, even though Whitman's homosexuality figures implicitly in his reaction to the Civil War propaganda regarding "masculinist" ideals of military valor. It is not a limitation I can excuse merely by claiming that nineteenth-century American culture was profoundly repressive in regard to sexuality or by arguing that homosexuality is not socially constructed as a marginalized social category until the end of the century, as a consequence of the Anti-Sodomy Laws in England and the trials of Oscar Wilde.

2. "Hamlet's Task": Emerson's Political Writings

1. Emerson, "An Address . . . on . . . the Emancipation of the Negroes in the British West Indies," in *Emerson's Antislavery Writings*, eds. Len Gougeon and Joel Myerson (New Haven: Yale University Press, 1995), p. 18. See also chapter 11 in this

volume, in which I interpret Hurston's retelling of this folktale about African-American origins in her *Mules and Men*.

2. Richard Poirier, ed., *Ralph Waldo Emerson* (Oxford: Oxford University Press, 1990), p. 612.

3. Gay Wilson Allen, *Waldo Emerson* (New York: Viking Press, 1981), p. 619.

4. Ibid.

5. Ralph L. Rusk, ed., *The Letters of Ralph Waldo Emerson*, 6 vols. (New York: Columbia University Press, 1939), vol. 3, p. 261.

6. To William Emerson, January 17, 1855, *Letters*, vol. 4, pp. 484–85. The lecture Emerson is preparing is the "Lecture on Slavery," which he delivered on January 25, 1855, before the Massachusetts Anti-Slavery Society in Boston.

7. Emerson, "Boston Hymn" (January 1, 1863), in *The Works of Ralph Waldo Emerson*, ed. Edward W. Emerson, 14 vols. (Boston: Houghton, Mifflin, 1883), vol. 9, p. 174. Further references in the Notes as Emerson, *Works*.

8. Len Gougeon makes a persuasive case for considering this antislavery speech by Emerson as the turning point in his career, "the transition from philosophical antislavery to active abolitionism," in both his "Historical Backgrounds" to *Emerson's Antislavery Writings*, from which this quotation is taken, p. xxx, and in Gougeon's indispensable *Virtue's Hero: Emerson, Antislavery, and Reform* (Athens: University of Georgia Press, 1990), pp. 69–85.

9. Emerson, "Voluntaries," in *Works*, vol. 9, p. 178.

10. Throughout the tumultuous years leading up to the Civil War, the appeal to "higher laws" would be made by abolitionists and transcendentalists alike, meaning in many cases that a "higher law" than the Constitution argued in favor of the abolition of slavery. The rhetorical strategy of abolitionists like William Lloyd Garrison and transcendentalists like Thoreau was to call attention to the Constitution's neglect of slavery as an issue. Such neglect opened the door for the appeal to a higher, usually divine or natural, law. By 1850, the reference to "higher law" was also a code word for those who supported abolition and defied the Fugitive Slave Law. In his speech in the U.S. Senate opposing Clay's Compromise of 1850, William Henry Seward, senator from New York, "argued that the moral law established by the Creator was a higher law than the Constitution and that the moral law was working everywhere in the civilized world toward the extirpation, not the extension, of slavery." Barbara Packer, "The Transcendentalists," in *The Cambridge History of American Literature*, vol. 2, 1820–1865, eds. Sacvan Bercovitch and Cyrus Patell (New York: Cambridge University Press, 1995), p. 550. Seward was mocked publicly by Webster and others as "higher-law Seward," to which Emerson and other abolitionists vigorously objected (ibid., pp. 550–51).

11. Eduardo Cadava addresses Emerson's use of climactic, regional, and geographical metaphors in "The Nature of War in Emerson's 'Boston Hymn,'" *Arizona Quarterly* (Autumn 1993), 49 (3): 21–58.

12. Emerson, "Voluntaries," in *Works*, 9, p. 179.

13. Emerson, *Nature*, in *Works*, 1, p. 33.

14. Ibid., p. 32.

15. Ibid., p. 25, emphasis mine. For a thorough discussion of Emerson's use of rhetoric of the feminine in his writings, see Eric Cheyfitz, *Emerson and the Trans-Parent* (Baltimore.: Johns Hopkins University Press, 1979).

16. Ibid., pp. 15–16.

17. Ibid., p. 76.

18. Gougeon, *Virtue's Hero*, p. 84.

19. Packer, "The Transcendentalists," *Cambridge History of American Literature*, vol. 2, p. 560.

20. Gougeon, "Historical Background," *Emerson's Antislavery Writings*, p. xxx.

21. The best argument in this regard is Howard Horwitz, *By Law of Nature: Form and Value in Nineteenth-Century America* (New York: Oxford University Press, 1991).

22. Bercovitch, *The Rites of Assent: Transformations in the Symbolic Construction of America* (New York: Routledge, 1993), pp. 312–13. Future references cited in text as: Rites.

23. Gougeon, *Virtue's Hero*, p. 337.

24. Ibid., pp. 340–42.

25. Gougeon and Myerson, *Emerson's Antislavery Writings*, pp. 206–7n1.

26. Emerson, "An Address . . . on . . . the Emancipation of the Negroes," in *Emerson's Antislavery Writings*, p. 18. Further references will be cited in the text as: BWI. The Women's Anti-Slavery Society included Emerson's second wife, Lidian, and Henry Thoreau's mother. Thoreau helped organize the lecture, which had to be given in the courthouse auditorium, because the churches in Concord wouldn't let them use their space. Thoreau had to ring the bell of the First Parish Church to announce the lecture, because the sexton refused to do so. Allen, *Waldo Emerson*, pp. 427–28; Gougeon, *Virtue's Hero*, p. 75.

27. Gougeon, "Historical Backgrounds," *Emerson's Antislavery Writings*, p. xii.

28. Emerson, "Self-Reliance," *Works*, vol. 2, p. 70.

29. It would not have been lost on his audience that this sixty-seven-year period matches roughly the sixty-four-year period (1776–1844) of American independence during which Americans had failed to abolish slavery. Of course, such rhetorical parallelism only reinforces the dangerous position Emerson ends up endorsing in this essay: that America ought to follow the example of British history and constitutional law—a notion difficult to imagine for the author of "Self-Reliance," "The Divinity School Address," and "The American Scholar."

30. Packer, "The Transcendentalists," *Cambridge History of American Literature*, vol. 2, p. 551: "The rush of Boston's mercantile elite to support Webster, on the other hand, elicited an outburst of contempt. 'I think there was never an event half so painful as occurred in Boston as the letter with 800 signatures to Webster.' "

31. Gougeon, *Virtue's Hero*, p. 84: "Emerson's address concludes on an optimistic and

inspiring note that shows his willingness to consider, now, the possibility of a collective rather than exclusively individualist development of society."

32. Ibid., p. 160.

33. Emerson, "Address to the Citizens of Concord" (May 3, 1851), in *Emerson's Antislavery Writings*, p. 57. Further references will be cited in the text as: Concord.

34. Gougeon, *Virtue's Hero*, p. 164.

35. Ibid., p. 165.

36. Emerson, *Works*, vol. 11, p. 277. Further references in the text as: "Civilization." See also Gougeon, *Virtue's Hero*, p. 279.

37. See chapter 5.

38. Emerson, "The Fugitive Slave Law" (March 7, 1854), in *Emerson's Antislavery Writings*, p. 77. Further references will be cited in the text as: Fugitive. In the Riverside edition of *Emerson's Works*, vol. 11, p. 211, this passage is syntactically clearer: "But he wanted that deep source of inspiration. Hence a sterility of thought, the want of generalization in his speeches, and the curious fact that, with a general ability which impresses all the world, there is not a single general remark, not an observation on life and manners, not an aphorism that can pass into literature from his writings." Myerson in his "Textual Commentary" to *Emerson's Antislavery Writings*, p. 171, points out that the Riverside edition makes "roughly a thousand variations" on the manuscript version of the speech, which is at the Houghton Library at Harvard and is the copy text for their version of the essay. Hence, I quote from Myerson and Gougeon's more authoritative text.

39. Emerson, *The Journals and Miscellaneous Notebooks of Ralph Waldo Emerson*, 16 vols., ed. William H. Gilman et al. (Cambridge: Harvard University Press, 1960–1982), vol. 1, p. 361.

40. Allen, *Waldo Emerson*, p. 558. Emerson's letter of October 7, 1851, was published in the *New-York Daily Tribune*, together with an account of the convention. As Rusk, ed., *Letters*, vol. 4, pp. 260–61, puts it: "Emerson said he would be kept from the convention by his work and was not sure, anyhow, that he could find a message worth bringing."

41. Allen, *Waldo Emerson*, p. 559.

42. Emerson, "Woman," in *Works*, vol. 11, pp. 338, 339, 340, 341. Further references will be cited in the text as: Woman.

43. In his Journal entry for February 1851, he recalls: "Some persons are thrown off their balance when in society; others are thrown on to balance; the excitement of company and the observation of other characters correct their biases. Margaret Fuller always appeared to unexpected advantage in conversation with a circle of persons, with more common sense and sanity than any other,—though her habitual vision was through coloured glasses." *The Heart of Emerson's Journals*, ed. Bliss Perry (Boston: Houghton Mifflin, 1926), p. 251.

44. Emerson wrote in "To the Citizens of Concord," p. 64: "The only benefit that has accrued from the [Fugitive Slave] law is its service to the education. It has been

like a university to the entire people. It has turned every dinner-table into a debating club, and made every citizen a student of natural law."

45. Bercovitch, *The Rites of Assent*, p. 348.

46. Ibid., p. 352.

3. ANTEBELLUM SLAVERY AND MODERN CRITICISM: EDGAR ALLAN POE'S *PYM* AND "THE PURLOINED LETTER"

1. The historical focus of this essay on Poe's proslavery sympathies does not depend exclusively on new arguments favoring Poe's authorship of the disputed review of James Kirke Paulding's *Slavery in the United States* and [William Drayton's] *The South Vindicated from the Treason and Fanaticism of the Northern Abolitionists*. This unsigned review of two proslavery "histories" appeared in the April 1836 issue of the *Southern Literary Messenger* and was included in *The Complete Works of Edgar Allan Poe*, 17 vols., ed. James A. Harrison (1902; New York: AMS Press, 1979), vol. 8, pp. 265–75. William Doyle Hull II argued in his doctoral dissertation, "A Canon of the Critical Works of Edgar Allan Poe with a Study of Poe as Editor and Reviewer" (Ph.D. dissertation, University of Virginia, 1941), that the surviving evidence did not support Poe's authorship but rather that of Judge Beverly Tucker, a proslavery advocate. Both before and after Hull's thesis appeared, however, scholars and critics have argued that Poe's writings and his personal beliefs were compatible with Southern aristocratic values, including the defense of the institution of and laws pertaining to chattel slavery. In this essay, this tradition of Poe criticism is best represented by Ernest Marchand's "Poe as Social Critic," *American Literature*, 6 (1934): 28–43; F. O. Matthiessen's "Edgar Allan Poe" entry in *The Literary History of the United States*, 3 vols., ed. Robert Spiller et al. (New York: Macmillan, 1947), vol. 1, pp. 321–42; Bernard Rosenthal's "Poe, Slavery, and the *Southern Literary Messenger*: A Re-Examination," *Poe Studies* 7 (1974): 29–38. Sidney Kaplan's "Introduction" to *The Narrative of Arthur Gordon Pym of Nantucket* (New York: Hill and Wang, 1960) discusses Poe's racism and explicitly refers to the disputed review, but without apparent knowledge that Poe's authorship had been disputed by Hull. And Harold Beaver's "Introduction" to *Pym* (Baltimore: Penguin Books, 1975) treats *Pym* as an allegory of Southern racism in the antebellum period. This tradition of Poe criticism has been strong enough, albeit marginalized by both literary historians (in part, as a consequence of Hull's thesis) and modern critical theorists, that it deserves renewed attention *as* a tradition that tells us much about Poe. Whether or not such new attention will lead to new scholarly discoveries that will revise Hull's thesis regarding the disputed review is less important, however, than continuing discussion of the ways in which Poe's major literary works are structured around racist, sexist, and aristocratic themes.

2. John C. Miller, "Did Edgar Allan Poe Really Sell a Slave?" *Poe Studies* 9 (1976): 52–53.

3. Joan Dayan, *Fables of Mind: An Inquiry into Poe's Fiction* (New York: Oxford

University Press, 1987), p. 3. Dayan quotes an 1856 review in the *North American Review* of Poe as a subversive author "who was 'like other revolutionists, desirous mainly of decapitating the sovereign, and debasing all of the blood royal.' " Further references in the text as: Dayan.

4. William Doyle Hull, "A Canon of the Critical Works of Edgar Allan Poe."

5. In "Paul de Man's Past," Christopher Norris argues in de Man's defense that "The articles have been mined for passages that show him up in the worst possible light, often by being juxtaposed with other items from *Le Soir* whose content bears no relation to anything that de Man wrote" (6). Yet it is just this latter point I would make about both de Man's wartime writings *and* Poe's work as assistant editor (primarily responsible for reviews) of the *Southern Literary Messenger*. Newspapers and journals are written by the authors of their different articles, but they nevertheless have a certain *corporate* authority that is familiar to even the most casual reader. Although this corporate authority sometimes takes the explicit form of an editorial, it is normally communicated by the *dominant political tone* of the periodical. Periodicals that encourage a wide range of opinions and subjects are not exceptions to this rule; they generally reflect a political attitude of liberal pluralism. For contributors, of course, this means that they must share responsibility with the other contributors for that corporate authority. For an editor of a periodical, that responsibility is even more binding. The political rhetoric of *Le Soir* during the German Occupation of Belgium is unmistakable: shrill German nationalism punctuated by the ugliest anti-Semitic and racist rancor. The *Southern Literary Messenger* is just as propagandistic when its anti-Northern, pro-Southern, and proslavery attitudes are added up.

6. Hervey Allen, *Israfel: The Life and Times of Edgar Allan Poe*, 2d ed. (New York: Farrar and Rinehart, 1934), p. 317.

7. Bernard Rosenthal, "Poe, Slavery, and the *Southern Literary Messenger*: A Re-Examination," pp. 29–38.

8. See Bezanson, "The Troubled Sleep of Arthur Gordon Pym," in *Essays in Literary History Presented to J. Milton French*, eds. Rudolf Kirk and C. F. Main (New Brunswick, N.J.: Rutgers University Press, 1960), pp. 149–75. See especially p. 169 on the curious water of Tsalal: "Even fresh water runs purple, and the use of the word 'veins' to describe its peculiar structure suggests a fantasy on negro blood."

9. G. R. Thompson, "Edgar Allan Poe," *American Literary Scholarship: An Annual/ 1974*, ed. James Woodress (Durham, N.C.: Duke University Press, 1976), p. 33.

10. G. R. Thompson, "Poe and the Writers of the Old South," *Columbia Literary History of the United States*, ed. Emory Elliott (New York: Columbia University Press, 1988), pp. 268–69. Given Poe's well-documented correspondence with Tucker (especially in the spring of 1836, when the disputed review was published), the disassociation of Poe from the proslavery sentiments in the Paulding-Drayton review seems even more improbable. In his edition of Poe's *Essays and Reviews* for the Library of America, Thompson includes Poe's review of Beverly Tucker's

George Balcombe, A Novel, which appeared in the January 1837 *Messenger*, only nine months after the Paulding-Drayton review. *George Balcombe* is an utterly conventional Southern chivalric romance, rendered thinly contemporary by setting the usual plot of misplaced wills and elusive fortunes primarily in the Missouri frontier. Poe judges it with his typical critical hyperbole as "upon the whole, . . . *the best* American novel. There have been few books of its peculiar kind, we think, written in *any* country, much its superior" (978). One of the few "philosophical" points that Poe challenges in the novel is Balcombe's (and, for Poe, the author's) view that "When truth and honor abound, they are most prized. They depreciate as they become rare." Poe responds in the manner of a Southern aristocrat: "But it is clear that were *all* men true and honest, then truth and honor, *beyond their intrinsic*, would hold no higher value, than would wine in a Paradise where all the rivers were Johannisberger, and all the duck-ponds Vin de Margaux" (978).

11. Thompson, *Poe: Essays and Reviews*, p. 1483. Although Poe's critical evaluations of Simms' works vary throughout the reviews collected in Thompson's *Essays and Reviews*, he is one of the most frequently cited writers and, like Tucker, receives one of Poe's longest reviews (for *The Partisan: A Tale of the Revolution*). In his review of Simms' *The Wigwam and the Cabin*, Poe writes, "The fiction of Mr. Simms gave indication . . . of genius, and that of no common order. Had he been even a Yankee, this genius would have been rendered *immediately* manifest to his countrymen" (p. 904).

12. Dana Nelson, *The Word in Black and White: Reading "Race" in American Literature, 1638–1867* (New York: Oxford University Press, 1992), p. 91. Dana Nelson's and my own interests in the history of the academic reception of Bernard Rosenthal's essay have independent origins in our respective interests in Poe's critical revaluation, but they coincided when both of us contacted Professor Rosenthal about his essay. I called Bernie in 1988 while I was preparing an original version of this chapter as a lecture ("Poe's *Narrative of Arthur Gordon Pym* and Modern Theories of Psychoanalysis") at a conference on *Pym* sponsored by Pennsylvania State University and held on the island of Nantucket in May 1988. Professor Rosenthal directed Cathy Davidson's doctoral dissertation, and Cathy in turn directed Dana Nelson's doctoral dissertation. Both Nelson and I thus benefited from Rosenthal's generous account of this interesting controversy, and I wish to acknowledge here my thanks to him (as Nelson does in *The Word in Black and White*, p. 162n2).

13. Ibid., pp. 91–92.

14. Nelson rightly identifies my approach to *Pym* in *Through the Custom-House* as characteristic of the poststructuralist approaches that depoliticized and dehistoricized Poe in the 1970s and 1980s. The critique of the poststructuralist position that I develop in this chapter was originally published in an earlier version in *Poe's "Pym": Critical Explorations*, ed. Richard Kopley (Durham, N.C.: Duke University Press, 1992), pp. 117–38, but it appeared in the same year

Nelson's *The Word in Black and White* was published. I could not expect Nelson to
have been familiar with that argument while Nelson was writing *The Word in Black
and White*.

15. John Irwin's *American Hieroglyphics: The Symbol of the Egyptian Hieroglyphics in the
American Renaissance* (New Haven: Yale University Press, 1980) devotes two-thirds
of its pages to Poe. Emerson, Thoreau, and Whitman serve as a kind of brief
prologue to the Poe section; Hawthorne and Melville are treated in two short
chapters in the book's final section. Irwin's rhetorical organization of the book
baffled many reviewers, but at least one important purpose was to treat Poe as a
center for American romanticism. Irwin's argument is thus implicitly directed at
Matthiessen, who barely treats Poe in *American Renaissance: Art and Expression in the
Age of Emerson and Whitman* (New York: Oxford University Press, 1941). Irwin's
strategy is in its own right a remarkable instance of criticism enacting an aesthetic
argument. By the same token, Matthiessen's neglect of Poe in *American Renaissance*
may have had more to do with Matthiessen's understanding of Poe's antebellum
Southern attitudes than we have previously thought. I address Matthiessen's
interpretation of Poe toward the end of this essay.

16. The rapid institutionalization of the post-Freudian psychoanalytical approaches
to Poe of Lacan, Derrida, and Barbara Johnson is well represented by the
publication of *The Purloined Poe: Lacan, Derrida and Psychoanalytic Reading*, eds. John
P. Muller and William J. Richardson (Baltimore: Johns Hopkins University Press,
1988). Further references to Lacan, Derrida, and Barbara Johnson on Poe will be
to this collection.

17. Poe, "The Purloined Letter," *Collected Works of Edgar Allan Poe*, ed. Thomas O.
Mabbott (Cambridge: Belknap Press, 1969), vol. 3, p. 974.

18. Marie Bonaparte's extraordinary *The Life and Works of Edgar Allan Poe: A Psycho-
Analytic Interpretation*, trans. John Rodker (London: Imago, 1949) revolves around
the psychic costs to Poe of John Allan's brutal treatment of him. For the
particular ways Bonaparte understands Poe to have incorporated Allan into the
Narrative of Arthur Gordon Pym, see pp. 295–97.

19. Derrida, "The Purveyor of Truth," in *The Purloined Poe*, pp. 173–212.

20. Lacan, "Seminar on 'The Purloined Letter,' " in *The Purloined Poe*, pp. 28–54.

21. In addition to Sidney Kaplan's and Harold Beaver's interpretations of *Pym* as an
allegory of Southern white fears regarding slave insurrections and Dana Nelson's
interpretation of the narrative as a Eurocentric colonialist fantasy, Kenneth Alan
Hovey's "Critical Provincialism: Poe's Poetic Principle in Antebellum Context"
(*American Quarterly* 4 [1987]: 341–54) complements my own approach to Poe's
writings. Focusing on Poe's criticism of Longfellow and other Northeastern
writers, Hovey argues that Poe endorsed an aesthetic formalism as a reaction to
Northern artists' "double error of didacticism and progressivism." For Hovey, Poe
"formulated a poetic principle which eliminated messages altogether. A 'poem
written solely for the poem's "sake"' could have no social implications. It might
be morbid, but it could never be incendiary or fanatical" (350). The combination

of Kaplan, Beaver, and Hovey's readings presents a convincing case that Poe's antebellum values are integral to his major writings and not just a matter for scholars deciding his authorship of an objectionable review. This is what I mean by recognizing anew the *tradition* of critical interpretation of Poe as Southern writer.

22. Poe, *Narrative of Arthur Gordon Pym*, in *Collected Writings of Edgar Allan Poe*, ed. Burton Pollin, vol. 1, p. 66.

23. Allen, *Israfel*, p. 317.

24. Eric Sundquist, *To Wake the Nations: Race in the Making of American Literature* (Cambridge: Harvard University Press, 1993), p. 69.

25. Dana Nelson, *The Word in Black and White*, p. 93.

26. David Reynolds, *Beneath the American Renaissance: The Subversive Imagination in the Age of Emerson and Melville* (New York: Knopf, 1988), pp. 241, 242.

27. John Carlos Rowe, *Through the Custom-House: Nineteenth-Century American Fiction and Modern Theory* (Baltimore: Johns Hopkins University Press, 1982), pp. 99–102.

28. Throughout my re-reading of *Pym*, I am indebted to the work of Scott Bradfield's revisionary reading of Poe in *Dreaming Revolution: Transgression in the Development of the American Romance* (Iowa City: University of Iowa Press, 1993), esp. pp. 68–82.

29. See the statement by members of the court, Jerusalem, Virginia, in the preface to *The Confessions of Nat Turner*, the twenty-page pamphlet published in Richmond in 1832, the year following Nat Turner's Southampton Insurrection. This document is conveniently reproduced in the section, "To the Public," in William Styron's *The Confessions of Nat Turner, A Novel* (New York: Random House, 1966).

30. Poe, review of Theodore Irving, *The Complete Works of Edgar Allan Poe*, ed. Harrison, vol. 8, p. 39.

31. Poe, review of Hall, *The Complete Works of Edgar Allan Poe*, ed. Harrison, vol. 8, p. 108.

32. In Hervey Allen's *Israfel: The Life and Times of Edgar Allan Poe*, Appendix 6, "History of Poe's Friend, F. W. Thomas," Allen reprints John Bennett, Esq., of Charleston, S.C., "Ebenezer S. Thomas: Book-seller, Stationer, Editor, *City Gazette*, Charleston, S. C." on pp. 706–9. In Bennett's account, Frederick W. Thomas' father, Ebenezer, is presented as a staunch defender of the Union and of the Jeffersonian party, of which he joined with Pinckney, Freneau, and Lehre, "they being dubbed the Triumvirs," and Thomas the " 'lever of the Triumvirate,' . . . [as] their official spokesman through the *City Gazette*: they were nicknamed Caesar, Pompey, and Lepidus by the Federal Party" (708).

An "ardent supporter of the Federal Union, and an antagonist of John C. Calhoun from the discovery of the end and aim of Nullification onward," Ebenezer Thomas had earlier supported Langdon Cheves for Congress in a campaign that "sent Calhoun, Lowndes and Cheves from South Carolina" (p. 708). Sometime after that campaign, Thomas published in the *City Gazette* "a political letter from M. M. Noah, attacking Jos. Alston, for alleged participation in Burr's so-called conspiracy, and for alleged misconduct of an election which made Alston governor of S. C."As a consequence,

> Thomas was prosecuted by Jos. Alston for libel, found technically guilty by the jury, was escorted from his prison by a brass band and parade of admirers; and *shot at through a window by some un-identified supporter of Alston's.*
>
> It was at Thomas's suggestion to David Ramsay, the historian, that the latter undertook his *Life of Washington;* . . . and it was at the very moment of the conclusion of Thomas's trial in the Charleston court that a *loud report of a pistol was heard from the street near by. . . when Ramsay was shot by one Lining whom Ramsay, as a consulting physician, had pronounced insane.* This is just incidental. (p. 708; my italics throughout)

Poe met Frederick W. Thomas, a minor literatus, in May 1840, when the latter visited the Poes in Philadelphia "on his way home to St. Louis from the Whig presidential convention held in Baltimore the same month" (Allen, p. 381). Thomas and Poe worked in the campaign for William Henry Harrison, the 1840 Whig campaign noted for its youthful exuberance, progressive hopes, and wild rhetoric against the Democratic incumbent, Martin Van Buren. As Allen points out, "while in Philadelphia in May, 1840, Thomas made a speech for 'Tippecanoe and Tyler too'—and was pelted by a mob of the Locofocos" (the radical wing of the Democratic Party, also known as the "Equal Rights" Party) (381).

Let me connect these historical details by way of a certain strategic condensation—that of the "lunatic or drunkard" Dupin places in the street to distract the Minister's attention from his switch of messages (Mabbot 3:992). Frederick Thomas may have told Poe about the shot fired anonymously at his father, as he left the Viriginia couthouse, and the coincidence of Dr. Ramsay's death by the shot of a lunatic on the day of Ebenezer Thomas' release from jail (and thus its simultaneity with the shot fired against him). Poe knew about the pelting Frederick Thomas endured at the hands of the Locofocos in Philadelphia. The threats to his friend, his friend's father (although the assailant was undoubtedly proslavery), and to his father's acquaintance Dr. Ramsay are all "mastered" by Poe in the "event" staged by Dupin in Paris. That these events belong to the "same" time that we have tried to vaguely locate in "The Purloined Letter" (1814–1815 to 1845) should not surprise us, because Poe/Dupin's enactment substitutes its own fictive temporality for the accidents of the empirical world—accidents that increasingly would provoke Poe's own paranoia about the uncontrollable savagery directed against him and his kind.

33. Orlando Patterson, *Slavery and Social Death: A Comparative Study* (Cambridge: Harvard University Press, 1982), p. 338: "The ideological inversion of reality was the creation of the slaveholder class, so it is not surprising that few of them expressed reservations about its veracity; almost all masters, in fact, genuinely believed that they cared and provided for their slaves and that it was the slaves

who, in the words of one southern ex-slave owner, had 'been raised to depend on others.'" Toni Morrison, *Playing in the Dark: Whiteness and the Literary Imagination* (New York: Random House, 1993), pp. 32–33, reads brilliantly the cultural significance of this penultimate episode in *Pym*: "The images of the white curtain and the 'shrouded human figure' with skin 'the perfect whiteness of snow' both occur after the narrative has encountered blackness. The first white image seems related to the expiration and erasure of the serviceable and serving black figure, Nu-Nu. Both are figurations of impenetrable whiteness that surface in American literature whenever an Africanist presence is engaged. These closed white images are found frequently, but not always, at the end of the narrative." See chapters 5 and 6 for further discussions of Patterson and Morrison in these contexts.

34. Barbara Johnson, "The Frame of Reference: Poe, Lacan, Derrida," *The Purloined Poe*, p. 248.

35. Ibid.

36. Arthur Hobson Quinn, *Edgar Allan Poe: A Critical Biography* (New York: Appleton-Century-Crofts, 1941), p. 695, concludes his biography with a eulogy to the cosmopolitan and thus supremely modern Poe: "His fame is now secure. . . . He has become a world artist and through the translations of his writings he speaks today to every civilized country. He has won this wide recognition by no persistent clamor of a cult, but by the royal right of preeminence. For today . . . he remains not only the one American, but also the one writer in the English language, who was at once foremost in criticism, supreme in fiction, and in poetry destined to be immortal."

37. F. O. Matthiessen, "Edgar Allan Poe," *Literary History of the United States*, eds. Robert Spiller et al., p. 328.

38. Ibid., p. 342.

39. Ibid.

40. See my "The Writing Class," in *Politics, Theory, and Contemporary Culture*, ed. Mark Poster (New York: Columbia University Press, 1993), pp. 41–82, for a fuller development of a postmodern "hermeneutics of class."

4. A Critique of Ideology: Herman Melville's *Pierre*

1. Henry A. Murray, Introduction, *Pierre, or The Ambiguities*, by Herman Melville (New York: Hendricks House, 1949), p. xcvi.

2. Mark Poster, *Critical Theory of the Family* (London: Pluto Press, 1978), p. 144.

3. Philippe Ariès, *Centuries of Childhood: A Social History of Family Life*, trans. R. Baldick (New York: Knopf, 1965); Jacques Donzelot, *The Policing of Families*, trans. Robert Hurley (New York: Pantheon, 1979).

4. Sacvan Bercovitch, *The Rites of Assent: Transformations in the Symbolic Construction of America* (New York: Routledge, 1993), pp. 253–54.

5. Ibid., p. 257.

6. Emory Elliott, "Art, Religion, and the Problem of Authority in *Pierre*," *Ideology*

and *Classic American Literature*, eds. Sacvan Bercovitch and Myra Jehlen (New York: Cambridge University Press, 1986), p. 337.

7. Ibid., p. 342.

8. Ibid., p. 344.

9. Michael Paul Rogin, *Subversive Genealogy: The Politics and Art of Herman Melville* (Berkeley: University of California Press, 1988)

10. Carolyn Porter, *Seeing and Being: The Plight of the Participant Observer in Emerson, James, Adams, and Faulkner* (Middletown, Conn.: Wesleyan University Press, 1981), p. 65.

11. Poster, *Critical Theory of the Family*, p. 43.

12. Karl Marx, *Capital*, trans. Ben Fowkes, 3 vols. (New York: Random House, vol. 1, 1977, p. 471n26.

13. Raymond Williams, *Keywords: A Vocabulary of Culture and Society* (New York: Oxford University Press, 1976), p. 132, explains that the precapitalist family was often understood as "the household," rather than in terms of specific kinship relations. There is much disagreement among scholars concerning Williams' assumption that the nuclear family and the rise of the bourgeoisie are historically contemporary developments. I am not qualified to resolve these disputes, but I am struck with the central concern in the modern novel with adultery and illegitimacy and thus with the definition of "proper" family relations in terms of sexuality. Capitalism's judgment of ethical questions often involves the settlement of property rights. Kinship relations in the novel are almost always a function of property rights and the orderly transmission of those rights, rather than the other way around. And it is common that "proper" sexual conduct is determined first by property rights.

14. G. W. F. Hegel, *The Phenomenology of Mind*, trans. J. B. Baillie (New York: Harper and Row, 1967), p. 477, 479.

15. Herman Melville, *Pierre, or The Ambiguities* (Evanston, Ill.: Northwestern University Press, 1971), p. 122. Further references will be cited in the text as: Pierre.

16. Carolyn Porter, *Seeing and Being*, p. 65.

17. Hegel, *The Philosophy of History*, trans. J. Sibree (1899: rpr. New York: Dover, 1956), p. 161.

18. Rogin, *Subversive Genealogy*, p. 164.

19. Ibid., p. 165.

20. Hegel, *Phenomenology*, p. 479.

21. Bercovitch, *The Rites of Assent*, p. 296.

22. Carolyn Karcher, *Shadow Over the Promised Land: Slavery, Race, and Violence in Melville's America* (Baton Rouge: Louisiana State University Press, 1980), p. 94.

23. Hegel, *The Philosophy of History*, p. 161.

24. Ibid., p. 165.

25. Marx, *Capital*, vol. 1, pp. 451, 452.

26. Ibid., p. 452.

27. In *Pierre*, Melville makes a number of puns on Kant's surname as part of his more
general critique of transcendental idealism. Speaking of the idealists of various
sorts—painters, sculptors, students, German philosophers—inhabiting the
upper floors of the tower in the Church of the Apostles, Melville jibes: "While
the abundance of leisure in their attics (physical and figurative), unites with the
leisure of their stomachs, to fit them in eminent degree for that undivided
attention indispensable to the proper digesting of the sublimated Categories of
Kant; especially as Kant (can't) is the one great palpable fact in their pervadingly
impalpable lives" (Pierre, 267). Yet the only *negative* palpability of Kantian
idealism—its cant is its can't—finds its habitation in the "Titanic" tower that rises
out of the stores and law offices into which the old church has been divided.
Elsewhere, Melville judges these "theoretic and inactive" transcendentalists to be
"therefore harmless," but as neighbors with the commercial and legal powers of
the modern city these transcendentals must be said to serve some more active
and dangerous ideological purpose, even if such a purpose depends on their
apparent ineffectualness (Pierre, 262).

28. Ralph Waldo Emerson, "The American Scholar," in Emerson, *Nature, Addresses, and
Lectures*, ed. Robert E. Spiller and Alfred R. Ferguson (Cambridge: Harvard
University Press, 1971), p. 62, vol. I of Joseph Slater and Douglas Emory
Watson, eds., *The Collected Works of Ralph Waldo Emerson*.

29. Emerson, "Man the Reformer," *Nature, Addresses, and Lectures*, p. 152.

30. Ibid., p. 153.

31. Many critics agree that Plotinus Plinlimmon and his lecture on "chronometricals
and horologicals" is Melville's intended "satire on all shallow and amiable
transcendental 'reconcilers' of the 'Optimist' or 'Compensation' school," as
Willard Thorp put the matter in his Introduction to *Herman Melville: Representative
Selections* (New York: American Book Co., 1938), p. lxxxii. Extracted as
Plinlimmon's lecture is from a series of "Three Hundred and Thirty Three
Lectures" and qualified as "*not so much the Portal, as part of the temporary Scaffold to
the Portal of this new Philosophy*," Plinlimmon's very form parodies the Emersonian
lecture. The title itself, " '*EI*,' " is paronomastic of Emerson's identification of the
"eye" and the "I," in the famous "Transparent Eye-Ball" passage of *Nature*, for
example, as well as the spiritually generative qualities Emerson attributes to the
crossing of the "eye" and the "I." The latter connection involves a third
paronomasia: "*das Ei*," German for "egg," as in *ab ovem*. Connecting all of these
pedantic puns is their mutual philological source, the Greek philosophic term
eídos, which variously links appearance, constitutive nature, form, type, species,
and idea. I cannot recount here the complicated history of *eíde* in even the
restricted classical tradition from Plato to Aristotle and Plotinus, but I will simply
remind the reader that classical philosophical debates concerning the relation of
immanence to transcendence often focused on the particular status of *eíde*. F. E.
Peters in *Greek Philosophical Terms* (New York: New York University Press, 1967),
p. 50, notes that by Aristotle's postulation of "the *eide* as the thoughts of God, a

position that continues down through Plotinus . . into Christianity, and at the same time . . as immanent formal causes with an orientation toward matter . . an at least partial solution of the dilemma of immanence vs. transcendence was reached. But the problem continued as a serious one in Platonism, discussed at length by both Plotinus . . and Proclus."

32. Wordsworth's lines are from "Tintern Abbey," ll. 17–18. T. E. Hulme, "Romanticism and Classicism," in *Critical Theory since Plato*, rev. ed., ed. Hazard Adams (New York: Harcourt Brace Jovanovich, 1992), p. 729.

33. Bercovitch, *The Rites of Assent*, p. 265, reads the Memnon Stone as a reference to "the Egyptian hero Memnon," about whom Melville would have read in "Pliny's *Natural History*, where Memnon is associated with porphyrite, the purple-tinted royal stone of Egypt. According to Pliny, the porphyrite statue of Memnon, son of Aurora, rang a musical note each morning at the touch of the sun's first rays." Hegel reads the "Memnon stones" of ancient Egypt as signs of unrealized human spirituality, because the stone ("Memnon stones" were conventional decorative devices in ancient Egypt) "resounds at the first glance of the young morning Sun; though it is not yet the free light of the Spirit with which it vibrates" (Hegel, *The Philosophy of History*, p. 199). The hollow in Pierre's Memnon stone, like the empty pyramid "mined" in *Pierre*, suggest Melville's variation on the conventional romantic theme of manmade forms that have not yet incorporated their shaping power—whether human or divine. In the context of Melville's critique of American capitalism and Southern feudalism, the "monument" whose informing spirit or labor is "elsewhere" once again reminds us of the American history of stolen labor—from the theft of land from native Americans in Saddle Meadows to the large New York landowners' control of agribusiness in the 1830s, which led to the Renters' Revolt, suppressed by the New York State Militia.

34. Herman Melville, *The Confidence-Man: His Masquerade*, ed. Elizabeth S. Foster (New York: Hendricks House, 1954), p. 271.

35. Bercovitch, *The Rites of Assent*, pp. 270–72, connects Melville's reflections on "originality" in *Pierre*, of which the novel makes an obvious mockery, with Melville's critique of Emersonian individualism. Summarizing various passages from Emerson's Journals, Bercovitch concludes: "They constitute what remains the boldest claim of American individualism: that all history is not only at but for one's disposal; that the independent self, as the heir of the ages (like 'America' at large), must freely use the great works of the past—extracting whatever is relevant, discarding the outmoded, improving the imperfect—as a standing advertisement of an unbounded originality" (270–71).

36. Bercovitch, *Rites of Assent*, p. 257, provides an excellent complement to my reading here: "The descent into the pyramid is a metaphor not of absolute futility, but of the futility of absolute independence. The disciples who drew back the stone from Christ's sepulcher to see no body there found their faith confirmed. . . In this sense [Melville's] inquiry into the processes of mind devolves upon the theme of narcissism, which he repeatedly connects to the theme of incest." Such narcissism

and incest are at the heart of the ruling-class ideology in both Northern capitalism and Southern feudalism, as Melville makes clear elsewhere in the novel.

37. Porter, *Seeing and Being*, pp. 228–29.

38. See chapters 5 and 6.

39. Emerson, *Nature*, in *Essays: Second Series*, eds. Alfred R. Ferguson and Jean Ferguson Carr (Cambridge: Harvard University Press, 1983), p. 113, vol. 3 of Slater and Wilson, eds., *Works*.

40. Emory Elliott, "Art, Religion, and the Problem of Authority in *Pierre*," p. 346.

41. Ibid. Both characters are, of course, literally "locked in prison" at the end of their respective narratives, Vivia's foreshadowing Pierre's own end.

42. Rogin, *Subversive Genealogy*, pp. 179–80.

43. Elliott, "Art, Religion, and the Problem of Authority in *Pierre*," 341.

44. Ibid., p. 348. Much as Melville parodies sentimental romances of his day, he also borrows from them in often surprisingly effective ways. It would thus not be entirely accurate to claim that Melville's parody of popular literature is thoroughly negative, because Melville seems to learn from or at least use many of popular literature's devices. Bercovitch points out in *The Rites of Assent*, p. 296n, for example, how Isabel "is modelled on the victimized orphans and weaver-girls of sentimental fiction, where in fact this character type often serves as a focus of social criticism." Certainly ambivalent in his response to the contemporary sentimental romance, Melville seems fitfully aware of the sentimental romance's potential for political commentary and critique.

45. Bercovitch, *The Rites of Assent*, p. 304.

5. BETWEEN POLITICS AND POETICS: FREDERICK DOUGLASS' *Narrative of the Life of Frederick Douglass*

1. Carolyn Porter, "Social Discourse and Nonfictional Prose," *Columbia Literary History of the United States*, ed. Emory Elliott (New York: Columbia University Press, 1988), p. 359.

2. As Waldo E. Martin, Jr. demonstrates convincingly in "Images of Frederick Douglass in the Afro-American Mind: The Recent Black Freedom Struggle," in *Frederick Douglass: New Literary and Historical Essays*, ed. Eric Sundquist (New York: Cambridge University Press, 1990), pp. 271–85.

3. Russell Reising, *The Unusable Past: Theory and the Study of American Literature* (New York: Methuen, 1986), p. 256. Further references are cited in the text as: Reising.

4. Another is Gregory Jay's extended reading of Douglass in *America the Scrivener: Deconstruction and the Subject of Literary History* (Ithaca, N.Y.: Cornell University Press, 1990), pp. 236–76.

5. All scholars recognize the period 1851–1853 as the fictional construct of F. O. Matthiessen in his *American Renaissance* (1941), but there is no question that the decade of the 1850s continues to structure our thinking about nineteenth-century American literature and culture.

6. Eric Sundquist, *To Wake the Nations*, p. 86.

7. Ibid., p. 89.

8. Sacvan Bercovitch, *The Rites of Assent*, p. 370.

9. In addition to critics already treated in this chapter, like Bercovitch and Waldo E. Martin, Jr., several other critics have located Douglass in the tradition of New England enlightenment and transcendentalism, including Donald Gibson, "Faith, Doubt, and Apostasy: Evidence of Things Unseen in Frederick Douglass's *Narrative*," and Rafia Zafar, "Franklinian Douglass: The Afro-American as Representative Man," both in *Frederick Douglass: New Literary and Historical Essays*, pp. 84–98 and 99–117, respectively.

10. Although I find Cindy Weinstein's *The Literature of Labor and the Labors of Literature: Allegory in Nineteenth-Century American Fiction* (New York: Cambridge University Press, 1995) a valuable study in many respects, I also find it curiously narrow in the focus of its attention primarily on the representation of labor in classic American writers: Hawthorne, Melville, Twain, and Adams. This focus is all the more troubling insofar as Weinstein recognizes on several occasions that slavery was the central issue for those reflecting on issues relevant to labor in nineteenth-century America. As she points out, there was frequent discussion of "the conversion of persons into objects in slavery" in analogy with "the alienation of labor(ers) in a market economy" (p. 7).

11. Carolyn Porter, "Social Discourse and Nonfictional Prose," *Columbia Literary History of the United States*, p. 359.

12. Technically, of course, Douglass' freedom was purchased by Ellen and Anna Richardson of Newcastle, England, in accord with the political action of the English Abolitionists with whom they were associated. I am following Robert Cover, *Justice Accused* (New Haven, Conn.: Yale University Press, 1981), p. 184, in my contention that Douglass' purchase of freedom constituted an act of "self-purchase," which was designed explicitly to expose the contradictoriness of U.S. laws in regard to slaves as legal chattel.

13. Waldo Martin, Jr., *The Mind of Frederick Douglass* (Chapel Hill: University of North Carolina Press, 1984), pp. 127, 129.

14. "Letter to His Old Master," *The Liberator*, September 22, 1848, was reprinted in Douglass' *My Bondage and My Freedom*, from which these passages are quoted: Douglass, *Autobiographies*, ed. Henry Louis Gates, Jr. (New York: Library of America, 1994), p. 415. Further references are cited in the text as: Letter.

15. Douglass, *Boston Daily Whip* (1847).

16. As Sundquist points out in *To Wake the Nations*, p. 99, it is "not very important" that there was "no evidence. . .to support his accusation, later retracted, that Auld had turned out his grandmother, Betsy Bailey, 'like an old horse to die in the woods,' " because: "Brutality and sexual exploitation were common enough in southern slaveholding, and it was the institution, not Auld himself, that was Douglass's target." What Sundquist terms Douglass' critique of the institution of slavery over the individuals responsible for it should also be understood as part

of Douglass' consistent effort to make every detail of his writings serve representative purposes. Rarely was Douglass speaking of his own special freedom without invoking by contrast the millions without freedom or aligning himself with the few African Americans who had achieved freedom. Writing in this representative way, whatever the genre or style, should always be understood as literary.

17. Ibid., p. 93.

18. Arguing in favor of his preference for *My Bondage and My Freedom*, Sundquist acknowledges Douglass' inevitable reproduction of patriarchal ideology in the following way: "The language of the fathers offers two choices: capitulation and ignorance, or resistance and knowledge. Literacy is linked to the power to enslave and, alternatively, to the power to liberate and father oneself. [In *My Bondage and My Freedom*] Hugh Auld stands now more emphatically in the book's sequence of fathers that leads toward the revolutionary fathers themselves, against whom Douglass in the 1850s was working to define himself yet again as though in 'opposition to my master' " (*To Wake the Nations*, p. 107). The patriarchal and paternalistic attitudes are certainly present in Douglass' 1845 *Narrative*, subjecting it to the same sort of criticism that such a Freudian family-romance as Sundquist describes has elicited from recent scholars. Yet by rendering radically ambiguous his "father's" identity in the 1845 *Narrative*, Douglass at least opens the possibility of another kind of African-American cultural "authority," which I will argue in this chapter is often grounded in African-American *feminine identity*.

19. H. Bruce Franklin, "Animal Farm Unbound or, What the *Narrative of the Life of Frederick Douglass, An American Slave* Reveals about American Literature," *New Letters* 53 (1977), 44.

20. *Narrative of the Life of Frederick Douglass, An American Slave, Written by Himself*, ed. Houston Baker, Jr. (New York: Penguin Books, 1982), p. 113. Further references are cited in the text as: Narrative.

21. As quoted in Philip Foner, *Frederick Douglass: A Biography* (New York: Citadel Press, 1964), pp. 60–61.

22. Valerie Smith, *Self-Discovery and Authority in Afro-American Narrative* (Cambridge: Harvard University Press, 1987), p. 27, concludes her reading of the 1845 *Narrative* by indicting Douglass' definition of himself "according to the values of mainstream culture": "I would further suggest that the plot of the narrative offers a profound endorsement of the fundamental American plot, the myth of the self-made man. His broad-based indictments notwithstanding, by telling the story of one man's rise from slavery to the station of esteemed orator, writer, and statesman, he confirms the myth shared by generations of American men that inner resources alone can lead to success." Yet this by now familiar indictment of Douglass' complicity with the dominant ideology depends crucially on the interpretation of the 1845 *Narrative* as a conventional *Bildungsroman*. As I am suggesting in this chapter, Douglass does not unequivocally appeal to his "inner resources" as his means to freedom; by invoking the power of language to aid in

the quest for freedom, Douglass appeals to a common and culturally maintained resource potentially available to all.

23. Emerson, "The Poet," in *Essays: Second Series*, in *The Works of Ralph Waldo Emerson*, ed. Edward W. Emerson (Boston: Houghton, Mifflin, 1883), vol. 3, p. 37.

24. There is no sharp division between the Middle Passage and the "commerce" conducted by Jacksonian America in this context. Despite the outlawing of the slave trade by the United States in 1808, Americans conducted illegal slave trade on a major scale. As Sundquist writes in *To Wake the Nations*, pp. 200–201: "The great majority of slave ships were owned and outfitted by Americans, with the result, as DuBois wrote in his landmark study, that 'the American slave-trade finally came to be carried on principally by United States capital, in United States ships, officered by United States citizens, and under the United States flag.' "

25. I am thinking here of my discussion of Whitman's egotistical sublime in such poems as "Crossing Brooklyn Ferry," "The Sleepers," and "Passage to India." See my discussion in chapter 7.

26. Waldo Martin, Jr., *The Mind of Frederick Douglass*, pp. 263–64.

27. Sundquist, *To Wake the Nations*, p. 89.

28. Douglass, *My Bondage and My Freedom*, in *Autobiographies*, ed. Henry Louis Gates, Jr. (New York: Library of America, 1994), pp. 329–30.

29. William S. McFeely, *Frederick Douglass* (New York: Norton, 1991), p. 266.

30. Ibid., pp. 265–69.

31. Sundquist, *To Wake the Nations*, pp. 102–3n.

32. Philip Foner, ed., *Frederick Douglass on Women's Rights*, Contributions in Afro-American Studies, no. 25 (Westport, Conn.: Greenwood Press, 1976), p. 8.

33. In both Douglass' 1845 *Narrative* and Jacobs' *Incidents in the Life of a Slave Girl*, the African-American child occupies a special position. Both authors stress the terrible suffering endured by their young narrators, and the authors remind us that the psychological and sociological evils of slavery exceed the comprehension of the young Douglass and Linda Brent (only fifteen when she "gives herself" to Sands). Even so, the authors subtly allow these characters to see and know more than their years warrant, both suggesting the unnaturalness of slavery in childhood development and the special knowledge that comes to those whose very lives depend on such knowledge. The position of the African-American adolescent in these narratives is far more complex than romantic clichés about the "child as father to the man." It is a subject-position that is obviously based in part on fact and the authors' experiences but also controlled rhetorically in a manner that should be considered an aesthetic tour de force. It is certainly equivalent (and anticipates) more celebrated literary uses of the adolescent's perspective in Twain's *Adventures of Huckleberry Finn* and James' *What Maisie Knew*. For further discussion of this issue in Jacobs, see chapter 6.

34. Sundquist, *To Wake the Nations*, p. 95. Another reason Sundquist gives for preferring *My Bondage and My Freedom* to the 1845 *Narrative* is that Douglass makes his quest for the real facts about his paternity a central part of *My Bondage*

and *My Freedom*. Once again, I do not dispute Sundquist's important revaluation of *My Bondage and My Freedom*, but I want to pay close attention to the rhetorical strategies Douglass employs in the 1845 *Narrative*, rather than judging it, as Sundquist does, "a key work in any estimation of Douglass's life" but "not Frederick Douglass's 'masterpiece' " (89). In my judgment, the 1845 *Narrative* is a literary masterpiece, because it transforms personal facts and experiences into elements in a symbolic narrative explicitly linked to political praxis.

35. There is no factual ambiguity, because Douglass introduces this episode by writing that Captain Anthony's "farms and slaves were under the care of an overseer. . . Plummer" (50). Nevertheless, Plummer's name is not mentioned during Aunt Hester's whipping — only "he" and "master" are used alternately to suggest agency.

36. Sundquist, *To Wake the Nations*, p. 99.

37. See Thomas Virgil Patterson, *Ham and Japheth: The Mythic World of Whites in the Antebellum South* (Metuchen, N.J.: Scarecrow Press, 1978), pp. 70–74. In *The Legends of the Jews* (New York: Simon and Schuster, 1956), p. 80, Louis Ginzburg provides the following narrative account: "When Noah awoke from his wine and became sober, he pronounced a curse upon Ham in the person of his youngest son, Canaan. To Ham himself he could do no harm, for God had conferred a blessing upon Noah and his three sons as they departed from the ark. . . . The descendants of Ham through Canaan therefore have red eyes, because Ham looked upon the nakedness of his father; they have misshapen lips, because Ham spoke with his lips to his brothers about the unseemly condition of his father; they have twisted curly hair, because Ham turned and twisted his head round to see the nakedness of his father; and they go about naked, because Ham did not cover the nakedness of his father."

38. William McFeely, *Frederick Douglass*, p. 27, confirms that Sophia Keitley Auld "came from a poor family near St. Michaels; she is reported to have worked for wages as a weaver before marrying Hugh Auld and moving with him to Baltimore." Nevertheless, McFeely creates a "scene" in which Sophia's kindness to Douglass is clearly maternal: "As she sat with Tommy on one knee and [the Bible] on the other, she drew Frederick to her side, and read—or told—its stories to both boys" (26).

39. Deborah McDowell, Hortense Spillers, and Valerie Smith. As Smith puts the case in *Self-Discovery and Authority in Afro-American Narrative* (Cambridge: Harvard University Press, 1987), p. 27: "Surely he believes that American society requires widespread transformation. But the story of his own success actually provides counterevidence for his platform of radical change; for by demonstrating that a slave can be a man in terms of all the qualities valued by his northern middle-class reader . . . he lends credence to the patriarchal structure largely responsible for his oppression."

40. Jenny Franchot, "The Punishment of Esther: Frederick Douglass and the Construction of the Feminine," in Eric Sundquist, ed., *Frederick Douglass: New*

Literary and Historical Essays (New York: Cambridge University Press, 1990), pp. 141–65.

41. Valerie Smith, *Self-Discovery and Authority in Afro-American Narrative*, p. 25, connects his witnessing of Aunt Hester's punishment and his fight with Covey in just this way: "Indeed, if the sight of his aunt's wrongful punishment initiated him into slavery, one might argue that he emancipates himself by revising that earlier episode and refusing to be beaten."

42. Jane Tompkins, *Sensational Designs: The Cultural Work of American Fiction: 1790–1860* (New York: Oxford University Press, 1985), pp. 141–42.

43. McFeely, *Frederick Douglass*, p. 70, reports the familiar story: "In the privacy of the family, it was always said that Anna sold a featherbed to finance the journey, and having suggested that Frederick impersonate a sailor, altered his clothing to make it look like a seaman's."

44. Sundquist, *To Wake the Nations*, p. 102n.

45. McFeely, *Frederick Douglass*, p. 66.

46. Douglass to Mary Howitt, May 10, 1848, from *Mary Howitt's Journal*, vol. 1, p. 352, as quoted in Foner, *Frederick Douglass: A Biography*, p. 76.

6. RECONSTRUCTING THE FAMILY: HARRIET JACOBS' *Incidents in the Life of a Slave Girl*

1. Hazel V. Carby, *Reconstructing Womanhood: The Emergence of the Afro-American Woman Novelist* (New York: Oxford University Press, 1987), p. 27.

2. As Carby points out, Jacobs' frequent use of such conventions led John Blassingame to conclude in *The Slave Community* (1973) that "Jacobs's narrative is unauthentic because it does not conform to the guidelines of representativeness" (Carby, 45). Of course, Jean Fagan Yellin's careful scholarship in her edition of *Incidents in the Life of a Slave Girl* (Cambridge: Harvard University Press, 1987) demonstrates convincingly the authenticity of Jacobs' authorship and experience.

3. Such moments of cultural schizophrenia are often encountered in nineteenth-century American literature, both by African Americans and white Americans. Huck Finn's defiance of the Christian morality that protects Southern slavery is a well-known instance. In refusing to turn Jim in as a runaway slave, Huck rebels but still within the rhetoric of Christian morality when he says, " 'I'll go to hell, then!' " For Morrison, this contradictoriness is an essential component of an American literature that expresses repeatedly the cultural double-standards and contradictoriness of a white ideology for a multicultural U.S.: "This haunting, a darkness from which our early literature seemed unable to extricate itself, suggests the complex and contradictory situation in which American writers found themselves during the formative years of the nation's literature." *Playing the Dark* (New York: Random House, 1992), p. 33.

4. Dana Nelson, *The Word in Black and White: Writing "Race" in American Literature, 1638–1867* (New York: Oxford University Press, 1992), p. 133.

5. I am not arguing here for *Incidents* as the "first" novel or self-consciously literary

work of African-American women's writing. I agree with Henry Louis Gates, Jr. in his Introduction to Harriet Wilson's *Our Nig; or, Sketches from the Life of a Free Black* (Boston: by the author, 1859; rpr.: New York: Random House, 1983), p. xiii, that Wilson's novel is the first novel by a black writer, but Gates makes this claim on the basis of Wilson's use of the plot conventions of sentimental novels. As I will argue in this chapter, Jacobs establishes the African-American *women's* literary tradition by refunctioning such literary conventions specifically in the interests of an African-American woman's literary voice and authority. See also Carby, pp. 43–45.

6. Harriet Jacobs, *Incidents in the Life of a Slave Girl*, ed. Jean Fagan Yellin (Cambridge: Harvard University Press, 1987), pp. 56–57. Further references are cited in the text as: Incidents.

7. Dana Nelson, *The Word in Black and White*, p. 140.

8. Ibid., pp. 144–45.

9. As Carby puts it, "Jacobs developed an alternative set of definitions of womanhood and motherhood in the text which remained in tension with the cult of true womanhood" (56). In her "Introduction" to her scholarly edition of *Incidents*, Yellin discusses how for Jacobs "the madwoman in the attic sanely plots for her freedom" and "instead of studying self-control within a domestic setting, the young woman learns to engage in political action" (xxxiii).

10. Valerie Smith, *Self-Discovery and Authority in Afro-American Narrative* (Cambridge: Harvard University Press, 1987), pp. 2–4. Further references are cited in the text as: Smith.

11. As Smith writes: "Afro-American writers draw on both an oral and a literate tradition; their debts to the one influence shape them and distance them from the other. To focus on the texts' literariness, then, is to oversimplify their lineage, and to pay homage to the structures of discourse that so often contributed to the writers' oppression" (6).

12. Lindon Barrett argues in "The Singing/ Signing Voice and African-American Culture" (manuscript) that African-American culture is far more profoundly defined by the voice, especially as the singing voice, than by the written text and narratorial practices associated with Euroamerican "telling." What this means for Barrett is that concepts of "literacy" and "literature" predicated on textuality and narration based on written forms are likely to marginalize if not exclude valid modes of social communication and representation defined by performance and voice.

13. As Jane Tompkins has argued in *Sensational Designs: The Cultural Work of American Fiction, 1797–1865* (New York: Oxford University Press, 1985), pp. 144–46, Stowe's work culminates in a utopian vision of a new Christian matriarchy, epitomized by characters like Rachel Halliday, whose "Quaker kitchen" in Indiana is also a station of the Underground Railroad.

14. Orlando Patterson, *Slavery and Social Death: A Comparative Study* (Cambridge: Harvard University Press, 1982), p. 5, writes that "the most distinctive attribute

of the slave's powerlessness was that it always originated . . . as a substitute for death, usually violent death." Indeed, Linda's rebellion in this chapter will place her in such a relation to the Flints that Mrs. Flint "vowed . . . she would kill me if I came back" (76), turning this absolute of the slave's powerlessness into a genuine form of power for Linda. I am indebted to Abdul JanMohamed for his discussion of Patterson's relevance to the African-American literary tradition in "Refiguring the Master-Slave Dialectic: Some Black Perspectives on the Function of Death in Slavery" (manuscript).

15. Dana Nelson, *The Word in Black and White*, p. 136.

16. Dr. Flint does, of course, brutally punish Linda, usually in a jealous rage, as in this episode from chapter 14: "When Dr. Flint learned that I was again to be a mother, he was exasperated beyond measure. . . . He cut every hair close to my head, storming and swearing all the time. I replied to some of his abuse, and he struck me. Some months before, he had pitched me down stairs in a fit of passion; and the injury I received was so serious that I was unable to turn myself in bed for many days" (77).

17. Linda's awareness, even at fifteen, that social "propriety" is an important lie to white slaveowners may be another way to answer why she feels such "pain and humiliation" at the very moment she has achieved some measure of agency and identity by choosing Sands as the father of her children. Rebelling against such propriety, Linda exposes in her relation with Sands—reasonably well-known to gossips in the town—the fundamental miscegenation of Southern slaveholding culture. So much critical attention has been focused on the sentimental conventions at work in her transgressive behavior that readers have been distracted from the very practical purposes served by her conduct.

18. On the messianic and millennial aspects of Nat Turner's Rebellion, see Eric Sundquist, *To Wake the Nations: Race in the Making of American Literature* (Cambridge: Harvard University Press, 1993), pp. 67–83.

19. One reaction to the Southampton Rebellion throughout the South was for whites to close African-American churches on the grounds that they were likely places for organizing such rebellion. As Yellin points out, North Carolina made it a crime in 1831, the year of the Southampton Rebellion, for "any slave or free person of color to preach, exhort, or teach 'in any prayer-meeting or other association of worship where slaves of different families are collected together'" (Incidents, 270n5). The rhetorical links between Nat Turner's Rebellion and the African-American Church are made explicitly in this passage, but they are implicit in virtually all of Jacobs' references to Nat Turner.

20. Much attention is given in *Incidents* to the time and money wasted by vengeful slaveowners, like Dr. Flint, in punishing rebellious slaves or searching for runaways. Jacobs' attention to economic details like this is intended to remind the reader that slavery is an economically inefficient system, as well as a morally corrupt one. Her arguments are made more compelling for nineteenth-century readers by the contrast she establishes with the well-ordered, economically stable

lives led by free African Americans, like her grandmother, even though free African Americans were obviously very much victims of economic and social racism in the South.

21. At key moments, Linda refers impersonally to Sands. In this case, he is simply "the father" and in chapter 10, he is merely "a white unmarried gentleman" until she has made her full resolution to use him against Dr. Flint. Jacobs makes it clear to the reader that Linda rejects from the outset the authority of the father, especially when it works in concert with the slavocracy. Early in *Incidents*, when Linda's brother, William, is a child, he is called at the same time by Mrs. Flint and his father. When William goes to his mistress, instead of his father, the father criticizes him: " 'You are *my* child. . . and when I call you, you should come immediately, if you have to pass through fire and water.' " Linda concludes that "Poor Willie . . . . was now to learn his first lesson of obedience to a master," suggesting that the father's insistence upon his authority has the taint of a slaveowning mentality to it (9).

22. Linda's allusion to Payne's *Clari; or, the Maid of Milan*, works with several other efforts Jacobs makes to link the sufferings of African-American slaves with the ruling-class oppression of the European peasantry. In Payne's play, the peasant-woman, Clari, is seduced by a duke, with whom she lives until she longs for home and runs away from him. Linda opens chapter 6, "The Jealous Mistress," by contrasting her situation with that of Irish victims of the Potato Famine: "I would ten thousand times rather that my children should be the half-starved paupers of Ireland than to be the most pampered among the slaves of America" (31). As Yellin (266n.1) points out, this was a conventional comparison by Abolitionists. Such allusion and contrast both work rhetorically to remind readers that European feudalism and African-American slavery are historically linked and that the work of democratic emancipation in the United States has not been accomplished.

23. Dana Nelson, *The Word in Black and White*, p. 145, suggests that "Mrs. Bruce's well-intended actions" in buying Linda's freedom, for example, "call to mind Child's scheme for American postwar regeneration, whereby 'whites' would lift up ex-slaves into middle-class society through a system of patronage." Acknowledging the paternalism of committed Abolitionists and women's rights activists, like Lydia Maria Child, Nelson also shows how Jacobs criticizes such paternalism in the interests of creating "a communicative bridge" that might link together different groups within the abolitionist and women's rights movements. As Nelson points out, this "radical vision. . . depended on the willingness of its audience to listen and to accept the challenge of self-critique" (145).

24. Claudia Tate, "Allegories of Black Female Desire; or, Rereading Nineteenth-Century Sentimental Narratives of Black Female Authority," in *Changing Our Own Words: Essays on Criticism, Theory, and Writing by Black Women*, ed. Cheryl A. Wall (New Brunswick, N.J.: Rutgers University Press, 1989), p. 108, differs from this trend by interpreting *Incidents* as complementary with the work of nineteenth-

century male African-American writing: "*Incidents* writes a female version of the racial discourse by aligning black women's moral outrage at the sexual abuses of slavery with black men's petition for liberty." In effect, this is my strategy in reading Douglass' 1845 *Narrative* and Jacobs' *Incidents* in conjunction, recognizing the important supplement to and implicit criticism of Douglass' consideration of gender that is provided by Jacobs's account.

25. See Herbert Gutman, *The Black Family in Slavery and Freedom, 1750–1925* (New York: Random House, 1976).

26. Yellin points out that: "Punishment in North Carolina for harboring a runaway slave included fines and punishment" (Incidents, 275n3).

27. As Amy Post writes in her "Appendix" to *Incidents*, Jacobs "was grateful for the boon" of Mrs. Bruce's generosity, "but the idea of having been *bought* was always galling to a spirit that could never acknowledge itself to be chattel. She wrote to us thus, soon after the event: 'I thank you for your kind expressions in regard to my freedom; but the freedom I had before the money was paid was dearer to me. God gave me *that* freedom; but man put God's image in the scales with the paltry sum of three hundred dollars' " (204).

28. Tate, "Allegories of Black Female Desire," p. 110.

7. The Body Poetic: Walt Whitman's *Drum-Taps*

1. "Eighteen Sixty-One," *Drum-Taps*, in *Leaves of Grass*, vol. 2, *The Collected Writings of Walt Whitman*, 3 vols., eds. Gay Wilson Allen and Sculley Bradley (New York: New York University Press, 1980), p. 467. Further references are cited in text as: DT; and to *Sequel to Drum-Taps* as: Sequel.

2. Emerson, *Nature*, in *Nature, Addresses, and Lectures*, *The Works of Ralph Waldo Emerson*, ed. Edward W. Emerson, 14 vols. (Boston: Houghton, Mifflin, 1883), vol. 1, p. 35. Further references in the Notes to this edition are cited as *Works*.

3. Emerson, "American Civilization," *Miscellanies*, vol. 11, *Works*, p. 277. Further references are cited in the text as: "American Civilization." See also my discussion of Emerson's treatment of labor in "Man, the Reformer," in chapter 4.

4. Cavell, *The Senses of Walden*, expanded edition (San Francisco: North Point Press, 1981), p. 119.

5. As Betsy Erkkila demonstrates, in *Whitman the Political Poet* (New York: Oxford University Press, 1989), Whitman's utopian vision was communitarian and thus far more demanding in terms of what the poet had to acknowledge and incorporate into his thinking and poetic practice than the ego-centered transcendentalisms of Emerson and Thoreau, in which the "representative man" could stand metonymically for a people, community, or nation.

6. F. DeWolfe Miller, "Introduction," *Drum-Taps* (1865) and *Sequel to Drum-Taps* (1865–66), facsimile edition, ed. F. DeWolfe Miller (Gainesville, Fla.: Scholars' Facsimiles and Reprints, 1959), p. xxxi. It's worth pointing out that the first edition of *Drum-Taps* did include reference to Lincoln's assassination in "Hush'd Be the Camps To-Day," with its title note, "A. L. Buried April 19, 1865." Sculley

Bradley and Harold W. Blodgett point out in *Leaves of Grass*, Norton Critical Edition (New York: Norton, 1973), p. 338n, that this original title note was included "evidently under the misapprehension that interment, as well as the funeral, was to take place in Washington. In the 1871 and 1876 editions he corrected the note to ["May 4, 1865"], and also made a number of changes in the final stanza."

7. Timothy Sweet, *Traces of War: Poetry, Photography, and the Crisis of the Union* (Baltimore: Johns Hopkins University Press, 1990), p. 11.

8. In *Walt Whitman and the Citizen's Eye* (Baton Rouge: Louisiana State University Press, 1993), James Dougherty argues that Whitman adapts the dramatic monologues of "Song of Myself," in which he had "spoken on behalf of slaves and criminals, to draw them back within the spiritual commonwealth," to his own situation in *Drum-Taps*: "Now Whitman speaks as an outsider himself: a citizen whose democratic anarchism was affronted by the Union's suppression of political dissent and by the elitism of its military leadership, and whose human impulses were enraged by the suffering and human wastage he saw in the hospitals. . . . He begins to speak not as the president of regulation (as he had called himself in the 1855 Preface), but as the perpetual revolutionary" (p. 82). It is just this difference between his marginal poetic authority and the authority represented by Lincoln that he can no longer sustain in "Lilacs" and most of the *Sequel*. As Sweet points out, Whitman collapses his poetic purposes in "Lilacs" with a heroic Lincoln, who has been thereby "dehistoricized" and thus depoliticized (*Traces of War*, p. 77). In this regard, see also Mark Edmundson's "'Lilacs': Walt Whitman's American Elegy," *Nineteenth-Century Literature* 44 (1990), 465–91.

9. Although he makes the case a bit too reductively that "Whitman *was* an imperialist poet," Walter Grünzweig connects effectively Whitman's cosmopolitanism and internationalism, especially in the poetry of the 1870s and later, with U.S. expansionist policies in the later nineteenth century. See Grünzweig, "Noble Ethics and Loving Aggressiveness: The Imperialist Walt Whitman," in *An American Empire: Expansionist Cultures and Policies, 1881–1917*, ed. Serge Ricard (Publications de l'université de Provence, 1990).

10. Bradley and Blodgett, *Leaves of Grass*, Norton Critical Edition, p. 290n.

11. As Kent Ljungquist points out in "'Meteor of War': Melville, Thoreau, and Whitman Respond to John Brown," *American Literature* 61 (December 1989): 679, Whitman identifies his poetic voice with a meteor in "Year of Meteors" (the twenty-ninth poem in the first edition of *Drum-Taps*), probably in reference to the meteor shower reported in the Northeast in December 1859 and cited by many as a portent of war: "In typical Whitman fashion, he appropriates this image of the 'I' of the poem and asks: 'What am I myself but one of your meteors?'"

12. Of course, Whitman's various appeals in *Drum-Taps* for poetic foreknowledge of the war's necessity serve also to divert attention from his ambivalence regarding war in the early months of the Civil War. See Miller, "Introduction," *Drum-Taps*

and *Sequel to Drum-Taps*, facsimile, pp. ix–xvi, for an account of how Whitman's ambivalences about the War were treated by his contemporaries up to his death and Thomas Wentworth Higginson's obituary on Whitman in the *New York Post*.

13. See Sweet, *Traces of War*, p. 44: "In the context of the war Whitman found his own 'self' to be unstable. During his years as volunteer nurse in army hospitals he suffered physical and emotional breakdowns, in 1863 and again in 1865. . . . The grounding of poetics in 'myself' or in the 'body electric' as constructed in the first edition of *Leaves of Grass* was brought into question by the violence of the war."

14. Eric Sundquist, *To Wake the Nations: Race in the Making of American Literature* (Cambridge: Harvard University Press, 1993), pp. 9–12.

15. The appropriation of General Washington's authority by the poetic voice is perhaps subtly reinforced by the Whitman family's tradition that "one of the sons of Nehemiah Whitman, W[alt] W[hitman]'s great grandfather, lost his life fighting as a rebel lieutenant in this action," as Bradley and Blodgett note in *Leaves of Grass*, p. 295n.

16. F. O. Matthiessen, *American Renaissance: Art and Expression in the Age of Emerson and Whitman* (New York: Oxford University Press, 1941), pp. 599–600. Matthiessen's purpose, of course, in stressing Whitman's impressionistic techniques in these short lyrics, was to establish a connection between the later romantic and early moderns, especially T. S. Eliot. Dougherty's treatment of Whitman's pictorialism is a later and better interpretation, in part because Dougherty recognizes the narrativity of the impressionist lyrics in *Drum-Taps* and in part because he does not push Matthiessen's formalist thesis. See Dougherty, *Walt Whitman and the Citizen's Eye*, pp. 108–16.

17. Bradley and Blodgett, *Leaves of Grass*, p. 424n.: "The Fourth of the untitled twelve of the first edition, this poem was called 'Night Poem' in 1856, 'Sleep-Chasings' in 1860 and 1867, and 'The Sleepers' since 1871."

18. This is how Dougherty reads these short poems in *Drum-Taps* about soldiers' experiences in the field. See *Walt Whitman and the Citizen's Eye*, pp. 110–11. I don't disagree with this more literal treatment of Whitman's dramatic monologues, but I would argue that Whitman wants the reader to be confused about speaking voice in these poems, such that the soldier's literal experience and its poetic figuration become complements in the overall project of reconstructing Whitman's poetic identity.

19. Once again, I think that Whitman's revisions of *Drum-Taps* reinforce the emergence of this confident poetic voice, primarily by rearranging the narrative of the poems. Thus the 1891–92 edition of *Leaves of Grass* puts together and in this order "By the Bivouac's Fitful Flame," "Come Up from the Fields Father," and "Vigil Strange I Kept on the Field One Night." Read in this order, the three poems dramatize the transformation of the poet from mere observer of war ("By the Bivouac's Fitful Flame") to surrogate father ("Come Up from the Fields Father") to Christlike savior ("Vigil Strange I Kept on the Field One Night").

Such a reading depends crucially on treating the different voices of the dramatic monologues variously represented in the three poems as parts of the same overarching poetic voice.

20. Dougherty, *Walt Whitman and the Citizen's Eye*, p. 100, reads "Come Up from the Fields Father" as a conventional poem for its sentimentalization of the family's grief in the mother's death at the end of the poem. Yet when read as Whitman's substitution of his own generative powers for those either of the Union or the dead soldier's parents, then the poem escapes the sentimentality of such war elegies by problematizing our responsibility for the war dead. This does not by itself render the poem better on purely aesthetic grounds than Dougherty judges it, but it does make it far more *interesting* than the spate of conventional poems about Union dead from this period.

21. Sweet, *Traces of War*, p. 43. Sweet interprets the speaker in the poem as "the father of the dead soldier," a conclusion that if taken too literally distracts us from the Christological rhetoric of the poem—a rhetoric necessary for Whitman's poetic voice to claim to be both *father and son*, thereby achieving his own symbolic resurrection at the poem's conclusion.

22. Dougherty's reading of "Vigil Strange" in *Walt Whitman and the Citizen's Eye*, p. 102, also misses the rhetoric of poetic resurrection, but it does treat the poem as centrally concerned with the problem of voice: " 'Vigil Strange' is striking for the reticence of its soldier-persona. His I stands mute and passive in the presence of a Not-Me that exceeds his capacity to respond; and Whitman's imagination embraces that emptiness, not filling its void as he did at the end of 'Come Up from the Fields' " (102). As Dougherty recognizes, this is not the only poem in *Drum-Taps* in which Whitman uses silence, the inability to find poetic voice, and the poet's afflatus to remind us that his theme is at least as much the problem of rediscovering poetic voice as witnessing the War.

23. Sweet, *Traces of War*, p. 24.

24. For an excellent account of Whitman's use of his earlier poems in "Lilacs," see Helen Vendler, "Whitman's 'When Lilacs Last in the Dooryard Bloom'd," in *Textual Analysis: Some Readers Reading*, ed. Mary Ann Caws (New York: Modern Language Association, 1986), pp. 132–43.

25. I disagree with Kenneth Price, *Whitman and Tradition: The Poet in His Century* (New Haven: Yale University Press, 1990), p. 78, who argues: "In 'Lilacs' Whitman confronts the 'debris and debris of all dead soldiers' and resists even his own affirmations of faith in immortality. Nor does he take comfort, as he had earlier in his career, in the idea that an individual is one particle of the universal life and that death leads to endless regeneration of new life. Having witnessed amputations, gangrene, and piled limbs outside of Civil War hospitals, Whitman seeks release and praises death as the 'strong deliveress.' " "Lilacs" moves inevitably toward the "resurrection" of the dead President in the renewed vision of democracy that the poet offers his public. Such poetic transformation of grief into joy, dirge into "Victorious song" is typical of romantic elegy, even if

Whitman's version is an extraordinary example of the established form ("Lilacs," XVI).

26. Edmundson, " 'Lilacs,' " 491, effectively makes this point about "Lilacs" dehistoricizing and depoliticizing its ostensibly historical subjects.

8. FATAL SPECULATIONS—MURDER, MONEY, AND MANNERS: MARK TWAIN'S *The Gilded Age* AND *Pudd'nhead Wilson*

1. Mark Twain, *Pudd'nhead Wilson* and *Those Extraordinary Twins*, ed. Sidney E. Berger (New York: Norton, 1980), p. 115. Further references cited in the text as: PW.

2. See Arlin Turner, "Mark Twain and the South: *Pudd'nhead Wilson*," in the Norton Critical Edition, p. 282: "By 1894, the problems explored in *Pudd'nhead Wilson* had grown wearisome in the North as well as the South. More than a decade earlier the political decision had been made that the Southern states should solve the race problem without interference from the national government. As state laws were enacted in the early 1890s which decreed for the former slaves a segregated, non-voting status, no effective protest was voiced in either section. The public, valuing the peace which had been achieved, did not welcome disturbances, even in fiction. There is something of irony in that, by chance rather than intention, Mark Twain wrote his most perceptive and most impressive attack on racism and related doctrines at a time when his attack could stir no spark in the reading public." My argument, of course, attempts to lend Twain's "attack on racism and related doctrines" more relevance to late nineteenth-century, industrial America, North and South.

3. The "p'fessor in a college" so reviled by Pap Finn in chapter 6 of the novel is particularly hateful to him, because he can *vote* in "Ohio." Freedom and voting-rights are very often linked by Twain, which is why vote-buying is such an immoral "speculation" for him.

4. Michael Tadman, *Slavetraders and Speculators* (Baltimore: Johns Hopkins University Press, 1985), discusses the rise of speculative interests in slaves after the slave trade was formally banned in the United States. In other words, the consequence of that ban was simply to put greater pressure on the domestic market for slavery, although there was still considerable illegal international commerce in slaves, as I noted in chapter 5.

5. Mark Twain and Charles Dudley Warner, *The Gilded Age: A Tale of Today* (New York: New American Library, 1969), pp. 393–94. Further references are cited in the text as: GA.

6. While working as a surveyor and investor in a speculative scheme to develop a small Missouri settlement in advance of the railroad, Philip Sterling visits the New York offices of the company to find out why no funds for the workers' salaries have been sent. By the time he leaves these headquarters, he finds himself several thousands of dollars in debt and his workers considerably overpaid. The

accounting given him is a splendid parody of the rhetorical sophistry by which
commercial America would give objective credibility to its speculative fictions.

7. See my discussion of Twain's representations of parents and children in *Through
the Custom-House: Nineteenth-Century American Fiction and Modern Theory* (Baltimore:
Johns Hopkins University Press, 1982), p. 161.

8. Dixon Wecter, *Sam Clemens of Hannibal* (Boston: Houghton Mifflin, 1952),
pp. 68–72.

9. Wecter, p. 72.

10. As quoted in Wecter, p. 72.

11. If Percy and the Judge represent two "halves" of Judge John M. Clemens, then
David Wilson and Tom represent two "halves" of Twain's own personality. A
psychoanalytical reading of *Pudd'nhead Wilson* that would elaborate the literary
mechanisms by which Twain distances, represses, and still recognizes his kinship
with these two corrupt characters would be most welcome and helpful.

12. Perry McCandless, *A History of Missouri*, vol. 2, *1820–1860* (Columbia:
University of Missouri Press, 1972), p. 119.

13. McCandless, vol. 2, p. 138.

14. Philip Sterling finally overcomes his "speculating instincts" by working hard and
discovering shared labor with his workers in the coal mine he develops in the
latter part of the narrative. Henry Brierly's financial and romantic schemes lure
him into the clutches of Laura Hawkins, who uses him as an unwitting accessory
in her murder of the lover who had betrayed her. Finally released from prison,
Harry heads for San Francisco, apparently unregenerate, "to look after some
government contracts in the harbor there" (GA, 346). The morality of Warner
and Twain in *The Gilded Age* is heavy-handed and puritanical, but it provides a clear
background for Twain's indictment of the cancerous immorality of speculation in
Pudd'nhead Wilson.

15. *The Autobiography of Mark Twain*, ed. Charles Neider (New York: Washington
Square Press, 1961), p. 281.

16. *Autobiography*, p. 282. Of John Clemens' efforts to satisfy his creditors, Dixon
Wecter, *Sam Clemens of Hannibal*, p. 71, writes: "The code of the Virginia
gentleman permitted no other course to Mark Twain's father, and the pride which
the son took in his father's stripping himself to satisfy all claims—beyond the call
of duty, we are told, down to offering the forks and spoons, and every stick of
furniture—presaged a similar act in Mark's life half a century later."

17. Arlin Turner, "Mark Twain and the South: *Pudd'nhead Wilson*," p. 280, makes a
strong case for finding traces of Judge John Clemens in the characters of both
Percy Driscoll and Judge Driscoll.

18. Tom's cowardice throughout *Pudd'nhead Wilson* often has been noted by critics.
Tom's famous reflection in chapter 10 on his newly discovered identity as an
African-American slave seems only to intensify that cowardice by adding self-
contempt to the formula. Twain often noted that it was just this "slave-mentality"
that was white America's worst sin against African Americans. By the same token,

Roxy's will, cleverness, and moral righteousness all seem to come from her general imitation of white customs and attitudes. As potentially racist as Twain's distinction between Tom and Roxy seems to be, it's fair to note that Twain gives us virtually no means for generalizing about the "essence" of the "Negro" in *Pudd'nhead Wilson*. As Roxy's fantastic family genealogy suggests, the "Essex blood" of which she is so proud is traceable ultimately to "Pocahontas de Injun queen, en her husbun' was a nigger king outen Africa" (70). In her own fictional origins—the ones that are finally the important ones for Twain's characters, Roxy rediscovers her strength, intelligence, and will in native American and African roots.

19. Michael Paul Rogin, *Subversive Genealogy: The Politics and Art of Herman Melville* (Berkeley: University of California Press, 1983), p. 73.

20. Ibid., p. 73.

21. See Frederick Anderson, "Mark Twain and the Writing of *Pudd'nhead Wilson*," in the Norton Critical Edition, p. 285: "Aspects of Pudd'nhead Wilson's character and career, specifically his barren law practice, are based on that of Mark Twain's brother Orion and the crushing failure he encountered in his attempt to practice that profession." We might add the "crushing failures" that Orion's speculative and inventive schemes invariably encountered in his curious career. The character Washington Hawkins in *The Gilded Age*, chief victim of Colonel Sellers' fantastic schemes, is clearly modeled after Orion Clemens.

22. George M. Spangler, "*Pudd'nhead Wilson*: A Parable of Property," in the Norton Critical Edition, p. 303.

23. The anonymous reviewer of *Pudd'nhead Wilson* in *The Athenaeum* (January 19, 1895), reprinted in the Norton Critical Edition, p. 216, complains: "Why drag in, for example, all the business about the election, which is quite irrelevant? and the Twins altogether seem to have very little *raison d'être* in the book." It's fair to say that these are old complaints that have not been sufficiently answered by modern critics of the novel.

9. The Politics of Innocence: Henry James' *The American*

1. I make the argument for James' conscious bid to become an international author in *The Theoretical Dimensions of Henry James* (Madison: University of Wisconsin Press, 1984), pp. 30–57. See also my essay, "The Politics of the Uncanny: Newman's Fate in *The American*," *The Henry James Review*, 8 (Fall 1987): 79–90, which explores the psychological aspects of Newman's political and historical ignorance in *The American*.

2. Henry James, Jr., *Hawthorne*, English Men of Letters, ed. John Morley (New York: Harper, 1879), p. 42: "If Hawthorne had been a young Englishman, or a young Frenchman of the same degree of genius, the same cast of mind, the same habits, his consciousness of the world around him would have been a very different affair; however obscure, however reserved, his own personal life,

his sense of the life of his fellow-mortals would have been almost infinitely more various."

3. First published in *Macmillan's Magazine* (December 1887), this review-essay was reprinted as "Emerson," the first essay in *Partial Portraits* (London: Macmillan, 1888), pp. 2, 3, 8.

4. *Partial Portraits*, p. 31.

5. For reasons discussed later in this essay (see note 16), I am using the first edition of *The American*, rather than the much-revised New York Edition. Because James Tuttleton's Norton Critical Edition of *The American* (New York: Norton, 1978) uses the more authoritative London Macmillan edition of 1879 as a copy text, but records all variants between the Boston edition of 1877 and the London edition of 1879, I have chosen to use the Norton as an authoritative text for a study of the "first edition" of *The American*. All page references are included in the text.

6. Manfred Mackenzie, in *Communities of Honor and Love in Henry James* (Cambridge: Harvard University Press, 1976), provides brilliant structural analyses of these rites of inclusion and exclusion in James' fictional social worlds. Apropos of Newman's transformation of his ignorance of history and politics into his own private melodrama in *The American*, Mackenzie's following remarks are especially helpful: "If the Jamesian hero's quest for identity and honor implies another or a second go, then his story may very well take a one-two form. Insofar as this hero quests compulsively for being-unto-self, then his story may well turn into a fiction system that is by definition supremely unto itself" (p. 117).

7. William Stowe, *Balzac, James, and the Realistic Novel* (Princeton: Princeton University Press, 1983), p. 40.

8. James W. Tuttleton, *The Novel of Manners in America* (New York: Norton, 1974), p. 69.

9. *The American*, 300. In his letters written from Paris between 1875 and 1876, James mentions frequently his own habits of reading several papers to keep abreast of French social and political life. In his letter to his father, December 22, 1875, James writes: "I find the political situation here very interesting and devour the newspapers. The great matter for the last fortnight has been the election of seventy-five life-members of the new Senate, by the Assembly, in which the coalition of the Republicans, Legitimists and Bonapartists (which the attitude of the Orleanists has made necessary) had entirely routed the latter. The Left has carried the whole thing through with great skill and good sense, and there is a prospect of there being a very well composed Senate." *Henry James Letters*, ed. Leon Edel, vol. 2 (Cambridge: Harvard University Press, 1975), p. 15.

10. John V. Antush, "The 'Much Finer Complexity' of History in *The American*," *Journal of American Studies* 6 (April 1972): 88, discusses the sixteenth- and seventeenth-century French history in *The American* primarily in terms of the beginnings of a strong bourgeoisie that would replace the aristocracy: "Since the end of the sixteenth century, when the king of France began selling small parcels of his

authority to the highest bidder, the bourgeoisie, who alone held the purse strings for the economy of the nation, began to replace the aristocracy in key positions of power." Antush's rather broad view of French history causes him to treat nineteenth-century aristocratic political interests as relatively insignificant, thus reinforcing his interpretation of the Bellegardes—and Valentin in particular— as emblems of an anachronistic class: "However, the restoration of the Bourbon family to the throne of France in 1814 brought back only symbols and effected no serious change in the new political system." Nevertheless, Antush's essay deserves special mention as one of the few studies of *The American* to attempt to discuss in any detail the concrete historical details in the text. Like *The Aspern Papers* and many of James' other works, *The American* is full of such details, but the reader's surrender to the protagonist's perspective tempts us to repeat Newman's historical ignorance. James seems to take special pleasure in burying those concrete details that qualify drastically the mere impressionism of his central characters.

11. I am indebted to Professor Thomas Kavanagh, of the Department of French at the University of California, Berkeley, for this observation.

12. *Henry James Letters*, vol. 2, p. 30.

13. Edgar Holt, *Risorgimento: The Making of Italy, 1815–1870* (London: Macmillan, 1970), pp. 248–49. Holt describes the battle of Castelfidardo in the following terms: "The papal mercenaries fought well so long as they were facing the Italians on more or less equal terms; but as soon as Cialdini was able to deploy his whole army corps the issue was decided. . . . On the papal side 88 men were killed, 400 wounded and 600 taken prisoner. Castelfidardo was not a great victory. It was not comparable with Garibaldi's successes. But it gave the new army some useful prestige" (pp. 249–50).

14. Leon Edel and Ilse Dusoir Lind's "Introduction" to Henry James, *Parisian Sketches: Letters to the "New York Tribune" 1875–1876*, ed. Leon Edel and Ilse Dusoir Lind (New York: Crowell-Collier, 1961), p. 12. Further references are cited in the text as: PS.

15. As early a work as it is in James' career, *The American* remains the most carefully structured in terms of what we might term the "repetition-compulsion of revenge." The loss of any viable sense of historical reality by Newman might be explained as a consequence of his entrapment in the closed circle of this revenge-cycle. Newman's ostensible efforts to hold himself aloof from the chances at revenge in New York and Paris in no way liberate him from the cycle, because his renunciation depends upon denial and repression. Innocence of man's fundamental will to power/knowledge may be the ultimate ignorance for James' characters. The only way to break the revenge-cycle in James is to translate the sentimental sense of personal injury into political action. Very few of James' characters follow this course, although Hyacinth Robinson's suicide—the ultimate object of revenge is, of course, oneself—illustrates negatively how James offers his characters rather specific choices: the repetition-compulsion of

revenge, absolute renunciation that merely directs enmity inward at its original source, or political action that would turn blind repetition in the direction of conscious historical change. On the psychology of revenge in James' fiction, see Mackenzie, *Communities of Honor and Love*, pp. 94–126.

16. Tuttleton writes in "A Note on the Text," in the Norton Critical Edition of *The American*, p. 315: "Whatever one may think of James' revisions for the 'New York Edition,' it is clear that the 1907 edition of *The American* is so extensively revised that it is a substantially different book from the novel James composed in the mid-1870s. In reissuing the novel, the editor must therefore choose which of the versions—early or late—should be presented."

17. R. W. Butterfield, "*The American*," in *The Air of Reality: New Essays on Henry James*, ed. John Goode (London: Methuen, 1972), pp. 9–10.

18. There is a great deal of what appears at first to be rather conventional, even heavy-handed foreshadowing in *The American*. When reconsidered in terms of James' knowledge of the great European political events that were about to descend upon the characters in *The American*, however, this foreshadowing would be better defined as rhetorical prolepsis. We associate foreshadowing with suspense and plot, whereas prolepsis effects a certain equation between present and future. The duel between Valentin and the German, Kapp, certainly plays upon the popular understanding of the Franco-Prussian War as a useless war fought over airy honor. Bismarck's infamous use of the Ems Dispatch to whip up German patriotism and indignation over the behavior of the French ambassadors relied also on his understanding of French national honor. Nevertheless, James' connection of the duel and the Franco-Prussian War is intended less to trivialize the war (there were very real political and territorial stakes involved) than it is intended to give some legitimacy to Valentin's absurd gesture. Looking back from the vantage of 1875, James as much as says that Valentin's commitment to his social codes at least allows him to identify with some exactness his real enemies. In this regard, he has the advantage of Newman. Antush treats the duel as many other critics have: it is just another instance of how empty rituals have replaced the military power of the European aristocracy. See Antush, "The 'Much Finer Complexity,. . .' " 87–88.

19. *The American*, 306. When Tom Tristram first meets Newman in the Louvre, he asks: "What are you up to, any way? . . . Are you going to write a book?" (33). As the romantic melodrama usurps the realism of the early chapters, James has Newman increasingly figure his situation with metaphors of the popular romance, the arts, and other stylized representational modes.

10. THE ECONOMICS OF THE BODY: KATE CHOPIN'S *The Awakening*

1. Kate Chopin, *The Awakening*, ed. Margaret Culley (New York: Norton, 1976), p. 37. Further references are cited in the text as: KCA.

2. Edna's sense of heightened excitement and then unaccountable lassitude often

occur in contexts suggestive of masturbation. As I shall argue throughout this chapter, Edna's moments of private reverie and/or masturbatory "self-touching" should be read doubly as potentially narcissistic and yet striving to define and constitute a self otherwise severely attenuated by the ideology of Creole (and U.S.) culture.

3. Sandra Gilbert, Introduction to *"The Awakening" and Selected Stories*, ed. Sandra M. Gilbert (New York: Viking Penguin, 1984), 19–33.

4. Chopin's "naturalism" refers more often to the deterministic qualities of Creole ideology—its entanglement of patriarchy and economic hierarchy—than to her conscious affiliation with a contemporary literary school or movement. Thus the conflict in *The Awakening* between romanticism and naturalism is less a consequence of Chopin's inability to control her technique than her representation of the conflicts experienced by women like Edna in such a society. These conflicts are by no means comparable with the suffering experienced by Linda Brent in Jacobs' *Incidents* (discussed in chapter 6) or Douglass in his 1845 *Narrative* (discussed in chapter 5), but they have certain analogies with the subject under slavery insofar as Edna, Linda, and Douglass all come to understand the fantastic qualities of an ideology that is built upon contradiction and hypocrisy. How to salvage the imagination and thus creativity of the individual subject from such a deeply conflicted social situation becomes a common problem for all three, and it involves centrally a reconsideration of the body as the site of self-expression, just as it is the primary site of ideological domination.

5. Emerson, *Nature*, *Nature, Addresses, and Lectures*, in *The Works of Ralph Waldo Emerson*, ed. Edward W. Emerson, 14 vols. (Boston: Houghton, Mifflin, 1883), p. 16; Thoreau, *The Journals of Henry David Thoreau*, eds. Bradford Torrey and Francis H. Allen, 14 vols. (Boston: Houghton Mifflin, 1906; rpt: New York: Dover, 1962), vol. 1, pp. 141–42, seems to anticipate Edna's evening with the mosquitoes while avoiding Léonce on Grand Isle: "Would it not be a luxury to stand up to one's chin in some retired swamp for a whole summer's day, scenting the sweet-fern and bilberry blows, and lulled by the minstrelsy of gnats and mosquitoes? . . . Say twelve hours of genial and familiar converse with the leopard frog. . . . To hear the evening chant of the mosquito from a thousand green chapels, and the bittern to boom from his concealed fort like a sunset gun! Surely, one may as profitably be soaked in the juices of a marsh for one day, as pick his way dry-shod over sand"; Whitman throughout *Leaves of Grass*, but especially in the "twenty-nine" bathers section of "Song of Myself," *Leaves of Grass*, eds. Sculley Bradley and Harold Blodgett (New York: Norton, 1973), poem 11, p. 38: "Dancing and laughing along the beach came the twenty-ninth bather, / The rest did not see her, but she saw them and loved them."

6. The father subsequently acquires a Mississippi plantation, so that any possibility of Kentucky as a "border-state" of the South and Creole culture must remain an increasingly distant memory of Edna's lost childhood.

7. Elaine Scarry, *The Body in Pain: The Making and Unmaking of the World* (New York:

Oxford University Press, 1985), pp. 243–77. In *The German Ideology*, ed. C. J. Arthur (New York: International, 1970), Marx and Engels repeatedly stress the equivalence between "ruling ideas" and "the ruling material force of society," which "is at the same time its ruling *intellectual* force" (p. 64). It is a commonplace to conclude, then, that for Marxism the transformation of society must begin with those ruling material conditions, and I am arguing that Chopin, by no means a Marxist, recognizes that the transformation of patriarchal society begins for women with an equivalent transformation of the "ruling material conditions." For Chopin, the "ruling material conditions" can be experienced first (and thus transformed first) in the *body* of the subjugated woman.

8. Scarry, *Body in Pain*, pp. 252–53.

9. This late nineteenth-century anxiety is, of course, the basis for later modern and postmodern cultural anxieties regarding "biological engineering." It may be that Marx and Engels once again deserve criticism for endorsing too readily the emancipatory possibilities of technology, but it may also be the case that our failure to comprehend the body as a natural technology has allowed us to maintain the split between nature and culture and thus to grant exclusive rights to the control of technology to ruling interests.

10. Frederick Engels, *The Origin of the Family, Private Property, and the State* (New York: Penguin, 1985), pp. 113–14.

11. Walter Michaels, *The Gold Standard and the Logic of Naturalism* (Berkeley: University of California Press, 1987), p. 67.

12. Engels, *Origin of the Family*, p. 113.

13. Georg Lukács, *History and Class Consciousness*, trans. Rodney Livingston (Cambridge: Cambridge University Press, 1985); Thorstein Veblen, *Theory of the Leisure Class; An Economic Study in the Evolution of Institutions* (New York: Macmillan, 1899).

14. Carolyn Porter, "Reification and American Literature," in *Ideology and Classic American Literature*, eds. Sacvan Bercovitch and Myra Jehlen (New York: Cambridge University Press, 1986), p. 189.

15. In this case, the significance of such languor and torpor as masturbation would overdetermine the meaning of frustrated sexuality as the psychosexual equivalent of the worker's alienation from his or her own economic production.

16. Karl Marx and Frederick Engels, *Capital*, trans. Ben Fowkes (vol. 1) and David Fernback (vol. 2), 2 vols. (New York: Random House, 1977, 1981), vol. 1, pp. 340–53.

17. In *Capital*, the worker's right to "time in which to satisfy his intellectual and social requirements" is considered a measure of "the general level of civilization," agreeing in effect with what Marx and Engels claimed in *The German Ideology* is the new human "need" that comes with history— socialization. See *The German Ideology*, pp. 93–94.

18. Like Linda Brent, however, Edna's powers of negation are insufficient to constitute a genuine subject-position. Brent goes on to take action, negating

negation, as it were, by virtue of her seven years in her grandmother's garret, but Edna never achieves this degree of self-representation. See chapter 6.

19. Dale Bauer and Andrew Lakritz, "*The Awakening* and the Woman Question," *Approaches to Teaching Chopin's "The Awakening,"* ed. Bernard Koloski (New York: Modern Language Association, 1988), p. 51.

20. In this case, the specific taboo against divorce in Catholic Creole society helps foreground patriarchal hierarchies in the nineteenth-century U.S. family that Chopin by no means wants to restrict *only* to Southern Creole society.

21. Engels, *Origin of the Family*, p. 145.

22. Marx and Engels, *Capital*, vol. 1, p. 874.

23. Stanley Clisby Arthur, *Jean Laffite, Gentleman Rover* (New Orleans: Harmonson, 1952), pp. 261–66.

24. Eric Sundquist, *To Wake the Nations: Race in the Making of American Literature* (Cambridge: Harvard University Press, 1993), p. 185.

25. Kate Chopin, *The Complete Works of Kate Chopin*, ed. Per Seyersted, 2 vols. (Baton Rouge: Louisiana State University Press, 1969), vol. 2, pp. 697–99.

26. In this case, the eroticism is clearly associated with her being alone and thus euphoria and lassitude together suggest masturbation, but now in a context that is clearly emancipatory rather than narcissistic or frustrating.

27. Gilbert, Introduction, *The Awakening* (Penguin), p. 30.

28. Scarry, *Body in Pain*, p. 255.

29. Ibid., p. 256.

30. Chopin, *Complete Works*, p. 704.

31. Ibid.

32. Ridley Scott's *Thelma and Louise* (1991) makes this point just as clearly as *The Awakening*. Pursued by the police to the edge of the Grand Canyon, Thelma and Louise choose to drive off the edge in their outlandish, symbolic 1966 Thunderbird. Frozen in flight just as they leave earth and hanging suspended over the canyon, Thelma and Louise only "commit suicide" in our realistic expectations of an action that continues beyond the frame of the cinematic work. Their suspension in the film's conclusion allows the viewer to ask the question about their desire for emancipation—a question that criticizes the limitations of the society that has provoked their rebellion (in the case of Thelma and Louise, a culture in which violence against women is enacted daily from psychic abuse to rape).

11. THE AFRICAN-AMERICAN VOICE: WILLIAM FAULKNER'S *Go Down, Moses*

1. There are two exceptions to this pattern in the epigraphs to the chapter of *The Souls of Black Folk* of linking music from African-American spirituals with quotations from literature associated with the traditions of Western civilization. Chapter 6 quotes an extract from Omar Khayyám's *The Rubáiyát*, but Du Bois specifies Edward FitzGerald's Victorian translation. Most scholars consider

FitzGerald's translation to be such a free adaptation as to constitute an original and very European work. Chapter 7 begins with an extract from the Song of Solomon, but this Old Testament text has long been considered an instance of European Orientalism in the readings that displace the erotic love song with an allegory of Christ's union with the Church. For a complementary reading of the epigraphs, see Eric Sundquist, *To Wake the Nations: Race in the Making of American Literature* (Cambridge: Harvard University Press, 1993), p. 533.

2. W. E. B. Du Bois, *The Souls of Black Folk*, ed. Donald Gibson (New York: Viking Penguin, 1989), p. 5. Further references are cited in the text as: Souls.

3. Sundquist, *To Wake the Nations*, p. 525.

4. Ibid., p. 533.

5. Henry Louis Gates, Jr., "Afterword: Zora Neale Hurston: A Negro Way of Saying," in Hurston, *Mules and Men* (New York: Harper-Collins, 1990), p. 294. Further references are cited in the text as: Mules.

6. Du Bois's arguments in *Souls* for African-American emancipation through cultural self-representation never address explicitly the educational and economic situations of African-American women as different from those of African-American men. Du Bois' blindness to gender hierarchies is one of the weaknesses of *Souls*. Hurston is thus a much-needed supplement to Du Bois' otherwise progressive modern ideas about cultural work as part of political emancipation.

   Although Hurston undertook the project to "go and collect Negro folklore" at the urging of her mentor at Columbia, Franz Boas, she works carefully to undercut the scientific claims of modern anthropology throughout *Mules and Men*. Nowhere is this clearer than in part 2, "Hoodoo," in which she plays with white culture's obsessive interest in all aspects of "black magic," displaying on the part of white culture a far greater superstitiousness than it would ever find in the religious practices of African Americans in New Orleans or Afro-Caribbean culture in Jamaica.

7. Toni Morrison, *Playing in the Dark: Whiteness and the Literary Imagination* (New York: Random House, 1992), p. 13.

8. Ibid., p. 14.

9. Michael Millgate, *The Achievement of William Faulkner* (New York: Random House, 1966), p. 201.

10. See Millgate, pp. 201–2: "His answers to these needs were Isaac (Ike) McCaslin and the numerous other members, black and white, of the McCaslin family; and the fact that there exists a McCaslin family tree, drawn by Faulkner himself, is perhaps suggestive of the degree to which the family was created for a specific purpose, not evolved slowly from Faulkner's original conception of the world of Yoknapatawpha County."

11. Most critics agree that Ike's Christological associations are ironized by Faulkner in ways that question both Ike's and Christianity's redemptive powers. As Lewis Simpson puts it in "Isaac McCaslin and Temple Drake: The Fall of New World Man," *Nine Essays in Modern Literature*, ed. Donald E. Stanford (Baton Rouge:

Lousiana State University Press, 1965): "I would agree with Robert D. Jacobs" that Ike "in his total aspect" is " 'a pathetic figure, slightly comic, certainly ineffectual.' He represents only the nostalgic possibility of modern man rising in the guise of New World man to a new and better moral condition."

12. Millgate goes to some trouble to account for what he considers the apparently "disturbing" "shifts in period, setting, theme, and personnel which occur" in *Go Down, Moses* (Millgate, 203). These disparities are almost always explained by Millgate's appeal to the "novelistic" features of the collection. These qualities are, in turn, established by the nearly exclusive consideration in Millgate's interpretation of Ike's education in the hunting stories.

13. Susan Donaldson, "Contending Narratives: *Go Down, Moses* and the Short Story Cycle," in *Faulkner and Short Fiction: Faulkner and Yoknapatawpha 1990* , eds. Evans Harrington and Ann J. Abadie (Jackson: University Press of Mississippi, 1992), p. 129.

14. Donaldson, p. 147.

15. The four stories I wish to treat as critical readings of the three hunting stories are: "Was," "The Fire and the Hearth," "Pantaloon in Black," and "Go Down, Moses."

16. Faulkner, *Go Down, Moses* (New York: Random House, 1970), p. 364. Further references are cited in the text as: GDM.

17. Ike is thinking specifically of miscegenation, although he must be thinking of the social *acceptance* of miscegenation, since the African-American woman who prompts this reflection is the mother of a son fathered by Roth Edmonds. She is the granddaughter of James Beauchamp ("Tennie's Jim").

18. See chapters 5 and 6 in this regard.

19. Toni Morrison, *Beloved* (New York: Knopf, 1987), p. 110.

20. Like Hurston in *Mules and Men* and her work on Jamaican voodoo, *Tell My Horse*, Morrison is invoking a tradition of alternative cultural expression that has been particularly demonized by Euromerican culture. That "zombies" are somehow religious figurations of the African-American and Afro-Caribbean communities that will not be crushed by colonial domination is made quite clear by Hurston in both *Mules and Men* and *Tell My Horse*.

21. See Craig Hansen Werner, " 'Tell Old Pharaoh': The African-American Response to Faulkner," *The Southern Review* 19 (October 1983): 711–36, and Eric Sundquist, "Faulkner, Race, and the Forms of American Fiction," *Faulkner and Race: Faulkner and Yoknapatawpha*, eds. Doreen Fowler and Ann J. Abadie (Jackson: University Press of Mississippi, 1987), pp. 1–34.

22. Joseph L. Blotner and Frederick L. Gwynn, eds., *Faulkner in the University: Class Conferences at the University of Virginia, 1957–1958* (Charlottesville: University Press of Virginia, 1959), pp. 117–18.

23. See Millgate, p. 203: "Dated January 10, 1949, [an unsigned letter from Random House] mentions plans for reissuing *Go Down, Moses*, recalls that Faulkner had emphasised in conversation the fact that he considered it a novel rather than a

group of stories, and asks whether, when the book was reissued, he would like to insert chapter numbers in addition to the titles of the individual sections. That Faulkner did not accept this suggestion may have been due in part to his familiar reluctance to return to work which was behind him. . .; but he may also have recognized the force of the observation, also made in the letter, that it might be a mistake to eliminate the section titles altogether because of the way in which they had become accepted as part of the text."

24. Werner, " 'Tell Old Pharaoh,' " p. 725.

25. In the quest for literary forms appropriate to African-American culture and experiences, African-American writers have often written short story sequences and other works that challenge traditional genres of prose fiction. I begin this chapter with discussions of Du Bois' *The Souls of Black Folk* and Hurston's *Mules and Men*, both of which rely on a wide range of literary devices and yet remain difficult to classify according to traditional literary genres. Langston Hughes' "Jesse B. Simple" stories, collected in *Simple Speaks His Mind* and *The Ways of White Folks* are also examples of the modern African-American literary tradition's transgression of traditional genres. Perhaps the most self-conscious contemporary version is Ishmael Reed's *Mumbo Jumbo*, which mimics the popular detective novel and scholarly anthropology while substituting its own version of U.S. history.

12. REVIVALS

1. Richard Poirier, *The Renewal of Literature: Emersonian Reflections* (New York: Random House, 1987), p. 48.

2. Louis Althusser, "Ideology and Ideological State Apparatuses," in *Critical Theory Since 1965*, eds. Hazard Adams and Leroy Searle (Tallahassee: Florida State University Press, 1986), p. 241.

3. John McAleer, *Ralph Waldo Emerson: Days of Encounter* (Boston: Little, Brown, 1984), p. 573.

4. Poirier, *The Renewal of Literature*, p. 70; Kant, *Critique of Judgment*, trans. James Creed Meredith (Oxford: Oxford University Press, 1961), p. 161.

5. Poirier, *The Renewal of Literature*, p. 93.

Index